Kay Boyle

KAY BOYLE

Artist and Activist

SANDRA WHIPPLE SPANIER

PARAGON HOUSE PUBLISHERS
New York

First paperback edition, 1988.

Published in the United States by

Paragon House Publishers
90 Fifth Avenue
New York, New York 10011

Library of Congress Cataloging-in-Publication Data

Spanier, Sandra Whipple, 1951–
  Kay Boyle, artist and activist.

  Bibliography: p.
  Includes index.
  1. Boyle, Kay, 1902–   . 2. Authors, American—20th
century—Biography. I. Title.
PS3503.09357Z88 1987   813'.52 [B]   87-9023
ISBN 0-913729-97-3 (pbk.)

for Graham

Contents

Illustrations

Preface

Early in her career, as an avant-garde writer in Paris in the 1920s, Kay Boyle was singled out by Katherine Anne Porter as one of the strongest and most promising talents of her generation, as one who "sums up the salient qualities of that movement: a fighting spirit, freshness of feeling, curiosity, the courage of her own attitude and idiom, a violently dedicated search for the meaning and methods of art." As spirited and "violently dedicated" as ever, Kay Boyle has continued to earn high esteem within small circles to the present day.

Interest in the "lost generation" has been keen for some time now, and interest in the overlooked contributions of women to American literature is burgeoning. Yet in a single recent year, while the *MLA Bibliography* listed seventy-six new studies of the work of Ernest Hemingway, fifty-four of F. Scott Fitzgerald, and twenty-five of Gertrude Stein, Kay Boyle was not even named. Except for a few perceptive reviews of her books as they appeared and introductions to her work that has been republished, serious attempts at a critical assessment of Kay Boyle's career, spanning most of the twentieth century, have been limited to a handful of articles and unpublished doctoral dissertations. When other "minor" literary figures like Harry Crosby, Robert McAlmon, Nancy Cunard, and Djuna Barnes are subjects of entire books, it is most surprising that there has not been published before a full-length study of the life and work of Kay Boyle, their close associate, friend, and certainly artistic equal. A wider recognition of her achievement is long overdue.

When I sent the original version of this study to Kay Boyle asking permission to quote from her work, I expected a simple yes or no answer. Instead it was the beginning of an extensive correspondence. The present study draws upon scores of letters from Kay Boyle containing a wealth of new information about her life and work, unpublished documents and typescripts of works in progress, yellowed news clippings and book reviews she had saved over the years, and hundreds of pages of detailed notes in which she has reacted to my work page-by-page. She has set some facts straight; she has shared anecdotes about her personal relationships with William Carlos Williams, Gertrude Stein, Archibald MacLeish,

Peggy Guggenheim, Janet Flanner, Samuel Beckett, and many others; she has asked provocative questions about my readings of her work; and she has explained her own motivations and intentions behind her writing.

The danger, of course, in having the rare privilege of talking to an author about his or her work is that one may listen less attentively to what the work has to say for itself. The matter is complicated in this case by the fact that Kay Boyle identifies so closely with her fiction that she sometimes has objected to my interpretation of a character's actions or motives on the grounds that the actual person on whom that character was based—often herself—never would have behaved or felt that way. Writing this book has been an object lesson in what New Critics called the intentional fallacy, and I hope I have managed to evade it. Writing about a living author, knowing that that author will be reading one's work and most certainly will have some opinions about it, is another challenge in itself. I have been grateful many times that the bulk of the critical discussion was set down before our extended correspondence began and my growing personal admiration and respect for Kay Boyle might have altered my views of her work or inhibited their expression.

It should be noted that she has never hesitated to let me know when she thought my reading of her work to be "deeply right" or "completely wrong." (Her friend Janet Flanner, *The New Yorker*'s "Genêt," once said of her, "It was no good asking [Kay Boyle] what she thought, because she would tell you. If you didn't expect to know, you'd better not ask.") But she has been utterly fair in respecting my autonomy. A self-described "maniac about detail," she has written to me more than once that her intention in responding to my study with such "excruciating care" has never been to alter my thesis or my thinking about her work in any way, but simply to keep the record straight. When she has taken issue with details in my rendering of biographical and historical facts, I have checked her recollection against other sources and have found her almost always to be right. (Interestingly, only in those cases when what I have written might be seen as less than flattering to someone *other* than Kay Boyle have I discovered any inaccuracies in her recollection—the memories colored, perhaps, by a fierce and generous loyalty to friends and contemporaries no longer alive to defend themselves.) When my reading of a work has clashed with what she says were her intentions, I have carefully reconsidered my interpretation. In some cases I have come to a new and different understanding; in others I have not. In either event, I have identified the author's view as her own.

This study attempts to assess the achievement of Kay Boyle, from the first experimental stories and poems published in Paris in the twenties to her most recent fiction and essays on political and social issues. It traces the central themes that echo through and unify the diverse body of her work. It is intended first and foremost as literary criticism, but because her art, more so than that of most other writers, has always sprung so directly and so immediately from her personal experience, I have also paid a good deal of attention to biography as it relates to her development as an artist and illuminates her work. Kay Boyle herself refers to this study as her "biography," but she has led a long and exceedingly rich life—a "complicated life," she calls it—and a complete biography would be another book. The organization of this book is chronological, with biographical material serving as background and framework for discussions of her writing. The study also examines her treatment of female experience and offers some explanation as to why Kay Boyle's reputation has not matched the expectations of those who once considered hers one of the most promising talents of the "lost generation."

At first glance, this book may seem top heavy. I have devoted over one-third of its pages to Kay Boyle's life and work of the twenties and early thirties—a very small fraction of her career, measured in years. I have devoted a full chapter at the beginning to her life through the 1920s because it was such a crucial period in her personal and creative development. I have discussed individual works of the twenties and early thirties in more detail than most of her later works for two reasons. First, her early fiction is generally more complex than most of what she wrote during and after World War II. It calls for and bears the weight of a more intensive critical examination. Second, despite radical shifts in her material and style over the course of her career, Kay Boyle is a remarkably consistent writer. (She says herself that she finds it very convenient to have the same feelings now that she had at the age of eight or nine because she never has to deny anything she has ever written and say she didn't mean that.) The themes she explored in her very first volume of short stories have remained her central concerns to the present day. I felt that if these themes were clearly outlined early on, I might avoid belaboring those points in later discussions of her work.

With the publication of *Fifty Stories* in 1980, the republication of *Three Short Novels* in 1982 and *Being Geniuses Together* in 1984, and the appearance of three new books in 1985—a translation of René Crevel's *Babylon, Words that Must Somehow Be Said: Selected Essays of Kay Boyle 1927–1984,* and *This Is Not a Letter and Other Poems*—Kay Boyle's work is becoming increasingly accessible. But because so much of what she has written still is out of print, because a number of readers know her only for the short fiction that appeared in magazines in the thirties and forties, and because her work is not commonly included in literature courses, I have not felt that I could assume the reader's familiarity with individual novels, stories, poems, and essays. I have tried, therefore, to evoke the material and flavor of each piece while discussing the critical issues it raises. I hope that this book might serve as an introduction to Kay Boyle's considerable achievement for readers unfamiliar with her work without tiring those who "discovered" her long ago.

A final note: an English professor once told me that after Edmund Wilson's devastating review of Kay Boyle's novel *Avalanche* (her only bestseller) appeared in *The New Yorker* in 1944, he dismissed her from consideration as a serious writer and read no more of her work. Others have told me, in so many words, that I should forget the criticism in this book and concentrate on the biography—that Kay Boyle the woman is more interesting than Kay Boyle the writer. I firmly reject that notion. It is all too easy to view Kay Boyle simply as a fascinating woman who, in addition to writing over thirty books, had three husbands and six children and managed to be in the important places at the important times, participating actively in many of the major movements and events of our century. Her life *is* a compelling story. But to continue to overlook or downplay her considerable contribution to American literature—a distinguished contribution by even the most conventional measures of fellowships, awards, and membership in select bodies of writers and artists—is to do her a grave injustice. That Kay Boyle's name is not in the vocabulary of every student of twentieth-century literature is to some degree a political issue. Her lack of a wide reputation says more about the way our literary tastes and judgments are formed than it does about the "quality" of her work, and it is my hope that the next few years will see a fairer reevaluation of her achievement.

Acknowledgments

My debt to Kay Boyle is impossible to measure. Her graciousness and generosity in corresponding and meeting with me despite deadlines and difficulties of her own have made writing this book a high adventure and deep pleasure. I feel extraordinarily fortunate to have known her. I thank her, too, for her kind cooperation in granting permission to quote from unpublished materials.

Philip Young, Evan Pugh Professor of English at The Pennsylvania State University, has been an inexhaustible source of wise advice and warm encouragement. I am deeply grateful to him. I owe thanks, too, to Don Bialostosky, Peter Elbow, Hugh Ford, Robert N. Hudspeth, Ted Huston, David V. Koch, Charles W. Mann, and Peter White for their thoughtful readings of the manuscript at various stages.

I am grateful to the Morris Library of Southern Illinois University at Carbondale for allowing access to the Black Sun Press Archive, the Philip Kaplan Expatriate Collection, and to its extensive collection of Kay Boyle's papers, which were indispensable to this study; to the Sophia Smith Collection (Women's History Archive) at Smith College and to Elaine Sproat, executor of the Lola Ridge papers, for access to Kay Boyle's letters to Lola Ridge; to The Harry Ransom Humanities Research Center, The University of Texas at Austin, for making available the correspondence of Boyle with a number of literary figures, including Evelyn Scott, Katherine Anne Porter, Nancy Cunard, Caresse Crosby, Edward Dahlberg, William Carlos Williams, and Langston Hughes; to the Beinecke Library at Yale University for permitting access to the Alfred Stieglitz collection, containing letters Boyle wrote as an expatriate in the twenties and thirties; to The Pennsylvania State University's Pattee Library for making available several of her letters of the sixties and seventies; and to Professor Richard C. Carpenter for sending me a copy of a letter the author wrote to him in 1953. Cathy Henderson, Research Librarian at the Harry Ransom Humanities Research Center, and Louisa Bowen of the Morris Library at Southern Illinois University have been most helpful. David V. Koch, Curator of Special Collections at the Morris Library and compiler of a forthcoming Boyle bibliography, guided me through twelve cubic feet of her uncatalogued papers and has consistently been a valuable source of information. Professor Hugh Ford was kind enough to share with me a typescript of his own chapter on Kay Boyle before it was published in his book *Four Lives in Paris* (North Point Press, 1987).

In the age of computer-generated manuscript copy, Bronwen Heuer, Documentation Specialist for the Computing Center at the State University of New York at Stony Brook, has been the indispensable link between technology and the humanities. I am indebted also to my mother, Maxine Whipple, for her generous help in preparing the manuscript, and to those good friends whose more than polite interest in this work has continuously fueled my own. And finally, my deepest thanks to Graham Spanier, for his total support in this and everything else.

Kay Boyle

Prologue: "The Crusading Spirit"

"It was in the late twenties that I went to live and work in Paris, and I was then still a French citizen (through my marriage). These two facts would seem to disqualify me as a member of the lost generation or as an expatriate. But I was there, in whatever guise, and even if a bit late" (*BGT,* 11).[1] So begin Kay Boyle's memoirs of that decade.

She certainly *was* there, and she was very much a part of that group of expatriate writers that has since come to be known as the "lost generation." Her work appeared in the avant-garde magazines alongside that of Ezra Pound, James Joyce, Gertrude Stein, Hart Crane, Djuna Barnes, and Ernest Hemingway. Her circle of friends included Joyce, Crane, William Carlos Williams and Archibald MacLeish as well as Black Sun publishers Harry and Caresse Crosby, *transition* editor Eugene Jolas, *This Quarter* editor Ernest Walsh (he was the father of her first child), and Robert McAlmon, who published Hemingway's first book and whose own enormous influence on the Paris literary scene has not been widely remembered.

Kay Boyle's career got off to a promising start. Harry Crosby declared in 1928, "I think she is the best girl writer since Jane Austen—I say this without exaggeration."[2] Besides being her first publisher, he sought her criticism of his own poetry and acted on her advice. After reading Boyle's book of short stories, brought out in a limited edition by the Black Sun Press in 1929, Archibald MacLeish offered his congratulations to publisher and author, declaring: "She has the power and the glory. I believe in her absolutely when she writes—even when I want not to. I talk of her everywhere—not that it can do her any good. Simply that I must."[3] In 1931 Katherine Anne Porter wrote in a review of Boyle's second story collection and first novel: "Gertrude Stein and James Joyce were and are the glories of their time and some very portentous talents have emerged from their shadows. Miss Boyle, one of the newest, I believe to be among the strongest."[4]

Her career has stretched far beyond that decade, however. Her sub-

1

jects range from the psychological trials of an expatriate in Europe in the twenties and thirties to the causes and effects of World War II to social injustice in modern America. She is the author of over thirty books, including fourteen novels, ten collections of short fiction, five volumes of poetry, three children's books, two essay collections, and several edited, translated, and ghostwritten volumes. Hundreds of her stories, poems, and articles have appeared in periodicals ranging from the little magazines published in Paris in the twenties to the *Saturday Evening Post* and *Ladies' Home Journal,* and she was a foreign correspondent for *The New Yorker* from 1946 to 1953. She has been awarded two Guggenheim fellowships, won the O. Henry Award for best short story of the year in 1935 and 1941, and is a member of the American Academy of Arts and Letters.[5] In 1980, she received a Senior Fellowship for Literature from the National Endowment for the Arts, one of eight grants given to "individuals who have made an extraordinary contribution to contemporary American literature over a lifetime of creative work."

For some reason, however, Kay Boyle has not received the wide attention and acclaim that her contemporaries of the twenties and early thirties assumed would be her due. Today, while her name is mentioned in many of the myriad memoirs and studies of the expatriates, it most often appears without elaboration as one of the "other" writers in Paris in the twenties. In the face of intense continuing interest in the lost generation and the widening awareness that women's accomplishments in literature too often have been underrated or ignored, Kay Boyle is a prime candidate for "rediscovery." The present study assesses the achievement of this distinguished and prolific writer whose career has spanned the better part of the twentieth century and whose contribution to American literature has not been adequately recognized.

In 1929, Kay Boyle was among the sixteen expatriate writers who signed a proclamation calling for the "Revolution of the Word." It declared, among other things, "The writer expresses. He does not communicate," and "The plain reader be damned."[6] Yet in the seventies she wrote to a young poet that she hoped to help her students realize that their lives are not unique and lonely voyages unless they close the doors and thus bring all communication to an end. She asks rhetorically, "Writing *is* communication, isn't it?"[7] While these statements mark the ends of the spectrum through which she has passed in her career, they are not as incompatible as they may seem. In a 1963 essay the author defines what she believes to be the role of the serious writer: to be "the spokesman for those who remain inarticulate around him," an "aeolian harp whose sensitive strings respond to the whispers of the concerned people of his time." The writer, she believes, is "a moralist in the highest sense of the word," whose part has always been "to speak briefly and clearly of the dignity and integrity of individual man."[8] This belief in the moral responsibility of the artist is the unbroken thread that runs through the variegated fabric of Kay Boyle's work and makes it of a piece.

"One of the essentials that is asked of us as writers," she says also, "is not to separate ourselves from our time."[9] She always has lived immersed in the moment. In the twenties when the young expatriate writers she knew in Paris were struggling "against all literary pretentiousness, against weary, dreary rhetoric, against all the outworn literary and academic conventions," she dedicated her talents to the creation of "a grandly experimental, furiously disrespectful school of writing in America."[10] Her own early works are intensely individual expressions of intensely personal experiences, and she soon earned a reputation as a brilliant and innovative stylist. Yet when the pressures of the external, social world came to bear so heavily on private lives in our century that they could not be ignored, she began to expand the scope of her vision, vibrating to the note of the new times to affirm on a broader scale the same basic values—the "dignity and integrity" of the individual. From the thirties to the present day, she has taken as her subject matter the rise of nazism, the French resistance, the occupation of postwar Germany, and the Black Panther party, writing in a far more accessible style in order to communicate her urgent convictions to the widest possible audience. In the course of her career, her characters and concerns, chameleonlike, have taken on the shades of the times through which she has passed. Yet they have never completely merged with their backdrops; she has never lost sight of the individual dramas acted out against the panoramic scenery.

The sum of her art is a chronicle of the twentieth century. Yet at the same time, her works are products of Kay Boyle's unique individual experiences. Nearly everything she has written has sprung immediately from her personal life—from her first novel, *Plagued by the Nightingale* (1931), in which a young American bride struggles to adjust to life with her repressive in-laws in Brittany, to her latest, *The Underground Woman* (1975), based on a middle-aged writer's arrest and imprisonment following a demonstration against the war in Vietnam. In an attempt to explain the shifts in focus of her art—from her earliest work, never published, reflecting her involvement in the radical labor movement as a teenager in Cincinnati, to her experimental and introspective work of the late twenties and early thirties, to the overtly political work she has published since the beginning of World War II—the author herself speculates that "once I had solved to a degree my own individual distress (through my marriage to Laurence [Vail] and the security of a family life)

I returned to the wider predicament of all women and men."[11] For Kay Boyle, the personal, social, aesthetic, and political are nearly indistinguishable and absolutely inextricable.

In the 1963 article in which she defines the role of the serious writer, she also quotes Camus' statement that "a man's work is nothing but a long journey to recover through the detours of art, the two or three simple and great images which first gained access to his heart."[12] In Kay Boyle's long journey, a few themes remain constant: a belief in the absolute essentiality of love—whether on a personal or a global scale, an awareness of the many obstacles to its attainment, and a tragic sense of loss when love fails and the gulfs between human beings stand unbridged. Along with E. M. Forster, she would exhort humanity, "Only connect!"

The barriers to contact are many, both natural and manmade. In some of her fiction, bonds are severed by death. In other works, would-be lovers are kept apart by a blood relationship; love's fulfillment is simply made impossible by biological facts of life. In still others, love is thwarted or blocked by idiosyncracies of individual psyches or by conflicting sexual orientations. Yet the author often presents a more assailable villain. She finds many barriers to connection to be as arbitrary and immoral as the social conventions that cause Huck Finn's "conscience" to torment him as he helps his friend Jim escape from slavery. An obstacle she attacks repeatedly is a narrow-mindedness which blinds an individual to the inherent dignity of others—an egotism that in the plural becomes bigotry and chauvinism.

Looking back over her career, Kay Boyle has said, "I think I have that kind of mother-complex—that protective thing which really has been the motivation of my writing. I wanted other people to know what was going on in life: at least, how this person could be helped, or this person would be understood, or how awful the English are, how we must do something about enlightening and illuminating their spirit, you see. The crusading spirit, I'd say."[13] While her causes have ranged from the liberation of language from a stale and inhibiting literary tradition to the liberation of minority groups from an oppressive social system, Kay Boyle's writing has always been fired by this "crusading spirit." (It is indicative of her profound respect for womanhood that she defines it as maternal.) As an artist she has felt a moral responsibility not only to reflect human life but to improve it:

> Perhaps there are no absolute answers, but I feel that in our time it is not the writer who must seek to be accepted by the world in which he finds himself, but the world that must be transformed to acceptability by the higher standards of the individual. For the artist's, the writer's, concern has always been not only with what is taking place—although that may be the frame within which he

states the tenets of his faith—but with the dimensions of what *might,* within the infinite capacity of man, be enabled to take place.[14]

While her material and style have changed with the times, the body of her work is a "fervent prayer"[15] offered up to the hope of humanity's salvation through love and understanding, the hard irony coloring so much of it testimony to her disappointment that men and women so often have failed to live up to their "infinite capacity." Although she is too much a realist to deny that the individual may fall victim to chance, or fate, or history, Kay Boyle believes there are still responsibilities to be taken, choices to be made. Her world most often is a grim place, but it is not a Waste Land. Despite the bitter realities of life in the twentieth century, Kay Boyle still will grant human beings the possibility of redemption through their uniquely human power to love, if only they would.

1

Beginnings: St. Paul to Paris

"In my childhood," writes Kay Boyle, "I thought of my family as quite a usual American family, but obviously we were not, for we had no fixed dwelling place, and my father had neither a profession nor a trade."[1] Kay Boyle was born on February 19, 1902, in St. Paul, Minnesota.[2] The timing and geography were right, but her childhood was not the middle-American idyll common to most members of the lost generation. She never really had a hometown. Her family left St. Paul when she was six months old, and she spent her childhood in Philadelphia, Atlantic City, Washington D.C., the Pocono Mountains, and Cincinnati. Her grandfather, Jesse Peyton Boyle, who had studied for the priesthood in England but instead became a lawyer and cofounder of the West Publishing Company in St. Paul, was "the life force of our family as well as the provider," according to the author, and thanks to his affluence, the family also "travelled expensively and dined expansively in a great many different countries" (*BGT,* 19).[3]

Kay Boyle comes from a strong line of independent women. Her grandmother, Eva S. Evans, became one of the first women to work in the Federal government when she took a position in the land-grant office in the Department of the Interior in 1874. Her aunt, Nina Evans Allender, a political cartoonist, produced almost 300 pieces on the suffragist campaign and was the first to depict the suffragist as an attractive young woman instead of a maiden lady of uncertain age. Her drawing of Susan B. Anthony appeared on a 1936 postage stamp, and her suffragist art is now part of the collection of the Library of Congress. Even today her work is frequently reproduced in newsletters of the National Woman's Party. Kay Boyle's mother, Katherine Evans Boyle, had disturbed the author's conservative father and grandfather with her liberal political activism and avant-garde artistic interests, running for the Cincinnati school board on the Farmer-Labor ticket in 1919 and introducing her young daughters to the works of Joyce, Stein, Brancusi, and Duchamp. Years later, Katherine Evans Boyle and Nina Evans Allender were "honorary co-chairmen" of the World Woman's Party, founded in 1939 by Alice Paul, the object of which was "To raise the status of women throughout the world."

The author describes her grandfather Boyle, the family provider and patriarch, as "one of the few charming reactionaries whom I have ever met," a man who "insisted that the lives of those about him be of his making."[4] Her father, Howard Peterson Boyle, was "one of those very silent and introverted people who suffered very much." He had little contact with his daughters "because he was a frustrated person who couldn't communicate his feelings," she says. "He probably resented my mother very much, which we didn't realize then—resented her ideas, which were extraordinary. God knows where they came from."[5]

Although Kay Boyle put in some time at Miss Shipley's School in Bryn Mawr—which she labels "another abortive attempt" at her education (*BGT,* 19)—and later would study briefly at the Cincinnati Conservatory of Music, the Ohio Mechanics Institute, and the Parsons' School of Fine and Applied Art in New York City, her formal schooling was sketchy. Her mother alone, "with her modest but untroubled intuition about books and paintings and people, had been my education," she says (*BGT,* 18).

In the evenings Mrs. Boyle would read aloud to her two daughters while they drew illustrations for every book she read, and in 1913, took Kay to the Armory show in New York. When Kay's father—a graduate of the University of Pennsylvania law school and for a while director of the Children's Homeopathic Hospital in Philadelphia—brought home colleagues for dinner, Mrs. Boyle would read aloud to them from Gertrude Stein's *Tender Buttons,* "believing that men advanced in the study of medicine would be enthralled by such evidence of the parallel literary advances of their time" (*BGT,* 19). One evening, however, a particular doctor laughed so hard over Stein's work that he became ill and had to be taken upstairs to bed.

Mrs. Boyle's artistic emancipation and her liberal politics went hand in hand. While running for election to the Cincinnati Board of Education on the Farmer-Labor ticket in 1918, she would read aloud to the labor union organizers the early chapters of James Joyce's *Ulysses* being published in the *Little Review.* She encouraged her teenaged daughter's literary efforts—works with titles like "Arise, Ye Women" and "The Working Girl's Prayer"—often embarrassing Kay by reading them aloud, too, at political meetings.[6] She served dinner to Lincoln Steffens and escorted him to the lecture hall, ignoring the menfolk's silent disapproval. When a large group of youngsters taking part in the Children's Crusade marched through Cincinnati on their way to Washington to protest the fact that their fathers, political prisoners, were still in jail although the war was over, Mrs. Boyle took some of them in. Her husband and father-in-law packed overnight bags and went to a hotel. "Because of my mother, who gave me definitions, I knew what I was committed to in life; because of my father and my grandfather, who offered statements instead of revelations, I knew what I was against," the author explains (*BGT,* 18).

A reverence for art, a social conscience, an independent spirit, and unflagging support for Kay's development as a writer were Katherine Evans Boyle's great gifts to her daughter. The doctor who had laughed himself sick over Gertrude Stein at the Philadelphia dinner party had missed the second half of the evening's cultural program: readings from Kay Boyle's diary of her trip to Germany the previous summer. Kay Boyle attributes her own accomplishment as an artist to her mother's encouragement:

> Mother accepted me and my word as she accepted James Joyce, Gertrude Stein, or Brancusi, or any serious artist. Because of her, I knew that anyone who wrote, or anyone who painted, or anyone who composed music, had a special place in life. And so, when I got to Paris, and really met these people who were accomplishing things, I felt I belonged with them, because my mother brought me up in that quite simple feeling.[7]

The dedication page of her first novel, published in 1931, reads "For my Mother and Her undying Flame."

In 1916, the family suffered a financial reversal and moved to Cincinnati, where Kay Boyle's father opened a garage. Her education took a prosaic turn. She studied architecture at the Ohio Mechanics Institute from 1917 to 1919, worked as a switchboard operator and cashier in her father's office, and put herself through secretarial school at night.

"The teenage etiquette of the period . . . decreed that a girl must be popular or die of shame, and I construed this as meaning a different date every night," she recalls.[8] She wrote to her sister, who had left home to work in New York, that she enjoyed "a dance with Schelley, a walk with George, a theatre with Ralph, a luncheon with the university boys," but she was in love with a French exchange student at the University of Cincinnati, Richard Brault.[9] With Richard she took long walks talking about "everything from the science of eugenic living to the brutality of doctors and skimm[ing] over birth-control and other kinds of control and life in general and us in particular."[10] They planned to marry after his graduation.

Even as a teenager, Kay Boyle was characteristically outspoken and unconcerned with convention. Her sister refused to double-date with her, insisting that young men were not interested in discussing Einstein's theory of relativity nor the diameter of the star Betelgeuse. One evening in June, 1921, an "enormous cop" accompanied by three other "huge men" came upon Kay and Richard smoking in a parked car and threatened to report the scandal to her parents. Kay (who later claimed to have been terrified) coolly informed them that she had lived in the East, where society women smoke in their limousines right on Fifth Avenue. "My friends, may I offer you some of my cigarets?" she had asked, and the crisis dissolved into "much jollification."[11] (The next day she was "rabid" when the officer telephoned and attempted to blackmail her into going out with him. "Hounded by the police! My gawd!" she wrote to Joan.)

Kay Boyle joined her mother as an active supporter of the radical labor movement in Cincinnati. Each evening after work, Kay and the family's Model T were at the disposal of the Farmer-Labor party or any other radical organization needing her services. Night after night she drove the speakers from street corner to street corner and distributed literature to passersby. During the imprisonment of Eugene Debs she spent weeks collecting signatures on a petition calling for his release and pardon. She was outraged when a dictation exercise in her secretarial course consisted of a business letter from a mayoral candidate to an influential businessman calling for the extermination of socialism in this country and for government control by the Republican Party. "This to the ignorant young stenographers who have no ideas of their own and who will swallow it whole," she complained to Joan. "I am becoming more radical everyday. Absolutely *red*."[12]

Kay Boyle supported a radical movement in art as well as in politics. At nineteen she made her first contribution to a national magazine, Harriet Monroe's *Poetry: A Magazine of Verse*. It was a letter to the editor, decrying the gap in innovation between the music and the poetry of the day, blaming it on "the complacency of the reactionaries of the musical world" who had insisted that music remain "more than a little antiquated, scented with lavender, while the contemporary arts are keeping pace with the complexities of civilization." Citing several of the newer artists (Sherwood Anderson and Picasso among them), she wrote with the passion and stylistic flair that would become her hallmarks: "Whether or not they gain a foothold is as much our concern as theirs, for they *are* ourselves, our explanation, the story which the future generations shall read of us. And meanwhile music stands like a Boston *bas-bleu,* her skirt a little shortened because of the influence of Korsakov and Dvorak, but still wearing her New England rubbers."[13] Kay Boyle's first publication was portentous in another way, too. In the 1921 volume of *Poetry,* her letter appears alongside the work of others whose lives would come to intertwine with hers: William Carlos Williams, Robert McAlmon, and Emanuel Carnevali—lifelong friends and mentors; Ernest Walsh, the father of her first child; and Laurence Vail, her future husband and the father of their three daughters.

But in 1921, in Cincinnati, Ohio, Kay Boyle could scarcely have dreamed that. At home relations were growing increasingly intolerable between "the allies" (Richard, her mother, and herself) and "the belligerent powers" (her father and her grandfather, whose nickname was "Puss"—short for "Gran'puss"). "Sometimes I could commit murder without a qualm," she wrote to her sister in December. "We sit at the table and every time Mother opens her mouth you might think that a maniac was beginning to speak from the sweet and forebearing silence which immediately falls upon the masters of our house. . . . Why a liberal idea is a black and unforgivable sin, and the Indians can die like cattle in boxcars and the miners be killed in West Virginia, and the unemployed starve and yet we here must not talk of these things but of Fatty Arbuckle. And Puss had the damned nerve to sit back in his chair the other night after gorging three bananas and five pastries and a dozen or so doughnuts, pat himself comfortably and say: 'Do you know Howard, I think there must be people starving in America today?' I said: 'Think?', and left the table."[14]

When she had completed the secretarial course, Kay notified Puss that she was quitting work in the family business to take a job as secretary to a wholesale jeweler in Cincinnati. By the spring of 1922 she had saved enough to follow her sister to New York. She would never see her father or grandfather again.

Joan Boyle was working as an illustrator for *Vogue* and provided Kay with the connections to become secretary to a fashion writer so she could earn a living while taking a writing class at Columbia. But before the semester was over, Kay had found a job with Lola Ridge, American editor of *Broom* magazine, "probably the handsomest and arty-est of any literary publication of its time, printed as it was on very elegant paper and published in Italy by Harold Loeb, Alfred Kreymborg, and a number of other temporarily expatriate writers" (*BGT*, 14). "I naively took some of my poems to the *Broom* office, found Lola Ridge alone there trying to handle all the work, and we loved each other instantly," she recalls.[15] Lola had asked Kay to be her assistant and wrote at once to Harold Loeb for his approval to give her a salary of $18.00 a week.

Richard Brault soon followed Kay to New York, and on June 24, 1922, they were married at City Hall with a large group of other couples. He "rather disgruntledly" went to work as a meter inspector for the New York electric company, having hoped to do better than that, "armed with his fine degree" (*BGT*, 13). The morning after their wedding, Kay received a special delivery letter from her father forbidding her to marry until Richard could support her, and two weeks later, Richard got a cable from his family in Brittany saying that unless the couple were immediately married by a priest, they never wished to see him again.

Kay Boyle's developing social conscience was nourished by her association with Lola Ridge. An Australian poet born in Dublin, Ridge in her own work "expressed a fiery awareness of social injustice" in "a woman's savage voice," and Kay Boyle claims to have borrowed from Lola's conscience and poetic vocabulary when she wrote her own poetry. "Mother and those she loved were a part of every decision I took," she later would write, "and now in New York Lola had joined that company of the great" (*BGT*, 22).

Lola Ridge also provided her with important literary contacts. Every Thursday afternoon and perhaps one evening a month, she held open house in the New York office of *Broom*—the basement of the house at 3 East Ninth Street where Marjorie Loeb, divorced wife of the magazine's publisher, lived. Kay found herself serving tea and cakes and listening in "silent awe" to the readings and conversations of those who gathered there: Marianne Moore, William Carlos Williams, John Dos Passos, Elinor Wylie, Waldo Frank, Babette Deutsch, Edwin Arlington Robinson, Glenway Wescott, and "countless others" (*BGT*, 18). It was at one of Lola's gatherings in 1919 or 1920 that Robert McAlmon and William Carlos Williams had met, and they had gone on to found *Contact*, a literary magazine with an anti–literary establishment credo. In June, 1923, Kay Boyle was proud to have one of her poems published beside theirs in that magazine.

In late May, 1923, she and her husband, fortified by a big-splurge breakfast of sausages and wheatcakes at Child's on East Fourteenth Street and a $250.00 loan from Marjorie Loeb, boarded the SS *Suffren* at the French Line pier for a summer visit with Richard's family.[16] In Brittany Richard planned to look for a temporary job, and Kay would begin her novel. The advance she would receive from a New York publisher for the first few chapters would pay for their return tickets, they thought. They would be gone for about three months, or, at the most, four. It was the beginning of Kay Boyle's eighteen-year expatriation.

Crossing the Atlantic, Kay looked forward to being alone in France with Richard that summer. Away from the distraction of other people, she intended to do a great deal of writing. While others aboard got seasick, she was enraptured by the movement of the waves and wrote to Lola: "Why do they call people rebels who are swinging into the wide, hot rhythms of life? The real rebels are the ones who build themselves tight little houses, and sit within them all their years. And we who really live actually take life exactly as we find it—moving easily with its motions. One *can't* be seasick—or life-sick—when one really understands."[17]

"If I had come down the gangplank wearing a gray suit, it is possible everything might have turned out differently between the family and me," Kay Boyle says of her landing in Le Havre on a beautiful June morning (*BGT,* 42). Immediately upon the couple's arrival, her in-laws began to inquire of Richard as to whether she even owned *un tailleur gris,* the only decent costume in which a lady could travel. There was immediate tension between Richard and his family, who, except for his favorite sister Charlotte, represented every rigid, narrow-minded, bourgeois value the couple despised. On the way home to St. Malo that first day in the chauffeur-diven limousine, they stopped at Rouen for lunch, and Richard's father took him aside to complain that "ladies don't put paint on their mouths, and they don't wear earrings as big as cartwheels" (*BGT,* 47). Kay was wearing a blue challis dress with red roses strewn over it and a crimson scarf, an outfit that William Carlos Williams had admired when she and Richard had visited him and Florence Williams in Rutherford, but Richard's father privately told him that the family would borrow on their house in the country, if necessary, to get her a gray suit. The next morning she put away her lipstick and white plastic Woolworth's earrings (which today she admits "must have been awful")[18] and attempted to fit into the "impenetrably sealed universe of the family's daily life" (*BGT,* 64–65).

They lived with Richard's family in their modest home across the road from the grand estate Charlotte shared with her husband, Jean, and their children. Papa made Kay's breakfast coffee every morning, beating an egg in the cup "with his own hands" (something he had never done for anyone before in his life, the others told her), and each day Maman stood in the garden and called, "Good morning, Kay," so that the first words she would hear when she awoke would be English instead of French.[19] But while the family was "dear and devoted," Kay was frustrated. "Their conversation and reactions make me impatient," she confided to Lola. "They feel that if I am left to myself for five minutes that I shall feel myself neglected. But whenever the darling Richard is able to keep them off, I write."[20]

As the summer wore on, Richard occupied himself with schemes for job hunting so that they might free themselves from financial dependence on his family, while Kay "entered into a sly and secretive life and entered it alone:"

> I lived for the letters that Mother and Lola wrote me, and for the writing of letters to them. William Carlos Williams' white chickens and red wheelbarrow, with the rain shining on it, were in every farmyard that I passed, and night after

night I listened to the silences of Marianne Moore's far nightingale. "What time is it in New York now?" I'd keep asking Richard, and when he had worked it out for me, I would enter again my delitescent life. (*BGT,* 67)

As Richard grew increasingly bitter in his rebellion, Kay outwardly conformed to the family's ways while continuing her secret life, reading ravenously and working on a book "about all that had happened to me as I grew up in Philadelphia, in Atlantic City, in the Pocono Mountains, and in Cincinnati, as if a recounting of these experiences must finally reveal to me who I was" (*BGT,* 68). Yet she recalls she cried herself to sleep every night of that summer that they lived with Richard's family.[21]

Although Kay longed to return to New York and Lola offered to take up a collection to pay their passage back, their return would have meant "the Edison Company and consequent hell for Richard." Thanking her for her generosity, Kay wrote to Lola that "though life in New York is vital and stimulating to me, I do feel that as long as Richard and I have thrown in our lot together in a spirit of understanding and love and wisdom that we should work it out on the most colourful and happy lines."[22] Finally, in September, 1923, Richard's sister Charlotte provided the means for their escape. One afternoon on the beach at St. Malo, she had given Richard three thousand francs and had assured him that he would be certain to find a job in Paris. She was not thinking of herself in enabling them to go away, Charlotte told Kay, for she wondered what would become of her without the two of them for companionship, but she realized their desperate need for independence.

In Paris, while Richard spent the days looking for work, Kay explored the city and even stood outside Sylvia Beach's book shop on the Rue de l'Odeon, hoping to catch a glimpse of James Joyce or George Moore, but she lacked the courage to go in. She did decide to look up Harold Loeb, and it was when she had met him one afternoon at the Café de la Paix that she was introduced to Robert McAlmon, whose work she had long admired. He would become "something of an older brother and mentor," in one critic's words.[23] Over forty years later, Kay Boyle would edit and republish his long-out-of-print memoirs, *Being Geniuses Together* (1938), interspersing alternate chapters of her own recollections to create what the book jacket calls "A binocular view of Paris in the '20s."[24] She would also write the afterword for his short story collection, *A Hasty Bunch* (1922), when it was reissued in 1977 by Southern Illinois University Press.

"God's got to be a good poet or a good composer before I'll genuflect," McAlmon had declared that afternoon (*BGT,* 87). Although Kay Boyle had been too nervous to find anything to say to him, their meeting inflamed her imagination. She returned to their hotel room to tell her husband "in virtuously drunken accents" that "we must find our people and commit ourselves to them," and that "it behooved us now to *know*" (*BGT*, 105). " 'Know *what*?' Richard had asked me with a good deal of sense; but sense at this moment affronted me," she reports, and she had run off through the Paris night to spend it finally on a park bench by the lake in the Bois de Boulogne. The following afternoon, she bought and read a paperback copy of George Moore's *The Lake*, filling with emotion when she read " 'There is a lake in every man's life, and he must ungird his loins for the crossing' " (*BGT*, 108).

When she returned home that night, Richard had announced that he had found a job in Le Havre; "So we journeyed to Le Havre, and there, as if it were the most natural thing in the world, we became members of the proletariat," she recalls (*BGT*, 121). The couple lived in a dingy flat without running water. Moving into 5 Rue des Jardin on a rainy Tuesday in October, Kay cheerfully had opened the kitchen cupboards to find every dish piled with rotting food and then discovered in the bedroom the chamber pot so thickly encrusted with dried urine that she had to get it out with a knife. Her grandfather's subsequent sentimentalization of their poverty infuriated her. "He thinks of me mooning on sand-dunes, returning to a sweet little abstract apartment, Richard helping with the dishes—all on 30 cents a day," she wrote to her sister. "One is liable to get raped or pneumonia on the dunes, we have nothing but oil cloth—ripped cracked oil cloth that never stays clean—on our floors, not one easy chair, [and] five days out of the week one can't use the middle room because the week's wash is up and *never* dries." Jean's chauffeur, sent one day by Richard's family to deliver fresh fruits and vegetables, had been shocked by their living conditions and had stood in the flat "twisting his hat with one of Richard's shirts hanging over his shoulders and dripping quietly on his forehead. Too embarrassed to move." Yet, Kay said, "Wouldn't I rather shiver and write what I want about life and the capitalistic system than have my remarkable 'earning power' amazing three continents?"[25]

It was a bleak autumn and winter. Charlotte and her unborn baby had died. Fighting depression and despair, Kay Boyle resumed her writing, and she began a rich correspondence with Emanuel Carnevali, a poet dying of encephailitis in Italy whose work she had admired in *Broom* and *Poetry*. (She later would commit herself to compiling and publishing his autobiography, although it took until 1967 to find a publisher.)[26] It was in Le Havre that she finished her first novel, which besides being "autobiography, pure and simple," included as background descriptions of the labor movement in Cincinnati—"that nest of reactionary stagnation."[27] In 1928 she gave the only copy of it to Robert Sage, a columnist for the Paris edition of *Chicago Tribune* and an associate editor of *transition*. He sent it to a Chicago publisher who mislaid the manuscript—"and it has never been heard of since," she reports (*BGT,* 129). During the twelve hours of every weekday that she was alone that winter, she also wrote poetry and began a second novel, the story of her husband's family in Brittany, which would be published in 1931 as *Plagued by the Nightingale.* Ignoring the fact they had written to say they would only be passing through Le Havre on their way to Paris, she made elaborate preparations for the visit of "Bill" and "Flossie" Williams. In an ambitious effort to beautify the windowless room behind the Café-Restaurant de l'Univers where they had moved in December, she followed a suggestion of Carnevali's and spent days attempting to fabricate a "window" on an inside wall by gluing on it a mosaic of colored bottle glass she had gathered from the beach. Her labor was a testament to her loneliness and her longing for a richer life in the dismal port town. And her reaction to her disappointment, when she realized the Williamses really would not have time to visit their place, reveals a fundamental respect for individual integrity—an attitude central to nearly all her writing:

> I learned this simple thing: that people of dignity are not to be dragged by the hair of their heads into the precincts of one's life, and that to attempt this is to violate their probity. That threshold lying at the entrance to each man's and woman's life, I knew without equivocation now, must be recognized and genuflected before. Neither strangers nor friends could be urged to cross it, not even as onlookers were they to be invited to view the spectacle of one's avidity for love and one's inexcusable despair. (*BGT,* 144)

"It turned out to be quite an intellectual winter, as if life were offering me a compensation for what had taken place," she writes (*BGT,* 144). She read "as a textbook" Rebecca West's *The Judge,* which gave her courage to pursue her own writing. She says of West, "All that mattered to me was that she was a woman, and that she had written a novel, a very long novel, which was what I was seeking to do" (*BGT,* 145). In her effort to understand Norman Angell's *The Political Conditions of Allied Success,* she paraphrased the book in blank verse and claims that his thoughts and words "became an uneffaceable part of my awareness, or of my unawareness, and shaped my predilections, which were, indeed, hope for the democratic process and despair for national particularism" (*BGT,* 145). For Christmas, her mother sent her Waldo Frank's *Holiday* and Evelyn Scott's *Escapade.* Kay was unimpressed by Frank, who professed realism but who had written her "amazedly" from Paris wondering why she would choose to winter in Le Havre. ("Of course no one would choose to 'winter' in Le Havre any more than one would choose to do one's own washing," she wrote to Lola Ridge.)[28]

But although she felt that Scott's other books were "pose, pose, pose," Kay was "deeply thrilled" by *Escapade* and "mad with a tense wild recognition for weeks" after fininshing it. Within months, Evelyn Scott joined the company of Boyle's intimate correspondents. Yet their relationship would come under strain by 1927, when Evelyn issued an ultimatum to Kay that she either stop defending Robert McAlmon, whom Evelyn disliked for his lack of a consistent social ideology, or their own friendship must end. Kay Boyle would come to feel, like McAlmon, that (in his words) Scott's mind was "a collegiate one, dealing with abstractions and ideas rather than with actualities." ("I'm so tough and hard that I not only chew nails for breakfast but I distrust idealism with a friendship-breaking clause," McAlmon would tell Boyle.)[29] Decades later, Kay Boyle would write of her impatience with Evelyn Scott's "constricted gaze" and "her helplessness in that narrow world:" "I had come to demand a great deal of women, and more of women writers than I was able to express. It was an actual pain in the heart when they failed to be what they themselves had given their word that they would seek to be. I think I never forgave Evelyn for this" (*BGT*, 151).

During that long, "bitterly lonely" winter of 1923–1924, Kay Boyle also wrote prolifically and discovered strength in her solitude. "I have come through a wide and deep period of being," she wrote to Lola. "I have lost a very peculiar sort of faith I had in circumstances, and I have shed a final skin. And since the final skin has dropped, I feel that I am at last able to write, that an inner and unrarefied strata, a pure inner strain, has come to the surface and can never again be submerged or corroded."[30] For months Kay had hoped to be able to return to New York for the summer, but by the spring of 1924, she had come to realize that that would be an easy escape from a challenge she must face. Although she longed desperately to see her mother and Lola, coming to France had meant to her "the assertion of a new faith and the beginning of a new tradition," and now, she explained to Lola, "the material expression of it must be solved."[31] There was something strange, she felt, about all the young moderns who were writing, who seemed "mortally afraid of getting away from the center of action, from their cliques." "They seem to go all to pieces when they are weeded out from the central poles of action in New York and Paris and are tossed aside to grow by themselves."[32]

In May, 1924, Kay and Richard moved inland to Harfleur, where there was "no sign of prosperity anywhere around" (*BGT*, 146). They lived there for two years, and she writes that she became "totally French" (*BGT*, 146). The setting gave her the material for another novel, published in 1933 as *Gentlemen, I Address You Privately*. She set aside *Plagued by the Nightingale* half-finished to begin the next book "because all the details of Le Havre and the sea, and Harfleur and the land, were clamoring in my mind." She wanted to express what she had learned in that "unhappy town" while her experience was still fresh (*BGT*, 149).

Her poem about Le Havre, "Harbor Song," was accepted for *Poetry,* although "much mutilated" because Harriet Monroe could not "risk" the word "buttocks" nor the section entitled "Whore Street."[33]

She does not remember the exact date, but sometime in 1925 she received her first letter from Ernest Walsh. He had seen some of her poems in *Poetry* and *Broom* and got her address from Carnevali. He was starting a literary magazine entitled *This Quarter,* coediting it with a Scotswoman named Ethel Moorhead, and he wanted Kay Boyle to contribute to the first issue. It would be dedicated to Ezra Pound and would also contain work by Robert McAlmon, Gertrude Stein, Yvor Winters, William Carlos Williams, Ernest Hemingway, James Joyce, Emanuel Carnevali, Bryher (then married to McAlmon), and others. After she sent him some poems and excerpts from *Plagued by the Nightingale,* they began a steady correspondence. In the winter of 1926, the harshness of the climate finally took its toll on her health; she suffered a prolonged lung ailment that a local doctor eventually diagnosed as tuberculosis. As the winter wore on and her condition deteriorated, she became increasingly desperate to get out of Normandy, and even Richard's family sent money, saying she must find a way to get some sun. Ernest Walsh's cable from the south of France, where he and Moorhead lived, was a godsend: " 'Insist that you see my lung specialist in Paris. I will take care of everything. *La vie est belle.* We want you to join us here. Come quickly.' " With the help of a 1000 franc advance for *Plagued by the Nightingale* from "the angelic Ernest Walsh,"[34] Kay and Richard were able to scrape together the necessary sum, and at the end of February, she left Harfleur "for a month or six weeks, not longer" (*BGT,* 155–56).

Ernest Walsh and Ethel Moorhead had found a modest room for her in a *pension* not far from their villa in Grasse. Walsh himself suffered a lung ailment after surviving the crash of an Air Force plane he was piloting in Texas, but he assured Kay Boyle that first night, after a few drinks, that he had another five years to live. Ethel Moorhead, in her forties at the time, had been active in the women's suffrage movement in England, and a few years earlier she had "rescued" Michael (the name Ernest Walsh preferred his friends to call him) when he was ill at the Claridge Hotel in Paris and unable to pay his bill. Walsh had always dreamed that one day he could be the editor of an avant-garde literary magazine, Kay Boyle explains, "and Ethel Moorhead was able to realize that dream for him."[35]

In the South Kay's spirits soared. "I am so happy and so spoiled in this place by these charming people," she wrote to her family. "They treat me like a very little Katherine and feed me American food—shredded wheat whose existence I had forgotten, and Heinz Baked Beans and Tomato soup!" With Walsh and Moorhead she felt "less expatriated and more American than I ever did in my life."[36] The three would spend their days driving in the countryside and working on the magazine. In the evenings they relaxed in the villa. Walsh would read poetry, his own as well as Joyce's, McAlmon's, and Carnevali's, while the toilet on the second floor flushed mysteriously of its own will about every ten minutes—a detail Boyle includes in her novel about this period in her life, *Year Before Last* (1932).

"All would have been delightfully simple," Kay wrote to Lola in March, "had I not realized that what had been missing from me since I began was some very exciting and necessary quality in life which Ernest Walsh had got."[37] One evening after they had received word that her ailment was not tuberculosis, Boyle was typing in her room at the *pension,* hoping to finish *Plagued by the Nightingale* before she returned to the North, when Walsh came in to say that Ethel Moorhead had seen what was happening to the two of them and had packed her things and left. He wondered if Kay would mind taking him on. "And I, who had preached fidelity and denounced betrayal, accepted faithlessness as if it were the one thing I had been waiting for," she remembers. "At that moment I gave not a thought to what would become of Richard or whom Ethel would turn to now, for nothing mattered to me except Michael's beauty and his courage, and I wanted to pay homage to what he was for all my life" (*BGT,* 179–80).

A stormy relationship continued between Walsh and Moorhead, who had moved to Monte Carlo. As she held his beloved magazine hostage with her financial power, Boyle and Walsh began their life "on the run," moving from town to town, staying as long as they could in each, until a hotelkeeper would hear Walsh cough or clear his throat and ask them to leave. At the end of June they found themselves in Annot, a mountain village high above the Riviera, their energy and financial reserves nearly exhausted, desperately hoping they would be able to rest there. On the hotel terrace they were approached by a young Scots admirer, Archibald Craig, who had recognized Walsh from his photo in *This Quarter.*[38] (He claimed to have nearly memorized the magazine verbatim.) Through the efforts of Craig and his English cousin—the former Gladys Palmer, heir to the Huntley and Palmer biscuit fortune and now, through marriage, the Dayang Muda of Sarawak—Walsh and Boyle were given a room at the back of the hotel where his coughing could not be heard. Throughout the summer Walsh wrote letters, poems, essays, and book reviews "like one possessed" and, for the sake of the magazine, continued to hope for reconciliation with Ethel Moorhead.

In July Richard Brault wrote to Kay saying that he had found a good job with the Michelin tire company in Clermont-Ferrand, and he sent her money to meet him for the day somewhere not far from Annot so that they might "decide what we were going to do with our lives," she says

(*BGT,* 191). As it turned out, Kay persuaded him to spend his ten-day vacation among people he knew rather than alone, and "he and Michael were cordial from the first and got along very very well," Kay reported to her mother. When Walsh, after a round of parties and much champagne and merriment, lapsed into a series of hemorrhages, Richard "was marvelous all the days, waiting on him and doing errands, and allaying suspicions, and cheering me up, and talking to me because I couldn't of course leave the room for a moment."[39] Richard had Walsh's hemorrhage prescriptions filled pretending they were for himself, and one night when they had used all but the last injection, drove to Monte Carlo to buy more ampoules, returning at five in the morning. But Richard could not give Kay a divorce because of his family; he had told them nothing of the separation. "Maybe one day everything will change," he had said, and the matter ended there (*BGT,* 191).

By this time Kay Boyle was pregnant. She and Walsh enjoyed the good will of the townspeople, who were impressed by the couple's influential friends as well as charmed by Walsh. (An accomplished magician, he would perform tricks for the children on his evening walks, making lumps of sugar disappear from his palm and reappear in dogs' ears.) At the end of August, when the second issue of *This Quarter* was ready for printing, Ethel Moorhead paid Walsh a visit in Annot while Kay secreted herself at the Dayang Muda's villa for the day. Moorhead announced that she had decided to bring out the magazine alone. Walsh refused to hand over the material he had collected, Moorhead refused to show him the contributions she had brought with her, and Boyle returned to find on the floor pieces of the water carafe Walsh had thrown at his former coeditor.

In a hastily handwritten letter dated "October something," Kay Boyle wrote: "Dearest mama—I want to write you now when things are so intense with me because I want you to share with me from the beginning whatever's coming."[40] Walsh had been bleeding for a week, two hemorrhages a day, and his heart was too weak to tolerate another intravenous injection. The first night he had filled half a chamber pot with blood in five minutes and Ethel Moorhead "went to pieces," leaving Kay to "get his injections in his arm, ice and the doctor." Kay was convinced that Moorhead had brought on one of the attacks by her quarrelsomeness, and her presence greatly complicated matters. "Ethel is one of those hopeless people who drops everything before she gets it to you, knocks against the bed everytime she passes it, drops water down his neck, etc.," Kay told her mother, and whenever Walsh would ask for Kay instead of Ethel to do something for him, Ethel would become "fiercely injured." Yet, Kay acknowledged, "Christ knows what we would have done had she not been here to hand out checks to the specialists at 1200 francs a visit." Finally Moorhead arranged for an ambulance to take him to her villa overlooking Monte Carlo. There Ernest Walsh died on October 16, 1926, at the age of thirty-one, "with Ethel's renewed promises for the magazine in his ears and fresh confidence in his heart" (*BGT*, 191).

"I walk in the streets and want to tear the lungs and the hearts out of the people for his poor body," Kay wrote to Evelyn Scott a few weeks after Walsh's death. But she felt fortified by what they had meant to each other: "If Michael and I had not been together these last months—not through convention but through loyalty or pride—I should want to be dead now. But because as a salute to each other at once we became to each other the most beautiful the dearest the loveliest the fiercest it makes life now a clear thing with sharp edges when it might have been a dry grief at the heart."[41]

She resisted her first impulse to return to America, "back to my mother and sister, back to Lola, to the women I loved" (*BGT*, 191), and stayed with Ethel Moorhead in Monte Carlo, where they gambled together at the casino, decorated Moorhead's apartment, and were visited by her suffragist friends from England. It was a curious relationship. Ethel would mock Kay's ungainly figure by scornfully reeling through what she called "The Dance of Pregnancy," and as Boyle bathed, she would sit by the tub studying her body and puzzling aloud as to what Walsh had seen in her. ("If it were not for the Princess of Sarawak and [Archibald Craig] and the cat and the phonograph and this kicking mountain on my front, I'd go mad," Kay confided to Evelyn Scott.)[42] Yet Ethel also lied to the American consul in Nice, saying that Kay Boyle and Ernest Walsh had been married in her family home in Edinburgh so that Boyle could receive a pension as a veteran's widow. ("The pension from the U. S. Government never materialized, of course," she says today.)[43] On the morning of March 11, 1927, Archibald Craig having fainted in the corridor of the Clinique Ste. Marguerite in Nice, Kay gave birth to a "huge and healthy" girl. Ethel had held her hands all through it and "cheered the arrival of the brat," and together they named her Sharon, from the Song of Solomon.[44] Soon thereafter, "out of the greatness of her heart and in contempt for all official authority," Ethel perjured herself again when she registered Sharon at the Mairie de Nice as Ernest Walsh's legitimate child (*BGT*, 193).

It is hardly surprising that Kay Boyle and Ethel Moorhead could not continue to live together very long. Despite her kindness—McAlmon's friend, John Glassco, called her "incredibly shy and immeasurably shrewd" and said he would nominate her as literature's candidate for canonization[45]—Moorhead was difficult to live with. The several weeks that Kay spent at the clinic had been a welcome respite. "I wish you could know how happy I am in this clinique," she wrote to her mother while waiting for the baby to come. "A clean white room—much sun—

books—Picabia's watercolors—Ethel's watercolors—Michael's portrait—Steiglitz' photograph (taken out of 'Port of New York')—a 'bidet'—a shower—hot water—perfume, powder, eau de cologne—a pleasant nurse—and frequent callers . . . *I think the world is good to me.*"[46] When Sharon was born, Francis Picabia, who lived nearby, became her godfather. He told Kay that the baby was the image of Stieglitz and brought her "the most amazing blue silk and lace coat and bonnet you can imagine," Kay told her mother. ("Its use will be solely that of calling upon the Picabias. You would be quite startled by it really.")[47] Luxuriating in the peace and privacy of her sunny white room and writing endlessly (sometimes using her nursing baby as a desk), Kay had grown optimistic that she and Ethel would be able to get along together, united by their common interest in Sharon and in getting out the third number of *This Quarter,* a memorial issue to Ernest Walsh. But although she was busy (upon her return to Ethel's villa in Monte Carlo, she did nothing but "correct proof, feed Sharon, correct proof, change diapers, correct proof"), Kay found it a continuous struggle to live peacefully with the woman who considered her "the usurper."[48] Many years later she would say that her first recognition of Ethel's madness came when several of Ethel's British friends, who visited them from time to time, each took Kay aside to beseech her not to leave Ethel alone with the baby at any time, "as she was quite capable of dropping it out the window 'in error' or in getting rid of it in some other way."[49] When McAlmon came for a three-day visit that spring, Ethel enjoyed cattily speculating as to the identity of the baby's father and would say of Kay, " 'She has no ideas at all on any subject' " (*BGT*, 210). The day after McAlmon left them, he sent Kay Boyle a letter advising her to get away from Moorhead and offering her any money she needed to do so.

When Richard Brault had visited at Christmas, he had reported that he was being promoted to manager of Michelin in Stoke-on-Trent, England, and urged Kay to join him after the baby's arrival—to "live separately, write, and be merry."[50] Afterwards, he had sent money every week for the baby not yet born. Despite serious reservations about returning to Richard, Kay accepted McAlmon's offer and requested fifty dollars to get to England. "And so I go away sick at heart. But I can't stick it," she told Evelyn Scott. Living with Moorhead was "like being married to someone who gives you everything—consciously gives—and will have nothing in return. Not love, nor interest, or belief. And I leave E. M. quite alone—she has nothing but me and the baby."[51] After a brief visit with her mother and sister, then in London, Kay Boyle and her daughter joined Richard in Stoke-on-Trent. She would stay a year.

Ernest Walsh's obituary in the Paris *Tribune* calls him "one of the most brilliant poets of the younger generation, as well as an *animateur,* who has left his stamp on the literary history of his age" and notes that *This Quarter* was regarded by many as the most brilliant and advanced magazine in the Anglo-Saxon world. It concludes: "American literature loses in Ernest Walsh an intellectual whip. He opened up many channels for expression and facilitated the emergence of writers who were suppressed by a commercial criticism."[52] The author of the tribute was Eugene Jolas. On the day of Walsh's funeral, Boyle had received a telegram from him in Paris saying that he wanted to carry on Walsh's work. Jolas was going to start a magazine called *transition* and hoped that Kay Boyle would be able to send him some stories and poems as quickly as possible for the first number. It was through her correspondence and her writing, some of it with an eye to publication in *transition,* that she was able to give meaning to her life after Walsh's death. In the year she and Sharon lived with Richard in England, she finished *Plagued by the Nightingale* and returned to *Gentlemen, I Address You Privately,* while endlessly writing letters to Jolas, Lola Ridge, Evelyn Scott, McAlmon, Carnevali, and her mother.

Her loneliness was eased also by her lively, conspiratorial friendship with Germaine Garrigou, the French wife of one of the Michelin engineers. The women, whose friendship was "instantaneous" thanks to Sharon, would spend the weekdays confiding in each other, drinking white wine before lunch, and discussing the new spring fashions (the black Kay wore in mourning was not good for the baby, Germaine insisted). In Stoke-on-Trent, Kay Boyle kept alive her political interests as well. On August 22, 1927, she set off for the American consulate with Sharon in the baby carriage, intending to burn the American flag to protest the execution of Sacco and Vanzetti, set for the next day. On the way she sang lines of poetry to her daughter, as she always did on their walks, but on that day it was her own work that came to her—poems she had written for Ernest Walsh both before and after his death, entitled "To America" and "To an American," and one she had just finished for William Carlos Williams called "The United States." Looking back, she writes, "As I pushed the baby carriage up one street and down another, Michael's and Bill Williams' country and mine, and its speech, and its people, formed a great wide avenue before me, so that I did not walk alone." She realized with sharp conviction that "America, the only America that would endure, . . . did not belong to Judge Thayer, or to Governor Fuller of Massachusetts, or the the President of the United States, who had refused a shoemaker and a fish peddler his word of clemency." The America that would lend her its direction forever now "was Lola's, and it was Bill Williams', and Mother's, and Michael's, and mine," and it was Sacco's and Vanzetti's as well (*BGT*, 218). She returned home with the flag untouched, neatly folded under the baby's blanket in the pram.

Already Kay had begun to look for a way to get back to France, feeling that she could not "inflict a platonic wife upon Richard for the rest of his existence" and wanting to take care of her daughter herself. Ernest Walsh was still a constant presence. "I am in the state of madness or loneliness which prevents me from having ever any feeling of being alone," she wrote to Lola Ridge. "I believe always that someone else is actually there, a glimpse almost of the coat in the corner of my eye, and everything new which Sharon does to be repeated to him even though I can only remember and not hear his laugh." It was a "particularly nauseous" kind of madness, she felt, "practical only because he still exists for me as a standard of achievement or attempt." She wondered what she could ever give to her daughter that would have "that actual flavour and reality" of Walsh: "How can I say to her with any hope in convincing her that he was the gayest, the bravest, the simplest and the most gallant of poets?"[53]

Kay Boyle had kept in touch with Archibald Craig, with whom she had planned for months to edit a yearbook of "the most adventurous and experimental poems" in the hope of focusing interest and attention upon "otherwise occasionally printed poets who thereafter decided to become insurance agents instead." She acknowledged that their main credential as critics was "a sort of ferocious enthusiasm which *ought* to have a value."[54] They intended their book to reflect what really was happening in poetry, "not the girly-girly off-moments of Harriet [Monroe]'s crew or the mouthings of Eliot."[55] The advertisement they placed in the summer, 1928, issue of *transition* promised it would be "not only the best anthology of poetry ever published, but the most read, sought after, and renowned." "It is perhaps unnecessary to add that the yearbook never appeared," she writes (*BGT,* 219).

In the spring of 1928, Craig wrote to her that his cousin, the Dayang Muda, wanted her to come to Paris to ghostwrite her memoirs. With that intention, as well as with the plan to work on the anthology, she left England with Sharon at the end of April. Again, it was to be only a temporary arrangement, but she writes that she and Richard "must have known then because of all the pain I had caused him, and the sorrow we had lived through, that what we had been to each other once had finally come to an end" (*BGT,* 219).

For two months Kay Boyle lived in opulence while writing the memoirs of the Dayang Muda. The princess's castoff haute couture clothes were altered to fit her, and each morning the French maid, Louise, brought her breakfast in bed. (She later discovered that all in the series of maids were called "Louise" for the princess's convenience.) But she found the project difficult. The princess, Boyle claims, was almost totally inarticulate, her mind "appeared to function in a state of shock," and she could remember no details of her own life. It was up to Kay Boyle, with a little help from her friends, to fabricate the life story of the Dayang Muda. "We won't be indiscreet about who wrote them," Robert McAlmon reports of the project. "We'll just say that two very bright-witted Canadian lads, and one American authoress, and myself did a great deal of chuckling together as we invented witty remarks which great men of the 1890s, or thereabouts, had made" (*BGT,* 274). Yet John Glassco, one of the "Canadian lads," who was hired to type the memoirs, concludes in his own, "All Kay Boyle's skill had been unable to make the Princess's absurd life interesting."[56]

Kay Boyle's literary connections were expanding. She was drawn into the artistic and social circles of the Left Bank, although she claims much of the lost generation legend is just that. Those expatriated artists were in Paris together mainly because of the favorable exchange rate, she insists, and she feels that "all this glorification of that wonderful Camelot period is absurd."[57] While maintaining her friendship with William Carlos Williams, she became closer to Robert McAlmon and made the rounds of Montparnasse watering places with him, talking long hours with Hilaire Hiler, Man Ray, the model Kiki, and Flossie Martin—professional café frequenter and the "Queen of Montparnasse." Constantin Brancusi became a close friend and he and Kay worked out together the design of the marble for Ernest Walsh's tomb.[58] Boyle met almost daily with Eugene Jolas for at least one meal and through him met Laura Riding, Robert Graves, and others. At a party she attended with Archibald Craig at the Jolas's apartment, she was introduced to James and Nora Joyce and sat with them as Gertrude Stein and her entourage entered like a "ceremonial cortege" (*BGT,* 241). The greats exchanged no sign of recognition across the room. And it was Jolas who took her to the Bal Nègre very early one morning to meet Harry and Caresse Crosby, whom Kay Boyle had heard of as the publishers of the Black Sun Press and whom Jolas fondly considered "madder than hatters and freer than the wind."[59]

There were two writers in Paris with whom Kay Boyle did not become friendly. Archibald Craig had taken her to tea at 27 Rue de Fleurus, and she had had a pleasant chat with Alice B. Toklas about cooking and recipes. But afterward Gertrude Stein had asked him not to bring her back again, finding her "as incurably middle-class as Ernest Hemingway" (*BGT,* 296).[60]

As for Hemingway, Kay Boyle had ample opportunity to meet him. Her sister Joan was working at *Vogue* in Paris with Pauline Pfeiffer, who would be Hemingway's second wife, and the two women visited Boyle and Walsh in Grasse. For a week before their visit, letters from Hemingway had arrived daily for Pauline. Joan explained to Kay that he was writing about special perfume and lingerie found only in Grasse and Cannes that he wanted Pauline to bring back as surprise gifts for his wife,

Hadley. But Kay knew what was going on and disapproved of Hemingway's love affair with his wife's friend. She refused to meet him on the grounds that he was a "bastard."[61] Nor did she like his writing, with the exception of *In Our Time* ("a book worth reading forever!"). In 1931 she would chide Caresse Crosby for reprinting *Torrents of Spring,* which she called "my first disillusionment with Hemingway as a writer." "The best he has he owes to Sherwood Anderson," she said, and "it is ignoble to take that writer and write such dull and stupid ridicule."[62] Hemingway did not care much for her taste, either. Ernest Walsh was the victim of his cutting sketch in *A Moveable Feast* called "The Man Who Was Marked For Death."

But Kay Boyle had more than social contact with the Paris literary scene. Her own work was beginning to appear regularly in the little magazines, especially *transition.* She was in the unusual position of being friends both with the "*transition* group" and with Robert McAlmon, who had little stomach for Jolas's mystical concept of literature as a journey into the "night mind." Jolas, who was from Lorraine and trilingual, had a "neo-idealistic" philosophy of literature. Of the two main threads he saw in literary tradition, the classical and the romantic, he was attempting in *transition* to "follow the evolution" of the latter. He objected to "rationalism" on the grounds of its "voluntary narrowness," and he had hoped to make his magazine "a haven for the imaginative spirit."[63] Jolas rejected the realism that he saw as the dominant force in contemporary American literature—"the sordid cynicism and objectivism of the Middle-Western school." He wanted "to encourage a sense of the fabulous in terms of the Twentieth Century, and to work toward a more flexible and lucid speech" which would recognize the primacy of the dream and unconscious over the "secondary 'thinking' processes" and in which the subjective and objective worlds would merge.[64]

The June, 1929, issue of *transition* contained a piece nearly as sensational as the long excerpts from Joyce's "Work in Progress" that were a mainstay of the magazine. It was a twelve-point manifesto entitled "Revolution of the Word." It declares, among other things, that "The imagination in search of a fabulous world is autonomous and unconfined;" that "Pure poetry is a lyrical absolute that seeks an a priori reality within ourselves alone;" that "The literary creator has the right to disintegrate the primal matter of words imposed on him by text-books and dictionaries;" that "Time is a tyranny to be abolished;" and that "The writer expresses. He does not communicate." The proper "expression of these concepts" could be achieved only through "the rhythmic 'hallucination of the word.' " The manifesto concludes: "The plain reader be damned." The proclamation was signed by sixteen leading literary figures of the day, including Hart Crane, Whit Burnett, Stuart Gilbert, Eugene

Jolas, Laurence Vail, and Harry and Caresse Crosby. The first name on the list is Kay Boyle's.

Robert McAlmon's literary views were rather different from those of the manifesto's signatories. He acknowledged that *transition,* under the editorship of Eugene Jolas, Elliot Paul, and Robert Sage, exerted a great deal of influence on the young writers of the day, but he says: "It was a constant example of how not to write. By the time these three boys had chased the hallucinatory word over the sleepwalking realms of a mythos, any balanced writer was apt to decide that either he or they were having delirium tremens, and to yearn for the normality of a simple and direct style in which words 'meant' something" (*BGT,* 252). The hostility between McAlmon and the *transition* editors was open. Kay Boyle believed (and "told Jolas constantly") that he did not publish McAlmon's work solely because McAlmon made fun of Jolas and *transition.* Jolas insisted that he simply did not care for McAlmon's work and that his rejection of McAlmon's submissions had nothing to do with personalities.[65] In an effort to expose the truth, Kay Boyle submitted some of McAlmon's poems to the magazine saying they had been written by a young poet named "Guy Urquhart" who lived in the Midwest. Jolas promptly accepted them. Ironically, they were published in the same issue of *transition* as some barbs by a group of New York literati directed toward American exiles, including McAlmon. One jingle, which Boyle reports gained "a certain amount of notoriety," went: "I'd rather live in Oregon and pack salmon,/Than live in Nice and write like Robert McAlmon" (*BGT,* 299). When she eventually confessed the identity of Guy Urquhart, Jolas was not amused.

Kay Boyle was able to maintain untarnished her high regard for both men, however. While always acknowledging her great debt to and affection for Jolas, she had the deepest respect for McAlmon as well. "He is the real thing," she told her sister in 1927, and she wrote of him in 1960, "It was McAlmon who, in liberating himself from genteel language and thought, spoke for his generation in a voice that echoes, unacknowledged, in the prose of Hemingway and that of other writers of his time."[66] Looking back, she is glad she had pledged her allegiance to no one group or school of thought, saying: "I was grateful then, and I am still grateful now, that I lacked the intellectual effrontery, and subsequent embitterment, that might have diminished my acknowledgment of all these two men stood for and all that they had done" (*BGT,* 299).

Kay Boyle worked for the Dayang Muda during May and June of 1928 and explains that by the time she had finished the memoirs, "my social conscience was in such a bad way that I decided to join Raymond Duncan's colony" (*BGT,* 292). Duncan and his group lived in a sort of commune in Neuilly, where they wore Greek-style tunics and lived mainly on goat cheese and yogurt. They supported themselves through sales in their two Paris shops, which carried sandals, tunics, and other "folk art," supposedly crafted at the colony. (Kay Boyle claims she never saw any evidence of such handiwork going on there and believes the items were left over from the time when Duncan and his late sister, Isadora, had worked in Greece several years earlier.) Boyle first met Raymond Duncan when he had arrived, tunic-clad and unannounced, at the Dayang Muda's one afternoon when Gertrude Stein and Alice B. Toklas also happened to be there. The conversation up to that point had been strained, and his arrival had saved the afternoon, for he and Stein had both grown up in Oakland, California. She took great delight in recalling his childhood clumsiness at baseball and his former taste for fine sherry, long dark cigars, impeccably creased trousers, and carnation boutonnieres.

Kay Boyle's decision to join Duncan's colony was as much a practical move on the part of a single mother as an ideological commitment. "Any other job I could not make enough to have Bobby with me and a maid, flat, etc.," Kay wrote to her mother, referring to her baby daughter by her nickname. "And I am interested—with qualifications—in what Raymond is doing."[67] Duncan's group provided food, lodging, and care for Sharon, and Kay Boyle was assigned to work in the colony's gift shops. Six days a week she opened one of the two stores on the Rue du Faubourg St Honoré and on the Boulevard St. Germain. Between customers she passed the time writing on any bits of paper she could find and talking with friends who dropped by. But by mid-July most of her friends—Craig and the Dayang Muda, Jolas, Brancusi, and McAlmon—had gone on summer vacation, and when the other colony members left for six weeks in Nice, taking her sixteen-month-old daughter with them, "off I went into the deep without any trouble," Boyle says: "In and out of every bar in Montparnasse I tripped and reeled and stumbled in my fine blue cape. . . . I consorted with this one and that one, love having nothing to do with it (love, indeed, the most uproarious joke of the century), probity scattered to the north, east, west and south (if such directions should still be recognized") (*BGT,* 317). To make matters worse, she discovered "there would be trouble to face nine months ahead, and who the happy and proud progenitor might be I was unable to determine." She decided that the child must not be born and writes, "Caresse helped me find the place and time, and Harry (who had no part in it) paid the enormous bill" (*BGT,* 320). Then the Crosbys left town, too.

The nightmare period that Kay Boyle calls her "collapse" was ended late in August by an attack of cerebral meningitis, which the doctors at the American Hospital in Paris credited to the filthy privy behind the shop. She was in the hospital for six weeks, where she was nursed by her mother (who was "inexplicably there") and finally was able to do some work on the poetry anthology. It was October before she was able to return to work, walking with the help of two canes. Although it was obvious that she had been dangerously ill, Duncan reproached her for a breach of loyalty, believing that she had been struck by "mother-sickness."

In early November, two American women walked into the shop and bought $25,000 worth of goods supposedly handcrafted at the colony, intending to establish a Raymond Duncan wing in a Kentucky museum. It was when Duncan bought himself a large American car with the proceeds that Kay Boyle decided she could not stay on in his group. Yet, she says, "I was not in the best of positions, actually, to take issue with Raymond's integrity" (*BGT*, 323). For one thing, the Crosbys had insisted on leaving their limousine at her disposal while they were away in America, and every morning the chauffeur would call at the colony to drive her into Paris, the "cracked and broken toes" of her ancient shoes "emerging shamelessly" from under the sable lap robe (*BGT*, 324). More important, however, she feared that there would be trouble over the custody of her daughter, since there had been previous lawsuits over guardianship of children living at the colony. Because Sharon's birth had been registered illegally in Nice, Boyle felt she had best make a surreptitious exit. Throughout December, 1928, she smuggled out her belongings and stored them in the Dayang Muda's apartment. Finally, in a prearranged plan, the Dayang Muda invited nine of the colony children to lunch on the last day of the year, and when the two taxis bearing them pulled up at the apartment and discharged the tunic-and-sandal-clad guests, Kay Boyle and Sharon remained in the cab and sped away to McAlmon's hotel. The three of them went that afternoon to Le Moulin, Harry and Caresse's place in the country.

"There were too many people at Le Moulin that December afternoon, and none of them—except for Caresse's two children, Polleen and Billy, who were twelve and ten—were the kind of people McAlmon liked," Boyle recalls (*BGT*, 326). After Harry had concocted a special drink for McAlmon, "which was intended to send Bob into poetic delirium for the next twenty-four hours," she reports that McAlmon had said to her: "It's too damned depressing . . . so depressing that I can't even get drunk. They're wraiths, all of them. They aren't people. God knows what they've done with their realities" (*BGT*, 328). She concurs that the Crosbys could be difficult company: "It was almost always the case in Caresse's and Harry's gatherings: one had to hold onto a clear knowledge of what they were seeking and what they had relinquished, sacrificed even, in that search, in order to bypass the people who surrounded them" (*BGT*, 326). The next December, Harry would be dead in a New York hotel room as a result of a bizarre suicide pact with one of his mistresses, whom he called "The Fire Princess." His end came twelve years "early": he and Caresse had planned a brilliant death for themselves for October 31, 1942, and she had changed her name from Polly (Peabody, by her first marriage) to Caresse, so that her name and Harry's could intersect in a cross. Their gravestone had already been carved and delivered to the Cimitière de l'Abbaye de Longchamp in Paris.[68]

In 1929 Kay Boyle began her life with Laurence Vail. They had met at the Coupole on the December afternoon that she and McAlmon were plotting Sharon's escape from the colony. Vail, who had earned the title "King of Bohemia," had called out to McAlmon and her to come have a drink and supper at the table he was sharing with his sister, Clotilde. Boyle is silent in print about the details of her early relationship with Vail. In *Being Geniuses Together,* her account of the year 1929 skips from New Year's morning at Le Moulin to the statement, "Laurence Vail and I celebrated the Quatorze Juillet of 1929 with Hart Crane in Paris" (*BGT,* 330). They began their life together in the village of St. Aulde with two children—Sharon Walsh and Sindbad, Vail's son from his marriage to Peggy Guggenheim. The author recalls walking through a deserted Paris on an August afternoon "in guilty contentment, knowing that, having found Laurence, I would never be alone again": "Our first child was going to be born in December, and there would be more children; and we would write books, and translate the books of the French writers we liked; and we would paint pictures, and climb mountains, and cross glaciers, and travel with all our children, forever together" (*BGT,* 331). The last two words are inaccurate, as she knew when she wrote them in the sixties. It would be by her choice that her life with Vail would end thirteen years later, but the thirties would be a happy and productive period for her. In the thirties, her career as a writer would begin to take off, but the people and places she had known in the twenties would provide the materials and shape the style of her work for decades to come. The twenties had been a time of sending out roots through which Kay Boyle would draw sustenance, personal and artistic, for the rest of her life.

2

The Revolution of the Word

"It may appear to have been a time without much humor in the avant-garde literary movement, but it must be remembered that it was a time of the gravest crisis in letters, of furious schism and revolution in the arts. . . . This was a serious business, and if one laughed a good deal over café tables, one did not laugh very loudly on the printed page," writes Kay Boyle of the twenties (*BGT,* 214). In the twenties and early thirties, Paris resounded with highly charged talk about art, and to Kay Boyle, as to many others, art was both politics and religion. Looking back, she describes it as "a time of peril" in which "gravity was demanded of writers who fought against the sentence of death, of oblivion, passed on their work by critics and publishers, and on the life term offered as alternative, to be served in the ancient strongholds of the established conventional forms" (*BGT,* 214). The little magazines abounded with declarations, definitions, and manifestos, and in the ideological battles that raged between their covers moderation was no virtue.

One of the most colorful examples of the vehemence with which the pens were drawn appears in the second issue of *This Quarter*. In the July, 1925, issue of *Poetry: A Magazine of Verse* (a publication of twelve years' standing), editor Harriet Monroe had reviewed the first issue of *This Quarter,* politely expressing her reservations as to the need for yet another magazine succeeding to *The Little Review, Broom, Others,* "and other radicals even less stable whose fitfulness or early demise have been lamented from time to time in these pages." She ends the critique with cute condescension: "And perhaps in the next number they will show us the promised land!" *This Quarter* did not appreciate the indulgent remark. Its second issue reprinted the entire review, adding this preface:

> The episode is taken note of here because it is typical rather than exceptional of the kind of thing THIS QUARTER means to make war on: namely the insinuating school of criticism; the weary critic; the bald-headed critic; the judicial critic; the polite critic; the malicious critic; the thousand and one kinds of critic that ought to *shut up*. There is only one kind of critic worth having and that is the *judge* possessing judgement rather than judgements who *values* rather than *discounts* and who *kills* cleanly but does not *poison* and who either loves or

despises. What cannot be either loved or despised is not vital enough to celebrate in print.[1]

In the third issue of *This Quarter,* Kay Boyle seconded the editors' pro-
nouncement by placing "Miss Harriet Monroe" on her "Unrecommended List"—a choleric regular feature of the magazine in which various contributors listed their least favorite books, bars, hotels, and
people.

Her ideology in those days is easy enough to piece together. She
clearly—in fact, stridently—outlined her moral/aesthetic stance (the two
were inseparable) in a number of articles. The fall 1928 issue of *transition*
published responses by seventeen expatriate artists—Gertrude Stein,
Robert McAlmon, and Harry Crosby, among others—to the question,
"Why do Americans live in Europe?" In her feisty reply, Kay Boyle
expressed her sense of alienation from her philistine homeland: "Americans I would permit to serve me, to conduct me rapidly and competently
wherever I was going, but not for one moment to impose their achievements upon what is going on in my heart and in my soul. I am too proud
and too young to need the grandeur of physical America which one
accepts only at the price of one's own dignity." "Each citizen functions
with pride in the American conspiracy against the individual," she declares, and with a proud jab at American softness and priggishness, warns
her compatriots: "Cling, gentlemen, to the skyscraper by toe-finger-eye-
lash, but do not come to Europe. Here nothing is done for you. You must
write your own literature, you must walk up and down stairs, and you
must drink like gentlemen."[2]

Of the artist, Kay Boyle demanded passion and originality. She
lauded Eugene Jolas, editor of *transition,* who had written, "Follow the
voice that booms in the deepest dream, deeper go, always deeper,"
calling him "a tireless stoker for a great wild fire" who "made a wondrous conflagration to warm cold nights and days." (The March, 1932,
issue of *transition* had been solemnly subtitled "An International Work-
shop for Orphic Creation.") Of Gertrude Stein, who taught people "to
fear the many-syllabled word and to mistrust the intellect," she writes:
"It would be well if, for her might, economy, and devotion, she were
sainted. I would be the first to bow the knee. Whether you will or
whether you won't, each word she writes is a stone cast after you."[3] Nor
was Kay Boyle's admiration of boldly original writers limited to her
immediate contemporaries: in 1931 she wrote, "I have no religion except that of poetry, and in Poe, Whitman, and William Carlos Williams
I recognize the apostles of America."[4]

She articulates her aesthetic values most completely in a memorial
piece she wrote a few months after the death of her friend Harry Crosby.

It begins: "To be living now, to be living, alive and full of the thing, to believe in the sun, the moon, or the stars, or in whatever is your belief, and to write of these things with an alertness sharp as a blade and as relentless, is a challenge that is a solemn privilege of the young." Harry Crosby stood "singularly alone" in her eyes in his "grave acknowledgement of that responsibility." "There was no one who ever lived more consistently in the thing that was happening then," she wrote, and she mused:

> Maybe it would be a good thing if history were never set down. It imposes a tradition of standards that has to do with the experiences of other people, and it makes criticism a literary right instead of a lonely deliberation of the heart. It puts judgment upon man before he is conceived even, and judgment on the life he has not begun to live. And if a man write down his poetry and his life, they are doomed before they are written by the poetry and the lives that have been done before.[5]

The stance was not original, of course. American writers had battled against a stale and inhibiting tradition the century before, and Emerson had already stated their case. For all their revolutionary talk, Kay Boyle and her contemporaries were more firmly grounded in a literary tradition than they perhaps recognized, descending in a straight line from American romantics like Poe and Whitman—not surprisingly, the very poets Boyle admired. What happened in the twenties was, after all, "a second flowering."[6] But Kay Boyle did not know of or did not recognize her antecedents. "You see," she explains, looking back, "I didn't have much of a formal education. I don't think I would have written all the books I did, over thirty books, had I realized that other people had already written everything there was to be said. I thought I had to tell people these things, because they hadn't been said before. That's why I felt compelled to write."[7]

Kay Boyle and her contemporaries plunged into their aesthetic revolution with religious zeal. Their mission was no less than to revive a desiccated English language:

> It is a sad time when the sap and the juice wither and dry in a language as when religion leaves the church and no longer resides in the symbols. But the English tongue was in for a long drought, and has been; parched and perished and written out as dry as sand. It has always been left to the poets to water the emotions, and when they sharpened their wits instead, it left the appetite high and dry.[8]

Many of Kay Boyle's poems, stories, and novels of that period are superb in their complex, innovative use of language and their authenticity of feeling. All of them were conscientiously wrought as offerings to the Revolution of the Word in which she so fervently believed.

In the beginning Kay Boyle considered herself a poet. In her estimation, poetry was the highest form of literature. "There is prose everywhere, giving the shape and smell of a man, but there is not enough poetry."[9] While she believed that "the short story and novel form are adequate finger exercises," she declared, "I, for one, am working towards a broad and pure poetic form."[10] The *transition* advertisement soliciting contributions to her poetry anthology expresses her romantic exuberance and her devotion to the genre. The first volume of *Living Poetry,* it said, would appear in September, 1928, under the editorship of Archibald Craig and Kay Boyle, *"who deny* that romance went out to the slow music of sewing machines and motor cycles. And *who affirm* that poetry is going on with a hot foot in a true stride." They wished to print not only the "perfect poem," but "even more the personal adventure, the contemporary escapade," which "come into the poet's life and out of the poet's heart with the same intensity that ever they did in more gallant ages."[11]

Kay Boyle was first known for her poetry and had published a number of poems before her first piece of fiction, a short story entitled "Passeres' Paris," appeared in the first issue of *This Quarter* (along with Hemingway's "Big Two-Hearted River"). She would receive a Guggenheim fellowship in 1934 to write an epic-length poem on the history of aviation (an abortive effort that resulted in a few published fragments). In the course of her career, she has published five volumes of poetry, the latest being *This Is Not a Letter and Other Poems* in 1985. And she still says that she prefers writing poetry because it is such a challenge.[12]

From the start, her poetic efforts were shaped by the belief that a poem should not simply convey a message in verse but should exist as an object of art on its own terms. Certainly, the idea was not her invention. Her friend Archibald MacLeish stated it clearly in "Ars Poetica" when he wrote, "A poem should not mean/But be." Samuel Beckett had written in *transition* that James Joyce was not writing *about* something, he was writing *something,* and Kay Boyle had been impressed enough by the piece to cite it in an interview some fifty years later as "a beautiful essay."[13] It is fair to assume that she espoused the aesthetics of her friend and mentor (and one of her "apostles of America"), William Carlos Williams, who declared that "the object of writing is to celebrate the triumph of sense" and that "in writing, as in art generally, sense is the form."[14]

Kay Boyle was also a close friend and long-time correspondent of Robert Carlton Brown. Inspired by a ticker tape machine, he had conceived of the "Reading Machine," a portable device that would liberate words from the convention of the printed page and revive "the optical end of the written word" by printing entire books on a single-line ribbon of paper to be unrolled beneath a magnifying glass.[15] His anthology of "readies"—pieces of poetry and prose stripped of such baggage as articles, pronouns, and connectives—was published by his Roving Eye Press in 1931 and included contributions by over forty of his literary friends, including Kay Boyle.

When she reviewed the *Readie Anthology* for *Contempo,* she cited as one of the best contributions a poem by Wambly Bald ("whose name in itself is an invention"): *"Dark a de rain a de cold a de bang a de bang the train like hell."* It has "design, orphic sensation, and optical sequence," she wrote. Innovation was a primary virtue in the prevailing aesthetic judgment, and her demands of the artist were uncompromising: "There should be a fire of shame that scalds the neck and ears and face from off a man if he in vanity set down words in a way that they have been set down before."[16]

Kay Boyle, using pictorial language, was seeking to capture in her own poetry the essence of an instant. An early critic said that "to enjoy her poems one must accept the theory of poetry which rules out utilitarian language, the familiar sequence of cues to the intelligence by which common ideas are refurbished and represented; which instead seeks by a 'flaming collusion of rare words' to induct one without the aid of reason into a realm of pure poetic pleasure."[17]

When she was good, she was very good. In a 1926 poem entitled "Hunt," she writes:

The buckhounds went on under the rain
with the wet fern swinging lace over their
eyes
and their skins hanging like crumpled
velvet.[18]

But as the same critic pointed out, "the weakness of the genre is that it is easier to run shallow than to run deep. If a phrase is not divinely right, it is nothing more than a silly waste."[19] The fresh image of the buckhounds is immediately followed by these lines:

the bucks shod with leaves like silk sandals
danced on chopsticks over the suey of red
lizards
              white stalks
              and caterpillars

When the image fails, the effort seems precious. As a later critic put it, at times "her style pirouettes stiffly before a looking-glass."[20]

The subject matter of Kay Boyle's poetry is kaleidoscopic. One poem was written "In defense of homosexuality" (1925), and she attacked the simplistic military mind in "The Only Bird That Sang" (1929). ("The corporal died knowing that if Debs/Had been president there'd be a german general/In every maiden lady's bed," she wrote.)[21] In "A Statement for El Greco and William Carlos Williams" (1931), she pays homage to the artist who revitalizes our sense of our past. Other poems are intensely personal tributes. A number written in the late twenties are paeans to Ernest Walsh, although his name is rarely mentioned. They grieve for one who used to "Make sugars fly/up his cuffs after dinner find/potatoes hot in the dogs' ears"—for a "Young man who died one autumn."[22]

Kay Boyle was experimenting with form also. Her poems incorporate such varied devices as marginal glosses, parallel columns of dialogue, and prose paragraphs—sometimes printed in italics, alternating with lyrical refrains, or set apart with subtitles like "The Complaint in It," "The Story I Wanted to Tell You," or "The Spiritual for Nine Voices." Even her titles reflect an effort to define and extend the forms of poetry (as well as testify to how inextricably her art and personal life are meshed). Her first collection, *A Glad Day* (1938), includes "A Comeallye for Robert Carlton Brown," "A Confession to Eugene Jolas," "A Communication to Nancy Cunard," "A Christmas Carol for Emanuel Carnevali," and "A Valentine for Harry Crosby." It is hardly surprising that the book never became popular with "plain readers," but even critics felt the poems were too personal to be accessible to those outside her circle.

She did not much respect such evaluations, feeling the critics had not read carefully enough to grasp her universal themes, but Kay Boyle *was* continually frustrated by the elusiveness of a satisfactory form for her poetry. She wrote to William Carlos Williams: "Some kind of poetic form has to be found or I'll go crazy. I can't go on taking what you (and others) make possible and beautiful. I think I've got lots to say in poetry and no, no, no form. Lousy—loose—*no punch*—no shape—no agony of line like the back-side or a lovely thigh or whatnot."[23] But he was facing the same problem himself. In his response, a complete treatise on poetry (which he intended to publish in his revived magazine, *Contact II*), Williams agreed that "There is no workable poetic form extant among us today." In his own frustration he had turned to prose, he said, "since I didn't know what to do with poetry." He wrote: "Poetry can be a laboratory for metrics. It is lower on the literary scale. But it throws up jewels which may be cleaned and grouped."[24]

Kay Boyle's own prose writing would throw up far more jewels in the long run than would her experiments with poetry—although there are some to be found there. As early as 1932, *Contempo* called her "one of the best living short story writers."[25] It is primarily as a writer of fiction, especially as a first-rate short-story artist, that Kay Boyle gained her reputation and made her finest contributions not only to the aesthetic revolution of the twenties but to American literature of the twentieth century.

Perhaps *Wedding Day and Other Stories* (1930) cannot precisely be called Kay Boyle's "germinal" work of fiction. For one thing, it is not her first book; that was a slim volume unpretentiously called *Short Stories* (1929), published in a deluxe limited edition of 165 copies by the Crosbys' Black Sun Press. For another, it is not an organic composition. *Wedding Day* consists of the seven pieces in *Short Stories* plus six more. The stories were written over several years, and nine of the thirteen had been published previously in little magazines from 1927 to 1930. Nonetheless, *Wedding Day and Other Stories* is a significant book deserving a close look as a way in to a study of the author's entire canon: in these early stories she outlined and explored the themes central to nearly all she wrote for the next fifty years, and she did it with a skill that later she would at times be unable to match.

As the title suggests, the stories in *Wedding Day* concern love—generally lost or lacking, however. They are products of pain; it is perhaps significant that all were first published after the death of Ernest Walsh. Kay Boyle chose not to include in the book her first three published short stories—"Passeres' Paris," "Flight," and "Collation," which appeared in little magazines in 1925 and 1926—all rather mannered vignettes of artistic souls in exile. In fact, they have never been collected. Perhaps she felt the material was derivative, that her baptism by pain— the unfortunate requisite for many artists—gave her work substance. Soon after the book was published, she wrote: "There should be a lacking limb that grows to seize the pen and write only when man has passed through deep corridors of humility and death, and still survived."[26] If Kay Boyle's experimentation with language was not unique in that heyday of "orphic creation," the material in *Wedding Day* was her own—forged in her personal passage through "deep corridors" of loss and despair.

While her perspective is thoroughly romantic in the sense that she mistrusts the intellect, places her faith in intuition, and depicts the external world as a reflection or projection of the perceiver's consciousness, it most assuredly is not romantic in the sentimental sense one might expect of a book called *Wedding Day*. These are no ordinary love stories. A reviewer in 1932 noted that Kay Boyle's fiction deals with "the distress of human beings reaching for love and for each other, under the cloud of disease, or the foreknowledge of death. . . . The short stories particularly revive for us the painful brilliance of living. Here is poison—in the small doses in which arsenic is prescribed for anemia."[27] Still, love is clearly the author's primary concern. She finds it the one element essential to a meaningful human existence, and in the stories of *Wedding Day* she explores the tragedy of its unfulfillment, whether the barriers to contact be imposed by society, by one's own psyche, or by the biological inevitabilities of life itself.

Four stories of *Wedding Day*—"On the Run," "Portrait," "Vacation-Time," and "Spring Morning"—are complex, psychological studies of a young woman's responses to the death of her lover, who strongly resembles Ernest Walsh. In each of these stories, the man has coughed and hemorrhaged his way to death; it is obvious that the author was painfully familiar with the details of such a disease. Written in the years immediately following Walsh's death, the stories capture in white heat the agony, terror, and despair of her loss. They deal with the ultimate betrayer of love—death—the obstacle that could not be overcome even if people *were* always sensitive, honest, and strong.

It is in these four stories that Kay Boyle makes her most daring and perhaps most brilliant contributions to the Revolution of the Word. As she attempts to capture with absolute accuracy a state of consciousness or the precise course of an exchange, comparisons with the work of her friend James Joyce are hard to avoid. Margaret Atwood has said that Kay Boyle's is a "solid world solidly described, but it is also a world in which matter is merely a form of energy." Her writing approaches "the hallucinatory, or rather the moment of visionary realism when sensation heightens and time for an instant fixes and stops."[28] The stories are also important as her first working through of material and techniques she would use later in two novels exploring her life with Ernest Walsh and its devastating aftermath: *Year Before Last* (1932) and *My Next Bride* (1934).

In "On the Run" the situation is simple. A rootless young couple, drifting from one Alpine village to another, tries to conceal the man's consumptive disease from a suspicious hotelkeeper so they can settle down for some badly needed rest. As in many of Kay Boyle's works, the external landscape in this story takes on the shadings of the perceiving consciousness. As the couple's train pulls into Saint-André-les-Alpes, the objective is rendered subjectively by an unidentified but not unbiased narrative voice, and we know their stay will not be a pleasant one: "The crest of little alps was burning across the roofs of the town, with the dry crumbling finger of the church lifted and the sky gaping white and hot upon decay" (*WD*, 103).[29] We next see the ill man at the hotel ordering with feigned vigor pigs' feet grilled in batter in order to convince the *bonne* of "the natural beauty of his hunger" (*WD*, 103–4). But the fairly conventional narrative style is abruptly broken as the man speaks quickly and desperately to his companion in the English that the *bonne* does not understand: "Get her out of here he said I am going to cough Christ is this where the death will get me take the cigaret and when I cough walk around the room and sing or something so they won't hear me" (*WD*, 104).

Subtly, but with bitter irony, the author expresses her contempt for the bourgeois hypocrisy that makes a show of mourning yet gives to callousness the name of propriety. She describes the interview between the young woman and the proprietor, a middle-aged woman clad in the rich black costume of perpetual mourning: "The sweet sorrow of the crucifix faced them the rosary hanging like false-teeth on the bed-stead the sacred smile the Christ bled with artistry in the well-rounded arms of the Virgin. 'Madame,' she said without any hesitation, 'your husband cannot die here,' she said, 'we are not prepared for death' " (*WD*, 106).

When the young woman returns to her lover, he scolds her for leaving him for "a hundred years" and then says into the pillow, speaking to Saint André, "I'm a sick man, I'm afraid. This time I'm afraid to go on." The story ends poignantly with a long, disjointed declamation by the woman that reveals her terror and love. As she packs their bags, she babbles to cover up the sound of his coughing. She is not whistling in the dark; she is shouting into it in desperation:

> You you afraid listen here packing the bags again the hairy-legged pointed ampoules as beautiful as earrings bottles of ergotine and striped pajamas we're going on somewhere else and have pigs' feet grilled and champagne and peaches with flames running on them this hole dries the guts in you do you remember Menton last February and every time you read Umbra the cabinay flushed may the Gods speak softly of us in days hereafter and the very small sausages for breakfast at the Ruhl
>
> Saint-André-les-Alpes you're a perfectly ordinary pisspot
> With a blue eye painted in the bottom of it
> Fit only to be put in a cheap room under the bed
> With education refinement and all the delicate bellyaches
> Here's to bigger and better pigs' feet

The story ends: "Keep on keep on keep on he said maybe I'm going to bleed" (*WD*, 107).

On first reading, "Portrait" is a puzzling story, as Kay Boyle continues to explore what Jolas called the "night mind" and to experiment with the language of hallucination. The protagonist, again a young woman, waits alone in a dark hotel room for her lover to return from an evening out. They both know he is dying. The story is a bizarre dialogue between the woman and a voice in the dark that she calls "Tara." The author captures the woman's tension and fear while waiting in bed watching the room "through her eyelids," singing to herself a psalm-like lyric of her lover's return. "There would be a long time to wait and the voice of Tara would sit in the dark by the bed, fingers clasped lightly and elbows in black lace masks resting on the arms of the chair" (WD, 86). Tara speaks of death, of women and their lives without men, and asks her, "Someday if he does not come back to you what will you do?" The room takes on a strange animation: "when lights passed in the street the darkness stirred like a slow fan and the smooth mirrors were ruffled" (WD, 87). The woman imagines the joy of his return, and subject and object merge in her consciousness until the imagery loses contact with "reality:"

> He would come and he would sing in the room to you, holding his notes up in his fingers as though his song were a bouquet of flowers. Or dance in the room on his thin feet, picking gestures from the air and fitting them to his body. And the geranium leaves at the windows would lean in and clap their palms together. His breath would be new strange wax-cool odor shaped with the designs of his absence. His kisses would be lettuce leaves on your fingers. (WD, 88)

He would tell her fantastic stories to make her laugh and then "He would cough in his chest and sit a long time coughing and he would say 'Once I heard a man cough this way and in a few months he was dead.' And you knew there was no truth in that either" (WD, 89). And when Tara would assure her it was true, "you knew it was only that she wanted the blood up out of his veins and carried away in china vessels from the room" (WD, 89). In the final sentence of the story, Kay Boyle captures the young woman's rebellious refusal to acknowledge Tara's grim, serene pronouncements of reality and the fresh, if naive, relief that she knows will accompany her lover's return: "And you would beat the pillow and scream at her that his voice would be sudden cold glass in the hall, saying 'sacred Jesus . . .' he would bruise the points of your slippers because his boots were always longer than he remembered, he would come in and Tara would be your black silk gown over the chair, and the room would sit up in the light like a sleepy child" (WD, 89). The quality of nightmare vanishes in these lines and the simple objects in the room, personified into grotesque beings by the woman's loneliness and fear, return to their comprehensible states. It is a skillful and original exercise in capturing the complexities created when the imagination gets out of control and creates other, terrifying, worlds.

In Wedding Day, "Portrait" is followed by "Vacation-Time" and "Spring Morning," and the sequence corresponds to the events that have taken place in the young woman's life. The waking nightmare of "Portrait," half-amusing when dispelled, is triggered, of course, by the all-too-real fact that the lover's absence is soon to be permanent. And, as the author herself slipped into a two-month collapse a year and a half after Ernest Walsh's death, so does the protagonist of her stories. "I was walking around like a nut in the streets after the train had gone off, and the black was all running down my face from my eyes. I was going like a crazy-woman from one place to another thinking that tonight I must get into something deeper, the eyes full, the mouth full, to be sunk in it, to wallow like a sow" (*WD*, 91). So begins "Vacation-Time." In it Kay Boyle captures in hallucinatory, stream-of-consciousness prose the despair that engulfs the woman after her lover's death. She grasps for any contact, pouring out her soul to a stranger at a bar, babbling, "I am not able to sit home in intellectual quiet I am beginning to get tired of what is sensitive unable to acclimatize I am for the gay the biddy a great thing it is to roll home in the furnace of anybody's mouth blasting rust like wine all night and no sleep but the brain too going hot as a black bottom" (*WD*, 92). Like the author, she attempts to lose her grief in drink and promiscuity, yet she is haunted by the details of her lover's death. Like Walsh, he had died of consumption in Monte Carlo. Still at the bar, the woman carries on a bizarre mental dialogue with the district gendarmerie of Monte Carlo, trying to recall her lover's exact last words, and finally, on her third try, she is able to say clearly what had happened: "He did not draw himself up to his full height as a poet he sagged in the middle there was a bright fan of red velvet fluttering from his mouth and he was saying speak louder for Christ' sake the cocaine is ringing like hell in my head" (*WD*, 94). It is as haunting and devastating a scene as the one Emily Dickinson created when she obliterated the anticipated glory of death with a fly's buzz. The protagonist's rock-bottom despair is manifest as her mind returns to the present surroundings of the bar: "I looked into the bottom of my glass of and I murmured to the soft blue clouds of gin I too I too should have spat my way to heaven with him" (*WD*, 94).

Raymond Duncan had refused to leave Kay Boyle's daughter with her when the colony went en masse to the South of France in the summer of 1928. "I actually felt the end of the world had come when they took Sharon to Nice," the author says.[30] The story's protagonist has just sent her little girl off to the South, too. As she is on her way to the Seine in a taxi, thinking, "I've got a heartful of misery to spill out I've got a long blue cape on that'll go down quick young feller," she tells herself, "And here is where you might have cheated, . . . just here you might have insisted upon love" (*WD*, 95). Yet in a passage that is either brutally honest or bitterly ironic, she regrets that she cannot feel the maternal love that might have been able to soothe her aching longing for her lover:

Oh wonder-wonder mother-love why didn't I have a bit of you instead of this fierce agony which betrays me this decision of the soul which is decided for happiness and which results in complaint. Oh wonder-love which holds you by the throat until your breath is a red-white-and-blue celluloid rattle I will not have you warming your bottom on my heart. Oh wonder wonder mother-love how comfortable you would have made me instead of this thing scratching its thin back against a lamp-post. (*WD*, 95)

But the taxi-man will only take her home, not to the "dark Swanee Seine for which my heart was parched." Unable to drown her sorrows, she goes home alone, and we are left with a wrenching portrait of her grief. Beating on a mirror with her fists, biting her mouth until it is filled with blood, in an awful parody of her wish to have spat her way to heaven with her lover, she finally finds herself lying against the glass: "All night long I was lying against the mirror because it had a human face to it, lying with my arms around the mirror soothing the sad old face that was crying in the glass" (*WD*, 96).

The bitter irony of the title "Spring Morning" is apparent when the reader finally breaks into its difficult hallucinatory language—there are only two periods in the story for punctuation—and realizes that he or she is inside the consciousness of a woman awakening with "the latest corpse in the bed" with her (*WD*, 97). She is praying to the gods that she will find some sign in the room to give her a clue to his identity before he wakes up. The woman, whose lover has died, has found another human face with which to spend the night, but this one in the flesh is not much more comforting than the one in the mirror in "Vacation-Time." She says of her bedfellow that he is "as much a corpse as the one they lifted off the bed in his night-wear one morning and let fall into the coffin from a height that sent his arms wide open and his jaw dropping down and him grunting out loud" (*WD*, 97). Again, Kay Boyle will spare us no illusion that the death of a young poet is romantic. She introduces a third "corpse" to the story as well, slipping in a caustic commentary on a living poet, probably Ezra Pound, with whom *This Quarter* had had a falling out (the third issue retracted the second issue's dedication to him). The protagonist calls her night's companion "as much a corpse as the gentleman a timorous generation relies upon for brilliance Poetry he wrote is not to reveal the h'emotions but to protect them from abuse I have them does he add in the false bottom of me derby the rabbits to appear with pinker eyes the eggs with thinner crusts" (*WD*, 97–98).

From his canvases "turned to the wall showing their numbered backsides," the young woman is finally able to identify "this stranger who slept dreary as a hog." When she finds the signature, "Pruter 1928," she becomes bold and awakens him: "it is Hans Pruter whom I have done violence to up up Pruter my love roust yourself and be my noble crossing the yard and the underwear for a quart of Perrier" (*WD*, 98). Then she notices a "gentleman photographed and framed" on his dresser and remarks that they have a friend in common. "If I had money I would buy him," she says, painting her face at the glass. When Pruter jokes that the man was easily bought and that she would not be the first to purchase him, body and soul, she retorts that she would buy him outright "with the contract that he not compromise" (*WD*, 99). When Pruter remarks that she is making a "grand show" of her friend, she reveals her deep love for the man in the photograph: "I was putting the rouge on and the black on my eyes is it the poor bugger's fault I said that he is purpose and pride when everything else is rejected through a sewage of emotions" (*WD,* 99). A heartless banter ensues until Pruter complains that she lacks decency and that they have said nothing of real importance to each other. Her response is brutal: "Lean out of the bed said I and pass me the dictionary lean over the biddy said I and pass me the words withal" (*WD*, 101). Pruter longs for "a woman appealing to me mentally as well as," he says, but her heart is scarred closed. That her hardness masks desolation and a desperate need for love is revealed in the final paragraph.

> I held my nose from the smell of Pruter rotting and still above sod a lively feeding ground I knew these hard iron rings of sorrow and contempt laid first one and then another in my throat I would survive but not the face photographed and framed. If I had money I would buy him I thought body and soul for the pleasure
> This I would never escape or find words to whisper
> *I have waited so badly I have waited but so badly I have waited so badly I have waited so badly for you what are you going to do* (*WD*, 101)

In a 1960 review of a book about Robert McAlmon, Kay Boyle identifies him as the man for whom she had "waited so badly." In response to her final questioning cry in the story, "What he did was to give me his typewriter, to keep, not to give back, so that I would write a book or two," she says.[31] As for Pruter's joke that "the man was easily bought," Kay Boyle explains that when McAlmon's wife, the poet Bryher, divorced him in 1927, her father, one of the richest men in England, settled such a generous sum on him that he became the butt of "scornful criticism," and was dubbed "Robert McAlimony."[32]

The remaining nine stories in *Wedding Day* are a catalogue of the ways in which love can fail. While the four drawn most directly from the author's relationship with Ernest Walsh explore the pain of love lost, the rest examine the anguish of love never gained. The obstacles to contact range from breakdowns in communication to repressive bourgeois proprieties to conflicting sexual preferences to the incest taboo. But whatever the cause, she consistently points to the thwarting of love as a fundamental tragedy of human existence.

From the first sentence of the title story, "Wedding Day," the reader senses that things are out of joint: "The red carpet that was to spurt like a hemorrhage from pillar to post was stacked in the corner." The wedding cake is ignored as it is carried into the pantry "with its beard lying white as hoarfrost on its bosom." "This was the last lunch," Kay Boyle writes, and the brother and sister "came in with their buttonholes drooping with violets and sat sadly down, sat down to eat" (*WD*, 25). Into the funereal atmosphere of this wedding day, she injects tension and bitterness. The son and mother argue as to whether the daughter will be given the family's prized copper saucepans, unused for twenty years. He mocks the decorum his mother cherishes when he commands her not to cry, pointing his finger directly at her nose "so that when she looked at him with dignity her eyes wavered and crossed" and "she sat looking proudly at him, erect as a needle staring through its one open eye" (*WD*, 26). As the mother and son bicker over who wanted the wedding in the first place, the bride-to-be is conspicuously silent. Finally, as he snatches away each slice of roast beef his mother carves until she whimpers her fear of getting none herself, the boy and her sister burst into laughter. He tosses his napkin over the chandelier and his sister follows him out of the room, leaving the mother alone "praying that this occasion at least pass off with dignity, with her heart not in her mouth but beating away in peace in its own bosom" (*WD*, 28).

Having delineated the tension between children and mother and suggested the exclusive camaraderie between brother and sister, the author shifts both mood and scene and describes in almost incantatory prose the pair's idyllic jaunt through the spring afternoon in the hours remaining before the wedding:

> The sun was an imposition, an imposition, for they were another race stamping an easy trail through the wilderness of Paris, possessed of the same people, but of themselves like another race. No one else could by lifting of the head only be starting life over again, and it was a wonder the whole city of Paris did not hold its breath for them, for if anyone could have begun a new race, it was these two. (*WD*, 29)

The incestuous overtones are strong. "It isnt too late yet, you know," the brother insists as they stride through the streets, take a train into the *Bois*, and row to the middle of a pond. "Over them was the sky set like a tomb," and as tears flow down their cheeks, the slow rain begins to fall. Landscape and emotion correspond perfectly, external phenomena mirroring the characters' internal states. The rain underscores the pair's frustration and despair as they realize the intensity of their love and the impossibility of its fulfillment:

> Everywhere, everywhere there were other countries to go to. And how were they to get from the boat with the chains that were on them, how uproot the willowing trees from their hearts, how strike the irons of spring that shackled

them? What shame and shame that scorched a burning pathway to their dressing rooms! Their hearts were mourning for every Paris night and its half-hours before lunch when two straws crossed on the round table top on the marble anywhere meant I had a drink here and went on. (*WD*, 32)

The inevitable wedding itself forms the final segment of the story, and the lyrical spell binding the pair is broken the instant they set foot in the house again to find their mother "tying white satin bows under the chins of the potted plants" (*WD*, 32). The boy kicks down the hall the silver tray for the guests' calling cards, and his mother is wearily certain "that this outburst presaged a thousand mishaps that were yet to come" (*WD*, 33). The irony of the story lies not only in the reversal of expectations the title may have aroused in the reader but in the discrepancy between the different characters' perceptions of the same situation. The self-pitying matron worries only about the thousand little social mishaps possible when a major emotional disaster—the wedding itself—is imminent. But the guests arrive "in peace," and the brother delivers his sister to the altar. Yet the author captures magnificently the enormous gulf between the placid surface and the tumultuous inner reality as she takes the reader inside the bride's consciousness:

> This was the end, the end, they thought. She turned her face to her brother and suddenly their hearts fled together and sobbed like ringdoves in their bosoms. This was the end, the end, the end, this was the end.
>
> Down the room their feet fled in various ways, seeking an escape. To the edge of the carpet fled her feet, returned and followed reluctantly upon her brother's heels. Every piped note of the organ insisted that she go on. It isn't too late, he said. Too late, too late. The ring was given, the book was closed. The desolate, the barren sky continued to fling down dripping handfuls of fresh rain. (*WD*, 33–34)

The mindless repetition of the phrase "the end" and the blind panic of the bride's imaginary flight have an intense psychological authenticity. The recurrence of the brother's phrase "It isn't too late" and its distortion in "Too late, too late," along with the continuing rain, are evidence of the skill with which Kay Boyle has woven motifs seamlessly into the fabric of the story.

"Wedding Day" ends with dancing. But in an ironic counterpoint to the flight she had imagined at the altar, the bride's feet "were fleeing in a hundred ways throughout the rooms, fluttering from the punch bowl to her bedroom and back again" (*WD*, 34). By repeating and transforming the flight image, the author underscores the fact that the bride henceforth will move within narrow limits. While the brother, limbered by the punch, dances about scattering calling cards, his mother, "in triumph on the arms of the General, danced lightly by," rejoicing that "no glass had yet been broken" (*WD*, 35). "What a real success, what a *real* success," is her only thought as her feet float "over the oriental prayer rugs, through the Persian forests of hemp, away and away" in another absurdly circumscribed "escape" that is yet another mockery of the escape to "other countries" that the pair had dreamed of that afternoon on the lake.

In its ironies and incongruities, "Wedding Day" is characteristic both in style and theme of Kay Boyle's work. She displays her ironic sense of humor in the son's cruel but not entirely unamusing taunting of his mother—an unsympathetically drawn embodiment of all the petty proprieties that keep people politely isolated from each other. But the author deals in dramatic as well as verbal irony, and the discrepancy between the way things seem and the way they are is at the heart of the story. Like "Vacation-Time" and "Spring Morning," the title "Wedding Day" arouses pleasant expectations which are promptly dashed. Within the story, too, there are gulfs between the different characters' views of the same events. In "Wedding Day" she juxtaposes a *real* loss of love with the surface gaiety of a wedding that celebrates no love at all, but which the mother terms "a *real* success." In Kay Boyle's world, what is real depends largely on one's perceptions, and the fact that different perceptions of the same situation result in disparate and often conflicting "realities" creates a disturbing world in which individuals collide and bounce off one another like atoms.

"Theme" is another story of thwarted love with incestuous overtones, exploring the fierce love of a mother for her son. Her emotions encompass the purest maternal tenderness, a fear of loneliness, nebulous sexual desires, and self-loathing. The mother is sitting in her kitchen awaiting her son's return from work. As in much of Kay Boyle's fiction, the action is psychological. The story lies in our realization of the pitiful contrast between the woman's rich inner life—her sharp intellect and passionate emotions—and the drab surface she actually presents to her son. All day she fantasizes. She imagines chatting brightly with her son across the dinner table about the Russian writers, "leaning over the table in the kitchen to him so that her breasts hung down in points . . . passing the bread over to him with her head on one side smiling" (*WD*, 39). Yet, as these rich thoughts occupy her, we see her cracking roasted chestnuts in her big teeth and drawing the worms out with the point of a pin: "She had a long face like a horse's face and she would sit eating the chestnuts slowly in her mouth with her long chin swinging back and forth under her face" (*WD*, 38). The contrast between her inner sensitivity and her bestial appearance is shocking, and we realize the tragedy of her existence when her son actually returns and she falls silent: "All day she had been talking to him but now there was nothing to say between them" (*WD*, 40). Because she is powerless to communicate with her son, he never has an inkling of the intelligence and love within her but sees only a crone with "full eyeballs tied with veins and the heavy old flesh hanging down on her jaws" (*WD*, 39).

The mother is painfully aware of the incongruity: "Ah, but if he knew what there was in her blood, she thought, he would be afraid to be in the room with her" (*WD*, 41). Yet these raging emotions are reduced to expression in whimpers and tears. When he announces he is going up to Chicago at the end of the month, she thinks, "I am a fierce woman. I am a fierce woman who is not afraid of solitude. I am a black wind, boy. I am lean and gaunt and strong as the wind." What she says aloud is, "I am an old old woman, what shall I do with myself when you leave me?" (*WD*, 41–42). The tragic gulf in understanding between the two is underscored when he charges, "You never wanted a son." The story ends: " 'Yes, yes,' she said. 'Yes, I wanted a son' " (*WD*, 44).

The exchange is intriguing. Is the son insensitive and blind to his mother's inarticulate but consuming love for him, or is his comment instead an acute one, revealing an insight that she wants not a son but a lover? In the first case, the failure of love may be blamed on the son, and we pity his unappreciated mother; in the second, the screw turns a notch and we suddenly sympathize with the son who has sensed some unhealthy sublimations in his mother's self-centered "love" for him and who has been deprived of pure maternal love. Kay Boyle herself postulates "Might not the son more likely be disturbed by guilt, by his inability to respond to, as well as being revolted by, his mother's love rather than being 'insensitive and blind'? I believe that is why he left, not for a moment because of his unawareness."[33] The reason for the gap in understanding between the mother and son is less important than the fact that it exists. What ultimately matters in Kay Boyle's work is the sad fact that human beings so often relate blindly with one another and that, instead of making contact, they skitter cold and lonely across the unpenetrated surfaces.

The bald facts of consanguinity are partly responsible for the failures of love in "Wedding Day," "Theme," and "Uncle Anne"—a story of a young girl's futile infatuation with her uncle, the black sheep of the family, who has impregnated the servant girl but who tells his favorite niece, "Whatever I have done is because I wanted always a thin wife with pink nostrils and little red apples in the points of her eyes" (*WD*, 84). In "Madame Tout Petit," Kay Boyle examines another obstacle to love: a conflict in sexual orientation. In bohemian Paris of the twenties, it would have been a familiar issue. Her poem, "In defense of homosexuality" (1925), and her full-length treatment of homosexual love in the novel *Gentlemen, I Address You Privately* (1933) indicate that she had more than a passing interest in the subject.

The narrator of "Madame Tout Petit" is a young woman who lives with her small daughter in an English boarding house. Through her we view the relationship between a lonely traveling salesman also boarding there and the proprietress, Madame Tout Petit, who does not love her husband but is infatuated with the salesman. On Friday evenings the traveler would come to the parlor and speak to the narrator of his lonely life on the road among men who laugh at limericks he finds "rather rum." Madame, smelling like a fresh rose and stitching at her embroidery, would listen "sweetly and sharply with her head" to their incomprehensible English, laughing "because the words collapsed before she could make any sense of them" (WD, 48). In the lulls of their conversation, Madame would quickly speak up, "brightly dropping her words through whatever his silence was suggesting," to complain of her husband's coarse ways. "I cannot tell you what took place in me," she says, recounting how her husband's hair was so curled and dandied on their wedding day that "the priest himself was slapping holy water on it to make it lie flat." The impossibility of communication between Madame and the traveler, already established by the language barrier between them, is wonderfully portrayed in their conversation, in which the import of each sentence slips past the other person until the exchange collapses in confusion:

> The priest himself. She shouted delicately with laughter. She looked at the traveling-man with her laughter scarring her face. *Bande de salauds.* Oh, rather, said the travelling-man. Oh, dear, dear, the Jesuits! He skipped across the room like a Nancy-boy. Madame Tout Petit's pure virtuous creed flamed in her face. I was speaking of my husband and the others, she said in confusion. He handed out cigars to them all to keep them from making jokes about marriage. I cannot tell you, she said, what took place in me. (WD, 49–50)

Later, as the salesman and narrator are rummaging through her grandmother's old dresses to find costumes for a dance that night, he produces a letter Madame Tout Petit had sent him, hinting at her unhappiness with her husband. The traveler, cynical and unmoved, comments that "her husband is rather a good sort," adding, "And I prefer her husband" (WD, 51). The narrator's account of the masquerade dance reveals, under the grotesque surface merriment, the painful clash of Madame's love for the salesman and his indifference toward her—and the pathetic loneliness of each:

> We were dancing together, and he would hop about on his feet with his legs doing the Charleston in the French way as if he could not afford to be ungraceful. And my old grandmother's shoulders had been fuller than his so that the sleeves slipping down he would keep putting back with his fingers. It is not a life, he said, it is not a life consisting of sleeping on a board. Madame Tout Petit clapped her hands and screamed with false delight. Oh, what a beautiful

woman he is, screamed Madame Tout Petit, and her sorrow and her love for him were ready to fall in tears from her eyes. (*WD,* 52)

Even Madame now realizes the traveler's homosexuality; it is a measure of her desperation that she asks nevertheless if the narrator would intercede for her with "a word or two concerning the eternal constancy of a *femme honnête:*" "I can forgive him, she said, anything. And if he still refuses to respond, I shall ask the priest to employ me with charitable work in the parish. I shall succor the young, she said" (*WD,* 53). "*J'ai un cafard horrible*" is Madame Tout Petit's final statement. We can presume that while the homosexual traveling man's need for love will go unsatisfied in his life on the road among coarse he-men, Madame's longing for him will be channeled henceforth into charity work and sick headaches. They are two more individuals in Kay Boyle's world who cannot give away the love surging but dammed within them.

Madame Tout Petit—a woman who claims that on her wedding night "I pinned the curtains of the canopy from top to bottom with nursery pins and myself in the middle like a jelly-roll" (*WD,* 50)—represents a type that often infuriates the author, whose own introduction to France was made miserable by a mother-in-law horrified that she had not arrived clad in the requisite *tailleur gris.* The mother in "Wedding Day" is another example. The "lady," who is repressed by bourgeois morality and religion and who self-righteously attempts to inflict her inhibitions on others (usually younger members of her own sex), is a sort of villain in a number of Boyle's works, for proprieties that deny one's humanity in favor of sterile codes are yet another barrier between human beings in need of contact.

A prototype of this genteel monster may be found in "Summer," a vignette of sexual repression and frustrated desire. Like many of Kay Boyle's works, it is the unraveling of a psychological situation rather than a tale with a plot, and it contains some fine examples of her technical skill. It focuses on the thoughts and feelings of a presumably plain young woman caring for an old lady at a sanatarium. A young man, his eyes bright with disease, resides in the next room. The girl must suffer the old woman's constant denunciations of the man because he and a young lady are seen together setting off on long walks into the hills. The old woman rages that she is not too old "to still feel resentment against the abuses of decency, decency," and she demands to know what good anyone could be at in the hills all day. "A good brisk walk is another thing," she adds.

That night, as the girl is reading to her elderly charge, she hears the young man enter his room. A second set of footsteps follows. Inner and outer worlds merge as the author moves away from objective reality to try to capture in physical images the girl's state of consciousness. Her awareness of the events "a hand's breadth" away on the other side of the wall takes over her mind and finally shapes and animates her perception of the concrete objects in the old woman's bedroom:

> The voice of the young man was sounding as though heard over water, a deep swaying bell swinging down like a tool on metal. And the silence of his companion hung between the two rooms, stirring back and forth between them like a soft soft hammock hung under strong trees. Everything in the old lady's room was meticulous and sharp to the girl, neat and small corners and legs of furniture tossed up like little boats on the terrific water which went on under and about them sending them dancing like crazy men, sending the little white tufts of cotton flapping like burnt butterflies over the quilt. The girl sat reading out the words; and the great dancing orgy of silence wove and tore strongly in the room, tossed up the little grunts of the old lady's breath like corks on the smooth mouth of the horizon. (*WD,* 61–62)

After his companion has left the room, the young man's coughing fit begins. Kay Boyle describes it brilliantly through the metaphor of a fox, an image that she uses in several stories and in her novel *Year Before Last*—especially haunting when one realizes that her skill in recreating the torment of the dying is rooted in her own painful intimacy with the details of Ernest Walsh's disease and death. The girl listens to the "lean shriveled heart of the sound as it beat alone in the middle of the room." "And then it began to run in a frenzy in his room patting with quick hard paws on the glass of the windows. It was a trapped fox barking in a frenzy to get out of the room, and flinging down with its soft gasping belly on the young man's belly, its worn thin bark snapping its teeth at his chest" (*WD,* 63). In her heart, the girl calls to him, "But cry out, cry out, cry out, my love," until the sound dwindles down "in a point, even the sounds of the springs whistling like bats, and the point to become a long needle of pain in her" (*WD,* 63–64). The girl's desire is trapped inside her, and, as the man is held in the grip of his disease, so she is powerless to free herself from the repression the old woman personifies.

"Summer" is significant not only as an example of the author's continuing thematic concern with failed connections, but because she employs the protagonist to articulate her aesthetic stance. The book the girl is reading at the old woman's bedside is a conservative one: "The healthy school is played out in England," the girl was reading, "all that could be said has been said; the successors of Dickens, Thackeray, George Eliot have no ideal, and consequently no language" (*WD,* 59). Yet she would "wonder about language and if there were perhaps some now so new and so incomprehensible that it could serve only to wound them." Like her creator, the first signatory of the manifesto for the Revolution of the Word, the girl takes language seriously: "She wanted to believe in a language that burned black the tongue of the one who spoke and scarred the one who listened. She would demand nothing of it, but to serve it, and be humble before it" (*WD,* 60). The conformism that oppresses language parallels that which stifles a healthy acknowledgement of human needs and desires, and the girl's heart cries out in quiet desperation against both types.

While Kay Boyle's opinion of the "lady" generally borders on contempt, it would be a serious distortion not to emphasize her respect for woman. Two stories in *Wedding Day* are evidence of an understanding of very different types of women. "Episode in the Life of an Ancestor" and "Letters of a Lady" are, in Katherine Anne Porter's words, stories in which "an adult intelligence plays with destructive humor on the themes of sexual superstition and pretenses between men and women."[34] Sexism is one more obstacle to contact.

From her earliest short stories to her latest novel, *The Underground Woman,* she has written of the power of women. Often a strong woman of expansive spirit will play opposite a man made weak by egotism, narrow-mindedness, and petty possessiveness. Most of these men are nearly as pathetic for their limitations as they are despicable for their attempts at domestic tyranny. This is the theme of "Episode in the Life of an Ancestor," which she chose as the opening piece of both *Wedding Day* (1930) and her most recent collection, *Fifty Stories* (1980). The author apparently based the heroine of this story on her Grandmother Evans, a Kansas schoolteacher who at sixteen had married the superintendent of schools and later left him to go off to work in the Land Grant Office in Washington, D.C., taking her two young daughters with her.

"Episode in the Life of an Ancestor" explores an incident in the girlhood of the narrator's grandmother, one of the best horsewomen in Kansas. Her father was proud of "the feminine ways there were in her," especially the choir voice she used in church, but "It was no pride to him to hear it turned hard and thin in her mouth to quiet a frightened horse" (*WD,* 2). Yet the local people "were used to seeing her riding with a sunbonnet on her head—not in pants, but with wide skirts hullabalooing out behind her in the wind" (*WD,* 2). Kay Boyle will not reduce her heroine to the stereotype of tomboy. She contrasts the girl's competence in a wide range of skills with her father's narrow and selfish expectations of her. Although in truth he has little control over this bold spirit, he clings to the illusion that he can mold his daughter into the kind of woman who will serve his needs: "To her father it was a real sorrow that a needle and thread were never seen in her fingers. His wife was dead and it seemed to him that he must set flowing in his daughter the streams of gentleness and love that cooled the blood of true women. The idea was that she be sweetened by the honey of the ambitions he had for her" (*WD,* 3).

After she rides away one evening, "hammering off through the darkness with nobody knowing what was going on inside her or outside her, or what she was filled with" (*WD*, 6), the father roams the house, thinking of her future, wondering if she will marry the schoolmaster, the only gentleman in the countryside. In all his masculine glory, he is not self-sufficient, for he draws his strength and sustenance from her; his image of himself is a distorted reflection of what power he thinks he has in shaping her. Wandering into her room, he discovers peeping out from under her quilt a poetry book "with pictures engraved through it of a kind that brought the blood flying to his face." It is opened to a passage that begins, ." . . To the Nuptial Bowre/I led her blushing like the Morn" (*WD*, 9). (He does not recognize it—nor does the author identify it—as *Paradise Lost*.) Inside, he finds the schoolmaster's signature. "You fine example to the young, screamed the father's mind. You creeping out into the night to do what harm you can, creeping out and doing God knows what harm, God knows." And in his mind the schoolmaster's image balloons to monstrous proportions, the pores on the wings of his nose and the black hairs that grow between his eyes clearly visible.

The scene shifts to the young woman riding alone on the prairie in the quiet night. Suddenly, impatient with the tameness of the ride, she kicks the horse into fury in a passage that is unmistakably sexual—with the female in the role of mastery.

> Suddenly he felt this anger in the grandmother's knees that caught and swung him about in the wind. Without any regard for him at all, so that he was in a quiver of admiration and love for her, she jerked him up and back, rearing his wild head high, his front hoofs left clawing at the space that yapped under them. She urged him to such a frenzy of kicking that he was ready to faint with delight. Even had she wished to now she could never have calmed him, and she started putting him over bushes and barriers, setting his head to them and stretching him thin as a string to save the smooth nut of his belly from scraping, reeling him so close to the few pine trunks that streamed up like torrents that he leapt sideways to save his fair coat from ripping open on the spikes of them. It was a long way to travel back, but he never stopped until his hoofs thundered into the barn that had shrunk too small for him. There he stood in the darkness, wet and throbbing like a heart cut out of the body. (*WD*, 12)

When she strides into the room where her self-pitying father is wondering how he will ever know what had become of her, he wants to ask her what she had been up to, to say "that he had seen the schoolmaster walking out early in the evening up the road that led nowhere except out into the prairie." But the "grandmother" stalks over to the table and reclaims her book in silent anger (in this time warp, Kay Boyle gives her power and stature by conferring on her the more venerable title). The father is powerless to speak. His thoughts turn again to the schoolmaster, but now his image of the man he had suspected of defiling his daughter shrivels and actually caves in before our eyes: "With this woman in the room with him he was beginning to see the poor little schoolmaster, the poor squat little periwinkle with his long nose always thrust away in a book. He began to remember that the horse his daughter had been out riding all night had once backed up on just such a little whippersnapper as was the schoolmaster and kicked his skull into a cocked hat" (*WD*, 14). The father must turn his eyes away from the sight of this woman who stands "with her eyes staring like a hawk's eyes straight into the oil lamp's blaze." The story ends: " 'What have you done to the schoolmaster?' he wanted to say to her. The words were right there in his mouth but he couldn't get them out" (*WD*, 14).

"Episode in the Life of an Ancestor" demonstrates Kay Boyle's skill in rendering the psychological states of her characters, as she simply presents without comment the protean images that fill their consciousnesses. The story also makes a statement about the nature of true power in a relationship between a woman and a man who would dominate her, exposing the brittle frailty of a rigid male ego when confronted by a woman's uncharted strength.

A self-proclaimed "crusading spirit," Boyle has little patience for emotional timidity, or even prudence, when it obstructs genuine passion. In "Polar Bears and Others," she takes a strong romantic stand. The story focuses on a young woman who feels threatened by her husband's interest in another woman, yet, interestingly, despises him for lacking the courage and conviction to pursue his heart's calling. The story begins in the tone of a fable. The first two paragraphs describe the plodding existence of polar bears who cannot adapt to the imitation-icicled caverns, false snows, and warm water pool of the zoo. The author's intention is obviously allegorical:

> They came from a country which is a small country because it is all alike, and they came from it with life only if their country and their ways be repeated for them. They came with their prejudiced bodies and their jaws gaping out for fish in empty water. They are like people who live in small countries and who go out of them with their small grudges strapped to their backs. In America, and in Russia, the big countries, there are little men but on them even there is a smell of romance. (And I believe in romance: that it should be snatched from the buttonhole where it has withered too long, so that reality can make a fresh thing of this poor faded flower.) (*WD*, 67–68)

The story then shifts into a first-person narrative. The protagonist's husband wishes to go the next day to have lunch with a woman passing through Le Havre to catch a boat back to America. "Because he stayed out in the garden with his thoughts I became afraid of this woman," she says. Her husband is disturbed because she will not come with him to lunch, and when he insists she must accompany him, she feels she could strike him in the face for this falseness. They go to bed with their backs to each other, and the narrator is bitter that she is something to be relinquished; yet she awakens the next morning feeling "a piercing gentleness for others which comes from life and not from innocence." "Innocence is obscene somehow, you know, but gentleness is the great wisdom of the emotions," she says (*WD*, 71). When the man decides to forego his trip, she is contemptuous:

> "I'll be something more than sacrifice and bitterness to you," I cried. "Go on, get out!"
> I knew when it was my turn I'd be off without a thought for him. "Listen," I said, "when it's my turn, I'll be off without a thought, so you'd better go now."

"Some other day maybe. Some other time," is his reply, and she retorts, "And maybe a tragedy would be as big as life, but you'd never see it" (*WD*, 72). She goes upstairs and screams in the empty room "thinking that perhaps here was a great love passing him by, and he not even going after it" (*WD*, 73).

The issue here is much larger than whether a man is going to have lunch with a woman not his wife. What Kay Boyle is speaking out against in this story is a rigid, narrow view of life that denies the emotions in favor of safe proprieties. She lacks respect for those "who must have a way prepared to dignity," those "who do not know what it is to go off and for yourselves be lost and lost and lost to all old dignities." "You do not know the humble way of beginning or of growing a new skin when the old one is ripped from your flesh," in the words of the young woman in her story (*WD*, 74).

In the author's view, dignity must be attained—through difficult confrontation with essentials, through loss of innocence, through pain—not simply maintained by preserving one's childish innocence intact. Such a dignity, guarded by remaining in one's own back garden, is no more than plodding provincialism, such as the polar bears exemplify. One can imagine Kay Boyle cheering Melville as he wrote to his friend Hawthorne, "I stand for the heart. To the dogs with the head!"[35] This stubborn romanticism would pervade and, in the opinion of some, taint much of her writing over the course of her career. Robert McAlmon had said she would be a good writer if she would not go so "Irish-twilighty" (*BGT*, 11). (He said the same of James Joyce regarding *A Portrait of the Artist as a Young Man*.) In her sixties, she admitted her romantic tendencies in the last line of *Being Geniuses Together*. After citing McAlmon's comment that she, come hell or high water, had to romanticize every situation, she concedes, "This may very well be true" (*BGT,* 332). From the very beginning, Kay Boyle believed that the heart's callings ought to prevail over convention and common sense, no matter what the consequences.

Finally, another story in which the barrier to love is internally imposed is "Bitte Nehmen Sie Die Blumen." The narrator, a woman with a baby living with a Frenchman named Peleser, has been scarred by the death of someone she had loved. The story is set in England in a company town where the men talk of rubber at the dinner table. The story revolves about the young woman's feelings for an Englishman living in the same boarding house, whose cool self-assurance both infuriates and infatuates her.[36] The woman is wary of love, and the author hints at what has jaded her: "I knew I had turned like an old maid now, when I met a man I wanted to wound him. I would think of the scars that death had put between my eyes, and I would think that even my love could not tell him of all that had dried up in me. Too much has happened that even my heart could not explain to you, I would think" (*WD,* 17–18). It would have been a familiar feeling for Kay Boyle at that time. This story first appeared in *transition* in December, 1927, a year after Walsh died; in *Being Geniuses Together,* she tells how she had closed off her heart to men after his death. Speaking of her friend in Stoke-on-Trent, Germaine Garrigou, Boyle recalls: "She would study Michael's photograph (which I kept at the bottom of a suitcase), and seek to learn his poems by heart, agreeing with me in a passionate whisper that I should never embrace another man and that I should wear black for the rest of my life" (*BGT,* 215).

Yet the narrator finds it impossible to stifle her feelings for this Englishman: "Everything in me was against him and I thought that I would not be beginning again but would get my mind off this man. And here I was . . . thinking that for a turn of his body I would be leaving Peleser and making a new life with this man" (*WD,* 20). When she finds herself on the boarding house stairway with him, her conflicting emotions surge forth. She cracks nuts and drops the shells on the stairs, knowing how it will disturb his English sensibilities, and as he picks them up, her hostility explodes in a psychologically authentic passage that eschews the conventions of "realistic" writing:

> Listen I said you're perfectly safe all right seeing yourself always in situations where you can go upstairs and close your door and spend the evening deploring deeply deploring regretting lamenting unfortunate interviews but for God's sake don't begin doubting that you've got all the superiorities because then you'll be something else again. He said please, please, wearily with his hand lifted and I went past him up the stairs to my room it is impossible he said you insist upon too much what I said was. (*WD,* 23)

In her room the woman brushes back her hair, puts on extra lipstick and goes down to dinner in a sleeveless dress. As she cuts her meat, she will not lift her head to look over or around the vase of marigolds and ferns that blocks her view of him, sitting opposite her at the table. The story ends in a fine example of the banal charged with significance, reminiscent of scenes in Joyce's *Dubliners*:

> They were serving us spaghetti and I didn't know if he were cutting it up or twisting it on his fork and when the pudding came on he put his head around the flowers. When he looked at me I felt that my flesh lit like a candle. I looked at him as if I could never see enough of his face and I saw that he was humbled and that he was silenced by the sad proud humility of his heart. He was handing the menu to me and I didn't know if I were taking it in my fingers or letting it fall, and across it he had written Aber Gott Bitte Nehmen Sie Die Blumen . . . (*WD*, 24)

The story closes with this quiet illumination, a Joycean epiphany. It is about as close as Kay Boyle comes in this book to a happy ending, for one senses that the Englishman's request to please take away the flowers will be the gentle blow that will crumble the defenses keeping the woman from the human contact she so desperately needs. Among Boyle's characters, she is a lucky one. It is perhaps significant that she is so closely identified with the author, who herself passed through great pain *and* the "formal feeling" and finally was able to open her heart again to love. It is also noteworthy that the man who is so infuriatingly and indelibly English speaks the most significant line in the story—if the title is a fair indicator—in German, a neutral language for the pair. Perhaps this indicates that he is willing to abandon *his* defenses, his standoffish Englishness, and open himself completely to the possibility of real communication without barriers.

Wedding Day and Other Stories is hardly a budding writer's rough-edged first attempt in print. Contemporary reviewers were positive, although one paid the author a backhanded compliment at the expense of some of her coterie:

> *transition* was a brave venture and in that respect demanded and obtained one's sympathy—but it is a good thing for Miss Boyle and one or two other contributors that it is no longer able to confound their genius with (let us be kind) the high spirits of the mathematical sign writers. It was a cocktail with too much kick in it for most of us, and served only to hide from our muddled vision those works which deserved a more serious consideration.[37]

But the most insightful—and glowing—review was Katherine Anne Porter's, in which she termed Kay Boyle one of the strongest and most promising talents to have emerged from the shadows of James Joyce and

Gertrude Stein. She says of Boyle, "She sums up the salient qualities of that movement: a fighting spirit, freshness of feeling, curiosity, the courage of her own attitude and idiom, a violently dedicated search for the meanings and methods of art." Yet Porter was the first to see, too, the concern for love at the core of Kay Boyle's work—the theme that is her *own* and that makes her work far more than just a fine example of a prevailing artistic movement: "Miss Boyle writes of love not as if it were a disease, or a menace, or a soothing syrup to vanity, or something to be peered at through a microscope, or the fruit of original sin, or a battle between the sexes, or a bawdy pastime. She writes as one who believes in love so fresh and clear it comes to the reader almost as a rediscovery in literature. It was high time someone rediscovered it."[38]

Wedding Day and Other Stories is a sampler of Kay Boyle at her best. Through these stories we gain insight into the method of her art. By probing the individual experience—most often drawn directly from autobiography in all its idiosyncratic detail—she extrapolates the larger patterns of human existence. By rendering with scrupulous honesty and precision the particular experience, she in turn gives voice and flesh to her universal themes. The finely wrought style that in time would lead some critics to pigeonhole her as a mere virtuoso is evident in its full range and power in these first works. Her reverence for the Word and her skill in manipulating it are demonstrated in her ability to capture an instant with the crystal clarity that matches William Carlos Williams' snapshot of a red wheelbarrow; in subjective descriptions of landscapes that are projections of a perceiving consciousness; in flowing, lyrical plays with the sounds of language; and in complex experiments in rendering streams of consciousness through the "language of hallucination." But besides contributing brilliantly to the Revolution of the Word, in these stories she introduces the theme that echoes through the entire body of her work for six decades: that love is a fundamental human need and that tragedy results when this vital force is thwarted, stifled, or destroyed.

3

More Fruits of the Twenties:
The First Four Novels

In her first four novels, all published in the thirties but based on her experience of the twenties, Kay Boyle continues to explore the human need for contact. She continues, too, to experiment with language. The novels are not as radically innovative (or "difficult") as some of her short stories of the period, but they are, nonetheless, subtle, complex, intensely personal works skillfully crafted. Clearly, the author still was more concerned with the aesthetic integrity of her work than in making it palatable to the "plain reader."

Her first published novel, *Plagued by the Nightingale,* chronicles the failed connections among the isolated members of a "close-knit" family. If the book seems a remarkably smooth continuation of the themes and styles of the short stories in *Wedding Day,* it is because they were written concurrently. Although not published until 1931, *Plagued by the Nightingale* was begun in Le Havre in 1924 and finished in Stoke-on-Trent in 1927. Like many of her novels, the finished version of this one was preceded in print by a shorter treatment of the same material. The third number of *This Quarter,* which came out in the spring of 1927, featured a thirty-nine-page piece entitled "Plagued by the Nightingale" that loosely corresponds to the first quarter of the novel. The piece ended with the promise "To be continued." It was not. Ernest Walsh had died the autumn before, and this was the last issue Ethel Moorhead edited before selling the magazine to Edward Titus. What happened to serialization plans is unclear, but in an autobiographical sketch she wrote in 1931, Boyle lists her aversions as "big cities, small towns, grand hotels, crowded beaches, radios, and Edward Titus."[1]

William Carlos Williams' response to the work in 1927 had set her "walking on air." He had read it late into the night until he was weary-eyed: "Then I went to be disgusted with my own novel that I am finishing," he wrote to her. "I wanted to tear it up. My sentences seem boorish, infantile, beside your beautifully informed inventions. What eyes you have! I am blind by comparison."[2]

By the time the novel finally appeared in print after being rejected by three publishers, the author had lost interest. In a 1931 letter she tells Kate Buss, "I wrote *Plagued by the Nightingale* so many years ago that I feel it has nothing to do with me now."[3] But even if she herself was not interested (to this day she cannot bear to read her books once they are in print), a number of her contemporaries were. Katherine Anne Porter called it "a magnificent performance" and added, "as the short stories left the impression of reservoirs of power hardly tapped, so this novel, complete as it is, seems only a beginning."[4] Hart Crane wrote to Caresse Crosby from Mexico, "Kay's novel Plagued by the Nightingale (and how they please over here!) impressed and delighted me immensely."[5] The book also has stood the test of time better than most of hers, in terms of its reputation, at least. In 1966 it was republished by Southern Illinois University Press (at the same time as D. H. Lawrence's *The White Peacock*) to launch its Crosscurrents/Modern Fiction series, dedicated to reviving significant works of modern fiction out of print or difficult to obtain in the United States. In the introduction to this edition, Harry T. Moore asserts that no one since Henry James has handled the theme of the clash between Americans and Europeans more successfully and concludes, "This is simply a first-rate novel that has been too long overlooked" (*PN*, x).[6]

In the fragment published in *This Quarter*, Christine, a young American three months pregnant, has come to France with her husband, Nicolas, to spend the summer with his family. It appears that the central tension in the finished story will be the widening rift between Christine and Nicolas, whom we see growing increasingly bitter as he gradually comes into his "inheritance": a creeping bone decay that debilitates the males of his family. The supporting cast is Nicolas's family. Living at home with Maman and Papa are three unmarried sisters, Annick, Alice, and Julie. Nicolas's beloved older sister, Charlotte, is married to her first cousin, Jean, already crippled, and they live in a chateau across the road with their four children. Pierre, Nicolas's older brother, is a doctor in Rennes.

Clearly, Nicolas's family is Richard Brault's. The names and personalities of Annick, Pierre, Charlotte, Jean, and their children appear undisguised. While the bone disease is the author's invention, Nicolas has in common with Richard a financial dependence on the family and a jaded outlook. "Richard was a rebel, a *rouspéteur*, incurably bitter about the Catholic Church, in which he had been raised, and about his father's army career," Kay Boyle recalls (*BGT*, 13). Charlotte, she says, "was the richer side of Richard's nature, for she was undimmed radiance and tenderness while Richard had already begun to mistrust the look of men" (*BGT*, 41). From her own experience, Kay Boyle carries into fiction the young man's bitterness, the couple's exasperation with the family's conservatism and pettiness, and their own desperate struggle for independence.

In the 1931 novel Boyle has transferred the pregnancy from Nicolas's wife (renamed Bridget) to his sister Charlotte. Aside from the irrelevant fact that in "real life" it was her sister-in-law Charlotte who was pregnant, in making this change Boyle expands and more satisfactorily motivates the story's conflicts. Now the young couple must fight not only the creeping destruction of the disease, but the family's obsession with respectability.

On his first day home, Nicolas outrages Papa—a blustery retired colonel who likes to think he is master of the household (and is indulged in this delusion by his sweetly indomitable wife)—by cynically declaring that he does not intend to inflict his disease on posterity. Papa offers the couple fifty thousand francs to have a child, money they desperately need if they are ever to escape the family's stranglehold. As Katherine Anne Porter summarizes the story in her review of it, Nicolas "hates his dear good sweet people who are so warmly kind in small things, so hideously complacent and negligent in the larger essentials. He needs help, restitution really, from this family that has brought him disabled into the world."[7] The burden of redemption, however, will fall to Bridget, his wife.

Nicolas is trapped socially as well as biologically, and bitterness begins to consume him like a cancer. He wishes he could have been born a German to have had the pleasure of marching through Brittany and murdering the family, "ripping Papa up the middle" and "slowly killing Maman, extracting her front teeth slowly" (PN, 33). The family's conditional, manipulative brand of "love" is destroying Nicolas's spirit as surely as their bone disease is his body. "Down, down, down to the bottom of the pond, to the valley of the river, had they pressed his heart with their thumbs; down, under the torrents of bridge games, under the grim Sundays of thunderous mass" (PN, 47–48). The day Papa makes his proposition, Nicolas disappears. After many hours Papa concludes that one of two things has happened: he has either gone off with another woman or he is dead. Papa's preference for the latter possibility reveals all there is to hate about the family. When Nicolas finally returns that night, he offers no explanation for his absence.

As he progressively withdraws into silent resentment, Bridget comes to the startling realization that "Nicolas was somebody else": "Until this moment she had thought of other people, outside, strangers, and as herself and Nicolas one sign and signal of purpose and youth, one figurehead carved against the surf of the world, one spirited high will. Now she knew that they were not" (PN, 50). It is a painful discovery. Bridget, a warm, sensitive, spirited woman, needs the sustenance of human contact. She regrets that her own family were "separated people." She wishes she had come from "a loving Jewish tribe, to be all the more fierce for each other because there is the same flesh on our bones." She seizes any connection with others: "I am afraid to be alone, she thought. There is no necessity to be one person alone, unrelated. I am afraid to have no family at all, she thought; no one, nothing, I am afraid. Gently she put her hand through her mother-in-law's arm as she sat talking beside her. The responding pressure gave her a curious assurance" (*PN*, 63). As Bridget attempts to live peacefully with the family, Nicolas begins to identify her with the enemy, and he turns against her, too. He viciously suggests that she find another man to father a healthy child in order to get the fifty thousand francs.

Her painful situation is complicated when the family's tidy routine of days on the lawn and nights around the bridge table is joyously shattered by the annual visit of Luc, golden-haired young medical partner of Nicolas's brother Pierre and life-long friend of the family. All assume that this is the year he will choose one of the three daughters as his bride. Against the parlor drama of the family's attempts to force his decision, Luc finds himself powerfully attacted to Bridget. Their compatibility does not go unnoticed. Nicolas cruelly asks Bridget in English in front of the others, "What do you think of Luc as a father of the race?" When Bridget and Luc are finally alone (on a walk engineered by one of the sisters so that Bridget could speak to him of her suitability as his wife), Bridget longs to warn him to fly the family's snares. She wants to cry out, "Do not give them one moment of your life, one drop of your rich blood" (*PN*, 121). He interrupts her prepared speech on Marthe's behalf to tell Bridget that if it were not for her, he probably would have spoken for one of the girls that year. When he tells her, "You can do whatever you want with me," she dreams for a moment of escaping with him into a new life, away from the stifling family and Nicolas's consuming bitterness, Luc's "bright beauty holding the world at bay" (*PN*, 123).

Only Charlotte holds the family together with her genuine graciousness and warmth. She even promises to speak to Jean about getting Nicolas a place on his *estancia* in North Africa. And as the pressure intensifies for Nicolas and Bridget to have a child, she announces that she is expecting her fifth. Despite her history of miserable confinements (which Nicolas attributes to the poison of Jean's inherited disease), Charlotte is cheerful, saying, "One more won't matter. . . . It's my life, isn't it?" (*PN*, 134). But even though she suffers more wretchedly than usual, the family is unalarmed and scorns Pierre's advice that she be put on a proper diet and moved to his clinic. Maman huffs that "all women suffer" and Charlotte is perhaps being dramatic. Jean does not want his child to have to point to a clinic as his birthplace. Together with Papa, they form a proud alliance against the encroachment of science on the family's domain. Charlotte deteriorates rapidly, and by the time the family finally consents to her hospitalization, it is too late. When Charlotte dies (as did Kay Boyle's sister-in-law), she is indeed, as Oncle Robert maudlinly proclaims at the funeral, a "poor martyred child" (*PN,* 190). She has been martyred to the family's smug narrow-mindedness and to their selfish expectations of her.

In the aftermath of her death, the family disintegrates. Papa slips into senility, Nicolas's sister Annick plans to enter a convent, and Luc, to the family's horror, announces his intention to open a clinic in Indo-China. "Gradually, gradually, thought Bridget, were they all making their escape" (*PN,* 198). But Charlotte's death has also dashed her brother's hopes of escape to an African *estancia,* and when Oncle Robert blithely ignores his last desperate hint for financial help, Nicolas reaches the rock bottom of his despair. He tells Bridget that he hates everyone, that "there is not a person alive that matters" (*PN,* 195). But finally he turns to her and pleads, "Help me, mountain. I don't know what to do, I don't know what to do at all" (*PN,* 195). "At this moment Bridget decided what it was that she would do," we are told.

In the final chapter Luc confronts Bridget and tells her that she must come away with him. She assesses what she has given to this golden, godlike man: "The tenderness that shook him, the sweet bright soft rebellion in his eyes were gifts to him, thought Bridget, gifts she could spare to him who had been a poor man with no intention but to marry in a small ungracious way" (*PN,* 201). The novel ends with Bridget's reply: " 'It's too late for that. Do you know what I am going to do?' she said. 'Nicolas and I are going to have a child' " (*PN,* 202).

It is an intriguing ending. The few critics who have discussed it have reached different conclusions. Katherine Anne Porter writes that Bridget, "who has wavered, been pulled almost to pieces by the tearing, gnawing, secretive antagonisms and separate aims of the family, comes to her conclusion—a rather bitter one, which in the end will solve very badly the problem. Of her own will she takes to herself the seed of decay."[8] Richard C. Carpenter apparently lacks faith in Bridget's resolve and assumes she will leave Nicolas despite her final statement.[9] The novel is a parable of youth and beauty defeated by age and corruption, he believes. In the most recent discussion, Frank Gado postulates that Bridget "will have Luc father the healthy child which will allow Nicol freedom on terms he can accept."[10] This interpretation is complicated by the fact that Kay Boyle added the entire subplot involving Luc after the novel was originally completed. That she did not intend Luc to play the critical role that Gado suggests is apparent in a 1931 letter to Bob Brown, who was having some problems writing a book of his own. "From the point of view of great popularity, you might have to change the personal side of the story," she writes and advises that he inject a bit of romance. "I tell you darling," she continues, "I had to re-write 'Plagued' completely before anyone would touch it. Fadiman, Friede, and Jonathan Cape all turned it down without a word. Just rejection slips. . . . And I don't doubt it was a better book before I dragged in a love interest."[11]

I would suggest that Bridget's final statement be taken at face value, as an indication of her faith that she can redeem Nicolas's spirit and persuade him to have a child despite the biological consequences. An unqualified happy ending would be uncharacteristic of Boyle's work, in which the individual nearly always finds himself or herself in a situation of painful and inevitable compromise with harsh realities. Yet redemption, albeit limited, is possible through love. The only victories Kay Boyle allows are gained through loss, and love's redeeming power requires sacrifice. Through her unconditional generosity of spirit, Charlotte had brought joy to others, and by her death she liberated them. Bridget, it seems, will assume the same role. She already has liberated Luc. The passion she "set ringing in his blood" (PN, 91) has made him see that to have married one of the sisters "in a small ungracious way" would have made a travesty of something sacred. Simply by igniting his emotions in a way he had never before experienced, she has taught Luc to follow the wisdom of his heart and to resist the sterile traps of convention, convenience, and common sense.

Yet Bridget lets pass her own chance at freedom and chooses to remain behind and save Nicolas, too. The bone disease that he dreads to inflict upon future generations is only an intensified form of the eventual decay and death that is every child's inheritance. But although these are the facts of life, to live in cynicism and bitterness is no life at all. This is what Bridget, through her unflagging love for her husband, even at his most unlovable, must teach him. Midway through the novel, he had perversely waited until the last second to wade ashore on his weak legs before the sea made its daily charge down a narrow river channel. As Bridget pleads for him to hurry, he calls, "Why shouldn't I want to be killed?" It is only when she cries in true desperation that she could not live without him that he suddenly yields and allows her to pull him to shore. His reaction is revealing: " 'Why didn't you let me be killed, Bridget?' he said. But the usual despair had left his voice" (PN, 131). We can only assume that at the end of the novel, when Nicolas begins to realize the power of Bridget's commitment to him and her determination to save him, he will soften his stance against bringing children into an undeniably flawed existence and will realize that a life of compromised happiness is all a human being can expect. Nicolas's acceptance of life on its own terms will be his liberation, Bridget's gift to him.

The title is taken from a poem by Marianne Moore, which Kay Boyle quotes as the novel's epigraph: "Plagued by the nightingale/in the new leaves,/with its silence . . . /not its silence, but its silences." What plagues Bridget is that the qualities the nightingale represents—youth, vitality, passon, imagination, freedom of spirit—are silenced by respectability and convention. Liberty of thought is anathema to Nicolas's family. Papa confiscates and burns Charlotte's copy of a book by Anatole France, dangerous reading for one of her impressionability. When Maman confides to Bridget the scandal of Oncle Robert—he had married a Creole woman not knowing that she was pregnant with someone else's child, and later she divorced him—she is sure Bridget will share her view of the woman's depravity: " 'Passion it was she had for him,' hissed Nicolas's mother. 'Passion, passion' " (*PN,* 50). Clearly, to the family, love is a commodity to be arranged for, negotiated over, and purchased. When Oncle Robert adds fifteen thousand francs to Annick's dowry (in the expectation that she will nurse him in his old age), Luc's choice of bride is a foregone conclusion within the family. Marthe, the middle sister, even begs Bridget to have a child, collect the fifty thousand francs, and make her a loan to even her chances to be Luc's wife.

The nightingale is a fluid symbol. In all other years the trees by the pond had been "thick with nightingales," and there was always one in the acacia tree outside Charlotte's window, but this year they are absent. The author associates the nightingale's silence with the growing estrangement of Bridget and Nicolas; as Bridget and Charlotte approach him in the garden after searching in the bushes for any signs of a nightingale, he turns his back to them, "avoiding Bridget's eyes, turning away, and setting new silences between them" (*PN,* 59). Charlotte, too, is plagued. As her confinement drags on, she repeatedly laments the bird's absence. To cheer her up, Bridget buys her a nightingale in a wooden cage, but he will not sing. On the night Charlotte dies, the centuries-old acacia tree outside her window crashes down in a thunderstorm.

The nightingale is associated with Luc, too. As he and Bridget study the caged, silent bird, he tells her that its heart is probably breaking "for love, or for the lack of it" (*PN,* 167). Bridget sees the similarity in the nightingale's plight and Luc's. Thinking of the family's demands on Luc, she replies that "Instead of bits of grousel and grains of corn," she would like to give the nightingale its freedom. In the end, when Luc asks her to escape with him, she realizes that her wish has been fulfilled, for "Even the words in his mouth were gifts to him which would be his forever": "What was the nightingale's small liberty to the deep wide exemption she had given Luc, she thought" (*PN,* 201).

Like a number of her contemporaries writing in the twenties, including D. H. Lawrence, whom she admired, and T. S. Eliot, whom she did not, Kay Boyle had an interest in myth. Inasmuch as it has proved a long-lived interest—her latest novel, published in 1975, features characters with names like Athena, Callisto, and Calliope—it is worth noting that even in her first novel Boyle was striving to imbue her strongly autobiographical fiction with mythological associations in order to universalize her material. Luc is presented as a cross between an Apollonian god of light and a fertility god returned to revitalize a barren land. Like Apollo, he is a healer, a doctor, "a perfect instrument against death" (*PN*, 55). Bridget even calls him "The twilight attempered Hyperborean Apollo . . . gleaming at times with a supernatural brightness, and exposing to those who love him a golden thigh" (*PN*, 155).[12] Luc's name suggests the Latin *lucere*, "to shine." He is fertility god as well. As "this gleaming god-like man" comes toward her, "bearing the sun in the roots of his hair even," Maman thinks that somehow "his flesh must be grafted to them all, be one rich fruitful bough upon the decaying family tree" (*PN*, 98). His annual summer return is welcomed with "enormous feasts" (*PN*, 71).

The nightingale, too, has a mythological association. In the English literary tradition and in *The Waste Land*—a work Boyle knew—the nightingale is a symbol of both incestuous and adulterous love. In her novel, the author loosely associates Charlotte with the tongueless nightingale of the Philomela myth. As her condition deteriorates, her tongue becomes black and so swollen that she cannot speak. Her last words are "the acacia," the tree abandoned by her beloved nightingales. The night the acacia topples, Charlotte dies, poisoned, in effect, by an incestuous union: her husband is her first cousin. As a symbol of adultery, the nightingale's association with Luc is also appropriate. Bridget is plagued by the possibility, at least. F. Scott Fitzgerald calls up both the adulterous and incestuous implications of the symbol when a slightly drunken observer in *Tender Is the Night,* very likely alluding to Boyle's novel, suggests that the young screen actress in love with Dick Diver is "Plagued by the nightingale . . . probably plagued by the nightingale."[13] Not only is Diver a married man, but his relationship with the starlet, famous for her role in "Daddy's Girl," is loaded with incestuous overtones as well. (An experience with incest also plagues Nicole, Diver's troubled wife.)

Nearly every contemporary reviewer of Kay Boyle's first novel remarks upon its style. Katherine Anne Porter is again among the most articulate as well as the most enthusiastic: "The whole manner of the telling is superb: there are long passages of prose which crackle and snap with electric energy, episodes in which inner drama and outward events occur against scenes bright with the vividness of things seen by the immediate eye."[14] Through her precise word choice and fresh metaphors, Kay Boyle can render a scene with startling clarity, as in this sentence: "How Luc managed to turn the rabbit over, to get the rascal who was running like quicksilver through his fingers, over and flat on his side, over and pressed perfectly flat with its teeth nosing through the neat split in its upper lip, was a thing that rattled the girls together like the sticks of a fan" (*PN*, 54).

Her method of characterization is to stay entirely out of sight and let the person unselfconsciously reveal himself through dialogue. Thus with his own words she fixes the eccentric nature of Oncle Robert, a man so blatantly self-centered and sexist that he is almost amusing. Defending his contribution of fifteen thousand francs to Annick's dowry, hoping Luc will choose her as his wife from among the family's three daughters, he says:

> I love Luc as I do my own dear boy, and rather than see him united with that absolute serpent of a Marthe who would consume him so completely that there would be no virility left to pursue his high career—or with that guffawing graceless creature who is half man and the remainder quite indescribable, I refer to Julie, of course—rather than see him united to either of those two monsters of womanhood who shy like skiddy horses at the sight of a man, I prefer to sacrifice my entire fortune, small though it may be, and enable him to marry a good and lovely woman who has washed enough behinds in hospitals to take a husband as a matter of course. (*PN*, 153)

Or, she delineates character by reporting actions without comment, as when she describes Oncle Robert at the funeral: "The mass for Charlotte's soul was being sung when he leaned close to ask them if Maman were serving chicken or duck for the lunch" (*PN*, 188).

Kay Boyle also has a keen sense of the grotesque, which she sometimes uses to great comic effect, as in her description of an English party picnicking on Castle Island. At the sound of their tour leader's whistle, the men and women split neatly and disappear into the woods. When the whistle sounds again a short time later, "immediately men and women alike began to wander back to the clearing, nonchalantly talking of the clear weather and the view, for all the world as if they had not but two minutes before been poised in the most awkward positions behind the trees" (*PN*, 85). But her sense of the grotesque can also be horrible. After Charlotte's death she writes: "In the afternoon the grave-digger came to the family to tell them that he had opened the vault and found that it was flooded. Jean's mother and father, it appeared, were quietly barging about underground" (*PN*, 183). The bilious Nicolas "could not refrain from mentioning the famous trip by river from Saint-Malo when Jean's father had distinguished himself by his gallant manipulation of the sails." During an electrical storm, while the ladies had "retched in unison over the heaving side," he had brought them safely to harbor. Nicolas adds, to the family's horror, "He's probably much better off cruising about that way" (*PN*, 184).

Richard C. Carpenter has remarked that in Kay Boyle's better work "we float on a placid, shimmering current, all the time aware of the cold, black rushing depths beneath."[15] Certainly there is a violent undertow below the surface of the simple domestic scene in which Charlotte's young son Riquet asks if the booties his grandmother is knitting are for him:

> "No, no, not for Riquet," said Maman as she curved fatuously over him. "For a little, little brother or sister who will come to play with Riquet. Maman is going to buy him this winter at the Galeries Lafayette," she said.
>
> In his small strong fist Riquet grabbed and held firmly the pleat of flesh that sagged in his grandmother's throat. The blood rushed to her face and her words were strangled in her mouth. She sat in her chair with her face swollen, gurgling as her grandson strangled her. Charlotte leapt to her feet and slapped his rosy hands. (*PN,* 139–40)

Margaret Atwood has said that Kay Boyle's work approaches "the moment of visionary realism when sensation heightens and time for an instant fixes and stops." While her writing has sometimes been spoken of as nearly surreal, Atwood feels that if one were to pick a painter whose work corresponds to Boyle's, it would not be Salvador Dali: "One thinks rather of Brueghel, a landscape clearly and vividly rendered, everything in its ordinary order, while Icarus falls to his death, scarcely noticed, off to the side."[16]

One can best appreciate the magnitude of Kay Boyle's achievement and how rapidly and how far her skill advanced by comparing the style of the *This Quarter* fragment with the brilliant, polished subtlety of the finished novel. A chapter of the fragment begins with this paragraph:

> The church was new, with a broad white nave and wooden saints whose cheeks Annick had refreshened too vividly. A wave of shame rose in her, suffusing her throat and face, confusing her when she passed the gaudy *Christophe* in the vestry door. In time it would wear away and the saints would fade to human colors, but now it was so, and at each mass she must face them and be shamed by their sharp complexions.[17]

She reworked the passage in the 1931 novel to read:

> The church was new, with a broad white nave. The wooden saints that flanked it had faces as red as fire. More shame to Annick, said Papa. For it was she who had been obliging enough to retouch their faded countenances. A wave of shame rose in her whenever she passed the gaudy *Christophe* in the vestry door. In time they would fade, but to her it was a source of great anguish that while Charlotte's children were small, at least, this would be one of the family jokes and jibes. All through their childhood they would hear Papa talking about it, and somehow this might alter their opinion of her. It might even give them a frivolous conception of religion. It might in some way lessen the dignity of God. (*PN,* 30)

In this version Boyle has indicated in strong but subtle strokes the "little murders" committed daily within the family fold, has deftly suggested the element of vanity in Annick's piety, and has made her own ironic comment on religion. Contemporary reviewers praised her style as "dainty" and "delicate."[18] Kay Boyle's style is as dainty as the thrust of a stiletto, as delicate as the slice of a scalpel.

Although *Gentlemen, I Address You Privately,* published in 1933, was the author's third novel to appear in print, it actually was completed prior to *Year Before Last,* published in 1932. While living in Harfleur, she had interrupted work on *Plagued by the Nightingale* to begin another novel "simply because all the details of Le Havre and the sea and Harfleur and the land were clamoring in my mind," she says. "I did not want to have wiped from my memory the things I had borne witness to, and the things I had learned in this unhappy town" (*BGT,* 166–67). In that dismal part of the country, where she lived from 1924 to 1926, she had become intrigued with the word "imponderable": "Imponderable, meaning 'that which cannot be weighed or measured,' was the word I used now in rebuttal of the ponderability of the France of which I had become an inextricable part," she recalls (*BGT,* 168). Like her first novel, *Gentlemen, I Address You Privately* centers on the struggle of the human spirit to maintain its vitality despite the heavy "ponderability" of mundane surroundings. It chronicles the fight of hope and vision to stay alive in a banal and sordid world.

Kay Boyle took the title from a poem by Ernest Walsh. She quotes the full line as the book's epigraph: "Gentlemen, I address you privately and no woman is within hearing." Besides serving as a memorial to Walsh, calling attention to his badly neglected poetry, the title is appropriate to the book's male homosexual characters.

As in Kay Boyle's other works, shifting emotions and relationships rather than external events provide the action of this novel. Munday, an English priest expelled from his order for playing "Poème de l'Extase" during the collection, finds himself an exile in Le Havre giving piano lessons for a living and gingerly, "with a grim elation in his blood," tasting freedom for the first time in his life (*G,* 12).[19] Ayton, a lusty Cockney sailor with "an uncommon pretty face" (*G,* 15), seeks his companionship. The ex-priest, whose newly acknowledged sexual desires are complicated by his reverence for his mother and the Virgin, is powerfully attracted to the other man. The two develop a homosexual relationship. Because Ayton has deserted his ship to be with Munday and has stolen some goods, the pair go into hiding outside town at the cabin of squatters, Quespelle and his wife, Leonie. During the months that the four live together, Leonie, who has come to despise her brutal husband, falls in love with Ayton as Munday looks quietly on. Three Alsatian friends of Ayton are frequent visitors: Blanca, a beautiful and aggressive lesbian, and her lovers—Sophia, daughter of the local madam, and Annchen, one of the whores. Ayton, the restless sort, finally goes off to Italy with them, leaving behind the man and woman who love him. He has stolen Munday's beloved piano to finance his journey and has left Leonie pregnant.

Contemporary reviewers were unenthusiastic. One called it "a complex of perilous stuff got off the breast by a writer intoxicated by its peril, and fascinated by the shapeless confusion that pluck [sic] the strings of being to no purpose and for inadequate cause."[20] In the only attempt at critical analysis of the book, Richard C. Carpenter calls it a "chiaroscuro" in which "we see everything through a glass most darkly, so much so that it is difficult to realize what the theme is."[21] Kay Boyle herself wrote to her friend Bob Brown, "I know this homo book is too over-written, out-written, inside out written. I've gone over and over and over and over and over and over it, drunk, sober, married and single, for the past six and a half years. And probably no-one will want it anyway."[22] It is difficult on first reading to discern a theme running through the bizarre tangle of relationships that make up the novel, but it is there.

Here again, she exposes the rifts in understanding between lonely people who fail to make meaningful contact with each other. From the beginning Munday and Ayton perceive their relationship differently. When the sailor first comes to the former priest for counsel and companionship, Munday innocently places his hand on Ayton's shoulder, but "the priestly gesture which his blood recalled and made had set Ayton to shaking in his skin" with desire (*G*, 24). After Munday has given his friend a seal ring that he had admired, Ayton announces that he is staying ashore to be with him. Now tormented by his own rising desires, Munday curses him: "For the little charity he had given, the man was taking him for something else, and he would have none of it" (*G*, 63). After meeting the Alsatian girls, he denounces Ayton's hedonistic aimlessness, saying, "you must have somthing to give your life a shape," and as the two walk together, "The soundless black torrent of the roadway coursed between them; a wide stream of invisible and seemingly unending night. On one side Munday walked, and on the other Ayton, separate, unassailable, as if the flood between them were never to be spanned" (*G*, 100). Even though the two do connect soon thereafter in a physical consummation of their relationship, the gap between them will not be bridged completely. Munday will always be the selfless, devoted partner while Ayton casually engages the affection of many others.

At the center of the novel is Munday's struggle to find something he can believe in. As he has already discovered, ready-made religion will not suffice. He rejects the Church, saying, "It was not made for men of spirit, but for the fishermen and the ignorant who had no other vision, such as the humble men of Galilee" (*G*, 140). Yet he believes that "All men must guide their life toward some image" (*G*, 141). "Mine is music," he claims. But ascetic devotion of this sort will not do either—and here the author takes a jab at her avant-garde contemporaries who had made a cold religion of art. In this work, as in her others, only love will satisfy a human being's longing for something beyond the self in which to place one's faith, and she is not particular or prudish about the form it takes.

Kay Boyle, who while disliking the author thought *A Farewell to Arms* a fine book, surely would agree when Count Greffi reminds Frederic Henry that love is a religious feeling. Ayton had first come to Munday seeking a new life through his companionship, and their love revitalizes Munday as well. After they have consummated it, the ex-priest knows he must have sinned, but his heart is unconvinced: "Abomination, he said in himself, but his heart was brimming still with wonder; abomination and sin, he repeated, seeking to give them meaning, but the glamour remained undefiled" (*G*, 110). Ayton acknowledges his own resurrection through Munday, whispering to him, "God, y'see, they say is Love. . . . And that is what Love does, y'see" (*G*, 142). Leonie's life, too, has been renewed through her love for Ayton, and she recognizes love's transforming power. "If a man has all his wishes and hopes set on one thing, it alters his face completely," she tells Munday. " 'Love,' she said softly, 'changes the look of anyone. I believe in it, you know' " (*G*, 175–76).

Kay Boyle's concept of love is Christian not in name but in the value it places on selflessness, on surrendering one's life in order to gain it. Munday is angry when he learns that Ayton is a thief as well as a deserter, but he quiets his own anger by asking himself, "if you have a child in your heart would you abandon him?" and "if anything like love has come to you would you drive it out into the desolation and cold?" (*G*, 156). Soon thereafter he perjures himself to the police to protect Ayton.

Paradoxically, by surrendering himself to another, Munday has gained a new, strong sense of his own identity. When he faces Quespelle in a showdown over whether the squatter will wantonly shoot his own dog after some rabbits are found killed, it is a critical moment for him: "Something will happen now, some decision come, he thought, but he himself, having taken his strength so long from other places, was weaponless" (*G*, 281). The Church and music are "like two pale sisters with their hands laid on him, detaining the wild blood that bound and unbound its mesh of power in his veins," but finally Munday's own *human* power, realized through his fleshly, human love for Ayton, is unleashed and gives him the strength to knock Quespelle to the ground. Later, thinking back on the incident, he explains to the others: "I am taking shape, I am coming little by little to life. I, myself, I was put aside for a long time, and now I have to dream or remember how I should be. Now it might be that things have been restored to me" (*G*, 288).

By the time Ayton is finally gone, both Munday and Leonie have been made whole and strong through their connection with him. Even after Leonie has stopped believing in Ayton, her spirit remains enriched: "So went the river of her love flowing, drifting through the afternoon as though there were many afternoons before them, and the stream never to run shallow" (*G*, 339). The squatters, finally put off the land, plan to move on to Dieppe, but Leonie, by now obviously pregnant, begs Munday not to leave them. For the first time in his life, Munday feels himself succumbing to a woman, "the river of her voice . . . submerging him like the waters of willing death" (*G*, 340). But he rouses himself and says, "But there's yours and Quespelle's child. Whatever happens next has nothing to do with me" (*G*, 340). When Leonie responds that he must have known it was not Quespelle's child, he is baffled, and as she opens her mouth to speak, the truth dawns on him. The novel ends: " 'No, no, don't say it!' and he suddenly began to laugh" (*G*, 341). Ayton has saved both Munday and Leonie. By giving them each a new sense of their own untapped powers through love for him, he has brought them together. Although he has gone, the man and woman are left with rich possibilities for a new life with each other (we assume Leonie feels no obligation to remain with Quespelle). Their capacity for love is Ayton's gift to them.

Kay Boyle is concerned with the need for understanding on the social as well as on the individual level. The failed relationship of the husband and wife, Quespelle and Leonie, has implications for all relationships between men and women. Quespelle displays a pride in ownership and need to control that seems a particularly masculine brand of egotism. As he surveys his land and animals, "his face was black with conceit, with an evil pride," and "everything he possessed he talked into pride to himself, because it was his own" (*G*, 33). Kay Boyle, whose grandfather meant to engineer the existences of all in his household until she, her sister, and her mother left home, was not unfamiliar with the type, although the squatter in her novel has none of her grandfather's compensating qualities. Quespelle boasts of his ability to kill rabbits with a single blow "in the narrow crotch" between their ears, and he demonstrates his technique on a pregnant rabbit—in callous disregard for the little bracelet Leonie had placed around her paw to mark and protect her. It is a deliberate plundering of the female. He boasts also of his father's mistreatment of women, and when the group goes to see a traveling show, Quespelle's coarse laugh is loudest during a burlesque wedding night scene that upsets and shames his wife. She looks to Munday, the ex-priest, "in appeal now that all she had been taught by other women to believe special and pure was being defiled" (*G,* 194).

Only military chauvinism is capable of moving this man's heart. When he hears the cannon ring out from the munitions factory in Le Havre, Quespelle proudly declares that never again will his nation be caught unprepared. He is oblivious to Munday's ironic observation that "They're like as not filling orders for the tribes in mutiny in Morocco:" Quespelle "made as if he had not understood him, for he had no time for anything that interfered with the way his mind was made" (*G,* 35). At the traveling show, Quespelle's raucous laughter at the burlesque so distressing to the woman abruptly gives way to maudlin tears when, in another skit, Napolean, booted and spurred, appears on stage.

Kay Boyle was no great admirer of T. S. Eliot, but in *Gentlemen, I Address You Privately* she makes use of some of the images and mythic elements at the heart of *The Waste Land.* In her novel the town lies "like the valley of death, sinking, settling into the ice of the marshes, with the people concealed in its shadow going without deviation toward death" (*G,* 54). Besides depicting, like Eliot, an "Unreal City" peopled by the living dead, Boyle employs his image of a great rock to suggest the land's awful barrenness and desolation. Describing the dwelling of the squatters, she writes: "A bosom of rock swelled there, offering no milk of kindness to the shy sweet dawn. Under it thrived a midnight more obscure than any, and in that chasm Quespelle's cabin stood in foreboding with its sackcloth waving outward in the morning breeze" (*G,* 159).

Just as *The Waste Land* concerns the return of the fisher king to the barren land, Ayton comes from the seas into the barren lives of the celibate priest and Leonie, who has been unable to have children. He acts as a catalyst, an amoral natural force that frees the elemental powers trapped within the others. Through him, Munday realizes his own natural sexuality, and Leonie becomes pregnant with the child that will provide her escape from a sterile, loveless bond with Quespelle. At the book's end we might speculate that she and Munday will establish a "natural" heterosexual relationship.[23] Ayton also restores to fertility the squatter's land as he masters the soil in explicitly sexual terms:

> It was the supreme authority in Ayton's flesh that humbled Munday; the appalling, the brutal power of his penetration into the land. Each thrust of his spade was so much more fervor given to his passionate advance. He would have the whole of it in tumult, clump upon clump uprooted and turned to fallow land. He had no time for speech, nor even to turn his head to Munday. The urgency of his flesh was driving the thing before him now, subduing it in assault, his greed insatiably renewed between each stroke, scarcely appeased when the attack was through. (*G,* 179)

Ayton's total abandon to natural forces takes on mythological dimensions, and he becomes a sort of fertility god. As he walks with Munday through the winter-bound forest sowing acorns, he sings aloud, "Oh, I could spend my best years showing the elements how to go or come or stay quiet. . . . If the shadow of the earth should fall on the sun or on the moon, I could drive it off myself with arrows" (*G*, 268). Like Dionysius, Ayton has a dual nature, both good and evil, and he teaches others to yield to the ecstasy of natural forces. But he also is linked to the Phoenician sailor of *The Waste Land,* for he had once dived off Panama and come up with a pearl necklace. He is like Lazarus, risen from the dead, as he travels on the passport and money of his dead friend, John Harpy (who had believed he himself had been born twice before and would live again). Kay Boyle suggests a number of mythological and biblical parallels to Ayton while at the same time identifying Leonie with the Virgin and Munday with Christ.

The truth is that it is difficult or impossible to sort the references into any consistent symbolic pattern. Perhaps it is here that her material slips out of control and the book becomes, as she sensed, "over-written, outwritten, inside-out written." Still, it is significant that in this novel begun so early in her career she has attempted to give her work mythological and allegorical dimensions, for she would try it again with varying success in a number of later works, including *His Human Majesty* (1949), *Generation Without Farewell* (1960), and *The Underground Woman* (1975). Thus *Gentlemen, I Address You Privately,* while a flawed work, continues several major threads that run through the body of Kay Boyle's fiction: a concern for the gaps in understanding that separate human beings, an almost religious belief in love as humanity's only salvation, and an interest in universalizing particular experience through allegory and myth.

Year Before Last (1932) was Kay Boyle's second novel to appear in print. In the chronology of her own experience, this story of her relationship with Ernest Walsh in 1926 follows the stay in Le Havre and Harfleur that inspired *Gentlemen, I Address You Privately. Year Before Last* is also the work of a more sophisticated stylist, but it was published first for practical reasons. In a 1931 letter to Bob Brown (who had not particularly cared for *Plagued by the Nightingale*), she reports having received a letter from her publisher "telling me what a disappointment my fairy book has been to himself and all my ardent admirers whom he has shown it to in N. Y." She continues: "He even suggests letting it hang over as he fears it will, because of its lack of strength, harm my reputation. So there we are. You were right, you see, I'm not such a hot lady novelist. However, I'll let it go to press, I think, with a few changes to jack it up here and there and let the next book be better."[24] But Kay Boyle did delay publication of *Gentle-*

men, I Address You Privately, and the next book *was* better. She was given a thousand-dollar advance on *Year Before Last* from Harrison Smith in New York, and the book was published simultaneously in London by Faber and Faber. Caresse Crosby republished it in her Crosby Continental Editions paperback series, Boyle received inquiries for translation into German, it was translated into French in 1937, and there was even some talk of making it into a motion picture.[25] In 1969 it was the second of her early novels to be republished in Southern Illinois University Press's Crosscurrents/Modern Fiction series.

The author was pleased with her novel, too. In a letter to Bob Brown, she quotes a long passage from her work in progress and tells him, "I'm going to have fun typing out the book for you. It's so much better than *Plagued* that it relieves my soul."[26] It was born of her love for Ernest Walsh, and contemporary reviewers who commented on the power and sincerity of feeling in the novel must have sensed Boyle's emotional investment in her material. In a letter of February 2, 1932, she tells Caresse Crosby that she is "hurrying madly" to finish *Year Before Last* and thinks it is a book her friend will like: "It is infinitely better than either of the other two novels, and sometimes I feel so close to you as I write it that I feel we must have gone through some terrible thing together sometime, somewhere."[27] Caresse, who also had recently endured the untimely death of the man she loved, was "absolutely overwhelmed by its beauty!" "Annah [sic] and Martin are so real and thrilling and heartbreaking that they have become part of life," she told her friend.[28]

Although the novel opens with the conventional disclaimer that "none of the characters herein depicted have any connection with actual people, dead or living," it is obviously autobiographical. Hannah, a young American, has left her French husband in Le Havre and come to the south of France to recuperate from a lung disease. She has made the trip on the invitation of Martin Sheehan, an ailing young poet, and his Scottish aunt, Eve Raeburn, who coedit a literary magazine. Hannah and Martin fall in love, and she leaves her decent husband, Dilly, with hardly a thought. But it is more difficult for Martin to cast off the hold of his jealous and indignant aunt, for his beloved magazine is wholly dependent on her financial backing. He is torn between his love for Hannah and his love for his art. At the same time his worsening consumption sends the young couple into flight from one hostile town to another and finally into a losing race against death itself. Thus the tensions within this unusual triangle are played out against the backdrop of a universal conflict: the individual spirit versus the inevitability of decay and death.

Hannah is a thinly disguised Kay Boyle. Their similarities extend from their innocent departures from French husbands and subsequent spontaneous love affairs with black-eyed poets right down to their Irish eyes and the cheap plastic hoop earrings they wear. It is interesting, although probably not particularly significant, that in the typescript of *Year Before Last* the protagonist's name is Bridget, as it was in *Plagued by the Nightingale,* and that in both novels the French husband has a Tante Dominique. Martin Sheehan, like Ernest Walsh, is an American poet of Irish descent, Cuban upbringing, and tempestuous temperament. A plane crash injury in the war had triggered his consumptive ailment, and he coedits a literary magazine with a well-to-do Scotswoman who had once bailed him out of the elegant Claridge hotel in Paris when he had been unable to pay his bill. Although Ethel Moorhead was not Walsh's aunt, she is the model for Eve Raeburn, who, like her, is a sturdy suffragist who dotes on the younger man, despises his illicit love affair, frequents Monte Carlo casinos (often wearing an embroidered coat from the days of the Boxer rebellion), and holds the magazine hostage in a tug-of-war over the man's soul.

Like Kay Boyle's other early works, *Year Before Last* is much more a novel of character than of events. One reviewer found Martin Sheehan "an insufferable person" and, apparently unaware of its autobiographical source, called the book "a chronicle that was never in any danger of being too much like 'real life' "; yet he had to credit Boyle for the authenticity of her characters: "That the characters are unreal I do not assert: nervous and brittle as they are, they are vital enough in their own way, and perfectly at home in the world Kay Boyle has made for them."[29] The author has done a marvelous job of capturing their complex, idiosyncratic natures. Although the novel is written in the third person (a change from the fragment called "Written for Royalty," which appeared in the summer, 1928, issue of *transition*), Hannah is still the sensitive filter through which perceptions reach the reader, and her own personality is unobtrusive beside the dazzling eccentricities of Martin, Eve, and several minor figures.

In his preface to the 1969 republication of the novel, Harry T. Moore remarks that Hemingway's "nastily cruel sketch" of Ernest Walsh ("The Man Who Was Marked for Death") in *A Moveable Feast* misses entirely his "enthusiasm and Celtic gaiety" (*YBL,* viii).[30] Kay Boyle, who was in love with the man, does not. Walsh was a man of fiery temperament, if the postscript to a letter he wrote in 1926 to Kate Buss is any indication:

> How in hell do you expect the postmaster of Cannes to deliver letters addressed to "Michael" Walsh, to Ernest Walsh? Your letter addressed to "Michael" Walsh reached me by a miracle. I being the miracle. I happened to see your handwriting and insisted the letter was for me although I found it very difficult to convince the man that Michael and Ernest were the same person. He asked me for "Michael" Walsh's carte d'identité and since there is no official record

of "Michael" Walsh I could not produce it. NEVER address letters to people using their nicknames. Don't forget my name is Ernest Walsh, not Michael Walsh.[31]

Yet he had a generous spirit as well, and in a 1922 letter to Buss he speaks fondly of Ethel Moorhead, who had nursed him "with unequalled devotion," saying "my debt to her is too great to ever repay."[32]

Kay Boyle captures both the volatile and the gentle sides of Ernest Walsh in her characterization of Martin Sheehan. Although Martin is leaving her to visit Eve for the day, he (most unreasonably) becomes furious with Hannah when she does not insist on accompanying him: "Have your solitude, he said politely. I couldn't wouldn't deprive you. I wouldn't think of. Have your solitude my dear. Wash it and scrub it clean and hang it up to dry. But before I go may I speak my mind in passing, may I utter? You have no life, stamina, strength. You have nothing I can rely on. Shine the floors, do the silver, don't let me deter you" (YBL, 51–52). Nearly every meeting he has with Eve becomes a wild shouting match, and his jibes can be vicious. Once, when he has been detained at the police station after an auto accident, she comes to rescue him, but in her haste to get there has forgotten to bring the car registration papers that he needs. From the station window he shouts across the street to her: "My God. . . . You had time enough to doll yourself up like Queen Victoria! . . . You look like a trained nurse in that outfit!" (YBL, 65).

Yet Martin delights in making sugar cubes appear from dogs' ears to entertain the village children, likes to do jigs in front of mirrors with his hands in his pockets, and succumbs to "helpless pity" when he stops to help an injured priest beside the highway. He is a "strong gay man" with "the gift of the gab" (YBL, 27). He and an indigent friend had once talked their way in and out of the Blackstone Hotel in Chicago, staying overnight in its most comfortable room and ordering two kinds of marmalade for breakfast, without spending a penny. Another time he had "skipped, skedaddled, decamped" from a sanatarium "full of other dough-boys coughing their way out of the picture, with gramophones and everything else about to make it pretty" (YBL, 139). When a doctor reminds him that he should not smoke with his lung condition, he replies, "Yes, I know. Or drink. Or talk. But still being alive I find it hard to dispense with the gestures" (YBL, 139). As he is about to die, he asks the hotelkeeper to bring champagne and caviar along with the doctor, and on one of the last nights of his life he throws a party, although he is flat on his back and the cork shoots out of the bottle just as a needle slips into his arm. Hannah says of Martin, "Poetry can open his eyes like fire, and the words of a stupid man turn him white as frost" (YBL, 55). Kay Boyle writes of Walsh that in his presence she learned that "to be gay is one of the postures of courage" (*BGT,* 197). She has captured her lover's indomitable spirit in her portrait of Martin Sheehan.

She also captures the contradictory nature of Ethel Moorhead in Eve Raeburn. Eve, "tough as a bean" (*YBL,* 5), was a brave feminist in Britain who had been to prison for her beliefs and had been force-fed during a hunger strike. She had burned churches and had rejected a title from a government that did not give women the vote. Yet in her bedroom, where a pink light burns all night so she will not be afraid, a grand collection of bisque dolls in satin dresses covers her bed, and she has led "a single virgin life" for fear of "what men might be after" (*YBL,* 6). "She had been half-killed for suffrage for women, but she was irritated to sit out in a café with a woman alone or to walk into a restaurant even with another woman," we are told. Even as she spurns Martin and Hannah, there is something pathetic in her pride. She sends them a letter saying that she is having a wonderful time in Monte Carlo with Lady Vanta. But Lady Vanta is in town with the couple. "How could the evil insinuating fury fit the sad lonely grief that invented a friend and friendship to take the edge off any pity they might feel?" Hannah wonders (*YBL,* 185).

The minor characters, too, are memorable. Kay Boyle captures the *haute* nonsense of avant-garde hangers-on in her picture of Lady Vanta, who hovers about the young couple to "warm her hands at the flame" while hoping they will publish her clever stories (*YBL,* 34). On her first visit with Hannah and Martin, "The third cocktail sent her sliding on the leather armchair under the table, and she too indolent to recover sat with only her white lashes remaining and her hand lifting now and then over the edge to fetch the almonds to her mouth" (*YBL,* 29). She reveals with canny subtlety her ulterior motive in befriending the pair: "My loves, she said, my loves. She plucked off a scarlet flowerhead and tossed the petals down before them. It's like stepping from winter and old age into the heart of spring, she said. My darlings, my lovely ones, when do you go to press, my loves?" (*YBL,* 39). This *artiste* cannot bear the silence and solitude usually requisite for serious creation. She has a "pale smiling mouth curved up like a bark for setting sail in conversation," and "When she sat on the terrace alone, rather than have it empty, she patted it full of yawns with the tip of her hand" (*YBL,* 187).

Harry T. Moore says of the novel, "One of its principal and most attractive features is its style, as always in the writings of Kay Boyle" (*YBL,* viii). Nearly all the contemporary reviewers, too, agreed that it was magnificently written.[33] As before, her metaphors are fresh and original. As Hannah travels out of the frozen North into the lush, warm Mediterranean region, she notices, "There were many fancy little trees, twisted as if they had been taken out of glass jars with a fork, and everywhere the soft flowing country broken, tossed-up, dammed and bursting over rocks, rushing up in high peeling waves" (*YBL,* 10). As in many of her short stories of this period, the landscape reflects the state of consciousness of the perceiver. When Hannah and Martin are driven back into the hot mountains by Eve's fury and hotelkeepers' suspicions of his illness, the scenery, too, becomes alien and hostile. The valley they climbed "was like the throat of hell": "Up and around the spiral brink they drove, like a fly on the parched lips of a crater" (*YBL,* 164). External reality is distorted to surrealistic dimensions in the scene in which the exhausted couple tries to make a smooth exit from a crowded hotel terrace before Martin succumbs to a coughing fit. Reflected in Kay Boyle's looking glass they became "A comic couple walking with dignity towards the door that receded and jumped back, that retired as they came": "Their feet lagged, the sun rose, the faces of the women sewing lifted and turned away. And down the terrace Martin and Hannah went, pursuing the small black haven of the door which fled. Once on the threshold, the opening grinned wide, withdrew, shrank to a keyhole, and then roared open like a furnace and let them in" (*YBL,* 191–92).

Kay Boyle's work is not generally heavy with symbolism, but when she does employ a symbol it is imbedded so subtly in the narrative that on first reading it seems just another surface detail. Soon after arriving in the South, Hannah sits close to Martin, drinking pernod and holding a little pink angel he has bought her: "Dilly and Eve were somewhere else, and she had no thought for them. She sat looking at her wax doll as purely as though she had ascended serene and blameless to this heaven." She whispers to Martin, "I am drunk with heaven" (*YBL,* 17). As they leave the café, he feels he must tell her what to do if he should begin to hemorrhage, but she tells him to shut up and puts her hands over her ears. As he persists in instructing her how to give him an injection to thicken his blood, the inescapable fact of Martin's illness and mortality is underscored by the symbol of the angel: "Will you look at your chateau ahead which is your home to you, and stop lying to me? she said with the little wax angel melting soft in her hand" (*YBL,* 18). The angel which just a moment before had represented her ecstasy, the "heaven" to which she had ascended with her lover, has quietly become an evil portent of quite a different kind of heaven, and Hannah does not wish to face how one gets there.

Kay Boyle is also skillful with foreshadowing. Throughout the novel Hannah stubbornly ignores the signs of Martin's illness, so obvious to outsiders, and becomes indignant when they refer to his health. A chilling scene takes place immediately before his final, fatal hemorrhage. He has just gotten out of bed for the first time in weeks so that the hotel coiffeur can cut his hair:

> I'm glad to see you up, said the coiffeur bending over. He parted the hair and laid it back and ran his scissors through. There's a superstition about cutting a man's hair in bed, he said, still smiling. The blades nipped near the temples and cut short the black silk hair. Sometimes we're called upon to do it. The steel ran through and laid the soft thick locks aside. After a man, he said, and he parted the hair on the other side and drew the comb through the depths of it. After a man has already passed on, he said. (*YBL*, 217)

As Martin lies down after the barber leaves, resting his "long white bones," "a bright thread of blood ran suddenly from his mouth, went writhing like a living thing over the white of his shirt," and his head went back "like a flower breaking from the stalk" (*YBL*, 218). "For Christ's sake," Martin says. "I'm dying, he said, and it seemed like an affront to him" (*YBL*, 219). The gleaming black locks that the barber had cut are lying all about the floor.

Year Before Last is at bottom another story of exile and isolation and the human need for contact with others. Its three principal characters are expatriates, and it is significant that Martin, living among the French, cannot speak or understand their language and that Eve is partially deaf. After Martin has finished reading William Carlos Williams' *The Discovery of Kentucky,* we are told: "This was the America with which Martin felt bondage, and the skyscrapers might never have been reared aloft. The country of Pocohontas. . . . Dostoevski's Russia, or Joyce's Ireland, the Italian poet's Italy to which he had returned ailing when America had broken him in two" (*YBL*, 130). Such alienation from one's homeland, even if voluntary and justifiable, is bound to be painful. Hannah notes how eagerly the English-speaking expatriates seek each other out and cling to the vestiges of home: "It was a terrible thing, thought Hannah, the sun that drew people from their own lands and set them off in isolation. In this part of the country every foreign ear was cocked for the sound of English, and when strangers found others who spoke their tongue they did what they could to move closer together" (*YBL*, 91–92).

Sensitive people long to transcend what separates them from one another. In this as in Kay Boyle's other works, they long to connect, and again, love is one means of transcendence. Soon after she took up life with Ernest Walsh, Boyle wrote to her mother, "I'm just full of all this slop about the healing power of love. The idea I *tried* to get over in writing. That love is a wide enormous tangible thing, and that if you hate anything, or any condition, you refuse the fusion in love. Michael is so enthusiastic about the idea that he has worked it out that he was dying because his ego had always been denied the one thing it needed to flatter it into health. Well, anyway for seven weeks he's been a bigger and better man."[34] In the novel, when Hannah first comes to live with Martin, he tells her:

I must have been dying, and that was what was happening to me. I was dying, for everything was drying and withering up in me. . . . I know that whatever death was in me was only in moments and now I am no longer in despair. The only relief is to be with you and who can say it does not matter as long as we two simply start out together on something, and not too serious about it either. Any interests in common as, what? I want the concern with something else again. (*YBL,* 3)

Art, too, is a "concern with something else" that transcends time and space and bonds isolated individuals, and for Martin as well as for his creator, poetry is a religion. He exalts the glory of the Word, saying, "words said one after another are in themselves a reason for existence." His belief in the power of poetry is mystical: "Measure the gold, the axis where the rails run into the sun. Take it home, measure the miracle. Put your finger on it, that's what I mean by making a poem up and getting it down on paper. It remains to be proved that there is any dimension to grandeur, or that an open door leads anywhere except beyond the threshold of a man's heart. That's what I mean by a magazine, he said" (*YBL,* 50). Martin spends much of his time reading aloud, and phrases of the poetry Kay Boyle herself loved echo through the novel. He savors Joyce's "Rain on Rahoon falls softly softly falling" and the words of Emanuel Carnevali, to whom the book is dedicated: "Tomorrow will be beautiful, for tomorrow comes out of the lake" and "Love, hear thou how desolate the heart is." Even though he is nearly destitute, he spends one hundred francs to send a telegram to "the poet in Italy" (Carnevali is not mentioned by name) saying, "Your gusto blows through the wasteland and other minor poems and sows them with rich crops" (*YBL,* 84).[35]

In Kay Boyle's view both love of another person and love of art are essential elements of existence. Martin's torment when Eve forces him to choose one at the expense of the other is the central conflict of the novel. It is an impossible decision, and he tells Hannah:

If I could give up one or the other. But that I cannot. Not you, nor Eve, nor the magazine and what it gives me. I love the best someone out there, beyond, whose name I do not know, wherever he is writing a poem, painting a picture. I love him more than I do you or as much as or else I could relinquish. But I shall, I must have you all. I shall jump, turn, sink, coil, twist with intention. Now you'll have me, now you won't. (*YBL,* 47)

But while offering art and love as the remedies for humanity's painful isolation, the novel explores the many obstacles to this sorely needed connection. The book's minor characters, Duke, Phyllis, and Lady Vanta—three writers who do more café-sitting than creating—represent a decadent spirit that threatens the integrity of art, that makes literature "a matter of tea-parties" (*YBL,* 161): "Each time I strike a key of my typewriter, said Duke with his whiskey blooming in his face, it means a cocktail at the Majestic" (*YBL,* 99). He attempts to ridicule Martin out of his fierce dedication to poetry and into a more "sensible" view of literature. Eyeing the rafters of his dining room, he asks Martin, "If you looked at this house . . . would you think it was built entirely of words, out of one sentence coming after another, would you think every stick and stone of it was an empty poetic idea put to a better use?" (*YBL,* 100). But Martin's dream "of raising other men into a perception of the infinite" remains undefiled, and he asks Hannah afterwards, "if Duke is a writer, then what am I? And if I am a poet, then what is Duke? And if Duke is real, then what am I after all?" (*YBL,* 110). The physical ailment that plagues Martin parallels his spiritual malaise. He tells the offensively healthy-looking English doctor sent by Duke and Phyllis that what might heal him is something no physician could provide: "It might be done by America restored to the Indians, or an entirely new race of proud men sprung up, or enough good books written out of the austere spirit of people who do not falter or conform" (*YBL,* 139).

Duke and Phyllis desescrate love as well as art. Martin is annoyed by Phyllis' cozy confession that she and Duke "are not married yet either," and she is eager to hear details of his and Hannah's romance. When she chummily asks Hannah what it is like to be in love with a poet who does not like to talk about love at the dinner table, Hannah "could not answer for shyness" (*YBL,* 105). She cannot abide the cheapening of one of the few things sacred to her. When Martin bitterly suggests that she go back to Dilly or find someone.else after he dies, she slaps him: "Whatever it is you've left me, she cried out, I'll keep for myself if I have to fight you for it! It isn't love, it's something the Dukes and Phyllises haven't had their hands on! It's something better than that!" (*YBL,* 112).

Through Hannah's discoveries the novel explores love's nature and its various faces. It simply exists. "If love is an element, like weather or wind, then it must go unchallenged," she believes (*YBL,* 67). Love must be allowed to flow free; it is destroyed when one attempts to claim small bits as his or her possession. Martin, a true "free spirit," warns Hannah against manipulative love, saying, "If you will remain with me, if you will stay by me, Hannah—cool, patient, quiet, possessed, I am yours forever, possessed, if you will have me devious. . . . If you remain Hannah—beautiful, gamboling, caressing along the brink of what I am I will always be there for you" (*YBL,* 47). Yet while he goes to Eve and for a time is even prepared to renounce Hannah for the sake of his magazine, he demands that she never lay eyes on her husband again, becomes violently upset when she receives letters from Dilly, and sobs in grief if she leaves his side for half an hour. He gives her words to describe himself—

"scamp," "scoundrel," "bully," or "wretch"—but she is willing to forego pride and possessiveness to love him on his own terms.

It is not easy. After Martin tells her that he has felt forced to choose Eve and the magazine over her, her response reflects her pain: "I knew that love is narrow as a coffin. It is not wide and warm, she said, like—like Whitman's love. It casts everyone else out. It is sharp and pointed, like a thorn" (*YBL*, 131). Hannah is the one character capable of true selflessness. She abhors the fact that she and Eve are at Martin like leeches, "two empty women turning to him and sucking him dry for a taste of life" (*YBL*, 89). Like the mother in King Solomon's court who would have relinquished her child before seeing him cut in half, Hannah would rather have her lover whole, though not for herself, than have him destroyed in a tug-of-war. When Martin knows he is dying and sends for Eve, Hannah is grieved that she has caused the painful rift between them. She prays that Eve will set aside her hard pride and come for his sake: "Eve, be his south wind, for I have been the north wind of privation. What has my love done for him but sent him shaking through the alleys? Let my hair go grey and my face lean without him, but bring him a cargo of plenty" (*YBL*, 202). Yet when Eve finally does come, she and Martin rage at each other in their familiar way, and Hannah realizes the complexity of love: "It had a furious face at times. It was a long steady pursuit that could not let the other be. There was no other life for Eve, except where Martin's interests were, and if she furthered or if she thwarted them, still it was love that drove her either way" (*YBL*, 207).

But these manmade threats to love—desecration by cheap sentimentality or ruination by pride and possessiveness—pale beside the ultimate obstacle of death, and it is the bitterest truth of all that the human failures and achievements in love do not change anything in the end. When Martin is dying, Eve forgets her animosity and clings to Hannah, and Martin's dream is fulfilled—the three of them are together under one roof. He says on his deathbed with a look of mischief, "After all, it's me that won" (*YBL*, 219). Yet the human transcendence of barriers ultimately counts for nought, for death brings irrevocable isolation. Martin, who has come close to it many times, knows this and says, "Close to it, Hannah, on the very threshold, there is no one else, you are quite alone" (*YBL*, 90).

The novel has a haunting ending. As Martin is borne into the ambulance that will take him to Nice—a tube for air in his teeth, "long deep shots of dreams" in his veins, and the two women he loves at his side—he is still quite alone. He had once told Lady Vanta as they sipped drinks in the dark that he was really a ghost, that he had actually died the night the nose of his plane went "six feet in the ground," taking one of his lungs "for a souvenir" and keeping his ribs "for toothpicks" (*YBL*, 181).

"There's nothing to me," he had said, "I'm not here at all. . . . That was the night I died" (*YBL,* 182). In the final passage of the book, Martin, in a drug-induced déjà vu, comes full circle to the image of his original "death," and in a scene reminiscent of "The Snows of Kilimanjaro," prepares for his final "flight:"[36]

> The back of the ambulance fell open and the stretcher slid in on runners.
> It's a hell of a day for flying, said Martin. He lay soft and white, like a dove fallen down in distress.
> Hannah climbed up over the little step and sat down on the stool beside him.
> Look at the pilot, he whispered. A beard like a bard, honey.
> He put the tube back in his teeth and drew a blast through it. When the motor started his mouth turned up and he smiled.
> It may make you sick the first time going up, he said. (*YBL,* 220)

Year Before Last is one of Kay Boyle's finest accomplishments. In it she has created rare and complex characters and rendered their conflicts in a brilliant style, exploring once more the perennial human need for "the curious agony of love."[37]

My Next Bride (1934) is the author's last full-length treatment of her experiences in France in the twenties. Like its predecessors, with the exception of *Gentlemen, I Address You Privately,* it is heavily autobiographical, drawing upon her stay at Raymond Duncan's Neuilly colony and her "collapse" of 1928. It is a novel with a dark view of life, and some critics took an equally dim view of the book. One called it "so much junk."[38] To another, however, it was "slight, charming, and pleasantly mad."[39] Once again, most agreed that her style was noteworthy, although their assessments of it range from accolade ("That Miss Boyle is an exquisite craftsman few are blind enough to doubt")[40] to charges that "Miss Boyle is guilty more than once of painful preciosity."[41]

The 1934 *Book Review Digest* synopsis reads:

> In her search for love and a livelihood, Victoria John drifted from the Middle West to New York and thence to Paris. There she became involved in the strange art colony of exiled Americans conducted by Sorrel. At night she wandered about Paris in company with Antony, a wealthy American whose whole devotion was given to his wife Fontana. Desperate because of her love for Antony, Victoria turned to promiscuity, became pregnant, and was finally rescued by Fontana.

The summary leaves out the important facts that Antony, a flamboyant bohemian, is also in love with Victoria, that he had left Paris immediately after retrieving her from a wildly promiscuous party, and that the book ends with the revelation of his suicide in New York. But it indicates that this book, too, has a very simple plot. Its action lies in the psychology of the characters and their relationships with one another.

My Next Bride is Kay Boyle's most bitter treatment of her prevailing theme, the human need for love. Like Kay Boyle's other characters, the individuals in this novel need nothing more than to bond with others in order to give their lives definition and purpose, but here Boyle is pessimistic about the chances.

That the protagonist is an exile from her own land—longing for the old, true America of the Indians and pioneers but estranged from its present-day philistinism—aggravates the sense of isolation she feels in her personal relationships. Victoria has drifted into Sorrel's colony simply because she had heard from two ancient and destitute Russian noblewomen in her boarding house that he will give anyone a free meal and work. Although the colony had been founded upon a dedication to simple living, Sorrel's sense of mission seems to have died with his wife, Ida, who had been a famous dancer. The colony members wear tunics and sandals, they are vegetarians, their ragged children are raised communally, and they support themselves by selling tunics, scarves, sandals, and rugs in a Right Bank shop. But although Sorrel still delivers weekly lectures on the virtues of simplicity to well-heeled American tourists, he is an empty man and his colony is floundering. Away from the podium, he speaks in a detached manner as if to himself or no one; his own daughter, thirsting for a truer purpose, has become obsessed with Catholicism; and his followers squabble among themselves, neglect their children, and live in idle squalor.

It seems to be the loss of love that has opened Sorrel to this decline. Victoria thinks as she looks at a photograph of his dead wife, "Whatever they were, they had been that thing together, and when she was dead it left room for the other things to come" (*MNB*, 65).[42] Sorrel eats fried potatoes and the "tender hearts of things" while the colony children starve on hard, boiled turnips. And when an American woman buys five thousand dollars worth of goods at the colony's shop, he does not spend the profits on the printing press he has always talked of needing, but on an oversized American automobile.

Long before Sorrel's moral bankruptcy becomes so obvious, though, Victoria is asking herself, "What am I here for, what am I doing here?" (*MNB*, 58). "Here" refers not only to the colony but to the world itself. When a colony member questions why she paints pictures of saints in her spare time, Victoria answers, "If I paint strong old men enough . . . perhaps something will happen to my own face. It's too small. It doesn't say anything" (*MNB*, 74). When Antony Lister breezes into the shop and into her life one day, she at first thinks she has found a person with a solid identity and purpose. Again, it appears to be love that saves the dangling individual. "You must meet my wife," he tells Victoria, and she thinks, "This is the way people speak . . . when love is not a name anymore but has been recognized alive in somebody else's flesh. Because of her he walks into strange places, stops people in the street, carries books under his arm to implicate strangers into what they are together" (*MNB*, 104).

Yet as she gets to know Antony better and they fall in love themselves, his own identity crisis becomes apparent. He is a mad poet, a death-worshipper, a man who flirts and makes love to many women without ceasing to adore his equally flamboyant wife, Fontana. But apart from his standing as the black sheep of a wealthy Bostonian family, he does not know his place in life either: " 'It's like looking at a photograph of a ball-team sitting up to have their picture taken and trying to find yourself in it. Everyone's there I like,' he said, 'but I'm never there' " (*MNB*, 161–62). His terrifying sense of nothingness motivates a brilliant episode in which he and Victoria spend the night drinking then go to the rue Mouffetard to buy him a new suit of clothes and a new identity. After buying a working man's outfit, he finds that he cannot give away his own perfectly good suit in a neighborhood where many need clothing badly. One man to whom he offers the suit even threatens to call the police. Antony finally lays out his suit, "long and empty," in the gutter, "the loose limbs of it curved in weariness and the arms fallen open, the white shirt laid in at the neck, the jacket buttoned, as if the man who wore it had lain down there and wasted to nothingness within" (*MNB*, 216).

Neither Antony nor Victoria can turn to country or family to satisfy this longing for identity. Both yearn for an America that no longer exists; there is nothing to fill the emptiness of exile. "America," Victoria says, "I want to go back to you. I want a father with a voice like baked beans and corn to put his arm around me. I want a mother warm as cornbread to wash my ears at night" (*MNB*, 159). As they sit in a bar, Antony tells her:

> Every day I'm in Europe or wherever it is, I can see the map of America in my head and the mountain-ranges. I think of State lines and I can hear the people talking as well as I hear you and me. Nobody over there hears it or sees it the way I do, the men's spit hitting the stove in the hardware store or the corn popping makes too much noise. They can't hear what is going on the way you and I hear it sitting here in a bar kissing the rock of Plymouth, the stone breasts, the iron mouth of Plymouth, because I'm for Plymouth, I'm for the Puritan women and for the ancestors who were not afraid of beginning there. (*MNB*, 162)

"Keep on drinking," Antony continues, "and maybe something will happen. Maybe we'll recognize our own faces in the newspaper or in a mirror."

Yet despite their need for a home, they fear they would be out of place in America: "We'd have to act like everyone else and maybe we wouldn't know how," Antony says (*MNB*, 207). Still, he hopes to find a clue to his identity in his family and his native country: "I keep going home to Massachusetts to find some other aspect of me, thinking maybe if I lift a turkey's wing I'll find it like lice under the feathers" (*MNB*, 203–4). But after his return to America, Victoria sees the newspaper headline, "Prominent Young Club Man Cuts Veins in Father's Office," and in smaller letters below, "Antony Lister Takes Own Life. Wall Street Losses Rumored" (*MNB*, 327).

The novel's structure is loose, and the subplots at times threaten to overshadow the central issue of Victoria's search to find herself. The reader's attention is diverted by the antics of the Russian spinsters, Miss Fira and Miss Grusha, who cling to past grandeur while gracefully trying to fend off starvation in a rented room; by the opulent bohemian orgies on a boat anchored in the Seine; and by the tangled associations within the colony—a menagerie that includes wraithlike children claimed by no one, a pair of vaudeville dancers, a demonic Parsee, and the jealous wench who is Sorrel's mistress. Perhaps the chaos is to the point, however. This jumble of relationships illustrates the mad disorder that threatens to destroy the sensitive individual searching for sanity in an insane world.

Victoria very nearly does not make it. She awakens one morning still drunk, not remembering how she got home or to whom she has lost her virginity: "Victoria lay under the boarding-house sheet and the quilt that was stained with other people's living. I'd give the feel of my skin to anyone as a gift, she said. . . . I'd give the taste of my mouth to whoever asked for it, she said" (*MNB*, 243). As she is thinking that she would be saved if only she had clean underwear to put on, she discovers that her purse has been stuffed with "smooth, new, silky bills" (*MNB*, 246). She learns from Fira and Grusha that she had been returned home in Antony's limousine, although he had not come in. That was to be her last contact with him. When she later discovers that she is pregnant, the vaudeville dancer at the colony gives her pills to "bring it off," and Victoria is nearly destroyed physically as well as psychologically. The author is merciless in her descriptions of the sickness that takes her, reeling, time after time to the slimy green privy behind the shop. One morning she collapses on the Metro. Her head falls under the seats, "and the coffee she drank at the corner for breakfast came out at the other end" (*MNB*, 287). When she revives to find herself on a bench at the Place de l'Opéra station, a poor woman with shaking hands and warts on her nose gives her five francs and a clean handkerchief. Victoria hits rock bottom as she stands in the street across from the Café de la Paix watching

the waiters prepare for the Americans who soon would gather for breakfast on the terrace: "Victoria stood in the island, looking, and the traffic
passed wild as steers, and toward the west she said America's that way,
over there, and her teeth were knocking together. Listen, America, she
said, and her nose was running. America, listen, listen, she said, but there
was nothing more to say" (*MNB*, 287–88).

Kay Boyle will not allow readers of delicate sensibilities to shirk from
the dark vision of life she presents in the novel. The metaphor she chooses
for life itself makes her view very plain:

> The privy behind the shop was a deep, fecund green, and the hole in the pavings
> that stood forever like a corpse's eye was as much the earth's gangrened navel
> as a thing for any human use. Out of it issued the myriad, dark smells of the
> earth's bowels, incongruously dressed in the rags and tatters of the daily
> press. . . . It might well have seemed that the printed record of that year was
> day by day, and several times a day, being intentionally rammed down this foul
> tributary to the earth's most private recognition. (*MNB*, 279)

The despair she communicates in this novel is rooted partially in her
awareness of social injustices, a topic that would concern her more and
more as her career progressed. Victoria believes that there are two kinds
of people, the rich and the poor, and that the poor are finished from the
start. It is hunger that brings out the ugliness in Fira and Grusha and
poverty that makes Sorrel a greedy man. But as Victoria lies writhing in
sickness in the back room of the shop, she engages in a hallucinatory
dialogue with Antony and hears him saying that the rich and the poor are
not the issue: "it had to be something better than that or else he might as
well be dead. If you had no money at all, you were finished, but also if you
had money it was possible you were finished too. Rich or poor, everyone
was stabbing everyone else with hate, stabbing in envy and terror. 'It isn't
a great deal to ask, only that everyone put down their weapons,' Antony
said" (*MNB*, 282).

In part, poetry has the power to transcend the differences that keep
people apart and to keep the spirit alive. Antony is moved by the work of
Archibald MacLeish, and he and Fontana have scrawled the poetry of D.
H. Lawrence over the roadside walls leading to their country house. Had
he lived in Emily Dickinson's time, he would have climbed over every
fence in New England to get to her, he claims. The author herself opens
the third section of her novel with poetry, quoting these lines of Emanuel
Carnevali: "Bathe me in the vision of my youth, communicate me
forever. Do not let me go back with the rest to fornicate and forget"
(*MNB*, 241).

Ultimately, only the force of love can "communicate" the human spirit
"forever." Despite her unflinching scrutiny in this novel of life's sordid-

ness and emptiness, Kay Boyle holds fast to this ideal as humanity's only chance for redemption. In *My Next Bride,* as in many of her other works, women appear to be better equipped than men to form these healing bonds. Among Victoria's scanty possessions are framed photographs of three women who had shaped her youth. The first thing she does when she moves into her shabby furnished room is to set them on the chimney, where their images can lend her the courage to face her life alone in another country. The first photograph is of a tall, mannish woman who had taught painting in the Middle West. Victoria tells the framed face, "Your silence sent me out looking for whatever there is" (*MNB,* 16). The second is a portrait of Victoria's mother, and it is clear that Victoria's feelings for her are Kay Boyle's feelings for her own mother:

> (Everything I do you began somewhere and didn't have time to finish—dancing alone to the sound of music before strangers until I could have died of shame for you, speaking of poetry and sculpture as simply as if the colored servants loved them best. If ever I see the faces of Brancusi, or Duchamp, or Gertrude Stein, I shall look the other way in shyness because of the history of courage they made for you.) (*MNB,* 17)

The third face is that of a friend, Mary de Lacey, an Australian vaudeville singer who had taken Victoria freight-hopping with her to Montreal and later committed suicide. Victoria recalls how "the wings of [her] shoulderblades" and "the necklace of the spine" had felt in her arms as the two lay together in the boxcar, and she remembers Mary's advice: "Don't fall for the skirts, Victoria, not till you've given the boys a trial. You'll come to it anyway in the end. The best of us do" (*MNB,* 22). The scene is mirrored in the final chapter as Fontana lies down beside Victoria in her squalid flat and puts her arm around her neck: "they went to sleep abruptly and still smiling, as if some kind of peace had been suddenly and at the same instant given to their hearts" (*MNB,* 326). The next morning they read of Antony's death, and we can only infer that these two women will continue to cling to one another for the warmth and connection that will save them from a similar destruction.

Yet while she draws sustenance from the spirits of these women, Victoria knows that she still must forge her own identity, that no matter how firm the bonds with others, they cannot provide the entire definition of one's self. She articulates the author's belief in the strength of women as she compares her own moral struggle with that of the weaker Antony Lister: "Only women grow up, Victoria was thinking; men go on remembering the time when their families stood on guard about them, or the books on the table, or the silver, and there was no need for explanation. Haven't you learned that once cut out of the family's life you are a single thing given to yourself and other people, carved out separate to stand alone or not to stand at all?" (*MNB*, 212). In her quest for identity, Victoria must pass through fire—through virtual imprisonment in an art colony, through a period of madness and promiscuity, through an unwanted pregnancy and abortion. But unlike Antony, she survives. It is significant that she is saved in part through the love and friendship of another woman—Antony's wife, Fontana.

My Next Bride is dedicated to Caresse Crosby, obviously the model for Fontana. Once more, Kay Boyle has drawn fiction almost directly from autobiography, in all its idiosyncratic detail. Victoria's experiences mirror those of the author during the period in 1928 when, living in Raymond Duncan's colony, she had suffered a collapse, become pregnant, and with the aid of the Crosbys obtained an abortion. Sorrel is obviously Raymond Duncan, and Duncan's deceased sister, Isadora, appears as Sorrel's late wife, Ida, also a famous dancer. Antony Lister first meets Victoria as he enters the shop to buy his wife a scarf. Caresse Crosby presents an identical account of Harry's introduction to Kay Boyle in her autobiography, *The Passionate Years*. (However, the novel may actually have been the source of her memory, for Boyle claims her friend is mistaken, that she had actually met the Crosbys one wild evening at the Bal Nègre.)[43] The Listers do have in common with the Crosbys a bizarre social life, a background that enables them to take chauffeured limousines for granted, a penchant for black hounds, and a passion for the poetry of Lawrence and MacLeish. Of course, Antony's death is a barely disguised version of Harry Crosby's sensational suicide in New York in 1929.

Again, Kay Boyle's style is noteworthy. In this novel she once more displays her talent for evoking character through colorful dialogue, especially in the wryly and delicately rendered exchanges between the destitute Russian spinsters. She continues to experiment with complex stream-of-consciousness monologues, imaginary dialogues, and other psychologically realistic narrative techniques, and she remains a master at depicting a scene vividly and precisely. In her description of a party on the Lister's boat, she offers an evocative glimpse into the inner sanctum of bohemian Paris in the twenties:

> In the flat bottom of the river boat, the bedroom opened suddenly out. They had come down three ladders of steps to it, and suddenly it opened, miraculously flower-like, petaled, mauve and richly scented, lamps lit around it as if forcing it to bloom at night. The place was filled with smoke and the talk of the people, and the bed, wide as three beds, stood to the side against the ship's curved ribs, covered in velvet, holding the woman in it propped higher than the heads and bodies of the others who lay stretched, smoking and talking, in evening dress across it. (*MNB*, 171)

Finally, the title of *My Next Bride* deserves consideration. Antony refers to himself several times as a bridegroom. He adores Fontana and says she "is part of the bridal cortège that goes endlessly towards the altar." Although he imagines himself as the "eternal bridegroom" walking her to the annointed place "where the Holy Ghost is burning in his little cup," he fears that the Holy Ghost "does not burn night and day forever but expires," and therefore his marriage to Fontana cannot alone fulfill his longing for permanence and meaning (*MNB*, 164–65). He tells his friends on the boat, "Victoria's my next bride" (*MNB*, 174). But he cannot really hope to find fulfillment in his love for her either. He *is* already married, and in the frustration of her love for him, she has taken to promiscuity. Antony is ready to commit himself to something beyond this world. Like Harry Crosby, he is fascinated by death and its absolute permanence. He says to Victoria: "I ask everything. I ask that people give up their brides. The whole universe on a honeymoon of horror, wedded to their daggers, stabbing their way from one betrayal to the next" (*MNB*, 282). The novel's epigraph is a line written by Laurence Vail, who, disappointed in his lack of success in his work, made one attempt at suicide: "Knife will be my next bride." Antony does take the knife as his "next bride," clutching it to him in his father's office and dying in the consummation of the "marriage."

But the title might apply to Victoria's fate as well as to Antony's: it appears that her next "bride" will be Antony's original one, Fontana. The scene in the final chapter in which Victoria and Fontana fall asleep in each other's arms, peaceful at last, seems a striking repetition of the flashback scene in which Victoria and Mary de Lacey had lain embracing on the floor of the boxcar and Mary de Lacey had advised her friend, "Don't fall for the skirts, Victoria, not till you've given the boys a trial. . . . You'll come to it anyway in the end." It would appear that Victoria, having been failed by the "boys," *has* come to it in the end.

It is only fair to note that Kay Boyle herself calls this interpretation of the title "completely wrong:" "It applies only to Antony; in other words, death was his next bride." In a response that indicates how completely identified in her own mind are her life and her art, she points out that she has had many very close and warm friendships with women—Caresse Crosby, Lola Ridge, Germaine Garrigou, Djuna Barnes, Ann Watkins, Nancy Cunard, Janet Flanner, Muriel Rukeyser, Jessica Mitford, and Joan Baez, Sr., among them—and says that, while some of these women may have been lesbians, "It would be completely wrong to take for granted that these were lesbian love affairs." ("I am not being moral about homosexuality," she explains. "It was just an aspect of love that I was never moved to experiment with.") She wishes to make clear "that none of my very deep and enduring relationships with women had any lesbian under-tones or over-tones," and she had intended "no such solution as a sexual union" for Victoria and Fontana.[44]

Whether or not the relationship between Victoria and Fontana is physical as well as of the mind and spirit, it will be their salvation. Kay Boyle had wished to make a statement about the comfort and solace that being understood brought to Victoria, and this is one instance, she says, "in which love did not fail."[45] Whether or not one reads the title of the novel as a double entendre, applying both to Antony's and to Victoria's fate, it is a cynical twist of one's expectations. In Kay Boyle's perilous world, the "bride" that will bring joy and satisfaction takes a form unacceptable to most readers: relief comes either as annihilation, or as a form of love that will seem a desperate compromise in a culture that does not accept homosexuality. Her work is filled with bitter ironies.

Kay Boyle's first four novels express a Romantic's concern for freedom of action and imagination, but a cynic's view of the possibility for attaining it. The individual in her world is trapped by nature, for one thing: three of the four books feature an "unwanted pregnancy," and in *Plagued by the Nightingale, Year Before Last,* and *My Next Bride,* the protagonist's loved one either is stalked by death or actually dies. Love is the only reprieve in such an ultimately futile existence, yet too often it is tragically lost or was never found. The material of these novels is idiosyncratic, a direct outgrowth of the author's private experiences as an expatriate in France in the twenties. Her concern with the lonely, isolated individual in search of an identity and a meaningful context in which to live may well have its roots in her own proud and painful exile.

The focus of these novels is the individual struggle, but they also provide a forum for Kay Boyle's social and political positions, which she feels are implicit in nearly everything she has written:

> In *Plagued,* there is the obvious concern with false values, with class conflicts, with the abyss between the rich and the poor, with the essentially political attacks Nicolas makes on every aspect of the *status quo.* In *Year Before Last* there is again the schism between the haves and the have-nots, and the false barrier of "class," a distinction engrained in Eve's snobbish judgment of all mankind and womankind. *My Next Bride* is deeply concerned with material inequality, with Antony's lost battle to be a just and simple man, with the misery of too much wealth, and with Sorrel's hideous greed for it. The social distinctions and conflicts lead to the even more obvious presence of them in *Gentlemen.* There is the editor of the newspaper, who is running for mayor on the communist ticket, . . . and there are also the munitions factories he speaks of.[46]

Beginning in the thirties much of Kay Boyle's work would become overtly political. Yet it is important to remember that even in her earliest fiction she was concerned not only with "personal love" but with "the love of humanity which is expressed in political protest."

In these four novels, Kay Boyle was engaged in a Revolution of the Word as well as one of the individual and collective spirit. As in her short stories of the same period, she was not writing for the plain reader. Yet while they show her continuing experimentation with language, her novels are not as iconoclastic in style as some of her short stories. Kay Boyle's loyalties were beginning to divide between the avant-garde literary revolution and her concern for humanity, between her sense of language as a statement of rebellion and her sense of it as a "fervent prayer" offered up "for the salvation of man, for the defense of his high spirit, for the celebration of his integrity," as she would say decades later.[47] In time her need to communicate with her fellow men and women would outweigh her desire to merely express herself. But in 1932 she was at a crossroads. She wrote to her friend Bob Brown, whose Reading Machine was his contribution to the Revolution of the Word and who vastly preferred Boyle's short stories to her novels: "I'm afraid we shall go farther apart than ever on narrative form—I like it, and doing it, more and more. I get more and more long winded, and you will not forgive me until I combine that and invention. I've lost all my invention. Parked it in the vestry with my cape. I confuse human faces and the thing to do with words."[48]

1. Wedding picture of Boyle's parents, Katherine Evans Boyle and
Howard Peterson Boyle. Collection of Kay Boyle.

2. Kay Boyle and her paternal grandfather, Jesse Peyton Boyle, Germantown, Pennsylvania, circa 1906. Collection of Kay Boyle.

3. Kay Boyle, souvenir photo taken in Atlantic City, circa 1906. Collection of Kay Boyle.

4. Kay Boyle and her maternal grandmother, Eva S.
Evans, Germantown, circa 1907. Collection of Kay Boyle.

5. Kay Boyle, photographed by her mother, Beach Haven, New Jersey, circa 1912. Collection of Sandra Spanier.

6. Kay Boyle's original passport, 1923. The Kay
Boyle Papers, Morris Library, Southern Illinois
University, Carbondale.

7. Richard Brault, Boyle's
French husband, on the beach
at St. Malo, 1923. The Black
Sun Press Archive, Morris Library, SIU.

8. Lola Ridge, 1934. Collection
of Kay Boyle.

9. Ernest Walsh, 1925. Sylvia
Beach Collection, Princeton
University Library.

10. Cover of *This Quarter*, No. 2, 1925.

11. Emanuel Carnevali. This photograph originally appeared in *This Quarter*, No. 4, 1929. Reproduced from *Being Geniuses Together* (San Francisco: North Point Press, 1984).

12. Laurence Vail, 1928. Collection of Kay Boyle.

13. Harry and Caresse Crosby with Clytoris, a mate for their whippet Narcisse Noir, at Le Bourget, 1929, following a cross-channel flight. Seated in the grass-green Voisin is Auguste, the last of their chauffeurs. The Black Sun Press Archive, Morris Library, SIU.

14. From left: Countess of Polignac, Laurence Vail, Kay Boyle, Hart Crane, and Caresse Crosby on top of Le Moulin, 1929. Reproduced from *Being Geniuses Together*.

15. Kay Boyle and Harry Crosby at Le Moulin, 1929. The Black Sun Press Archive, Morris Library, SIU.

16. Robert McAlmon in the 1920s. Reproduced from *Being Geniuses Together*.

17. Eugene Jolas and James Joyce in Joyce's flat, 1939. Jolas is holding the first impression of the last issue of *transition*. Reproduced from *Being Geniuses Together*.

PROCLAMATION

TIRED OF THE SPECTACLE OF SHORT STORIES, NOVELS, POEMS AND
PLAYS STILL UNDER THE HEGEMONY OF THE BANAL WORD, MONO-
TONOUS SYNTAX, STATIC PSYCHOLOGY, DESCRIPTIVE NATURALISM, AND
DESIROUS OF CRYSTALLIZING A VIEWPOINT...

WE HEREBY DECLARE THAT :

**1. THE REVOLUTION IN THE ENGLISH LANGUAGE IS AN AC-
COMPLISHED FACT.**

**2. THE IMAGINATION IN SEARCH OF A FABULOUS WORLD IS
AUTONOMOUS AND UNCONFINED.**
(Prudence is a rich, ugly old maid courted by Incapacity... Blake)

**3. PURE POETRY IS A LYRICAL ABSOLUTE THAT SEEKS AN A
PRIORI REALITY WITHIN OURSELVES ALONE.**
(Bring out number, weight and measure in a year of dearth... Blake)

**4. NARRATIVE IS NOT MERE ANECDOTE, BUT THE PROJEC-
TION OF A METAMORPHOSIS OF REALITY.**
(Enough ! Or Too Much !... Blake)

**5. THE EXPRESSION OF THESE CONCEPTS CAN BE ACHIEVED
ONLY THROUGH THE RHYTHMIC " HALLUCINATION OF THE
WORD ".** (Rimbaud).

**6. THE LITERARY CREATOR HAS THE RIGHT TO DISINTE-
GRATE THE PRIMAL MATTER OF WORDS IMPOSED ON HIM BY
TEXT-BOOKS AND DICTIONARIES.**
(The road of excess leads to the palace of Wisdom... Blake)

**7. HE HAS THE RIGHT TO USE WORDS OF HIS OWN FASH-
IONING AND TO DISREGARD EXISTING GRAMMATICAL AND
SYNTACTICAL LAWS.**
(The tigers of wrath are wiser than the horses of instruction... Blake)

**8. THE " LITANY OF WORDS " IS ADMITTED AS AN INDEPEN-
DENT UNIT.**

**9. WE ARE NOT CONCERNED WITH THE PROPAGATION OF
SOCIOLOGICAL IDEAS, EXCEPT TO EMANCIPATE THE CREATIVE
ELEMENTS FROM THE PRESENT IDEOLOGY.**

10. TIME IS A TYRANNY TO BE ABOLISHED.

11. THE WRITER EXPRESSES. HE DOES NOT COMMUNICATE

12. THE PLAIN READER BE DAMNED.
(Damn braces ! Bless relaxes !... Blake)

— *Signed* : KAY BOYLE, WHIT BURNETT, HART CRANE, CARESSE CROSBY,
HARRY CROSBY, MARTHA FOLEY, STUART GILBERT, A. L. GILLESPIE,
LEIGH HOFFMAN, EUGENE JOLAS, ELLIOT PAUL, DOUGLAS RIGBY, THEO
RUTRA, ROBERT SAGE, HAROLD J. SALEMSON, LAURENCE VAIL.

18. Manifesto for "The Revolution of the Word," published in *transition,* No. 16–17, June 1929.

19. Kay Boyle, photographed by Man Ray, 1930. Collection of Kay Boyle; reproduced with permission of Juliet Man Ray.

20. Kay Boyle, Nice, 1930. Reproduced from *Being Geniuses Together*.

21. Baron Joseph von Franck-
enstein, Boyle's third husband.
The Kay Boyle Papers, Morris
Library, SIU.

22. Kay Boyle, photographed
by George Platt Lynes, 1941.
The Kay Boyle Papers, Morris
Library, SIU.

23. Kay Boyle, photographed
by Louise Dahl-Wolfe, 1943.
The Kay Boyle Papers, Morris
Library, SIU.

24. Kay Boyle with her daughters Sharon, Clover, Faith (held on her lap), Apple-Joan, and Kathe in a New York apartment-hotel. Photograph by Louise Dahl-Wolfe appeared in *Harper's Bazaar*, November 1943, with an announcement of the upcoming publication of her book *Avalanche*. Collection of Kay Boyle.

25. Kay Boyle with a Fighting French air force pilot in France, February 1945. Collection of Kay Boyle.

26. Kay Boyle with Ian and Faith in Carson McCullers' back yard in Nyack, New York, 1946. Collection of Kay Boyle.

27. Kay Boyle, Paris, 1946. Collection of Kay Boyle.

28. Kay Boyle at the MacDowell Colony, 1961. Collection of Kay Boyle.

29. Kay Boyle on a 1966 fact-finding trip to Cambodia with Americans Want to Know, a group representing a number of pacifist organizations. The Kay Boyle Papers, Morris Library, SIU.

30. 419 Frederick Street, San Francisco, Kay Boyle's home from 1963 to 1979 and a center for her political activism. Collection of Kay Boyle.

31. Kay Boyle with Joan Baez, Sr., Jacqueline McGuerkin, and Eric McGuerkin during a 1974 march to Modesta, California, led by Cesar Chavez to protest the Gallo Wine Company's refusal of a farm worker labor contract. Collection of Kay Boyle.

K.B.
1978

32. When Merla Zellerbach of the *San Francisco Chronicle* asked eight well-known authors in 1978 for a quick sketch of how they saw themselves, Kay Boyle sent this "self-portrait." Her caption read: "Since receiving several volumes of censored data through the Freedom of Information Act, I see myself as a dangerous 'radical' (they themselves put it in quotes) cleverly disguised as a perfect lady. So I herewith blow my cover." *San Francisco Chronicle,* 15 March 1978.

33. Boyle with her 1980 volume of short stories. The Kay Boyle
Papers, Morris Library, SIU.

34. Kay Boyle, New York, photographed by the author, 1983. Collection of Sandra Spanier.

4

The Thirties: Art and the Functioning World

In 1930 Kay Boyle advised her friend and fellow poet, Walter Lowenfels,

> If you are weary and gutted with the literary attitude of today, then avoid the literary attitude and write things that nobody hears about at all, except the people you love. The thing is that neither you nor I can ever under any circumstances write anything except the things we want to write, and that means we can never live, except through some miracle, on our earnings from our writings. WE CAN'T. Let's be good poets and let it go at that. . . . the present day reader is not worth a ha'penny bit and I don't care whether his judgments are prejudiced or not. Hell, I'm writing for posterity—I mean, I'm going to. I'm going to write a record of our age and posterity is going to know all about our age and they won't care if my name is Boyle or Murphy.[1]

Yet twelve years and eighteen books later, and after having fled war-torn Europe, she had done a dramatic about-face. She would write in 1942 that "There is at least one bitter fight which the sensitive and distinguished writer is foredoomed to make, and to make alone, and that is the fight to escape from those limits of sensitivity and distinction which his own nature and the nature of his work impose." Art suffers when the writer is insulated or alienated from the social world, she argues:

> This was the tragedy of Emily Brontë, who of necessity created an imaginary kingdom in which her imaginary people might survive, and who achieved but one good book during her life's despairing search for her own people and that people's cause. It was the tragedy of Henry James, who sought in England (as T. S. Eliot has since) not only the vocabulary but the very spirit to animate communication. It was the damnation of Poe, of Rimbaud, of Emily Dickinson that there was not—or that they failed to recognize the features of—a functioning world to which they could belong.[2]

In the thirties Kay Boyle was an artist in transition. She always had been a "political" writer in that she wished to challenge whatever was oppressive and believed in the power of the written word to transform existence. Nor was the Revolution of the Word purely a matter of aesthetics, she insists. "On the occasions when we did sit at café tables together in those far days in Paris, we didn't talk about literature or art (strange as that may seem), but about politics. After a drink or two, Jolas did not hold forth about his bi-lingual abilities, or his having been sent at the age of sixteen by his family to make his fortune in America and his apprenticeship to life working in an East Side grocery store," she says, but rather he talked "with a still burning outrage" about the Palmer raids he had covered after World War I as a newspaper reporter—the "witch hunt," as Boyle calls it, carried out by Woodrow Wilson's Attorney General A. Mitchell Palmer that served as a prelude to the McCarthyism of the fifties.[3] Boyle places the avant-garde expatriate writers and artists in Paris in the twenties in the "great political tradition" of European writers such as Anatole France, Victor Hugo, and Emil Zola, who believed that "the writer has the obligation to revolt not only in his writings but also to walk the picket line."[4] But in her fiction and poetry of the twenties she had expressed her rebellion primarily in terms of the individual struggle, drawing directly from unique personal experience and experimenting with what the *transition* manifesto had called "the language of hallucination." In the thirties, her commitment to the belief that "the writer expresses" would be superseded by her sense of obligation to communicate her concerns clearly and straightforwardly with her fellow citizens of the "functioning world."

The reasons for the change in her aesthetic stance were pragmatic as well as philosophical. On April 3, 1932, the Paris *Tribune* reported: "There were no wedding bells when Laurence Vail and Kay Boyle, American authors and for many years residents of Montparnasse and the Riviera, were married at the city hall in Nice this afternoon, but the knot was tied just the same. Moreover, the principals in the matrimonial venture were accompanied at the wedding by a ready-made family of four children."[5] In December, 1929, a daughter, Apple-Joan, had been born to the couple, joining the company of Sharon Walsh and Sindbad and Pegeen, Vail's children by his first marriage to Peggy Guggenheim. Kay Boyle and Laurence Vail would have two more daughters, Kathe and Clover, before the decade was out. The couple was attempting to make a living by writing, and family responsibilities were beginning to make writing as pure expression an unaffordable luxury.

In the thirties Kay Boyle was writing fast and furiously, and her short stories were beginning to appear in the popular magazines as well as in the "artistic" ones. The transition from high- to middle-brow was not entirely comfortable for one who not long before had called for the Revolution of the Word. In a letter of July 9, 1931, to Bob Brown, she reports that she had written one short story the day before and another that morning, describing them as "Pretty English." ("I hope they're English enough to sell," she adds.) She was enclosing a story for his appraisal along with an apologetic postscript: "Bob, don't show this story to anyone. It's rotten. I thought you would tell me how bad it is and then I won't write anymore like it."[6] A month later, she confesses to him, "I think . . . that I write my short stories too quickly, in the stress of wanting to make a little money, and that is a lamentable idea."[7] After selling a story to *Harper's* a year later for $225, she still had qualms about the change in direction of her writing: "Every time I write a story that I think particularly shameful, the better magazines think I'm worth a little money."[8] In retrospect the author candidly acknowledges that her attempt to broaden her readership had affected her style in the long run. "I left my experimental technique behind for a variety of reasons," she would write in 1953, "a compelling one being that most magazines suggested deleting the experimental parts before they would print the story."[9]

But there were emotional and ideological reasons, too, for the shift in her style and subject matter that began in the thirties and has extended to the present day. "I confuse human faces and the thing to do with words," she had told Bob Brown in 1931.[10] In the course of the decade the balance would tip in favor of the "human faces." When she left Paris in 1929 to live first in a village on the Marne and later on the Mediterranean coast with her husband and children, it seems that she had moved away emotionally as well from that city and all it had come to represent in the realm of art. As she descended from the esoteric heights of the Left Bank and entered a warm, pastoral world of family and friends, the humanist in her came to overshadow the aesthete. When the couple moved to Austria in 1933, she got a first-hand look at the political forces brewing toward cataclysm. Perhaps she began to sense, along with many other writers of the thirties, that the hermetic individualism of the twenties was already a relic, a self-indulgence that could not survive the onslaught of public events that would rock private lives in the new decade. While retaining a reverence for language, she began to feel an increasing need to impress upon her readers (plain ones included) her fervent belief in the absolute essentiality of compassion and understanding—in the "functioning world" as well as in the private sphere.

In the thirties Kay Boyle was extraordinarily productive. From the beginning of the decade until her return to America in the summer of 1941, she published six novels, three short story collections, a volume of poetry, a book of three short novels, three translations of novels, two ghostwritten volumes, an anthology, and a children's book. Dozens of her short stories appeared in magazines—the big as well as the "little" ones—beginning in 1930 when *The New Yorker* accepted "Kroy Wen." Two of her stories won O. Henry awards for best short story of the year ("The White Horses of Vienna" in 1935 and "Defeat" in 1941); three appeared in the O.

Henry annual anthologies ("The First Lover" in 1932, "Anschluss" in 1939, and "Poor Monsieur Panalitus" in 1940); and forty made Edward O'Brien's honor rolls in his annual *Best American Short Stories* volumes. In 1934 she received a Guggenheim fellowship to work on an epic-length poem about aviation.

In the spring of that year, she wrote to her agent that she was pregnant again (but wanted to keep it quiet so it would not affect her chances for a Guggenheim). "Having babies is really a nice kind of relaxation after the amount of typing one seems to do in life," she said.[11] By all indications Kay Boyle was as devoted a mother as she was an artist. In March, 1935, she wrote to the Browns that after a summer trip to England she would like to go to New York but did not know how she would ever be able to leave the children, even for a month. She despaired of even getting to England in the first place "with all our passportless children." ("Kathe is my first legitimate child and very smug about it," she notes.)[12] Even Peggy Guggenheim, who said of Kay Boyle, "we frankly detested each other," had to admit her maternal skill.[13] In her salty memoirs, *Out of This Century* (in the first edition of which Laurence Vail and Kay Boyle appeared as "Florenz Dale" and "Ray Soil"), Guggenheim writes that although the pair "did everything they could to separate me from Sindbad . . . my only consolation was that Ray was a very good stepmother."[14] When Sindbad was ill during one of his mother's visits, "Ray acted the efficient nurse and made me feel *de trop* as much as she could," she reports.[15] (Boyle frequently has denied that she "detested" Peggy Guggenheim. "I always felt sorry for this sad, self-centered woman who was so desperate for love, and who—I truly believe—was never in her entire life loved by anyone." She finds it revealing of Guggenheim's preoccupation with the impression she made that she was more concerned about feeling "de'trop" than about her son's serious illness).[16]

The Boyle-Vail family led a rather nomadic life in the thirties. Having left Bohemian Paris behind with the decade in which it flourished, they lived from 1930 to 1933 in Villefranche and on the Col-de-Villefranche near Nice. In the summer of 1933 they moved to Austria, living first in Vienna, then in the Tyrolean village of Kitzbühel. "Our peregrinations," Boyle says, "should be recognized as a continuous search for the most economical (or advantageous) countries to settle in at various periods."[17] They moved as the world financial markets fluctuated, settling wherever the exchange was in favor of the American dollar. When Laurence's Uncle George died, leaving him a sizeable sum, the family moved to Devon, England, for a year and rented a large house in Seaton between the summers of 1936 and 1937 in order to be near Sindbad, who was in Bedales boarding school. They then returned to France, settling in Mégève in the Haute-Savoie, where they bought their first home, a chalet that they christened "Les Cinq Enfants." The accuracy of the name was shorter-lived than the family's supply of printed stationery; after the birth of Clover in 1939, Kay Boyle would strike out the "Cinq" in the letterhead and type "SIX" above it.

Above all, life was full and hectic. The reams of letters she wrote along with all her published work in that period chronicle the colds, the insect bites, the measles, the piano lessons, and the birthday parties that accompany a houseful of children. In one of the few letters she wrote in longhand rather than on the machine McAlmon had given her, she explains to Bob Brown, "I can't type because the kids are asleep—and it makes Laurence think I'm working."[18] In another (typed) letter, a bit soiled, she apologizes, "Every bit of paper I have seems to have fallen partially at least into the soup. That's what comes of eating with one hand and writing with the other. I don't know which I like doing best."[19]

Her energy and spirit seem irrepressible. A 1931 letter to Bob Brown is worth quoting for its sheer exuberance and *joie de vivre*:

Dear Bob;

Here's the story.
Dear Bob:

 I'm inspired. I'm inspired today. There's poetry in the air and I'm perfectly sober and inspired. We must all promise each other to get drunk together the first time when we've all fallen off the water wagon. It'll be a wonderful binge. A millionth heaven of enthusiasm.

 Today I feel like a great writer. It's a wonderful feeling. Only it lasts such a short time.[20]

The letters to Brown are filled with invitations to go mountain climbing soon or to meet for a beer in Nice and with fun-loving reminiscences of such meetings. They are sprinkled, too, with accounts of stories she has just finished or sold. In one letter, probably written in 1932, she tells him, "I'm working long, hard and desperate."[21] In another she says, "I've gone to bed in tears two nights just out of pushing all day and half the night—so silly, but really the only way to get things done. Writing goes in streaks, no doubt about it."[22]

Yet she seems to have maintained her good humor throughout the deluge. She wrote to Bob Brown and his wife, Rose (the letters are often affectionately addressed to "Dearest Rosebob"):

Laurence has been working top-speed to finish the German translation and I got busy on typing the finished copy for him—and beat my own record of typing eleven pages an hour for five hours yesterday—and the finished thing must go off tomorrow or Tuesday. It was promised for the first. Then I got a telegram, simultaneous with yours, asking if I would translate Radiguet's "Le Diable au Corps" by November first. I said I could, but I don't think anybody could.

AND, I'm trying to write an epic poem for Jolas. AND Jonathan Cape came down and spent eighteen hours with us. AND Emma Goldman arrived with eight people for dinner. AND Mary [Reynolds] and Marcel [Duchamp] are leaving for Paris this afternoon, and we're having a last meal together. AND can't you have dinner with us somewhere around the middle of the week—say Wednesday or Thursday night?[23]

And one can hardly blame her when she occasionally throws in the towel. "I simply cannot, will not, don't want to, get back to work," she writes a few months later. "I like to read and mull and sun and play with the children and the dogs, and go to market, and fuss around. I want to be a leisurely woman and have my corsets fitted and my eyebrows plucked, and I'll never write another line. I'll be damned if I do."[24]

Yet while the practical aspects of her literary career seem to have concerned her far more in the thirties than they had in the twenties (there were, after all, more mouths to feed), Kay Boyle certainly had not abandoned her reverence for art and for its creators. Her devotion still ran deep for those friends of the twenties, living and dead, who had had a special gift for art and for life.

She and Caresse Crosby had been intimate friends in the twenties and had helped each other through the devastating losses of the men they loved. Kay did not hesitate to tell her friend how much she had meant to her in the difficult time in Paris between the death of Ernest Walsh and the beginning of her life with Laurence Vail. She wrote in 1930: "I had really given up before you came back—I mean everything—not to write, or care anymore, but just to give up and go to America—and I'm simply boiling over with determination and conviction now—You've been the sun and the moon and the constellations rising and everything is going to begin again and be magnificent—I want to make you know this in some sounder way."[25] Several years later she would still say: "You are a wonderful miniature, bright and perfect, hanging in my heart all day and night."[26] The affection she expresses in letters to her "Darling Caresse" would continue unabated until her friend's death in 1970.

Her feelings are strong, too, for the others she and Caresse had known in the twenties. She wrote in 1930 that she had just received a copy of *transition* and was "proud to be on the same pages" with Hart Crane, Archibald MacLeish, and especially Harry Crosby: "I am proud of every tear that falls out of my eyes for him because they are the tears for a man who could never fall below his own high self." Harry Crosby was "a man whose personality alone would have made life for me worth living."[27]

Three years later, she made a pilgrimage with her husband to Bazzano, Italy, to visit the poet Emanuel Carnevali, with whom she had been corresponding for years. In a passionate and poignant letter to Caresse she describes the man and what he meant to her. Dated July 18, 1933, and sent from Cavalese, it is a letter she quotes herself in her preface to *The Autobiography of Emanuel Carnevali,* which she compiled and had published forty-four years later. She describes the effects of his encephalitis, saying, "On that bed is the most beautiful man, shaking completely, all over, like a pinned butterfly." In her eyes Carnevali was another of those vibrant souls who made life worth living:

> He is gay—he is the gayest person alive—the way Harry and Ernest Walsh were gay. He has a laugh that fills your heart—he says wonderful simple things. And we three sat and laughed and talked (how can I tell you that he made me feel gayer and bolder and more courageous than I have felt in years?) and drank two bottles of sickening sweet champagne in that ghastly filthy room which is his life. And in a little while, but only for a second, I was crying in his arms as I never cry with anyone except with you. No, there is no way to find the words to tell you. He is so tender, and he is so filled with love. It runs down his arms and out his fingertips. And he asks for nothing, nothing, for it is he himself who has everything to give.

Kay Boyle's romantic esteem for the individual who ranks the emotions above the intellect had continued to burn undimmed. Through the bills and the children and the publishing contracts, she had remained the same passionate woman who had written poems and stories in the twenties exploring the exigencies of the heart. She says of Carnevali:

> I know I should be with him always, for he is to me the last, the almost shattered remains of courage and beauty that are left. I don't know what to do—for I know that every day I live will be a rebuke to me, for I should be with him, and I have not the courage to say that everything else is a contortion except being with him. It is not as easy explaining this as love—it is a necessity, for if the thing he is did not exist and had never existed, there would be no reason to live at all.

"He is one of the last survivors of our faith," she tells Caresse.[28]

Finally, the letters chronicle the many literary projects Kay Boyle undertook in the thirties in addition to writing fiction. In May, 1931, she wrote to Caresse Crosby that she already had typed six hundred pages of notes for a long poem on aviation to be dedicated to Harry Crosby, a work which would include a section on the life of Count von Zeppelin.[29] Later she wrote to Bob Brown that her publisher, Harrison Smith, had said he wanted to publish all she wrote, but was particular about what she wrote. He feared that the air epic and biography would take at least two years to complete and that Kay Boyle would have to make a reputation for herself all over again.[30] In 1934 she received a Guggenheim fellowship to continue work on the project, but the poem was never finished, and only a few fragments have found their way into print.[31]

Once she had seen Carnevali, it became an "obsession" with her, she says, to compile his autobiography. She typed and retyped the bits and pieces he sent her and wrote to William Carlos Williams in Rutherford, New Jersey, to send her all the writing that Carnevali had ever sent to him. In August, 1933, she wrote to Caresse from Vienna, saying, "It must be placed, this book, or I will never write again."[32] Her friend tried to persuade Dick Simon of Simon and Schuster to bring out the autobiography as part of a three-book contract that also would include Ernest Walsh's poems and a novel of Kay Boyle's. "His failure to publish the three books caused Caresse to throw an ink-well at him, and it was the end of their rather long love-affair," Kay Boyle now reports.[33] In 1938 Boyle herself showed the manuscript to publisher James Laughlin when he was a house guest in Mégève and he accepted it on the spot, writing out a check to Carnevali for $250 as an advance. But his associates in New York persuaded him that it was not worth publishing, "and (millionaire though he was), he returned the manuscript to me and asked that the advance be returned to him," she recalls. "But poor and desperately ill Carnevali had already spent the money in joyous gratitude." In 1965 Edward Dahlberg asked her for the manuscript and took it to Coburn Britton and Ben Raeburn at Horizon Press, and the book finally was published in 1967 in a handsome illustrated edition.

Boyle was committed also to getting Ernest Walsh's poems published posthumously and found it a frustrating effort as well. Ethel Moorhead, as Walsh's literary executor (along with Harriet Monroe of *Poetry* magazine), guarded his works jealously and was being most difficult about their publication. Moorhead's long-standing antipathy toward Kay Boyle had turned rabid after she read *Year Before Last,* and Boyle knew that any word from her would be the project's death knell. Forced to remain entirely in the background, she corresponded with other literary figures in the hope that they would be able to help get the book published. A letter from Robert McAlmon to Boyle detailing his attempts to reason with Moorhead dramatizes the delicacy of the operation: "The moment she knows you're involved, she'll shoot herself or you before she'll sign anything, and it'd be you first." McAlmon finally was able to get the copies of Walsh's poems from Ethel Moorhead by assuring her that he wanted to publish them himself.[34] Kay Boyle believed that an introduction by a prominent writer was critical to the success of the book, and Archibald MacLeish agreed to write it. It was a totally selfless endeavor on her part. Upon receiving from MacLeish a carbon of the foreword he had just sent to the book's publisher, she was "frantic" that he had not followed her earlier request to delete a reference to Walsh's "being loved by a beautiful and gifted woman." Not only did she fear that Ethel Moorhead would stop publication of the whole book because of that sentence, but she also was distressed by the "ridiculous and tactless reference to something entirely outside and personal."[35] Her fears were well-founded.

"McAlmon wrote to me that Ethel Moorhead flew into a rage when she saw Archie's reference to me," Boyle recalls, "and tore the foreword to shreds."[36] Ernest Walsh's *Poems and Sonnets* was published by Harcourt, Brace and Company in 1934. The volume opens with "A Memoir by Ethel Moorhead."

Attempting to make a living at writing, Kay Boyle and Laurence Vail also took on several translating projects. She translated René Crevel's novel *Babylon* in 1930 for the Black Sun Press, although Caresse Crosby brought out the first chapter only, under the title *Mr. Knife, Miss Fork.* It was published in 1931 in a limited edition with illustrations by Max Ernst.[37] She completed two other volumes as well— *Don Juan* by Joseph Delteil (1931), and Raymond Radiguet's *The Devil in the Flesh* (1932)— but while working on the Radiguet book, she wrote to Bob Brown, "I can't afford to do this kind of thing again."[38]

Kay Boyle also did some ghostwriting. After leaving the Duncan colony, she had worked for a year as secretary to an American fashion writer in Paris, Bettina Bedwell—another woman who was to become a lifelong friend. Bedwell had plotted a mystery novel and written an outline of chapters, and Boyle wrote the book while living in Kitzbühel. In March, 1935, she told Bob Brown, "I'm working harder than ever—trying to make some money on a best-seller which will appear under someone else's name. No faith in it, really, but MUST make desperate attempts in every direction with all the needs and demands there are."[39] *Yellow Dusk* by "Bettina Bedwell" was published by Hurst and Blackett of London in 1937, and Kay Boyle earned $250—"a badly needed sum for us," she recalls.[40]

Her most portentous project of the thirties was an anthology she planned to edit with Vail. As she described this "great project on the boards" to her agent in January, 1934, it would be a three-volume work to be published annually.[41] The first volume, to be called *1934,* would be a 365-page compilation of newspaper and magazine cuttings on all subjects—"a symposium of the events which have interested the world, or have not, during 1934." The second 365-page volume would be entitled *Crime 1934* and would cover "outstanding murders, etc." and "small crimes . . . when interesting." The third book, *Short Stories 1934,* would consist of 365 pieces of fewer than 300 words each, contributed by many writers.

Despite her apparent enthusiasm at the time, the project was "completely and entirely" Laurence Vail's idea, Boyle says today. She longed to get on with her own writing, and editing the anthology would be yet another interruption. But she did not want to discourage her husband, "who was so discouraged about his career anyway," and in what she now calls a "bit of bravado," she assured Ann Watkins, "It may sound fanatic, but it's going to be good, and humorous, and full of life and the times."[42] Vail was openly excited and optimistic about the project. He had written to Caresse Crosby a month earlier: "Don't you think the Books are a good idea. And why not go on forever till 1999 once the machinery is underway. Knowledge, glory and money for all of us. . . . Kay should produce many diamonds and me some queer coal."[43] What resulted was a single book of 365 one-page stories edited by Kay Boyle, Laurence Vail, and a friend, Nina Conarain, entitled *365 Days* and published in 1936. It was a critical and financial failure.

Nevertheless, the project signals an important shift in the focus of Kay Boyle's art. In the preface the editors express their sense that 1934 had been "a desperately eventful year—a year that was to be characterized by almost universal unrest, by civil war, revolution, by strike and unemployment figures reaching monstrous proportions" (*365D*, xi).[44] They intended the book to be a fictional record of national and international events and of individual lives around the globe during that year.

The volume contains 365 stories of 300 words or less, one for each day of 1934. "Each story was to bear a date instead of a title," the editors explain, "for each story must belong not to an undefined period of time but peculiarly to the moment the writer had selected, the specified day and month of this particular year." They suggest that the reader approach the collection by first reading the newspaper headline or "journalistically noted fact" in the synopsis preceding each month's group of stories and then turning to the fictional account of that event, "in the same way that one naturally reads first the description referring to a printed reproduction or photograph in order that understanding be immediate and complete" (*365D*, xii).

This concern for the realities of the "functioning world" represents a dramatic change for a writer who just a few years earlier had signed a manifesto declaring "Time is a tyranny to be abolished." The editors' statement of the criteria used in selecting stories is also surprising. First and foremost, they explain, they intend that this collection "should fulfil the demand made of any single short-story—that it should entertain." Although Boyle maintains now that "entertain" was Laurence's word and that she never has believed that entertainment is the purpose of a short story,[45] the attitude conveyed in print contrasts sharply with the belief she expressed to Walter Lowenfels in 1930 that the taste of the present-day reader was "not worth a ha'penny bit" and ought to be ignored. While the list of 116 contributors to the book includes such contemporary literary figures as Bob Brown, Robert McAlmon, Emanuel Carnevali, Nancy Cunard, Hilaire Hiler, Charles Henri Ford, Henry Miller, William Saroyan, and Langston Hughes, it is perhaps significant that *transition* editor Eugene Jolas is not among them.

Kay Boyle herself was the foremost contributor. While Laurence Vail contributed forty-two and Nina Conarain eight of the 365 pieces, Boyle wrote ninety-six of them. (Her father and mother each contributed one, too.) In several stories she deals with standing concerns, continuing to express a high regard for poetry and the romantic perspective. She presents sympathetically an English waiter who struggles to write visionary poetry in the servants' quarters between calls for scotch and soda and a Transylvanian bride whose grief for birds killed in a gas-well fire baffles her prosaic new husband.

But while the author's ongoing concern with the tragic failures of understanding is implicit in nearly all of the stories, the overwhelming majority displays the concern for matters of the external social world not always apparent in her more personal fiction of the twenties. The stories are set anywhere from Cleveland to Tasmania, and they touch upon contemporary phenomena ranging from the Depression and the New Deal to the fame of the Dionne quintuplets. Nine of the stories Kay Boyle contributed to the anthology involve the European political climate of 1934, the year in which the Austrian chancellor, Dollfuss, had met increasing resistance from the swelling bands of clean-cut young patriots called Nazis and finally was assassinated. A number of the sketches deal sympathetically with fugitives, prisoners, and other assorted outcasts and misfits as the author champions the downtrodden victims of an unjust social hierarchy. Others satirize the shallowness, insensitivity, and genteel barbarism of those elevated at the other end of the scale.

Katherine Evans Boyle's single contribution is a dialogue between an unsympathetic employment agent and a "light coloured girl" who had quit a badly-needed job to avoid her well-respected employer's sexual advances. Several of Kay Boyle's pieces also deal with racial injustice. In a straight-faced report of a boiler explosion at a Rangoon rice mill, she states that while seven coolies were scalded to death, "the boiler came down on a piece of adjoining paddy land luckily doing no harm" (*365D*, 278)—a line reminiscent of the scene in *Huckleberry Finn* in which Aunt Polly inquires whether a blown-out cylinder head on the steamboat had hurt anyone and Huck replies, "No'm. Killed a nigger."

While the sketches are interesting for their diverse settings and subjects (and, in retrospect, for their eyewitness reporting of a momentous time in modern history), they do not, as a group, represent Kay Boyle's writing at its best. In these pieces as in her longer fiction, life is cruel, but in a 300-word story she cannot take the time to reveal that truth with the fine-tuned subtlety that marks her better work. Instead, she relies heavily on the grotesque and sensational incident to make a powerful impact in a short space. In one piece, the boundary wall of a two-hundred-year-old graveyard collapses in a rainstorm, deluging the thoroughfare below with mud and bones and injuring a passerby with a flying tombstone.

Other sketches rely on bald irony. A Scots pastor heatedly sermonizes against the superficiality of the "Amen," then absent-mindedly sings it at the end of the next hymn. An imprisoned conjurer who had once performed the Hindu rope trick before an audience of six hundred is executed by hanging. One critic who objects to the "O. Henry pattern of so many of these stories" quite rightly concludes that the method of obtaining material for the pieces in *365 Days* "leads to her treating people in situations about which she is limited in her knowledge, and the results, too frequently, have the flavor of fictionalized editorials."[46]

"I well remember going off and weeping myself (yes, feeling sorry for myself) when Laurence first described the idea of the three-volume work to me," Boyle says today. "I wanted so much to get on with my own writing, and the *365 Days* project was a burden I forced myself to grin about and bear. I don't think even Laurence knew how bitterly I felt about the demands of *365 Days*. But once I had accepted the unwelcome burden, I worked hard at it."[47] "It was perhaps a desperate way of trying to get his work in print," she explains, "for I felt guilty that my work was being published and he received only rejection slips."[48] The many stories they received from writers like Henry Miller and William Saroyan were the only compensation, she says. In fact, Saroyan, apparently misunderstanding the editors' request for 300-word stories, sent 365 stories. But they did not get enough unusual contributions to fill the book, and it ended with Boyle writing about a third of the stories under a variety of names. (She finds it odd that copies of the collection in which she listed her various pseudonyms inside the front cover now sell for as much as $125.)

Yet she still retains some regard for the book. Although it was, in her words, a "commercial flop," some of the earliest work of many good writers who later would become well-known was published in that volume. She used it as a text in her writing classes at San Francisco State in the sixties and seventies, believing it was "excellent discipline" for students to work within the 300-word formula. The one-page stories "are tremendously valuable in making students discard everything but the essentials," she says, and most of them liked the assignment, particularly when reminded that Hemingway learned that important lesson while working as a newspaper reporter.[49] And at a special session on her life and work at the 1979 convention of the Modern Language Association in San Francisco, she chose to spend half of her allotted time reading from *365 Days*.

While it certainly is not among her best literary efforts—from either a critical or a popular standpoint—it nonetheless is a significant one. For one thing, several of the sketches first published in the collection proved to be first workings out of materials she would later develop into short stories or scenes of novels.[50] More important, it marks the beginning of a new phase in Kay Boyle's career. *365 Days* reflects an increasing tendency to deal directly with political and social issues in her fiction as well as a new tendency to view her characters and their struggles from a greater distance. Yet it is characteristic of the author in the thirties that in the same year she was compiling and contributing to this parajournalistic anthology that heralds the future direction of her art, she simultaneously was composing an epic poem inspired by Harry Crosby and encouraged by Eugene Jolas—a work conceived in the heady aesthetic ferment of Paris in the twenties. In the thirties she was evolving into another kind of artist, but she had not entirely left the old ways behind.

Kay Boyle's short story collections of the thirties display the range of her interests and fictional techniques of that decade. Nearly every one of the fourteen stories in her 1933 volume, *The First Lover and Other Stories,* evidence the author's long-standing concerns with fresh language, the individual quest for identity, and the need for—and failures of—love. But a few chart new territory, moving away from the personal expression of personal experience toward communication of broader social concerns. She continues more firmly on the new course in *The White Horses of Vienna and Other Stories* (1936), a book in which the impact of the "functioning world" upon individual lives cannot be ignored.

Some of the *First Lover* stories are close kin to Kay Boyle's works of the twenties in their idiosyncratic material and experimental style. (She dedicated the volume to Eugene Jolas.) "Art Colony," for example, focuses on a disillusioned young woman trapped in a colony of toga-clad artists in Paris led by a man named Sorrel—material she would use in *My Next Bride,* published the following year.

"I Can't Get Drunk," largely a dialogue (written without quotation marks) between a man and a woman in a Paris bar, is the most radically experimental piece in the collection in terms of style, and it, too, is clearly a product of the author's experiences of the twenties. In fact, in 1960 she identified the man of the story as Robert McAlmon and the woman as herself.[51] The man, unable, he says, to get drunk but trying hard, is restless, unsatisfied, longing for something. It is clear that Kay Boyle knows what his problem is, even if he does not. The woman in the story says, "To see him with his lean mouth closed like a wallet, his eye like iron and as cold as, would it ever have come into your head that the mouth of his heart was open, was gaping wide like a frog's in dry weather, requesting that into it be drained not glasses with frost on their faces but something else again" (*FL*, 207–8).[52] The "something else" he needs is the nourishment of human contact. The fact that at the end he overturns his bar stool and has difficulty picking it up, coupled with the claim of the story's title, ironically underscores his desperation.

In "Rest Cure" we view an invalid writer sitting on a terrace in the south of France. Kay Boyle has said since that the story is based on the death of D. H. Lawrence, which had deeply moved her. She had been told that a well-known sculptor had gone down to the *midi* to visit Lawrence in his final days in the hopes of being able to do a head of him.[53] In her story, the ailing man, obsessed with the sun, breaks the red heads off the geraniums that block the afternoon light and snaps at a visitor standing before him—a publisher—whose "solid gray head had served to cork the sunlight." In response to the visitor's disingenuous pleasantries about the advantages of being a writer rather than a publisher, the irritated writer retorts, "Why be a publisher?" Closing his eyelids, he looks into "the black blank mines" of his childhood. Aside from flashbacks to his youth in England, his goading of the guest to respond to his question, and his expression of distaste for a live lobster his wife had bought for dinner, nothing "happens." The action is psychological. In morbid curiosity the invalid demands that the lobster be let out of its basket, and setting it on the rug across his lap, he examines it and decides that it looks just like his father: "There was the same line of sparkling dewlike substance pearling the *langouste's* lip, the same weak disappointed lip, like the eagle's lip, and the bold, suspicious eye." He lapses into a reverie, confusing images of the beast with images of the man who would come home at night "with the coal dust showered across his shoulders like a deadly mantle" and beer on his breath, swaying at the door as he fumbled for the latch. "I've got on very well without you," he thinks bitterly, but from the embarrassed reactions of his wife and guest he gathers that he has spoken aloud. Looking at them in bewilderment, he thinks that if they scold him, he will cry. He feels his underlip quivering. But then he pulls himself together:

> Scold me! he thought suddenly in indignation. A man with a beard! His hand fled to his chin for confirmation. A man with a beard, he thought with a cunning evil gleam narrowing his eye.
> "You haven't answered my question," he said aggressively to the visitor. "You haven't answered it yet, have you?"

His outburst over, he discovers that his hand had fallen against "the hard brittle armor of the *langouste's* hide" and he sees its eyes raised to his. "His fingers closed for comfort about the *langouste's* unwieldy paw. Father he said in his heart, Father help me. Father, Father, he said. I don't want to die." With this, we realize that the dying man's cantankerousness is his only defense—a mask to hide his vulnerability, from himself as well as from the visiting publisher who had come to exploit him in his helplessness—and as in other tragedies, we are moved to "pity and fear." Like many of Kay Boyle's stories, this one simply presents a situation without comment, peeling back layers until the bitter kernel of truth is exposed.

The remaining pieces in the collection represent a departure from the materials the author used in her fiction of the twenties. The characters are no longer rootless expatriates but Germans in Germany, Englishmen in England, and Americans at home. Yet apart from their new topicality, they are a by-now-familiar chronicle of missed connections between people hungry for contact but unable for a variety of psychological reasons to overcome their isolation from others.

The title story of the collection is a tragicomedy of such errors. In "The First Lover," three German girls vacationing in the south of France, daughters of a destitute professor, spy an astoundingly handsome and healthy-looking Englishman as he steps into the dining room of their *pension* one day at noon. Instantly they see his vigor as their redemption from poverty and defeat, and in their hopeful yearning, they contrive elaborate explanations to use in conversation with him to exempt themselves from Germany's suffering. After they have determined which sister will be his, she practices her introductory remarks and facial expressions before the mirror. Later, the man glances up from the garden and sees her in the window. When he asks if she could be one of the daughters of Professor Albatross, with whom he had once studied in Berlin, her fingernails turn white against the sill and she is speechless. He casually adds that he had just stopped off there for lunch, smiles, and bids them goodbye. The girls' intricate scheme for their future evaporates, yet they find themselves "in some kind of fury that had never possessed them before." "Their eyes were warm, and their teeth were strung like pearls across their faces. They had so much to say to one another that they didn't know where to begin" (*FL,* 43). While the author delicately mocks their maiden fervor, it is a sad indication of their need that such an insignificant encounter has meant so much to them.

Such irony demands an intellectual and emotional distance from the subject. But while this detachment marks a departure from much of her earlier work, Kay Boyle is still very much a champion of the feelings over the intellect. In "Kroy Wen" she exposes the egotism of a movie director so intent upon capturing the essence of humanity in his work that he is grossly inhumane. Having suffered a nervous breakdown, he is taking a boat to Italy from New York, following his doctor's order to take a leisurely vacation, a complete rest from his work. (One of his symptoms is seeing words spelled backwards; hence the words on the ship's hull become "Kroy Wen.") Yet when he spies a "picturesque" Italian couple in steerage, he is ecstatic: " 'There's color!' he said. 'I needed a few yards of a pregnant woman. God, what atmosphere!' he said" (*FL*, 21). In a grotesque climax, the filmmaker rages at the woman—who, conveniently for him, has gone into premature labor—for her stoic and unphotogenic endurance of the agony.

In "Three Little Men," Boyle continues her criticism of those whose overgrown intellects have smothered their capacities for emotion—a particularly masculine phenomenon, she seems to believe. Actually three independent vignettes marked by Roman numerals, the story is unified by a strong female voice expressing pity and contempt for three weak men. In the first sketch, which is rooted in autobiography, a father's lackluster romantic urges are observed by a daughter much tougher than he.[54] When the daughter discovers discarded bits of an anemic love letter that this "little man" had written, she tears at him in "silent anger": "I thought, oh, how pale are the flowers of your desire, my little father, how delicate is your need. . . . And I thought that I would place him on my strong wrist, like a falcon, and hood his small bowed head with my fingers so that he need not see the world" (*FL*, 64). The second section concerns a male poet who writes unconvincingly of a pale love, of the absence of "a pretty, pretty girl with the Chinese blue eyes" whose "absence was anybody's absence" (*FL*, 66). "If I had taken him in my hands and broken him up and scattered him over the logs, he would have made a sweet smell in the room" (*FL*, 65), the narrator says, and she would like to tell him: "I can make you a Jacob's coat, little fellow, I can give you a coat of agony to cover your bones. And a shirt of fire I can give you to warm your heart until it burns a black path through your body" (*FL*, 67). In the third sketch she speaks with a man who "had a reverence for art" but who "took art out of the flesh and made a grotesque of it" (*FL*, 69). He tells her of an artist in Siberia who had been writing a book on art but had had to abandon the project because he could find no reference books on aesthetics there. The narrator's retort surely would be the author's as well:

> Aesthetics, I said, are the soul of a man coming up again and again out of a hard ground in the cold, always coming up, like a new plant, with no sun but his own sap to warm him. But he would not believe this, or anything like it, because his mind could understand this, and he wanted something, as dull people do, that his mind could not easily understand. He would tell me never to be angry, and never to love, and he would say that I must quiet this ferocity in me because it was a spendthrift's way with strength and that strength must be conserved to twist it into perfect works of art. (*FL*, 69)

For Kay Boyle, the "ferocity" of emotion is essential if life or art is to have vitality and significance. Her narrator complains, "He would not listen to me when I said that perfect form was a carcase and that art was only an empty vessel in which to pour the torrent of a man's belief" (*FL*, 69).

Although in the twenties the author had focused on the missed connections between individuals, despising the customs and conventions that thwart heart-to-heart contact, Kay Boyle always had been sensitive to public issues. As a child she had witnessed and supported her mother's efforts on behalf of liberal causes, and her own early works had titles like "The Working Girl's Prayer" and "Arise, Ye Women." Her commitment to the Revolution of the Word was in itself a kind of political stand. Yet beginning in the thirties, she became increasingly concerned with exposing in her fiction the devastating failures of love in the world at large. Her method is to focus on the particular incident as representative of a sweeping disorder.

"Black Boy" is one of the few stories Kay Boyle mentions by name in her letters of the early thirties, when she was writing so many stories so quickly. She was thrilled when it "released huzzas" from Bob Brown, and she reported to him in detail her efforts to get it published. After several other magazines had rejected it, *Harper's* turned it down with the comment that some of its passages were "magical." "Maybe they aren't going in for magic this season," she comments.[55] She finally sold it to *The New Yorker* in 1932 for two hundred dollars, although "they pulled out the tendrils, the womb, and the back side," she said.[56] She has since expressed particular satisfaction with "Black Boy" because "it is completely simple, and moral without moralizing."[57] In the story a little girl in Atlantic City with a grandfather named "Puss" befriends a black boy who makes a living propelling tourists up and down the boardwalk in a push chair. In the early morning he sits in the sand under the boardwalk, and the girl often joins him to talk. "I seen kings . . . with a kind of cloth over they heads, and kind of jewels-like around here and here. They weren't any blacker than me, if as black," he tells her and adds, "I could be almost anything I made up my mind to be" (*FL*, 138). "If I was king," he continues, "I wouldn't put much stock in hanging around here" (*FL*, 139). The girl continues to visit her friend despite Puss's warnings that the boy might want to do her harm. One morning when she takes a horse down on the sand to try jumping over the jetty, she is thrown and knocked unconscious: "For a long time I heard nothing at all in my head except the melody of some one crying, whether it was my dead mother holding me in comfort, or the soft wind grieving over me where I had fallen. I lay on the sand asleep; I could feel it running with my tears through my fngers. I was rocked in a cradle of love, cradled and rocked in sorrow" (*FL*, 144–45). As the black boy wails, "Oh, my little lamb, my little lamb pie!" the narrator recalls, "I could feel the long swift fingers of love untying the terrible knot of pain that bound my head. And I put my arms around him and lay close to his heart in comfort." The story ends: "Puss was alive then, and when he met the black boy carrying me up to the house, he struck him square across the mouth" (*FL,* 145).

The White Horses of Vienna and Other Stories (1936) reflects in particular the author's experiences in Austria although it also contains stories set in England, France, America, and Ireland. Like *The First Lover,* it, too, is a watershed work, containing along with the more social pieces a number of stories that, for their exploration of purely personal struggles, would have been at home in the *Wedding Day* collection. Several of the stories in *The White Horses of Vienna* are studies of lonely individuals longing to make connection with others. But even in these "psychological" stories, Kay Boyle's style is generally more direct, less experimental than it had been in the twenties.

A notable exception is "Major Alshuster," on first reading a puzzling, seemingly disjointed work. A woman alone in England hears in a local pub of a nearby manor house for rent. She calls on the owner, Major Alshuster, who had served for twelve years in India and had never married. He is cold, recoiling at the thought of having to let his family home to a stranger (and a foreigner at that), and he shows her the place with tight-lipped efficiency. She is captivated—by the man as well as by the house. As in Kay Boyle's earlier stories the narrative technique is complex. Subject and object merge in the telling. As the major shows the woman around the property, external objects take on strange shapes. The greenhouse becomes a lush, sensuous Eden; the imagery is unabashedly sexual. "Here in this heart of glass, were cactuses besought to grow, wooed from the dark earth and rotting wood until they stood, leather-thick and coarse, with their soft yellow or long, silvery beards upon their bellies, rearing upward like snakes poised to strike" (*WHV,* 166–67).[58]

Although the young woman receives a letter soon thereafter indicating that "due to unforeseen circumstances," the major will be unable to rent the house to her, it is not the end of their relationship. The remainder of the story consists of accounts of their numerous rendezvous, in which he opens himself to her. The author continues to experiment with technique; "Major Alshuster" contains another story within the main narrative. The narrator confides to the major that she once had loved a boy who had been killed. She periodically interrupts her recounting of the tale to return to the present situation, detailing in parenthetical paragraphs the major's sympathetic reactions to the tragic story: " 'Blow your nose in my handkerchief. I'm in love with you,' he said" (*WHV,* 178). For several paragraphs the story even shifts out of the first-person point of view to report in the third-person a conversation between the major and the woman (now called "Mrs. Whatchername") on the rather suggestive topic of "pigsticking." The hunter must choose his own ground and never thrust at the pig, although that is his first impulse, the major explains to her: " 'You must just drop the point and hold it steady and let the force of the collision do the rest. If you thrust at him you'll miss him clean, nine times out of ten. Just set your spear and then wait, . . . And if your spear is sharp,' he said, 'it will go in like a hot knife into butter' " (*WHV*, 172–73).

At the end of the story, the woman returns two months later to the pub where she first had heard the major's house was for rent. The barmaid asks about her visit to Dower House in June: " 'Did you see Major Alshuster?' she said in a low voice. 'Was he still alive when you went there?' " (*WHV*, 180). Only then does the reader realize that the entire story has been the woman's fantasy—that she had met the man only once, on the afternoon he had shown her the house. But still the woman's imagination is undaunted. After taking another gin, she goes out in the dark up the cliff path she had trod many times with the conjured major, and again she meets him there. He pulls her against him, "and his mouth closed hard and hot upon my mouth," she says. The two cling fast to each other, looking straight "into the darkness which was England stretching invisibly away." The story ends: " 'To hell with the country,' he said. We stood close on the edge of it together. 'You belong to me, Mrs. Whatchername,' said Major Alshuster. 'I don't believe in death,' he said" (*WHV*, 182).[59] The tenacity of the woman's fantasy and the strength of her erotic imagination testify to her desperation.

"Maiden, Maiden," a story of tragic romance, relies on ironic twists in plot rather than on psychological complexities, foreshadowing the simpler narrative technique of most of Boyle's later fiction. An English doctor and his mistress, mountain climbing in the Alps, hire a local guide. The woman, weary of her three-year affair with the pragmatic physician, is cynical about love. But she and the guide are powerfully and instantaneously drawn to one another. The night before he is to take the doctor on a climb, they passionately commit themselves to each other and are transformed: "His mouth was fresh with wild new kisses, and here on the shelter's step was the heart of warmth and promise, and the dead abandoned world beyond bathed in floods of purest cold" (*WHV*, 245). "Holy blood, holy blood," the woman repeats to herself the next morning as she separates her things from the doctor's, preparing to leave him when the men return from their climb: "She felt it moving deep and exultant in her, the wondrous thrust of what was to begin piercing swift and blissful in her flesh." But late that afternoon a party of climbers returns, "and in their faces there was the shock and strain of warning." They had been hailed by a man whose partner had fallen, but he had called from such a distance that they could not say whether he was the guide or the doctor. Numbly the woman sets out alone across the glacier to follow the rescue party.

When the lone figure returning down the wide avenue of ice is finally identifiable, they call back "as if in comfort and assurance" to her, "The Englishman is on the ice! Your man, your man" (*WHV*, 251). There was nothing to be done for the poor chap by the time he had reached him, the shaken doctor says as he finally embraces her. " 'It might have been me Willa,' he said, holding her to keep the teeth from rattling in her head. 'It might just as easily have been me,' he said." He is precisely right. Fate could have taken him and spared the guide; the accident could just as easily have marked the beginning of a new love as the death of one.

It is an evocative tale, faintly reminiscent of the tragic Alpine episode in *Women in Love* by D. H. Lawrence, whom Boyle very much admired. But interestingly, given Kay Boyle's distaste for the man, it also has a strong flavor of Hemingway. In its blend of romance and fatalism it recalls *A Farewell to Arms,* especially the scene in which Frederic Henry watches ants on a burning log and muses on the cruel indifference of fate. And in one passage, after she and the guide have kissed for the first time, the heroine of "Maiden, Maiden" sounds remarkably like Catherine Barkley, who had cryptically announced to Frederic after their first kiss, "We're going to have a strange life": " 'We'll have a good life,' said Willa softly. In wonder she could feel it coming to life in the falling of warm tears on her face. 'Say that we'll have a good life, say it!' she whispered." (*WHV*, 245). Kay Boyle was familiar with Hemingway's novel, and while she thought him "unspeakable," she had said of his heroine: "He has no right to have such a wonderful woman as Catherine. Perhaps he made her up because he knew he could never have anyone so wonderful."[60]

"Maiden, Maiden" is laden with symbolism. The guide dies trying to scale a pinnacle called "The Maiden," a tall column of stone topped with a white face of snow—so named, he tells his new lover, "because not many men have been able to reach her" (*WHV*, 243). Willa and the guide commit themselves to each other beside a statue of a mountaineer and a woman in embrace; the guide had erected it in memory of his grandfather, who one night had taken leave of his wife and was killed in the mountains. Willa is searching for passion, and the author clearly takes her side. When she tells the doctor that she wants to find someone "who believes in the excursion of the soul," he laughs. When she sees the monument the guide had raised to this couple, she says bitterly of her own long affair, "If you think it's ever been anything like that!" (*WHV*, 236). "Why don't you tell him," the guide had quietly replied, "that you would like to fall in love?" Perhaps what Kay Boyle had found so attractive in Hemingway's Catherine Barkley was her total, almost religious, belief in love. Her own heroine shares that reverence and, like Catherine, who dies unexpectedly in childbirth, is cheated by a dirty trick of fate.

Pride is a self-imposed obstacle to a bonding with others, and in several stories Kay Boyle explores its destructiveness. She both pities and scorns those who envelop themselves in their pride and then suffer from the deprivation of human contact. For their cold snobbery they deserve the loneliness they get, but the author is sensitive to the pathos of their predicament. In "Natives Don't Cry," a proud British governess traveling in Austria with a well-to-do family spurns their warmth and friendliness. Instead, she dwells on tales of her own golden childhood as a civil servant's daughter in Burma (where natives "don't feel things the way other people do") and talks incessantly of Rudolpho, her gentleman friend back in London. Finally it becomes apparent that their love affair (if not Rudolpho himself), exists only in the lonely woman's imagination.

But the barriers to contact may be socially-erected as well and those who hide behind them victims of conditions beyond their comprehension or control. *The White Horses of Vienna* contains two Gothic tales of decaying nobility clinging blindly to the tattered remnants of social superiority and a grand style of living despite the harsh realities of the Depression. The characters in "Keep Your Pity" and "Dear Mr. Walrus"—close kin to Miss Fira and Miss Grusha, the destitute Russian spinsters in *My Next Bride*—are elderly aristocrats reduced to closing off portions of the family home to save on heat and to sizing up cats on the street for the meat on their bones. Both stories end grotesquely. In "Keep Your Pity," the wife refuses to accept her husband's death until a visitor months later discovers his decaying corpse seated upright at his desk, "working" on the invention that will restore their wealth. The police who come the next morning to retrieve the body are hit by a swinging object as they pass into the dark entry hall. The old woman has hanged herself and is kicking them in the face for their impudence. In "Dear Mr. Walrus," an elderly Fifth Avenue aristocrat finally completes his life's work—a ten-volume literary masterpiece—only to learn that his "publisher," a man who fifty years earlier had sent him a politely flattering rejection letter, had just died. He and his two ancient sisters cope with the disappointment by stretching out on the kitchen floor in their pyjamas and turning on the gas. In these stories the characters discover that their meticulously constructed private lives are fragile. Although they do their best to close their eyes to the crass realities of the functioning world, they are hit broadside by the facts and do not survive the collision.

Two stories obviously drawn from her own childhood again remind us that Kay Boyle's social conscience was not a new acquisition in the thirties. In "Security," a ten-year-old girl faces a difficult choice. To teach her the value of money, her grandfather, Puss, makes her a gift of a bond, "Union Iron and Steel, Preferred." The conflict arises when he asks his granddaughters to print a reactionary, pro-war article by him in the monthly mimeographed "magazine" they publish with his financial backing. The girls' mother, whose opinion they trust, considers it objectionable. The ten-year-old editor must choose between the financial security of her magazine and her principles. Her conscience wins and she gives up her precious bond to buy full ownership of the magazine—and editorial freedom—from Puss. This story does have a happy ending: "the dear gay little man, the sweet-tongued poet of Wall Street" ends up giving her another bond for her next birthday.

Another social piece with autobiographical roots is White as Snow," like "Black Boy," the story of a child's introduction to racial prejudice, set in Atlantic City. Again, Boyle effectively employs the first-person point of view of an innocent child to report the events without authorial comment. The reader is on his or her own to penetrate the peaceful surface and confront the ugly truth beneath. Simply stated, the children's light-skinned governess attempts to repudiate the facts of nature—wearing long gloves, referring to her "sunburn," and speaking with the proper disdain of the "colored element." But others will not let her forget what she is. When she goes to a movie on her first date with a boy, he must return from the ticket booth to tell her that there are not enough seats left for them to sit together—she will have to sit alone in the balcony. (Ironically, the film is *Birth of a Nation*.) The children in Carrie's charge are baffled by her sudden dejection and attempt to cheer her up with talk of the creamed chicken they will have for dinner, blissfully ignorant of the full significance of the afternoon.

While Kay Boyle was living in Austria from 1933 to 1936, she was an eyewitness as conditions of the social world began to encroach more and more insistently upon private experience. In one of her best-known works, "The White Horses of Vienna," winner of the O. Henry Award for best story of 1935, she exposes the evils of institutionalized bigotry. The story explores the relationship between a Tyrolean doctor, who has injured his leg coming down the mountain after lighting a swastika fire in protest of the current government, and a Dr. Heine, the young assistant sent from Vienna to aid him as he recuperates. The Tyrolean doctor is a compassionate, intelligent idealist who has willingly suffered repeated imprisonment as a member of the outlawed patriotic movement that he believes is his ruined country's salvation. Dr. Heine is a Jew.

The Tyrolean doctor is a clean-living, respected man. He had been a prisoner of war in Siberia and had studied abroad, but the many places in which he had been "had never left an evil mark:" "His face was as strong as rock, but such rains of tenderness washed over it that it seemed split apart with love: one side of it given to anguish and the other to shelter for everyone else alive" (*WHV*, 5).[61] In his personal dealings it is the compassionate side that dominates. When his wife asks in a desperate whisper what they will do with "him," he replies simply that they will send for his bag at the station and give him some *Apfelsaft* if he is thirsty. "It's harder on him than us," he tells her (*WHV*, 9). Neither has the wife's own humanity been extinguished entirely. When Dr. Heine's coat catches fire from a sterilizing lamp, she immediately wraps a piece of rug around him and holds him tightly to smother the flames. Almost instinctively she offers to try patching the burned place in the precious cloth, but then she suddenly bites her lip and stands back "as if she had remembered the evil thing that stood between them" (*WHV*, 12).

The situation of the Tyrolean doctor, described as a "great, golden, wounded bird" (*WHV*, 6), is counterpointed in a story Dr. Heine tells at dinner one evening about the famous Lippizaner horses of the Spanish Riding School in Vienna—still royal, "without any royalty left to bow their heads to, still shouldering into the arena with spirits a man would give his soul for, bending their knees in homage to the empty, canopied loge where royalty no longer sat" (*WHV*, 12). He tells of a particular horse that the bankrupt government had sold to an Indian maharaja. When the time had come for the horse to be taken away, a deep cut was discovered just above one hoof. After the cut had healed and it was thought that the horse could be shipped to the maharaja, an indentical slash was found just above another hoof. Eventually, its blood became poisoned, and the horse had to be destroyed. Who had wounded the animal was a mystery until the horse's devoted little groom committed suicide that same day. This after-dinner conversation is interrupted by the knocking of Heimwehr troops at the door, "men brought in from other parts of the country and billeted there as strangers to subdue the native people" (*WHV*, 16), and the identification between the doctor and the crippled steed is underscored. It is the doctor's wounded leg that saves him from having to guide the troops up the mountainside in search of those who have lighted that evening's swastika fires.

Dr. Heine is relieved that the rest of the evening will be spent with family and friends watching one of the Tyrolean doctor's locally re-nowned marionette shows. After staring out the window at the burning swastikas, Dr. Heine turns to the others, suddenly angry. He proclaims that the whole country is being ruined by politics, that it is impossible to have friends or even casual conversations on any other basis these days. "You're much wiser to make your puppets, *Herr Doktor*," he says (*WHV*, 17–18).

But even the marionette show is political. The characters are a clown carrying flowers who explains he is on his way to his own funeral, and a handsome grasshopper, "a great, gleaming beauty," who prances wittily about the stage to the music of Mozart. "It's really marvelous! He's as graceful as the white horses at Vienna, *Herr Doktor*," Dr. Heine calls out in delight (*WHV*, 21). Yet as the conversation continues between the clown, called "Chancellor," and the grasshopper, addressed as "the Leader," Dr. Heine stops laughing. The Chancellor has a "ludicrous faith in the power of the Church" to support him; the Leader proclaims that the cities are full of churches, but "the country is full of God" (*WHV*, 23). The Leader speaks with "a wild and stirring power that sent the cold of wonder up and down one's spine," and he seems "ready to waltz away at any moment with the power of stallion life that was leaping in his limbs." As the Chancellor proclaims, "I believe in independence," he promptly trips over his own sword and falls flat among the daisies (*WHV*, 23).[62]

At the story's conclusion, the young Viennese Jew is standing alone on the cold mountainside, longing to be "indoors, with the warmth of his own people, and the intellect speaking" (*WHV*, 24). When he sees "a small necklace of men coming to him" up the mountain, the lights they bear "coming like little beacons of hope carried to him," he thinks, "Come to me . . . come to me. I am a young man alone on a mountain" (*WHV*, 25).[63] Yet ironically, what Dr. Heine views as "beacons of hope" are carried by the Heimwehr troops, the Tyrolean doctor's enemies. As in one of her earliest stories, "Wedding Day," Kay Boyle presents a single situation and plays off against each other the characters' reactions to it in order to illustrate the gaps between individual understanding and the relativity of reality in our world.

His personal loyalties transcending his politics, Dr. Heine rushes to warn the family of the Heimwehr's approach. When the troops arrive they announce that the Austrian chancellor, Dollfuss, had been assassinated in Vienna that afternoon. They have come to arrest the doctor, whose rebel sympathies are known. "Ah, politics, politics again!" cries Dr. Heine, wringing his hands "like a woman about to cry" (*WHV*, 26). He runs outdoors and takes the doctor's hand as he is being carried away on a stretcher, asking what he can do to help. "You can throw me peaches and chocolate from the street," replies the Tyrolean doctor, smiling, "his cheeks scarred with the marks of laughter in the light from the hurricane lamps that the men were carrying down" (*WHV*, 26). His wife is not a good shot, he adds, and he missed all the oranges she had thrown to him after the February slaughter. And at this image of the Tyrolean doctor caged like an animal but still noble, his spirit still unbroken, Dr. Heine is left "thinking in anguish of the snow-white horses, the Lippizaners, the relics of pride, the still unbroken vestiges of beauty bending their knees to the empty loge of royalty where there was no royalty any more" (*WHV*, 27).

In "The White Horses of Vienna," Kay Boyle expresses hope, if not faith, that even in the face of divisive social forces, the basic connections of compassion between individuals might survive. In a work that is a testament to her humanity, she presents the Tyrolean doctor's plight with such sensitivity that the reader, like the Jewish assistant, is forced to sympathize with this proud man's search for a cause that will redeem his wounded people while at the same time abhorring the cause itself. The author sees and presents in all its human complexity what at first would seem a black and white political issue.

Yet she is no pollyanna. As the social conflict that motivates this story snowballed into world war and genocide, Kay Boyle saw with a cold, realistic eye how little survived of the goodwill among men she had hoped for. In many of her stories written from the mid-thirties to the present day, she has examined unflinchingly and sometimes bitterly the individual tragedies played out in the shadow of the global one.

In a letter to Ann Watkins from Innsbruck dated July 3, 1934, the author describes an incident that, had it been written as fiction, might be described as symbolic of the ways in which political concerns had begun to affect her art:

> It has been very exciting here and I wouldn't have missed it for anything. The trees and tables and chairs in the garden blown onto the nearby roofs, and all our papers (which were on the glass-enclosed balcony overlooking the garden) blown to the four winds. . . . The Nazis were after the anti-Nazi daily paper next door and put a time-bomb on the roof of the printing-works. The night watchman found it and threw it into the beer-garden—thus we got the whole thing—Two nights later, a second bomb, very much smaller, was found but extinguished before it exploded. We are now very much surrounded by Heimwehr troops all night who do sentinel duty up and down the roofs and gardens and one feels very warlike. . . . It was very funny to have police exhibiting pieces of February events "1934" with arrows and dates on them as probable evidence in the placing and timing of the bomb that night—and poor Laurence and me trying to pick up our remnants from the debris in despair—[64]

It is an incident she would use in *Death of A Man* (1936), the novel that grew out of her personal encounters with political activities in the Tyrol in 1934.

The dedication page of that novel is another piece of unintended symbolism. Like *The First Lover and Other Stories, Death of a Man* is dedicated to Eugene Jolas, but for a significantly different reason. In her 1933 story collection, the author had wished to honor the man "who wrote 'Follow the voice that booms in the deepest dream, deeper go, always deeper. . . .' " At the beginning of the 1936 novel she declares, "This book is dedicated to Eugene Jolas because we sat in the summer of that year in the wine-cellars and the Gasthauses of that town." The fact that in its dedication she had linked the name of the avant-garde editor with a topical reference to contemporary politics suggests that this book is a synthesis of Kay Boyle's aesthetic and social concerns.

Death of a Man is concerned with the necessity of love and with its tragic failures—on both the private and the public scale. In its landscape and characters, it bears some resemblance to the short story, "Maiden, Maiden." Set in the Tyrol, it centers on three characters: a cynical young American woman, her decent but boring English husband, and a handsome, vigorous man of the mountains to whom she is powerfully attracted. In the novel, the woman, who is actually married to the Englishman, leaves him in order to follow her passions, and it is the noble man of the mountains, not the Englishman, who is a doctor. He is also a Nazi.

The woman, Pendennis, is the embodiment of "an entirely youthful and spoiled conception of what is sophistication and what is enough, so commonplace in America that no one stops to look but startling when transplanted from its soil" (*DOM,* 136).[65] Dr. Prochaska comes to learn that his love for this foreigner and his fervent devotion to his fatherland are incompatible. The local Nazi organizer disapproves of their relationship, believing she is a hindrance to the doctor's political activities. In a climactic scene, after chastising Prochaska for being so blindly submissive, Pendennis packs her bags in the night and goes to Vienna, leaving no forwarding address. By the time both have come to the realization that "pride had no authentic place for existence between lovers" (*DOM,* 267), it is too late. When Dr. Prochaska finally learns her Vienna address and rushes to the capital to find her, she has gone. Bitterly disappointed, he returns home to Feldbruck, only to learn that the chancellor, Dollfuss, has been assassinated, a rebellion quelled, and that all Nazi sympathizers are being rounded up and jailed. The ending has a Romeo-and-Juliet quality of tragic irony. A fugitive, he sets off alone on a local night train toward the Italian frontier, unable to know that the express train flashing past in the opposite direction is carrying Pendennis back to Feldbruck to make her peace with him. Prochaska is a doubly defeated man. He has lost not only the woman he loves but his beloved country as well.

While Kay Boyle retains her long-standing romantic faith in intuition over intellect, she has become disillusioned about another tenet of romanticism: the belief in the absolute autonomy of the Self, in the unimpeded power of the individual will. *Death of a Man* is a story of human connections obstructed not only by stubborn personal pride but by external circumstances beyond the individual's control. In the end it makes little difference that Pendennis and Dr. Prochaska have undergone crises of conscience and have come to realize they need each other. There are more powerful forces governing one's existence—like the whims of fate and the changing course of history—and they can render impotent the decisions of the individual.

At least one critic has been troubled by "the ease with which Pendennis falls in love with Prochaska and sends off her English husband."[66] But it is perfectly consistent with the romanticism Kay Boyle had expressed in earlier fiction and, indeed, with her own experience that her heroine should disregard convention and common sense to follow the dictates of the heart. Dr. Prochaska and Pendennis recognize the improbability of their falling in love—she hard, cynical, and outrageous in the mountain village with her brown, bare legs and blood-red fingernails and he, as Pendennis puts it, "The man who believes in his country, and in women, and in love, I bet you. The genuine old article" (*DOM*, 80). "It's impossible what's happened" (*DOM*, 81), he tells her, yet both readily surrender to the reality of what has taken place.

The doctor's commitment to his political cause, too, is based on emotion rather than on reason. In what Mark Van Doren calls "the attempt by Miss Boyle to elucidate mystical fascism," (an analysis the author considers "absolutely right"),[67] Prochaska communes silently with Pendennis as they stand together staring at the swastika fire they have lit on the mountainside:

> Believe me it is not necessary to think, only to follow and to believe. It is not necessary to reason, only to feel the blood moving and to know. . . . Nothing having brought us here or together except the flesh of our bodies, the intoxication of movement, the mystery of the darkness together, nothing having any significance except those things we have not done before, our own knowledge of those things to be seized with the hands, the eyes, the lips, the limbs even while the mind is shed as cowardice is shed, disdained like caution, the mind cast off and even the reason for it cast aside and the direction of the body not lost but weaving magically, like a trumpet call unwinding through the flesh, the destination not even questioned, residing as it does in every instant, every breath that's taken, NOW. (*DOM*, 174)

If Dr. Prochaska, with his awareness of and commitment to the social world, is a new kind of character for Kay Boyle in the mid-thirties, Pendennis is not. Like many of her expatriate protagonists of the twenties, Pendennis is rootless, alienated, and suffering for her lack of connections. She is a child of the Waste Land. You're sentimental, you're hearts and flowers and I'm hard broken bits and pieces of things they threw out with the skeletons and cactus—" she tells her lover. "You belong to a permanent thing and to people that don't change, but that can't put me together. Too many parts are gone. . . . I've been left stranded somewhere" (*DOM*, 94–95).

The anchor her family might have provided has been dislodged. Her mother had been thrown by a horse while Pendennis and her twin brother had looked on, laughing, as she hurtled through the air and landed in a stream, not realizing that she had been killed. Her twin had hanged himself at seventeen, tormented by his impossible love for his sister. Her father makes toothpaste and money. She has been "left stranded" by her country, too, which despite vast prosperity and promise has failed to be anything she can respect. She kicks the silver-framed photographs of the doctor's beloved family off the table and cries, "My father's in Florida playing golf, yours is lying flat on his face on the rug there. God damn my speechless little country, Herr Doktor, it hasn't a word to say to yours" (*DOM*, 93).

Pendennis grasps at any connection that can lend her an identity. Even though she finds it absurd that a Jew should be excluded from a skiing competition, she cries in rage and recklessly shouts "Schwein" as the Heimwehr troops stamp out the swastika candles she has helped her lover plant in the snow. Her reasons for accompanying him on that political mission are neither ideological nor sentimental, she claims. "I'm doing it because I'm sick of the sight of my own face in the mirror and I haven't a book to read and there isn't a show worth seeing" (*DOM*, 139).

But despite her scorn of "romance," she will learn that only a commitment to something outside herself can give her life purpose. Alone in Vienna, she sees clearly for the first time what makes her different from her lover: "what he's never said to me is he believes in something . . . fighting like a fool for something . . . and I haven't even got that to make me look like a good imitation of somebody going somewhere and caring where they're going . . . so that I'm free all right; yes, sure, I'm free, so free I have nothing to do but take tonight or tomorrow night to a café table and stretch it out like a corpse on public exhibition" (*DOM*, 279).

What Kay Boyle saw in Austria in the thirties and what Pendennis must learn from the doctor is that one cannot, at will, remain separate from the world. The people of Prochaska's country have no personal lives. In a country in which young men take to the roads singing for a few schillings in order to eat, their only legacy despair, and in which many of the young people, such as the ski-instructors the author knew in Kitzbühel, "were among a generation that had never tasted meat in their entire lives,"[68] twenties-style individualism is not an option. Unfortunately the answer, the people think, is Adolf Hitler. The doctor's feelings toward the people's "savior" reflect a naïveté that is chilling in retrospect: "Because of one man we can now lift our heads again, we can remember our history without shame because of this promise made in our own tongue to us, not that we shall be conquerors, not that we shall be rich, envied, monstrously great, but only this, that I and every other man of my country will be able to put new shoes on for once in his life, hold a girl in his arms, be warm in winter, drink wine in the evening!" (*DOM*, 87). The peasant women speak affectionately of that man as "A.," and in their minds he has become "a figure so heroic that, in becoming the example each man set for himself and the man each woman carried in her blood, he was deprived of features, flesh and not alone of homogeneousness but even of reality, bearing resemblance in the individual mind to Plato, Gary Cooper, Lenin, or the Son of God, like a statue each one raised to love of man or love of liberty" (*DOM,* 132).

While the author intended the title *Death of a Man* to indicate simply her belief that "Prochaska was a lost man, his commitment to the Nazi cause his doom,"[69] this "deprivation of features," the submergence of individual identity in something beyond oneself, lends resonance to that phrase. Pendennis learns—too late—that the only meaning she has a hope of finding in her life will come when she surrenders her individual pride and merges with another human being. The doctor believes that he will find himself by losing himself in his love of country. Trying to make Pendennis understand his devotion to a political cause, he explains:

> Very well, the photograph is like this: granite hills, glaciers, and starvation in spite of what you're burning up and killing and throwing away into lakes over there. That's the picture, and I'm very big in the foreground of it, immense, enormous, very strong and without any cowardice, not even the ordinary amount of cowardice every man is entitled to, because I am no longer a man, do you understand? I am no longer myself even, believing as I do in the future. I am a signal, a sign of what is about to happen, I am, because I have made the choice between existing and not existing, the center of the photograph. (*DOM,* 91)

By coming to the judgment that he is "no longer a man" but "a signal, a sign of what is about to happen," by accepting the "death" of his identity as an individual, Prochaska believes he will live in a more significant way, as part of something transcending his own meager self. It is an interesting indication of the author's evolving values that one of the most unsympathetically portrayed characters in the novel is the local innkeepers's wife, who does not want to get involved in any outside cause. Apprehensive that any political commitment might hurt business, she forbids her more idealistic daughter to throw food up to the hungry Nazi patriots leaning out of the jail windows for fear the cakes might be traced to her gasthaus. In the author's view she is a coward and a philistine.

Kay Boyle was roundly criticized by some for her sympathetic portrait of Nazis in "The White Horses of Vienna" and *Death of a Man.* When "The White Horses of Vienna" was given the O. Henry Award, Clifton Fadiman, one of the judges, dissented on the grounds that it was pro-Nazi.[70] The author has never understood his protest, nor her sister's stand in not speaking to their mother for an entire year (although they lived in the same house) because Mrs. Boyle defended Kay's purpose in writing the story. "In writing *Death of a Man* and 'The White Horses of Vienna' I was seeking to find out, on a human level, what the almost inexplicable fascination of Hitler was," she explains. "Mother always understood. I remember her writing to me at the time, 'the true artist presents; he does not judge.' Whether completely true or not, it gave me great solace."[71]

It does appear that Kay Boyle, whose life-long dedication to human rights and the dignity of the individual is indisputable, might have been momentarily moved by the passionate intensity and promise of the early Nazis. In 1935 she had written to Bob Brown from Kitzbühel:

> Last night we sat up listening to Hitler on the radio (it is forbidden to listen to him in Austria but we get away with it in secret) and now we wonder how the Saar went and whether there will be trouble. It was strangely thrilling to hear the officials giving their directions to the inhabitants of the Saar how to "make their mark" on the ballots, and the really moving appeal of Hitler to them to return to the Fatherland. The French speeches were disgusting—all finance and big promises and wide arguments and assurances by slick-tongued diplomats. I prefer the emotional thing, and the Germans have got it in Hitler anyway.[72]

But any sympathy she might have felt for the "moving appeal" of Hitler was fleeting. At a time when "Heil Hitler" was the acceptable telephone greeting, when everywhere one went in Germany the greeting from waiters, hotel employees, gas station and shop attendants, doctors, and museum guards was invariably the same, Kay Boyle was considered lacking in humor by some of her American friends because she would not, even jokingly as they did, respond likewise. "I never could, and never did, speak those two words in greeting, but always answered with '*Gutentag*' in Germany, and (later) in Austria with '*Grüss Gott*,' " she explains.[73] She and Laurence Vail lived by choice in the only anti-Nazi hotel in Kitzbühel.

Yet, living in Austria in the early thirties, Kay Boyle was, of course, personally acquainted with Nazis and Nazi sympathizers. She recalls that while nursing her baby daughter Kathe late at night in Kitzbühel, she would discuss the evils of fascism with the young nurse they had for the children. It was she who described to the author how the swastika fires were lit on the mountainsides; she did it herself several nights a week. This nurse, "of whom I was very fond," Kay Boyle claims, had told her several times "that she had never met a Jew and would be incapable of remaining in the same room with one if such an unforeseen thing should occur." When Peggy Guggenheim came to Kitzbühel to bring her daughter Pegeen for the summer and to take Sindbad with her to Italy, Kay Boyle did not tell the nurse that their visitor was Jewish. She waited until after Guggenheim's departure, after the nurse had eaten a number of meals at the same table with Peggy, to reveal this fact. The nurse was deeply troubled. " 'Well, then, I have learned something about myself and my beliefs,' she said, and she never brought up again the question of the unbearable presence of Jews," the author recalls.[74]

Perhaps Kay Boyle's personal relationships with people like the young nurse account for the depth and authenticity of such characters as the Tyrolean doctor of "The White Horses of Vienna" and Dr. Prochaska of *Death of a Man*. The doctor of the novel, in fact, was not the author's invention. When first her daughter Sharon and then Laurence and Apple contracted diptheria in 1935, she spent several weeks helping to care for them in the *Infektionhaus* in Innsbruck while Laurence's sister Clotilde came from Paris to supervise the care of the other children back in Kitzbühel. It was at that hospital, in which much of the novel is set, that Kay Boyle came to know very well the young doctor "who was so persuaded by Hitler's promises of a better economic life for all Austrians." "It was his character, and his political problems, which constituted a large part of my eagerness to write the book," she says.[75] It is true that she has presented her Nazi protagonists with some sympathy. But what the critics apparently overlooked is that while she might have admired the fervent commitment of these men to a cause beyond themselves, she had expressed in her novel deep reservations about the cause itself.

Like Pendennis, who suddenly realized her need for commitment, Dr. Prochaska also experiences a moment of recognition near the end of the novel. On a nighttime mission for the local Nazi organization, he is awestruck by the stillness of nature, by the "inviolate, impersonal mountains winding from one country to another without barrier," and he comes to a mystical consciousness of "the mutability of existence, that interchange of substance which in exempting men and matter from individual being exempted them from death and annihilation and despair" (*DOM*, 293). Talking with a young Nazi courier, he finds himself interrupting the boy's verbatim recitation of Hitler's latest radio speech, not knowing that he was going to speak: "So what do you think will happen in the end? A lot of uproar and shouting and bloodshed in the streets, and then what will we come back to but this quiet, this absolute stillness of the mountains in the end? Where in the world do you think we're going . . ." (*DOM*, 298). That is the night he decides to abandon his party responsibilities in order to search for Pendennis in Vienna. Even the dedicated doctor doubts the value of his cause when weighed against the value of human love and the harmony of nature. Kay Boyle most definitely is not pro-Nazi or pro-war in this novel. What she does espouse is the need for a bonding between human beings, both individually and collectively, and she abhors the barriers of individual or collective pride that get in its way.

Kay Boyle the stylist is again very much in evidence in *Death of a Man*—too evident, some would continue to say. One of the more caustic reviewers wrote: "It should burn off, but will it? A writer needs some sort of whip of discipline and he needs solid ground under his feet; and Kay Boyle not only continues to go the fancy way of her own self-indulgence, she now gets absolutely over her head in all this land, ancestors, mysticism, and kraut." He adds: "in general she is so determined to be sensitive to scenery and mood at every turn that the god's truth is you can't see the forest for the prose."[76]

In this novel she does continue to experiment with language, respecting no distinctions between subjective and objective realities. At night a band of phantom mothers, psychological projections of their homesick children, winds through the ward at the Infektionhaus in a surrealistic parade. She continues to employ vivid and unusual metaphors, describing a dying boy, "his cheeks stained with fever and his body and limbs drawn hourly longer and whiter and thinner, with death holding him fast and grim by the feet and pulling and grinning, and life or what he knew or now remembered of it with her hands in his curls and pulling hard the other way" (*DOM,* 124). She is fascinated, too, by grotesque characters like the middle-aged lay nurse, Sister Resi, who is infatuated with Dr. Prochaska. In her wounded pride (he had once playfully posed for a snapshot with her, putting his arm around her and calling her "my girl"), she spies on him at night and reports his carryings on with Pendennis in an anonymous letter to the hospital administration. A vain woman, she cannot see in the mirror "the yellow skin and the few white locks and the long sly-seeming nose with the pores as thick as leather" (*DOM,* 59), nor the hump that "rides" on her back and casts a shadow "like a monstrous camel" on the wall of the ward as she snores in the candlelight beside a dying child.

The prose is at times incantatory, a virtuoso performance. In this novel Kay Boyle even begins to sound a bit like William Faulkner, whose influence on her style she later would freely acknowledge. The opening sentence reads:

> If it is Sunday the shops are shuttered and closed for the day and the doctor from the town hospital is that dark and hot-eyed young man moving quickly and singly along the solemn sabbatical streets, alone among the coupled others, his mountain boots and mountain corduroys on and his rucksack on his shoulders, seemingly without the time as well as the inclination to fix the women or the men in his bold nervous glance but going towards the country outside, his destination secret from them. (*DOM,* 3)

The Faulknerian flavor first evident in passages of *Death of a Man* would dominate her next book, *Monday Night* (1938).

There is nothing new about the concern for love or the celebration of the passions or the stylistic skill that Kay Boyle displays in *Death of a Man.* But the book does indicate a growing tendency to treat matters of the contemporary social world that in the next decade would come to supersede her commitment to aesthetic revolution. At least one critic of the time, Mark Van Doren, noted the change in direction, and although he feared that the author's work was "so topical" that "many of her pages would be unintelligible to one not conversant with the foreign news," he generally approved: "Always conspicuous for the detachment of her method, Miss Boyle now flings herself headlong into the stream of passing life and produces a 'significant' novel."[77]

In *Death of a Man* Dr. Prochaska tries to explain to Pendennis that there are "things that cannot be separated from myself" (*DOM,* 84). "I suppose there have to be ancestors, antecedents crowding the picture?" she retorts, and he tries to make her see that he is inextricably bound to family, to friends, to his entire nation, that he even has a role to play in history. Kay Boyle herself always had realized that the individual is part and parcel of all humankind, and by the mid-thirties she was moving away from the idiosyncratic vision she had expressed in her work of the twenties to focus her attention on the social world. It is not a journey she made alone. Many other writers were following the same course in the thirties. Hemingway is the obvious example, as the "separate peace" of *A Farewell to Arms* (1929) gave way by 1940 to the recognition in *For Whom the Bell Tolls* that no man is an island entire of itself. As the exiles returned and the solipsistic twenties became the socially conscious thirties, the direction of Kay Boyle's art paralleled the movement. The artist who had proclaimed in 1929, "The writer expresses. He does not communicate," wished now to communicate her deep concern for what was happening to her fellow men and women in the functioning world.

5

Interlude: *Monday Night* and
The Crazy Hunter

In the summer of 1936, Kay Boyle and Laurence Vail left the political
turmoil of Austria to spend a year in England. When they returned with
their children to the continent it was to the village of Mégève in the
French Alps, where the family lived in their chalet until war forced them
back to America in 1941. For a while, thanks to Laurence's inheritance,
Kay Boyle was free to write without regard for the marketability of her
work. These were vintage years in which she produced two of her finest
books, *Monday Night* (1938) and *The Crazy Hunter: Three Short Novels*
(1940). Based neither on her own experiences in exile nor on her observations of the broad social scene, they are unlike anything she wrote before
or has written since. The works are a perfectly balanced synthesis of her
long-standing concerns for the personal struggle and for aesthetic experimentation and her emerging tendency to deal in her fiction with matters
of the external world. As in many of her other works of the thirties, the
author distances herself from the conflicts she explores, and her characters live in what she later would term a "functioning world."[1] There are
topical references to the postwar poverty of Germany and Austria, to the
Spanish Civil War, and to the rise of Mussolini and Hitler. But unlike the
contemporary events that motivate the conflict in *Death of a Man*, here
they are simply stage props, lending the authenticity of a "real world"
context to the human drama at hand. In *Monday Night* and *The Crazy
Hunter* the author's primary focus is on the individual heart and psyche,
and she probes them with an acuteness and intensity and in an experimental style reminiscent of her best work of the twenties. And in the works
she produced in this brief interlude, she also makes some of her most
eloquent and explicit statements of the human need for love.

   Wilt Tobin, the protagonist of *Monday Night*, is a shabby newspaperman living in Paris who has been writing for twenty-five years. Citing
Sherwood Anderson as an example, he muses that maybe newspaper
writing is "where the real genius is today," and he tells his companion,
"Writing for a lot of people is just as good as writing for only a few people,

and it's just as ree-foined. . . . If you're dealing in words, you're dealing in words, and that's what counts" (*MN*, 35).[2] But his dream is to write a book. For twenty-five years the material has eluded him. Kay Boyle suggests that one problem may be his rootlessness, his lack of a people with whom he can identify. Perhaps he ought to have lived in another country, he thinks: "My heroes aren't French, maybe they're not Latin. Maybe they haven't any nationality or any fixed bivouac, maybe they don't exist any more, maybe they're all dead" (*MN*, 35). One Monday outside the Gare St. Lazare, he encounters Bernie (short for St. Bernard) Lord, a wet-behind-the-ears Chicagoan fresh out of medical school. He has come to Paris on a pilgrimage to see a Dr. Sylvestre, renowned toxicologist. Sylvestre is something of a legend in the medical world; on the sole basis of his expert testimony a number of men have been convicted of murder by poisoning and several executed.

When Wilt takes on Bernie as his companion and offers to help him locate the doctor, he thinks that he is on the trail of a hero, that he is finally about to discover the material for a book. The plot of Boyle's novel, stripped bare, is a detective story. We follow the pair through Paris and environs from Monday night to Tuesday morning in search of the elusive man whom Bernie has come to Paris to see, the man Wilt thinks will be the subject of the book he has been waiting all his life to write.

In a taxicab Wilt tries to explain to Bernie his long-standing intention to write a book about the young Johann Sebastian Bach:

"I'm going to write the life of this man, just this one man, but I'm going to do it so that in the end it might be anybody's life, your life or my life," he said. "This man, it might be you coming to Paris or me coming to Paris, wanting to see the right people at the right time, wanting the way every human being does to keep his head above water—not to get ahead of everybody else and do them in, but just to put over the special thing you've got. This fellow happened to be a musician, but he might have been anything, a writer, a doctor, but he just happened to be what he was. . . . The way I want to work the book out, it ought to come pretty close to poetry, to symbolism—something like an allegory. It's going to follow the outline, without plagiarizing, just in a vague loose way, of something like 'Pilgrim's Progress.' " (*MN*, 36)

Through Wilt Kay Boyle seems to have articulated her own aims in writing *Monday Night*. As he says, the story of one man's life "might be anybody's life," but the "one man" on whom she has based her protagonist she has identified as Harold Stearns. An American writer, he had come to Paris in 1921, where, according to one chronicler of the period, he "sat in cafés, drank his drinks, and read Anatole France without fear of the law." He supported his habits by covering the race tracks for the Paris *Tribune* under the name of "Peter Pickem."[3] He briefly figures in

The Sun Also Rises as Harvey Stone, sitting alone at the Select with a pile of saucers in front of him and needing a shave.

The only weaving Kay Boyle says she ever saw being done at Raymond Duncan's colony in the late twenties was her own repairing of the worn shirt collars and cuffs Stearns brought her, but "once he began to talk," she says, "you forgot the stubble-covered jowls packed hard from drink, and the stains of food on his jacket lapels, and the black-rimmed fingers holding his glass" (*BGT,* 291). She claims never to have questioned the truth of anything he said: "I knew if the things he described had not happened in his lifetime they had happened sometime, somewhere else, or else they should have happened; and if they had not happened to him, he believed by this time that they had, and one had no right by any word, or look, or gesture to take this desperately accumulated fortune of belief away" (*BGT,* 291). Besides identifying the "one man" whose story she would tell, Kay Boyle has made it equally clear that, like Wilt Tobin, she intends her book to be "something like an allegory," following the out-line "just in a vague loose way, of something like 'Pilgrim's Progress.' " She dedicates the New Directions edition of the novel to its publisher, James Laughlin, "Who, unique among publishers of his generation, deals with imponderables: 'What the artist calls good, the object of all his playful pains, his life-and-death jesting . . . the parable of the right and the good, a representative of all human striving after perfection.' "[4]

The book has a strong flavor of moral allegory. Wilt and Bernie clearly are engaged in a quest. Wilt sees a universal beauty in his companion's journey to Paris to meet the great doctor and compares it to Bach's having spent his last two ducats to get to Hamburg where he would hear a great organist play. The author also describes them as type characters—with her usual edge of irony—as she depicts a tireless Wilt leading his increasingly cranky friend through the streets of Malmaison in pursuit of Sylvestre, not letting him abandon his search to such banalities as hunger and fatigue: "he led Bernie down the side street, the hopelessness of the one drawn meanderingly in the wake of the other's purpose and resolve. Mutt and Jeff, Laurel and Hardy, names given to those qualities as familiar as the cent and dollar mark, symbol of the bewilderment and the vanity of one's being of which uproarious comedy or uproarious tragedy can be made" (*MN,* 44–45).

But what makes the story so intriguing and complex is the protean nature of Dr. Sylvestre, the object of the quest. To Bernie he is something of a god: "This man Sylvester, to me there's nothing like him, he's as great as anyone in history," he tells Wilt (*MN,* 52). When the proprietors of a local bar gossip of the doctor's miserable marriage to a hard English-woman, Bernie's image of the man is not tarnished but enhanced. Sylves-tre becomes "Quixotic in the flesh, an enigma to them, not comprehended and therefore betrayed" (*MN*, 53). "Of course he's hated!" Bernie protests, echoing Emerson's assertion that to be great is to be misunderstood. In his eyes Sylvestre is great because his faith in the truth "had quailed before none of the authorities: not before nature, nor science, nor the Law" (*MN*, 54).

But when Bernie and Wilt finally reach the doctor's home only to learn he is not there, they spend the night talking and drinking with his servants, and Wilt begins to reflect on what he knows about Sylvestre and the men his testimony has condemned. He slips into a long, intense reverie, and speaking in "a bewitched passive voice" begins to spin another history of the great doctor, arriving at quite a different "truth" about the man. The condemned had had in common perfect motives for their crimes. Each supposedly had killed for the sake of love—to inherit enough money to marry, for example. In each case, someone standing in the way of this fulfillment had suddenly and conveniently died of internal ailments, thought to be natural until Sylvestre had performed his autopsies on the victims. Every one of the accused had vehemently protested his innocence to the end. From the servants Wilt also learns that before his marriage, Sylvestre had been living for three or four years with a young Frenchwoman, a woman who had recognized his gift for science and "encouraged him not to let it stop there at just being a pharmacy owner but to go on and do what he had it in him to do." She had helped him set up a laboratory in a corner of their room in Montmartre "not caring about the muck and mess he made" as he pursued his dream of becoming a toxicologist, while she painted and sold lampshades "to keep body and soul together" (*MN*, 125). "He dealt in death," Wilt thinks, "and worse than that, with all the accoutrements and manifestations of unnatural death, while she was the purveyor or life to him" (*MN*, 130). Then Sylvestre had met an Englishwoman with money and abandoned the woman who had loved and supported him so selflessly—"dropped her like a hot potato," in the words of the Scots servant girl (*MN*, 130). Soon thereafter she had given birth to a son who died. "He can't look at a woman since it happened. I know that much aboot him," the servant girl reports (*MN*, 132).

Suddenly Wilt sees "the man they had created piece by piece among them": "Wilt saw him clearly as he must be now, afraid of youth, afraid of passion, afraid of people wanting or having each other because these were the names of the things he himself had lost" (*MN*, 133). He comes to the startling realization that the great toxicologist, embittered by the recognition of his own loss of love, has used his knowledge to destroy the lives of others in love. He sees a bitter irony in Sylvestre's exceptional expertise and his role as dispenser of justice: " 'That's a riot. That's funny,' he said. 'God himself making him a present of the one thing he could use to avenge himself on God' " (*MN*, 133). With this new recognition, the nature of Wilt's quest changes. He now takes it as his personal mission to expose the truth about Sylvestre—a man "scarred, pitted, revoltingly defaced by a misanthropy too savage to be repudiated" (*MN*, 144)—so that the doctor's victims still surviving in prisons might be freed.

The pilgrimage-turned-manhunt leads Bernie and Wilt back to Paris, where they call on a Madame Coutet, wife of one of the condemned. While it becomes apparent that Bernie is too rigid and narrow-minded to alter his long-held beliefs even when their foundations are shattered, Wilt demonstrates an unflagging idealism, a reverence for the truth, and a bottomless capacity for sacrifice. In a way, this "Pilgrim's Progress" becomes instead "Paradise Lost" and "Paradise Regained" as Wilt is beatified by his tireless, completely disinterested giving of himself to others.

He has abandoned his own work to take on Bernie's quest as his own, acting as his guide and refusing to let him give up. He shoulders the sorrows of Madame Coutet, whose husband has been in prison for seven years as a result of Sylvestre's testimony. He spends his last francs to rescue a trio of peasants from doling out their life's savings to an avaricious barman who has kept his place open three days and two nights so that they might continue to buy his drinks, and he gets a black eye in the effort. In his compassion for others, Wilt—the full-time Samaritan, unthanked, even scorned by the world—becomes almost Christ-like. In the world the author has created, this compassion is the only source of redemption, the only force powerful enough to confront the depravity of the man who once loved but fell from grace into "misanthropy too savage to be repudiated," the man who used his authority and learning to take "a good swipe at the rest of humanity because of what humanity hadn't done for him" (*MN*, 241).

Through Wilt Tobin, Kay Boyle comes as close as she ever does to stating directly in fiction her belief that love is the vital source of all meaning in human life, a force with the power to transform existence, the Holy Grail that all people seek but that few really understand or are able to find. Walking "with his lifted head bared in exaltation to the night's embrace," her shabby latter-day saint carries on an imaginary conversation with Bernie on the true nature of love:

> So love, he might have called back to the other man, still without turning, it is something you haven't had a taste of yet. You carry it, what you still think its essence is, like a flask on your hip and when you meet a skirt you pour what's left of the bottle into her mouth. It's like giving somebody an injection so they'll stop crying out, so their eyes will go wide and black with dope and they'll start dreaming the same dream you're dreaming. That isn't Love, Bernie, that isn't anything except what the biggest saps of all are satisfied to stop at. It's got to be something else, maybe something that was stamped there a long time ago,

before you came into the picture and will be still stamped there when you go out, something you can't get away from, like history, not a tune or an aria played one evening for two minutes on one string and a half and nobody very sure of the notes or who the composer was. I know what I'm talking about because I've been there the way only a few have been there and it's a one-way ride, Bernie, because you're never the same afterward even if you manage to get back. (*MN*, 94–95).

The author even appears to associate Wilt with Christ by giving him a wound sustained through suffering on behalf of humanity. He has a hideously mangled ear, which several people remark upon before we learn how it had happened. As Wilt tells it to Bernie, one night he had come home at one o'clock and could not find his own door, so he had cried, "Fire, fire!" up and down the stairs. In the scuffle with the concierge and the police, he had become, in the author's words, "emblem of man's persecution and mutinous despair." "That he had broken three windows and bitten the concierge through the arm were not so much manifestations of drunkenness as manifestations of that battle he had staged alone for the pity and sake of every other individual, in protest against the officiousness of what was authority or sanctimony or law" (*MN*, 41). "You don't have to give in," Wilt advises Bernie. "You don't have to be what they say, you can just keep on going the way you are. And in the end it'll happen. At the very end they'll see" (*MN*, 42).

But of course, at the very end, "they" do not see. Kay Boyle tempers her allegory of the redemptive power of compassion with a bitterly ironic conclusion. Wilt and Bernie finally learn that Sylvestre is in Lyons and make plans to catch the next train there. Wilt believes he is about to wrap up the case that will form the basis of the story he has waited a lifetime to write. At the station, just as they are about to leave Paris, he glances at a bystander's newspaper. The headline reads: "Eminent Toxicologist May Be Proven Criminally Insane . . . Master of Sciences Accused of Sending Innocent Men to Guillotine and Bagne" (*MN*, 271–72). Yet even though Wilt's hopes for his own future are shattered in that instant, his first thought is for Bernie. Lifting the newspaper out of the stranger's hands, he rushes to the third class waiting room where he had left his weary and exasperated companion only to find him gone. When he sits down to read the entire article, he is "not thinking that somebody else had got there first or thinking that he had known it when the others had not believed, but thinking I never thought to ask him what hotel so I won't be able to tell him and he won't think of buying a French paper so he'll go back to America maybe without knowing" (*MN*, 273). It is deeply ironic, too, that the original pilgrim in this journey (Bunyan called him "Christian"; Boyle names him "Lord") learns nothing. In the course of his quest, Bernie's mind has never risen above his concern over the number of francs the taxi will cost or the fact that it is past his regular mealtime, and he probably never will learn the truth about the man he had crossed an ocean to find.

Yet despite his ultimate failure, Wilt gains stature and glory through his idealism and his dedication to the quest for truth. And the quest has not been entirely futile. In the final sentence of the novel, he reaches into his pocket and takes out a glove belonging to Madame Coutet, reminding himself and the reader of the one thing he had accomplished that night. With no hope of ever seeing her husband again, Madame Coutet had sought relief from her loneliness first in a lesbian relationship with a woman who would dress up in Coutet's army uniform and later in a series of liaisons with faceless men. For years she had worked long hours to support the son born the day her husband had been condemned and whom he had never seen. By calling on her, Wilt had jolted her out of her numbed day-by-day existence and had reminded her of her commitment to her husband. "So now when he gets out there'll be something prepared for him, not finished, but something better than if I'd never—" Wilt thinks (*MN*, 260). The novel ends with a small victory—merely the resurrection of meaning in the life of one human being.

Monday Night is as complex and sophisticated in style as any of the fiction the author produced in the heyday of the Revolution of the Word. Its very first paragraph indicates that this will be no simple tale. In her description of a pharmacy window, Kay Boyle sounds a great deal like William Faulkner:

> Between two magnums of what was stamped Odorono in the familiar colors and print (but which was only tinted water bottled for display) were stacked the pastel rolls of the French imitations of Kleenex, protected by a cellophane so phony that it had torn of itself while lying at rest in the undecipherable jumble of syringes, quill tooth-picks, fards of the prevalent cheap French marks, tooth-brushes with renewable bristle sections, or Mickey Mouses on their handles, and the canvas and leather supports for hernia and corpulence. This already vast display was at least doubled by the mirrors which took the corners in three faces and reflected in painstaking detail the chaos of unrelated objects behind the plate glass as well as the chaos of pedestrians and vehicles that moved outside it. The four completely filled windows made the angle of the square and the street, and everything they held retreated in panic from the glass into what could with difficulty be distinguished as a reflection of the passing public and the passing traffic, a drop curtain of curious animation on which only the Gare St. Lazare and the buildings near it had been painted absolutely still. (*MN*, 3–4)

It is not only the syntax that is Faulknerian. In the same way that the reader must sort through the chaos of the window display to distinguish reality from distorted reflections of it, Wilt Tobin can arrive at truth only by piecing together constructions of his imagination. As Wilt lapses into a reverie and speculates in a "bewitched passive voice" on the doctor's past, the true nature of Sylvestre emerges through layers of conjecture. Wilt's long internal monologue and his exploratory exchanges with Sylvestre's servants are reminiscent of the Harvard dormitory dialogue between Quentin Compson and Shreve MacCannon in Faulkner's *Absalom, Absalom!* in which the youths imaginatively reconstruct one night the entire history of a century-old Southern dynasty.

While this novel has the strongest Faulknerian flavor of any of Kay Boyle's works, earlier pieces also suggest his influence. The aging standard-bearers of a dying aristocracy who people such Gothic tales as "Keep Your Pity" and "Dear Mr. Walrus" are close kin to Miss Emily Grierson in "A Rose for Emily." Passages of *Death of a Man* are written in a convoluted, incantatory prose that sounds more like Faulkner than Boyle. To be sure, not all the resemblances can be attributed to "influence." From the beginning, Kay Boyle had been creating characters and scenes of great psychological depth and authenticity, and for years she had written in an intricate, experimental style—a "language of hallucination" more readily traceable to the Left Bank than to Oxford, Mississippi. In fact, at the time she wrote the short stories, she recalls having read only Faulkner's *Sanctuary,* an advance copy of which the publisher had sent to her in Nice; she says, "I disliked it so vehemently that I determined then that I never wanted to read anything else of his."[5]

But there is no doubt that later Kay Boyle *was* inspired by William Faulkner. In the same year that she published *Monday Night,* she reviewed Faulkner's *The Unvanquished,* calling him "the most absorbing writer of our time" and herself "one who loves Faulkner's work and has followed it closely and impatiently." She praised in particular his "process of development, subtly, heedfully, skillfully accomplished through the seemingly inevitable metamorphosis of speech."[6] Years later she would say, "I believe Faulkner has influenced my style in several things I've written, particularly in 'Monday Night.' I admire him more than any living American writer."[7] Today she writes, "As for Faulkner's undeniable influence on my style (at least in certain unmistakable instances), let us say that I did not share Faulkner's political views, but that we apparently used the same thesaurus."[8] Others, too, have noticed the similarity between Kay Boyle's style at times and William Faulkner's. McAlmon saw it and disapproved: "Kay Boyle is overcome by the swooning moonlight of his precious moments to such an extent that she, often a fine writer in a sound sense, goes too, too fine for the ordinary mortal" (*BGT,* 253).

But another quality of Faulkner's writing that may also have drawn her to him is the faith in the integrity and worth of the individual that under-

lies his work, a reverence for humanity that he would express most elo-
quently twelve years after the publication of her novel. In his Nobel Prize
acceptance speech Faulkner said: "I believe that man will not merely
endure: he will prevail. He is immortal, not because he alone among
creatures has an inexhaustible voice, but because he has a soul, a spirit
capable of compassion and sacrifice and endurance."[9] These are Kay
Boyle's convictions as well. Faulkner had said in his speech that it is the
writer's duty to write about these things, that "The poet's voice need not
merely be the record of man, it can be one of the props, the pillars to help
him endure and prevail." Boyle would write in 1963 that the writer's role
"has always been to speak . . . of the dignity and integrity of individual
man."[10] It is clear that in 1938 she had recognized and responded to
Faulkner's humanism when she wrote in her review, "Faulkner and Poe,
set far enough apart in time, are strangely kin: unique in our history in
their immunity to literary fashion, alike in their fanatical obsession with
the unutterable depths of mankind's vice and even more with his divinity."[11] It is these "unutterable depths" of humanity's vice and divinity
that Kay Boyle herself has explored in *Monday Night,* and to this day she
calls it "the most satisfying book I ever wrote" (*BGT,* 291).[12]

Monday Night was followed two years later by *The Crazy Hunter,* a
collection of three short novels. "The Crazy Hunter," "The Bridegroom's Body," and "Big Fiddle" are stylistically sophisticated studies of
complex characters in desperate need of connection. The author's focus is
on the individual's search for a meaningful existence. But these works
differ from her more personal fiction of the twenties in that the people
and the conflicts she presents are products of her imagination rather than
of her actual experience. By achieving a fine balance between emotional
involvement with and intellectual detachment from her material, Kay
Boyle has endowed the personal struggles of unique individuals with
universal power and significance.

The protagonist of "The Bridegroom's Body" is a tough-seeming
woman who grows into a painful new awareness of her loneliness in a
world where women have no place. The one critic who has examined the
story in depth remarks upon the "brilliant evocation of milieu." The
setting—"the rain-drenched coast of southern England where the
Glouries live in their great, bare, stone manor"—is "an objective correla-
tive for the inner lives of the people in the story."[13] Now that her two
children have gone off to school, Lady Glourie lives alone with her husband on their country estate, where shooting and fishing, looking after
the family swannery, and worrying about foot-rot among the sheep are
the sum and substance of life. She is weary of this masculine world: "The
sound of men, all day, all year without a break, the sound of men: a man

serving at the table, a man in the kitchen, as if it were not only the wild cold countryside that drew men to it but as if all life itself and right to life were man's" (*TSN*, 149).[14]

Yet, isolated in this environment, she has absorbed its values and become estranged from femininity. Lady Glourie has cropped hair and a "big pair of shoulders strong as a wood yoke set across her freckled neck," and she smokes Gold Flakes (*TSN*, 144). She is proud that her daughter "had never liked dolls for a minute, mind you, never once, never at any time" (*TSN*, 155). When the swanherd's wife becomes ill in a difficult pregnancy, Lady Glourie sends reluctantly to London for a trained nurse, "a woman-sort-of-thing," although she fears they are "probably more trouble than they're worth" (*TSN*, 147). She writes "in a bold strong man-like hand," "I wouldn't be bother [sic] with women down here atall if it wasn't for this."

Yet the idea of a female companion gradually takes hold in her, and we begin to grasp the enormity of her loneliness. She walks the grounds engaged in imaginary conversations with the nurse she has never met, looking forward to the time she might speak to someone of the son and daughter who are gone. She imagines sharing with her new friend the poems she had written as a schoolgirl. Or, she thinks, "if you were not too old we might be able to laugh out loud, uproariously, senselessly, standing shouting with laughter at something the way men scream with laughter together" (*TSN*, 157). She confides, "Miss Smith, Miss Kennedy, Miss Forthright, there is nobody left, no one. . . . If I change the flowers every day and keep on talking to you, perhaps I can keep it from you for a little while that there is nothing left here, that everyone here has died" (*TSN*, 156).

But when the woman arrives she is not the middle-aged trained nurse Lady Glourie had pictured, with "parcels of pain tied up" in her legs "from having stood thirty years too long by bedsides" (*TSN*, 155). Miss Cafferty is a delicate Irish girl in a green silk dress and high-heeled shoes—a bitter dissapointment to the lady of the estate, herself given to tweeds and cardigans and "the heavy brogues a man might have worn" (*TSN*, 148). Lady Glourie gruffly warns her that the swanherd's baby must be a boy, for the swannery is passed on from father to son, and she snaps that Miss Cafferty ought to get better shoes for the country.

But a week later, as Lady Glourie passes the nests where the swans live in monogamous pairs, she experiences a shock of recognition. A "sudden and unforeseen vortex of compassion" for Miss Cafferty sweeps over her, and she thinks, "Even me, a woman, too hard, too defiant, so that she came into this domain of locked, welded mates an outcast, to be kicked up and down the hill from one wedded couple to another, the Jo Luckys, the Panrandalls, the Glouries, the violently mated swans, and nothing but suspicion offered her" (*TSN*, 173). Suddenly Lady Glourie sees her "gentle as a young lamb to be nursed in the heart" (*TSN*,173). Her tenderness for the young woman grows as Miss Cafferty's spirit, intelligence, sensitivity, and social conscience emerge in her conversations with the Glouries. At the same time, Lord Glourie, seeing that his attentions to the girl are unreturned, grows bitter and suspicious. When Miss Cafferty tries to explain to them that sometimes in the night she feels a "desperation of the heart as well as of the flesh," that she then must get outdoors and walk no matter what the weather is, Lord Glourie becomes testy. His small mind, with its narrow concept of women, can fathom only one explanation: she must be seeing the young farmer of the estate.

In the climactic scene, Lady Glourie battles the vicious old patriarch of the swans to retrieve the body of a young cob he killed in a struggle over the younger one's right to establish a nest for himself and his mate on the older swan's territory. Miss Cafferty looks on, paralyzed with terror, as Lady Glourie wades into the freezing pond to retrieve the body of the young "bridegroom" who had died for the love and protection of his mate—her white nightgown billowing up and trailing behind her on the water so that she herself resembles the swans who had battled to the death. The scene illustrates the skill and subtlety of Kay Boyle's craftsmanship at its best, the charged image woven into the narrative so that it seems at first a mere surface detail. Overcome with admiration for the other woman's strength and courage, Miss Cafferty bursts out in a sudden confession of passion that startles Lady Glourie and the reader: "Let me say it! I came out to think about you here alone where there might be something left of you somebody hadn't touched—some place you were in the daytime—some mark of you on the ground. . . . I couldn't sleep in the room. I couldn't bear closing the door after I'd left you, just one more door closed between what you are and what I am!" (*TSN*, 203). She had recognized Lady Glourie's loneliness and her entrapment in an existence devoid of women's tenderness. "Don't you think I see you living in this place alone," she cries, "alone the way you're alone in your bed at night, with butchers, murderers—men stalking every corner of the grounds by day and night? . . . don't you think I fought them all off because of you, because I knew that fighting them was taking your side against them?" (*TSN*, 204).

When the swanherd and Lord Glourie finally come upon them on the path, the women are staring at each other in the moonlight, transfixed. Then "Lady Glourie looked down at the nightdress clinging to her own strange flesh and suddenly she began shaking with the cold" (*TSN*, 205). The story ends there. Lady Glourie is shaken by the other woman's declaration of love and by this confrontation with the barrenness of her own existence. Yet in that charged moment we sense that the possibility of connection between these women will be their only hope for warmth and satisfaction in a cold, masculine world.[15]

"Big Fiddle," another story of an isolated individual in desperate need of love, ends less "happily." The protagonist is an American musician—we know him only as "Big Fiddle"—leading a rootless existence in Europe, drifting from one job to the next. He is isolated even from the other players in his act, his own countrymen:

> Even when the time came for him to walk out on the platform with the other Americans, the foreignness, not of nation or of race, but the unutterable separateness, the alien and seemingly incurable thing went with him. Even the instrument he carried was too big, too unwieldy, and when they began to play, the bass viol sobbed deeply alone: "Oh, cure me, cure me," while the others swung, "Life Begins at Oxford Circus, Give Worry the Bird, Things Look Rosy If You Know How to Look," banging the notes out, roaring their hearts out to cure him, to comfort him, to give him the remedy. . . . But in the end, their own bewilderment and shyness stopped the music, cut short the life-line of normal speech which had not managed to reach him quite. (*CH,* 211)[16]

When this group breaks up after their London engagement, Big Fiddle heads south on the advice of a neurologist who has prescribed rest for the shakes and quivers that have plagued him for a year.

As in "The Bridegroom's Body," the author uses setting to counterpoint the psychological state of her character. Big Fiddle awakens in "inexplicable alarm" in the strange boarding house of an English seaside town. Lying alone in a bed "as narrow and single as a hammock," he knows only by the "stamping of his heart" that "this wouldn't be the eternity box then . . . but just the dress rehearsal for it" (*CH,* 216). As in some of Kay Boyle's works of the twenties, external reality takes on the configurations of the consciousness perceiving it: "The street light was still lit on the esplanade outside and in relief against its bright white ambiance the curtain's coarse lace rose, webbed, convoluted, and like a dying breath expired" (*CH,* 215). In his mind Big Fiddle begins to compose "the nightly letter home," addressed to a Father O'Malley. He passes the sleepless night engaged in an hallucinatory dialogue with the priest of the orphanage where he had spent his childhood.

That afternoon he meets a young woman in a teahouse. Her manner and her readiness to abandon any plans and spend the rest of the day and night with him indicate that she is not unused to making the most of chance encounters with men, but after they make love in a field outside of town (in the shadow of a penitentiary), Big Fiddle believes he has finally found an object for the tenderness locked inside him. To him she has become "what still remained of pity's and salvation's corporeity" (*CH,* 250), and he plans to make the rest of his life with her. Grateful to have found at last the one who would truly understand him, he begins to relax and confide to her his troubled past. He had been raised in a Catholic orphanage and bitterly betrayed by the only girl he had ever loved. The darling daughter of Mrs. Carrigan, who ran the institution, she had made overtures to him when he was in his teens, and he had succumbed to the seduction. But the girl was already "in trouble," and to save her own skin she accused him of rape. He spent a year and a half in prison. "Eighteen months for doing nothing, for being a sap, for letting a damned little whore—" he tells his new love (*CH*, 254).

She is repulsed. Instead of responding to the injustice with sympathetic outrage, she scrambles to her feet and runs off into the darkness, crying, "You, jail-bird, doing what you did to me, and calling nice girls what you did—" (*CH*, 254). He hunts desperately all night for her but finally boards the boat to Capri, haunted by her memory. In a nightmarish, surrealistic passage the author accentuates his terrible loneliness and the devastation wreaked on his psyche by the endless deprivation of human contact:

> Once in the hotel room after lunch, the thing continued: the grotesquely masked and wigged, the enormous papier-maché figured and floated parade of reminiscence which had perhaps never halted but only digressed a little in its line of march went on; and he the solitary onlooker, the pressing sidewalk crowd of one, watched the gigantic mummers pass: Father O'Malley, frocked, and Mrs. Carrigan with the two white freckled folds of skin like curtains looped up at her throat, and the girls coming, the first one and the faceless nameless ones that followed, strutting and swinging and titubating singly or in formation down the avenue; until it was the moment for the English girl to come walking carefully and precisely past. He lay on the bed and watched her step fastidiously across the red-tiled Italian floor on which the flies were gathering thick as ants in the filtered pieces of hot light. The mosquito-netting hung from the ceiling and was spread around him, coarse, suffocating, white; the lengths of the wrong bride's veil, an ancient, simpering, painted bride who had spread it in wanton, Ophelia-cracked provocation around the surly reluctant groom. (*CH*, 275)

But "Big Fiddle," like *Monday Night*, is also a detective story of sorts. Beginning in the second chapter, even before Big Fiddle meets the woman in the teahouse, the narrative is mysteriously interrupted by fragments of conversation between an unidentified "Superintendent" in London and various lawmen elsewhere. An Italian count whom Big Fiddle had met on the boat coming to Capri and who had treated him coolly on board begins to seek out the musician's companionship, and Big Fiddle is flattered to a pathetic degree. Tension mounts as the reader recognizes a suspicious undertone to the unlikely friendship. When the count invites him to dinner, Big Fiddle is overwhelmed that such a man would be "asking a jail-bird, a delinquent, home" (*CH*, 271), and he eagerly accepts. An Englishman has also been invited. Over wine and hors d'oeuvres, Big Fiddle is lured into a conversation about his nerve problems, his interest in detective books, and his past relationships with women. The Englishman finally declares himself to be the Law. It seems the "little girl" Big Fiddle had picked up in the teahouse has been found dead and disfigured on the Downs near Brixton Beach. Big Fiddle is accused of her murder.

As the story ends, the voice of Father O'Malley, the orphanage priest, speaks the "pure, clear, exalted" words of the last rites as Big Fiddle, a victim once again, stands "swaying above the table at which the men still sat, holding to the chair's back for strength, and waiting, now that the voice had ceased praying, for the tears to gush, hot, childish, bitter from his eyes" (*CH*, 295). Once more he has been made vulnerable by his desperate craving for love, and again fate has slapped him in the face for attempting to establish the human contact that would give meaning to his desolate existence.

"The Crazy Hunter" is another impressively crafted testament to the human need for love. Again, Kay Boyle explores what one critic calls "the complex relation between a harsh and heartless external world and a tender, but sentimental and impractical internal world."[17] Nan Lombe, a seventeen-year-old girl, is back home in England on her family's horse-breeding farm after having spent the school year in Italy. She is restless within the confines of her childhood surroundings, aware now of a higher plane of existence, one peopled by students and artists. She longs to go back to that world in which "they are still on the adventure, looking for a thing nobody here wants or has heard of wanting: knowledge or the way to knowledge or else simply the way, because of what families and conventions want, of keeping curious and keeping free" (*TSN*, 9).

But she finds it impossible to communicate with her mother, to tell her how she has grown and changed. Mrs. Lombe is a strong woman, inaccessible behind her competence and confidence and common sense. On Nan's first day home, they go swimming together in a cold stream, and the silence hangs awkwardly between them. When Nan spots a bird dangling in a tree by a piece of fishing line it had swallowed, she is horrified, but her mother rescues it without fuss. The girl thinks:

> You can touch these things, you can touch death and wipe it off in your handkerchief afterwards and touch pain without shrinking from it but you cannot take me in your arms any more and when I am with you I am afraid. Mother, she said in silence not looking at the bird, come out of your stone flesh and touch me too and see how tall I am, my eye almost up to your eye, and how big my feet and hands are, like a woman's. But the cheek did not alter and did not color, and the girl made herself look down now at the bird. (*TSN*, 21)

Nan's father, Candy, is nothing like his wife. A bantam-like Canadian, he is a would-be artist who had married a frail consumptive girl with more money than he. After he had nursed her back to health in the high mountains of Europe, they had returned to her family home in England, where she gradually had become the strong, efficient horsewoman Nan has always known. Candy fills his days reading Woolworth paperback mysteries, meticulously grooming himself, and drinking. Long ago he had given up the pretense of sitting for hours paralyzed before a blank canvas.

As mother and daughter return from their swim, Mrs. Lombe confides to Nan her exasperation at Candy's latest foolishness. With strict instructions and some money, she had sent him to a horse fair, but, as usual, he had had a few too many drinks and had brought home a worthless gelding—a "crazy hunter" of a horse. But Nan will hear none of her mother's complaints about the man or the horse. As an act of defiance and a token of love for her father, she falls in love with the crazy hunter. Kay Boyle subtly but firmly makes a symbol of the horse and links it to Candy. When Nan first strokes her crazy hunter, she thinks (again in rather Faulknerian prose),

> Not my first horse or my second or even the third, but this time my horse in protest, my hunter in defiance; not with race and nervousness flickering down your crest and loins, but my bony-legged monster to gentle, to murmur alone to in fortification of my father's errors; the substance of identity and revolt and love to hold to, until I can see you like the oriflamme of what is nothing more violent than Candy and me walking down a street arm in arm together in another country, she said, the gloved hand moving on his neck under the mane's coarse glossy hair. With one finger she lifted the velvet of his lip and looked at the upper teeth laid bare in his mouth, breathing the warm hay-sweetened breath while the physical stab of love thrust in her. (*TSN*, 27)

The horse is "transformed to symbol for the separateness of two interpretations and two isolate despairs" (*TSN*, 39).

But suddenly the crazy hunter suffers a stroke that leaves him blind. The only sensible course is to destroy the animal. The local veterinarian, Penson, after examining the horse, says so, and the London doctor whom Mrs. Lombe brings in to satisfy her grief-stricken daughter concurs. But Nan and Candy square off against Mrs. Lombe and the veterinarians— irrational love versus common sense, the heart versus the head.

During the two-week reprieve Mrs. Lombe grants her daughter to come to her senses, Candy is torn between his loyalty to Nan and his own gut-terror of horses. He worries about her safety, and his fears are intensified when Penson is killed, kicked in the face by a horse he was treating. Nan clutches at any possibility to save her horse. She even writes for advice to an Irish student she had met at an afternoon tea in Italy. But like other inhabitants of Kay Boyle's world, she comes to a bitter realization: "She began seeing how it was now as a savage might have seen it and made a picture of it with berry stains, or some coloring as primitive, or stitched it toughly in beads or thread on cloth: the small helpless lone island of the self out of voice's call or swimmer's reach lying among the scattered inaccessible islands of those other selves" (*TSN,* 72). "She saw that unpeopled landscape and the vast waters washing forever unspanned between the separate islands, and she touched the bones in bed with her," realizing, "If there is any strength it is in these, it is here." In a world of isolated individuals, Nan can look only to herself for help.

In the course of the next two weeks, she steals into the stable every night, determined to make her horse understand that the world exists as it always had, even though he can no longer see it. She will teach him to walk, then be ridden, and finally to jump, in the conviction that with this evidence the standardbearers of common sense will be forced to recognize that his life has value. With hard work and love, she does begin to succeed in training the "worthless" animal. But the defenders of reason are not easily moved. When Nan receives an encouraging reply from her Irish friend saying he has heard of blind horses being successfully trained, Mrs. Lombe becomes bitter and exasperated. She tells the girl that she will not have her riding a blind horse and killing herself and the poor beast. "Thank God, there's a more humane way of putting it down," she says. Nan retorts: "Brigand's a He. . . . He's a man. You might speak of him like that." But her mother reminds her that the horse is a gelding: "There's no need to flatter it with a sex," she says (*TSN,* 81–82). Again we are subtly reminded of the crazy hunter's resemblance to Candy, himself "useless" and emasculated.

When Nan goes away overnight to attend a wedding in London as a guest of the Irishman, Mrs. Lombe finally sees the opportunity for reason to prevail. As Candy pours himself his first drink of the morning, he looks out the window to see his wife walking down the driveway with a stranger in khaki riding breeches. He knows what is about to happen, and in a way he is relieved. In his soggy reverie, Kay Boyle again makes clear that the situation of the crazy hunter, who has outlived his usefulness, is Candy's, too: "Horse, it's your turn to die. This time it's not Penson or me but you, horse not man, you blank-eyed espial spying upon the secrets of eternity, you milky-eyed deserter. You're no good to anyone, he said, but he was looking at his own face in the sideboard mirror" (*TSN,* 125).

But after the fifth glass of whiskey, he thinks of Nan and he knows what he must do. The story concludes in a dramatic standoff between Mrs. Lombe, accompanied by the man who had come to mark the lines in chalk on the horse's forehead, and Candy, who plants himself, pistol in hand, in the stall with the beast he fears, determined to wait it out until his "little girl" returns. Kay Boyle makes it plain that she considers Candy's rescue attempt an act of heroic proportions and universal moment—representing nothing less than the power of love standing up to the forces of desiccated reason that would have the parched heart wither away. Candy speaks thickly, leaning against the side of the stall:

> I'm waiting here for my little girl, I'm waiting, I'm on the side of civilization. This horse, he isn't a horse any moren any of us are horses, he's the forces of good against the forces of destruction, he's me, just as much me as artist, foreigner, just as much an outcast, he's freak and he's love, he's got something to do with love as it works out against—against this, this empire building and this susspression of the native, what you said the other night about Gandhi being so ugly himself, thin and his teeth out and his gums like that the way you would talk about a horse, you said he was such a freak you didn't care what his beliefs were and didn't think he could have any looking like—well, this horse is against that sort of thing. He's for love. (*TSN,* 133–34)

When the haulers come at eleven to remove the animal's body, Mrs. Lombe asks them to come back later. When they return in the afternoon, she requests their help in first removing her husband from the stall. Embarrassed and bewildered, but finally convinced the man is drunk, they begin to comply. Candy, confronted, shoots wildly into the air. The horse panics and rears, "while the little man lay pressed against the stall's side, his hands down, his head lifted, so far untouched and perhaps immuned by this passive, abeyant, this almost ludicrous posture of martyrdom" (*TSN,* 138). When at twenty past four Nan comes home, Mrs. Lombe quits the position she had taken outside the stable door and goes forward to meet her, "neither the thoughts or the words ready yet, nor the emotion nameable that shook her heart" (*TSN,* 139).

Candy, in his blind terror and blind love, pinned to the wood of the stable stall, is a ludicrous martyr, a freak—like the blind horse, like Gandhi, a bit like Christ. We are not allowed to forget that this is the act of a drunkard who must fortify himself in his heroic stand with draughts from his flask, who mortifies his wife throughout his sacred vigil by singing dirty jingles. His martyrdom is absurd—but truly noble. Once more, as she had in *Monday Night,* Kay Boyle allows love a small victory. In a work whose title coincidentally echoes that of another book published the same year by a woman who would come to be her close friend—Carson McCullers' *The Heart Is a Lonely Hunter*—she explores the insatiability of the human heart.[18] Candy has performed an act of awesome selflessness, confronting head on his own deepest terror in the name of love, ready even to die for it. The story ends ambiguously, Nan's reaction and the horse's fate left to conjecture. But in the "unnameable emotion" that

shakes the previously untouched heart of Mrs. Lombe there is the possibility of salvation. "The Crazy Hunter" is Kay Boyle's firmest and perhaps finest declaration of love's redeeming grace.

On June 27, 1939, the author wrote to her sister, "I think my 'Crazy
Hunter,' just finished two days ago is the best thing I've ever done, and I
do hope you'll like it."[19] In 1953 she would say of everything she had
written that "The Crazy Hunter" "remains one of my best, I think."[20] The
three short novels in the volume of the same name did not receive immediate recognition. "The Bridegroom's Body" "was rejected by every
magazine at the time I wrote it," she recalls, although it was finally
published in the *Southern Review*.[21] "Big Fiddle" first appeared in
another little magazine, *Phoenix*, and "The Crazy Hunter" was not published at all before appearing as the title piece of the collection. But in
1952 "The Crazy Hunter" was anthologized in Richard M. Ludwig and
Marvin B. Perry, Jr.'s *Nine Short Novels* in the company of widely acknowledged masterpieces by Conrad, Crane, Faulkner, James, Kafka,
Mann, and Twain.

The only heretofore published, in-depth critical discussion of her work
focuses on "The Crazy Hunter" and "The Bridegroom's Body," although the article did not appear until 1965, seven years after the pieces
were republished in *Three Short Novels*.[22] Not only is Kay Boyle a superb
stylist, the critic, Richard C. Carpenter, argues, but she is "an artist
deeply involved with one of literature's most enduring and significant
concerns"—what he calls "the perennial human need for love:" "Although on occasion she may have forgotten the artistic obligation in
exchange for sheer virtuosity (always a danger for the virtuoso), using her
style to bedazzle rather than to aid vision, or letting exotic setting obscure
the human situation with which she is dealing, in her better fiction, style,
setting, and theme form a seamless web in which all the threads are held
under a precise tension." "In two of her best pieces, the novelle *The
Bridegroom's Body* and *The Crazy Hunter*, she demonstrates this to
perfection," he adds.[23] These three short novels are reminiscent of the
works of Katherine Anne Porter in the subtlety and depth of their development and the "precise tension" of their craftsmanship. The 1940 edition of *The Crazy Hunter* volume is dedicated to her "in homage."

The balance between Kay Boyle's identities as aesthete in exile and
citizen of the functioning world already had begun to tip in her work of
the early thirties. Her fiction of the forties would become overtly political. But in her chalet in the Haute-Savoie, between the time she left the
political tumult of Austria and the time she would return to America with
war at her heels, she was able to write with deep sensitivity of the
struggles of individuals planted firmly in the social world. In that brief
interlude she produced some of her finest fiction. In *Monday Night* and in

the short novels of *The Crazy Hunter* she had achieved an exquisite balance between the psychological penetration and stylistic sophistication she had perfected in the twenties and the broader perspective of human dilemmas that had emerged in her less personal work of the thirties. They are complex, meticulously crafted works, exploring with subtlety and power the theme of "love that has been thwarted and shunted off into blind alleys"[24] but which still calls out strongly to the human heart.

6

The War Years: Politics and Potboilers

On the right-hand side of page five in the March, 1946, issue of the *Ladies' Home Journal,* a full-column advertisement depicts three wide-eyed women leaning over a backyard fence to watch their beaming young neighbor hang her laundry on the clothesline. "They turned *Green* with Envy the day I discovered Oxydol washes *White Without Bleaching,*" the banner above them proclaims. On the left side of the page in a column headlined "Undercover Stuff," Kay Boyle gazes out from a postage-stamp sized portrait—looking intense, serious, and rather glamorous with her arched eyebrows and large white earrings. She is flanked by a capsule review of her latest book, *A Frenchman Must Die.* It is a novel about France under fascism, "on the order of her popular AVA-LANCHE of a year or so back," according to the article, and the reviewer explains:

> These two books are a departure for Kay Boyle, the intellectual, whose books used to be distinctly of the long-haired variety. Before the war she was one of the small esoteric group of literary experimenters who appeared regularly in Transition, the Paris-American Little Magazine. She wrote poetry and short stories, beautiful but sometimes baffling. It's no doubt her return to easygoing, unexacting, wholesome America that accounts for the change.[1]

This observation of a change in Kay Boyle's work is absolutely accurate. The reviewer's speculation as to its cause probably is not, and it is unimaginable that many serious readers would have shared her satisfaction with the author's newfound "wholesomeness."

Edmund Wilson's review of *Avalanche* (1944) was scathing. Unfortunately for Boyle's reputation, it was the first review of a book of fiction that he wrote after succeeding Clifton Fadiman as the regular book reviewer for *The New Yorker* in January, 1944, and it attracted considerable attention. He called the book "pure rubbish," describing it as "simply the usual kind of thing that is turned out by women writers for the popular magazines." After wittily laying bare the novel's flaws—the type characters, the improbable climax, and the stylistic "tricks that Miss Boyle overworks with exasperating effect"—he said, "It is easy to be funny about *Avalanche* but it has its depressing aspect." What distressed Wilson was his sense that she had sold out, that she had reduced her artistic talent to the lowest common denominator of commercial taste:

> I have not read much else by Kay Boyle since her very early work, so that I do not have a definite opinion about the value of her writing as a whole; but I know from those early stories, written when she lived abroad and printed in the "little" magazines of the American *emigrés,* that she was at least making an effort to produce something of serious interest. Today she is back at home, and *Avalanche* was written for the *Saturday Evening Post.* I did not see it there, but I have been haunted since I read it by a vision of *Saturday Evening Post* illustrations, in which the ideal physical types of the skin-lotion and shaving-soap ads are seen posing on snowy slopes. . . . And I think about the days of *This Quarter* and *Transition,* full of nonsense though those magazines were, with a wistfulness it would have surprised me in that period to be told I should ever feel.[2]

The coming of World War II had changed everything for Kay Boyle as it had for millions of others. Individual concerns suddenly were obliterated in the tide of events engulfing most of humanity. The material and style of her work altered dramatically after the outbreak of war in France in 1939. Besides writing dozens of short stories and a long poem, she produced five novels in the forties and every one of them focuses upon the war and the values that she felt were at stake in the conflict. She would never return completely to the intensely personal subject matter and experimental style that had marked much of her earlier writing. The social conscience first manifested in such works of the thirties as "Black Boy," *365 Days,* and *Death of a Man* would dominate her work of the forties, and she wished now to communicate in simple terms with as many as she could get to listen.

The interlude of relative peace, financial security, and family stability in which she had written *Monday Night* and the short novels of *The Crazy Hunter* had not lasted long. As the Vail family returned from a year in England and settled into their chalet in the Haute-Savoie in 1937, civil war was already raging in Spain. Nancy Cunard and Langston Hughes, both covering the Spanish Civil War, were constantly in touch with their friends in Mégève, and Kay Boyle must have known it was only a dress rehearsal for the cataclysm that soon would rock the rest of Europe. She had picked her side. In October, 1938, she wrote to Bob Brown from Les Cinq Enfants that in March there would be "a sixth infant to brighten our lives." If the baby were a girl (it was) they would name her Clover, but she and Laurence were "stumped" for boys' names. "I'd rather like a Spanish one," she said, "but they are all so long—I mean the names of the Loyalist heroes are."[3] Kay Boyle not only took politics seriously, she took them personally.

In September, 1939, when Germany invaded Poland, France had declared war and mobilized, expecting to defend the Maginot Line. But nothing happened for eight months, and by the time the Germans finally did attack, the morale of the French forces had been sapped by Nazi propaganda, ambiguous loyalties, fatigue, and boredom. "Here half the world is skiing while the other half dies, and the night-clubs are open until three in the morning, and God knows how people can dance as madly as that and as late and be as happy as they are," Kay Boyle wrote to Caresse Crosby in February, 1940. "If only some high and noble solution to the whole thing were visible on the cold, chaste heavens."[4] The "solution" came more quickly than anyone had imagined, but she hardly would have viewed it as "high and noble." Ill-trained, ill-equipped, and demoralized, prepared to fight a 1914 war, the French forces were no match for Hitler's machine, and in June, 1940, the government in Vichy signed an armistice with the Germans. The sense of humiliation, outrage, and betrayal that Kay Boyle observed in the French people and her own disgust with collaborators who preferred the "well-bred," clean-cut fascists to the rabble they feared would take over a more democratic system would be a staple of her fiction for the next several years.

She ended her February letter to Caresse with a postscript saying that she was having a copy of *The Crazy Hunter* held for her friend at Ann Watkins' office in New York. It is an interesting addition, for the book of three short novels—her intricate and sophisticated explorations of the individual's need for love—published that very year, in 1940, was already on its way to becoming the last monument to a phase in her life and career that she was leaving behind.

Kay's mother had come to live with the Vails in Mégève, and of course, there was the new baby. At the same time that the family had increased in numbers, prices had risen. In April, 1939, Kay Boyle wrote to her sister in New York: "Of course, we ought to cut down and live on a different scale, but where to begin and how? I suppose Sindbad *has* to go to a good school in England, and the girls *have* to have their teeth seen to by a good dentist, and if I'm to get any work done, I *have* to have a nurse for the first months of Clover's life, and when Bobby [Sharon] goes to Annecy in June to take her examinations she *has* to have a decent coat and suit—and so it goes. I feel like the mother in D. H. Lawrence's 'The Rocking Horse Winner'—'There must be more money, there must be more money!' "[5] They also had been sending money to Carnevali in Italy, and Kay's mother, whose always-fragile health had been suffering, had been advised by her doctor that she must have a break of several months from the high altitude. Kay booked her passage on the *Volendam,* sailing October

8, 1939, for New York, where she would go to live with Joan, her husband, and their two daughters. "Unfortunately, I've wasted a lot of time on novelettes," Kay wrote to her sister, "which is the form of writing that fascinates me for the moment, but novelettes are not a magazine saleable length. . . . I shall have to stick to short stories and stick to them hard if we are to continue living in this house."[6]

Six months after the publication of her three short novels, Kay Boyle was waiting for a cable from Lisbon to advise her of openings on the Clipper planes to America. She planned to return to the United States with her stepson, Sindbad, in order to put him in school, and if she could find a place for the rest of the family to live and if life would not be too expensive there, she hoped that Laurence Vail and the rest of the children would join her soon. "Otherwise, I will come back here," she wrote to Caresse Crosby in August, 1940. "But I have a lot of business to do in New York—and Washington—and I want to make a lot of money—and I MUST do so. . . . The war changed so much in the things I had begun to write and now I cannot go back to them for my heart and mind are filled with newer problems."[7]

The "newer problems" were personal as well as political, as though the global upheaval were mirrored on a microcosmic level in her own life. The remaining two-thirds of the letter concerns a friend of hers, an Austrian, who also wished to go to America. The consul in Lyons had advised her that this man would need affidavits from persons in responsible positions in the United States attesting to his ability to support himself, and she begged Caresse to do what she could to help her. "This Austrian matter is very important. Caresse, it is important that you must perform miracles for me—I won't be able to do anything until I have succeeded in this," she writes.

The Austrian friend was Baron Joseph von Franckenstein, whom she had met in August, 1939. His mother had been a countess Esterhazy before her marriage, and his father was a descendent of the Hapsburg line. He would become Kay Boyle's third husband. An expert skier, a mountain climber, and a scholar of classical languages, with a Ph.D. from Innsbruck University, Franckenstein had left his homeland just before the Nazis annexed Austria. In Mégève he was teaching in a children's boarding school and later became tutor to Sindbad Vail and Kay's two oldest daughters. When France declared war on Germany in September, 1939, he had reported immediately to the authorities to enlist in the fight against the Nazis, only to find that the chauvinistic French were giving enemy aliens their choice of internment in a concentration camp or service in the Foreign Legion. He chose internment.[8] "Long before we fell in love," Kay Boyle says, "he was metaphor to me for all the European persecuted millions."[9]

There are no details in print of Kay Boyle's early relationship with Franckenstein. Among the papers she has donated to the Morris Library at Southern Illinois University are the hundreds of letters they exchanged until his death in 1963—sometimes writing three or four in a day during the war, when he served in the U.S. Mountain Infantry and later in the Office of Strategic Services (OSS). But she has stipulated that the collection remain sealed until ten years after her death. A single character, however, appears repeatedly in her short stories and novels of the forties—a tall, golden-haired Austrian skier, often a baron who had left his native country when the Nazis took over and who now makes a living as a ski teacher in a French resort town. He has fallen in love with a married American woman with children who lives in the same village in the Haute-Savoie. Several of the stories and two of the four novels Kay Boyle wrote about wartime France—*Primer for Combat* and *1939*—concern this woman's outrage over his internment by the French (or his induction into the Foreign Legion). In *Primer for Combat* (1942) she details the woman's tireless efforts—bicycling to the American consulate in Lyons, writing countless letters to friends back home who might have influence—to free her lover from his unjust confinement and get him to America, where they will begin a new life together. What Kay Boyle *has* said about her attraction to Franckenstein is that while Laurence Vail tended to take a cyclical view of political events, seeing the rise of fascism in the thirties as simply another phase in human history, Franckenstein viewed politics with a passionate sense of urgency that she shared.[10] Like her break with Richard Brault, it would seem that her separation from Vail was motivated at least as much by ideological differences as by any personal incompatibilities.

Franckenstein was interned until the fall of France in 1940, and when Kay Boyle, Laurence Vail, and their children finally returned to America via Lisbon in 1941, he was able to leave France by refugee boat in the same year. Peggy Guggenheim details their exodus in her gossipy memoirs, but it must not be forgotten that she also claims that she and Boyle "frankly detested each other."[11] She reports that "Ray Soil" and "Florenz Dale" had been breaking up for a year and that "Ray" was living with a new friend "whom she was rescuing from concentration camps." According to Guggenheim, "Florenz" was behaving like an angel to "Ray," who made him send telegrams and money to her friend, but he refused to travel to America with him, so Franckenstein crossed the Atlantic separately. The party was held up in Lisbon for two months arranging passage. (As Kay Boyle later described it to an interviewer, "Rich refugees literally pushed us aside—big rolls of money in their pockets.")[12] It was a strange combination of passengers who boarded the Pan American Clipper together on July 13, 1941, headed by four adults: Kay Boyle, Laurence Vail, Peggy Guggenheim, and Max Ernst. As Guggenheim puts it,

"We were eleven people: one husband, two ex-wives, one future husband, and seven children."[13]

Kay Boyle's version of the story is somewhat different. There was never any question of Joseph's flying to America with them, she says. As a man who refused a German passport, he had no papers and never would have been able to cross Spain into Portugal had he wished to. He left on a refugee ship from Marseilles several weeks before they left France for Lisbon. "Laurence was indeed a great and devoted help to me at the time," she writes, but it was Laurence's mother, Boyle's mother-in-law, who "rescued" Franckenstein when his ship was commandeered by the Dutch (the Allies needing ships) and all on board put into an internment camp in the Barbadoes.[14] After Joseph's cousin, Sir George Franckenstein, the Austrian Ambassador to the Court of St. James, had secured his release, Mrs. Vail had sent Joseph the money to fly to the United States. (After the war, when they all returned to France, Mrs. Vail became very fond of Joseph, Boyle adds.) But in Miami, Franckenstein fell into "the clutches of the FBI," as she puts it, for questioning about his relationship with a German communist (whom Franckenstein had never met or heard of) who had happened to be aboard the same refugee ship. In addition, he lacked the fifty dollars required of all aliens for entry to the United States and was detained for several days until Bessie Breuer and Henry Varnum Poor came to the rescue by sending him the money. They also shared their home in Rockland County, New York, with Joseph Franckenstein and Kay Boyle and two of Kay's daughters until Breuer found the couple an apartment in Nyack.

But Boyle and Franckenstein were not able to settle down together even then. Unable to find work nearby, Joseph finally took a job on a California citrus fruit ranch owned by an Austrian friend he had met while interned. Kay Boyle remained in New York, where she attempted to earn enough for them to live together and to raise money for the French cause by writing "day and night" and giving lectures.

Several of her letters of the winter of 1941 are appeals to Bob Brown and Ann Watkins to help her arrange these talks. Her subjects, she told them, would be creative writing (a "pragmatic" talk based on her experiences in teaching a writing class at an adult night school in Nyack) and France under the occupation. This lecture would consist of "actual stories of the defeat and of the people's reaction to occupation, scenes in which I participated myself, an indictment of the State Department, and of the Fascist element in every country," she explains. Her passionate commitment to the cause is apparent when she adds that the whole talk would seek "to demonstrate even further that nothing matters in life except the individual resistance and the individual protest." "My speech will not be a lady-like one," she warns.[15]

When the United States declared war after the bombing of Pearl Harbor, Joseph returned to the East and volunteered for military service. Kay Boyle and her children moved to Mt. Vernon, New York, to be near her old friends from Paris, Maria and Eugene Jolas. Upon her return to America in 1941, Kay also had eagerly looked forward to seeing another dear friend of the twenties, Lola Ridge, but found when she arrived that Lola had died just a few weeks before. Because of the vast differences in her two daughters' financial situations, Katherine Evans Boyle lived mostly with Joan, whose husband, Frank Detweiler, was a Wall Street lawyer. "But she did spend time with us in Mount Vernon during the war years," Kay reports, "helping with the children, and being—as always—my exciting, stimulating companion."[16]

In January, 1943, Kay Boyle wrote to Bob Brown from Reno: "I have been here a week with my two youngest babies—5 weeks and 3 years—and am here for the usual thing. When it is over, I am going to marry Joseph who is in the ski troops in Colorado."[17] They were married on February 24, 1943, in Salt Lake City. Mrs. Boyle accompanied Kay on one of her several trips to Colorado to see Joseph when he was in the Mountain Infantry, and on the last trip, before he was shipped with his outfit to the Aleutians in June, 1943, she was with Kay in Carmel, not far from Joseph's camp in Fort Ord. There she devoted her time to the children, Sharon, Clover, and Faith, while Kay, expecting her sixth child in November, wrote the last pages of *Avalanche*.

After taking part in the invasion of the Aleutians, Franckenstein was accepted by the OSS. He made a number of parachute drops into France, and in 1945 he and another agent infiltrated into Austria. Posing as German Army noncommissioned officers, they set up a ski-training school for recruits in the mountains near Innsbruck. His colleague, Karl Noveček, was killed the day the SS came to get them at Kemanter Alm—on the 28th of April. Joseph Franckenstein was kneeling beside the body riddled by machine gun bullets, still holding his friend in his arms, when he was taken captive. He was imprisoned at Reichenau, near Innsbruck, and tortured so that he would reveal he was an American officer, but he did not succumb. As Kay Boyle tells it, her husband and another prisoner—both of whom had been sentenced to death as deserters from the German army—managed to escape, and while his companion was shot and killed by guards, "Joseph, in a tattered German army uniform, was able to welcome the Americans as their tanks poured into the town."[18]

In the meantime, Kay Boyle and her youngest and oldest daughters had moved to New York City, where her two other daughters, Apple and Kathe, were living with Laurence Vail. Late in 1944 she was one of a group of writers and photographers on a two-month U.S. Air Force VIP tour of air bases in England, France, Italy, and North Africa. Although the object of the trip, she says, was to give the participants a first-hand look at the Air Force's activities so that they could write favorably about them afterwards, the author had her own reasons for going: "I accepted the invitation because I did not believe my husband, then stationed in London, would ever survive the London blitz or his parachute drops into Occupied France, and I welcomed the chance of being with him for the few weeks we were in England."[19] In Caserta, Italy, she had the "great good fortune" to meet Thornton Wilder, who was with the Intelligence Division there, and she earned the disapproval of the Air Force generals hosting the group by her visits to air bases of the Fighting French Air Force. From the Fighting French she was able to gather a great deal of material for *A Frenchman Must Die,* the novel she published the next year about the French Resistance and the Vichy-backed secret police. She never did write anything about the U. S. Air Force.

In 1941, Kay Boyle had come home to America after her eighteen-year expatriation eager to put into writing what she had witnessed in Europe. Upon her arrival in New York, she had told an interviewer that she had the material for dozens of short stories and that she wanted "to find a place in the country and do nothing for a long time but write:"

> I write very rapidly and thoroughly enjoy everything to do with writing. I even like the smell of carbons. I shall write many short stories. While waiting in Lisbon I read all the American magazines, but I suppose I'll have my old trouble when I try to write for the very popular magazines. I'd like very much to write for those with large circulation, but when I put down a sentence that seems to me the sort of beginning that an editor of such a magazine might like, I find something in that sentence that I must change so that my meaning will be exact—and then it is all over. The chance is gone.[20]

But despite her difficulties and frustrations in writing for a popular audience, she did manage to place dozens of her stories in the large magazines in the forties. Two of the five novels she published in that decade first appeared in serial form in the *Saturday Evening Post*. While her descriptions continued to be striking and vivid, only occasional passages of italicized interior monologues remained of her experimental style. All but one of her novels and many of her stories were drawn directly from her own experiences and observations in war-torn France; the remaining novel and stories concerned the war, too, but had an American setting. The better pieces focus on an individual's struggle with the problems created by war—the ultimate breakdown of human bonds. By sensitively portraying the personal drama enacted against the backdrop of sweeping forces, Kay Boyle endows a character's plight with universal significance. Her less successful stories are baldly didactic, the characters cardboard types speaking in cliches about patriotism and honor.

To be sure, she needed the money that popularized stories would bring in order to support Sharon and Clover and her two youngest children, born in 1942 and 1943, Faith and Ian Franckenstein. But she also was moved to appeal to a wide audience by her deep commitment to the cause of freedom. What she had to say to Americans about the effects of institutionalized hatred on human life was too important to her to be buried in little magazines for consumption by literary connoisseurs. Her view of the artist's role had changed radically since her Left Bank days. In 1942 she said of a fellow poet, a man she had known in Paris: "I am convinced that the only thing wrong with him . . . is that he is not a realist. He is mumbling and bungling about in a vague state somewhere and to a person of action it is most unsatisfactory. He is—perhaps completely—a poet, and has no place in this world of taking decisions and doing acts."[21] It was not easy for a former advocate of the Revolution of the Word to write for mass consumption. "It's only when I put myself through really agonies of self-contempt and shoddiness that I can write anything that sells," she told her agent in 1944.[22] Yet in the forties Kay Boyle was a "realist," and she did what she thought necessary in order to communicate her urgent message.

One critic assesses nearly all of her stories of the war years as being "implicitly didactic." "Also, when they are read in sequence," he adds, "the effectiveness of any one tends to be dulled by the author's tendency to repeat the moral message of the one read previously."[23] Perhaps the sense of sameness is partly due to the fact that a number of the works are set in the Haute-Savoie, that the hero is so often an expatriated Austrian skier and the heroine a slim American who wears white earrings and red nail polish and is married to another man. Also, in attempting to recreate the atmosphere of paranoia and despair in defeated France, the author tends to repeat the same anecdotes, what she calls "legends," that mysteriously circulated among the people: the story of the well-bred German soldier who had relinquished his bus seat to a Frenchwoman while seated Frenchmen looked dully on, or the accounts—always heard second or third hand—of the capsules someone had seen a German drop into water to transform it to petrol. And it is true, too, that most of her wartime stories, like the rest of her fiction, are variations on a theme: her concern for the integrity of the individual and her bitter despair over the failures of human beings to "connect."

Many of the short stories are vignettes of war, exposing the devastating effects of mass insanity upon the fragile individual spirit. A number of them appeared first in magazines, then were collected in *Thirty Stories* (1946). Others remained uncollected until the publication in 1966 of *Nothing Ever Breaks Except the Heart*. "Anschluss" was first published in 1939, just four years after Kay Boyle had won an O. Henry Award for

"The White Horses of Vienna," in which she had sensitively portrayed a good man fighting for the Nazi cause. But the tone of "Anschluss" is vastly different. An American fashion writer working in Paris makes her annual visit to the Tyrol to find the only man she has ever loved turned Nazi, a youthful, rebellious spirit turned bigoted and chauvinistic conformist. His final goodbye to her is a salute with his right hand lifted.

In "Men," the author explores the state of mind of members of a road gang—prisoners who have committed no crime other than to have been born in a country now at war with France. As their work takes them closer day-by-day to a simple house up the road, the cottage takes on symbolic significance, becoming "some sort of goal, almost an actual destination to them" (*TS*, 243).[24] When an Austrian baron is sent ahead to dig out a tree by the house, the girl who lives there offers him a cognac, and he walks her back inside, where she will be shielded from the other men's view and from their thoughts. His ideals and honor have endured despite his degrading circumstances. Yet when he returns after a few moments to his work to be greeted by another prisoner's lewd insinuations, he strikes the man across the mouth "at the same instant that the sentry came toward them, his gun lowered, up the broken road" (*TS*, 249). Despite her faith in the integrity of the individual, Kay Boyle is no pollyanna. We are forced to confront the harsh fact that those of dignity and honor may have difficulty surviving in an inhumane world.

She is not so simplistic as to cast only the Germans as villains in her work. She indicts French bigotry and elitism in "They Weren't Going to Die," a story of Senegalese colonials shipped to France to fight a war that has nothing to do with them. They do not know that the French have a cynical term for their kind, "one that covered the whole foolish, aimless-seeming catastrophe of them"—*chair de cannon* (*TS*, 250). A group of them is billeted in the stable on a count's property, and when the Germans fail to arrive for the war, the Senegalese are put to work in the garden. To highlight the absurd injustice of their position, Boyle stresses their childlike innocence. When one tires of his labor and disappears, he is found upstairs in the Count's house, sitting on a windowsill in order to dangle his bare feet in the water of a porcelain receptacle "that was there for another use entirely," and laughing out loud whenever he pulled the chain that brought water rushing up over his shins (*TS*, 252). When the Germans finally do appear, the African soldiers line up behind the garden wall with their guns and dutifully, if festively, pick them off their motorcycles as they round the bend one by one. But one rider sees the carnage and retreats. The Senegalese are disappointed: "It might have been just after six on Christmas Day, and the stockings emptied, the presents all opened, the candles on the tree put out. They hadn't quite got over it when the nimble little tank came down the road, its eyes, like those of a snail, fingering them out, nor when the second tank came down behind it and the piece of the garden wall suddenly blew in" (*TS*, 255).

As his men finish off the black survivors with machine guns, the scrupulously groomed German officer chats amiably with the French count, complimenting him on his "charming place" and apologizing for the damage to the wall. "The Count put his pince-nez on with a hand that did not tremble, and as the thought struck him with singular force, *Gentlemen, actually well-bred men this time,* he said aloud: 'The bodies removed?' " (*TS*, 256). But the German, touching the Count's tweed sleeve with his kid glove, replies that they will be buried instead. He turns to his men and snaps, "Right where they are . . . sniper's burial." The Count is shaken, but we suspect he may be disturbed not so much by the slaughter of the Africans as by the disruption of his garden. The story ends with the Count "thinking confusedly of the potato plants and the strawberry flowers, but he could not bring himself to turn and look at them again" (*TS*, 256).

Kay Boyle's disgust with the complacent French who did not object strenuously as the "well-bred" Germans overran their country also gave rise to her story "Defeat." In 1941 it earned her her second O. Henry Award for best short story of the year. Originally published in *The New Yorker,* "Defeat" presents the tragic defeat of spirit and principle that infected all of France after its fast capitulation to the Germans in 1940. The author vividly captures the mood of the time as she summarizes tales of the survivors who trickled down from the north after the armistice, having somehow survived the onslaught of the "bright-haired blonde demi-gods" who had marched row on row, arms linked, singing, with their trousers immaculately creased:

> Legends or truth, the stories became indistinguishable in the mouths of the Frenchmen who returned: that the Germans were dressed as if for tennis that summer, with nothing but a tune to carry in their heads, while the French crawled out from under lorries where they'd slept that night and maybe every night for a week, coming to meet them like crippled, encumbered miners emerging from the pit of a warfare fifty years interred, with thirty-five kilos of kit and a change of shoes and a tin helmet left over from 1914 breaking them in two as they met the brilliantly nickeled Nazi dawn. They said their superiors were the first to run; they said their ammunition had been sabotaged; they said the ambulances had been transformed into accommodations for the officers' lady friends; they said: "*Nous avons été vendus,*" or "*On nous a vendu,*" over and over until you could have made a popular song of these words and music of defeat. (*TS*, 258)

The story proper is a flashback, a tale told by a bus driver sitting in a café in September, 1940. He tells of the retreat and of his capture and escape from prison camp with a companion. He describes the tracts that

had showered down from German planes, saying, "Frenchmen, prepare
your coffins! Frenchwomen, get out your ball dresses! We're going to
dance the soles off your shoes on the Fourteenth of July!" (*TS*, 260). Yet
when the escapees had taken refuge in a schoolhouse, they found the
schoolmistress decorating the room with bunting and French flags in
honor of the coming holiday, and she had scoured the neighborhood for
food and civilian clothing for them. "A country isn't defeated as long as
its women aren't," one had remarked. (*TS*, 262). A few days later, on the
Fourteenth of July, they had been taken in by a garage owner in a strange
town, given dinner, and shown to an upstairs room overlooking the town
square. They had laughed to see the dance pavilion with strings of colored
lights that the Germans had erected in the empty square and the enemy
soldiers "hanging around in expectation." For a while, the bus driver tells
the travelers in the café, there was not a woman anywhere, but then he
continues:

> "They had fruit tarts, it looked like, and sweet chocolate, and bottles of lemo-
> nade and beer. They had as much as you wanted of everything," he said, "and
> perhaps once you got near enough to start eating and drinking, then the other
> thing just followed naturally afterward, or that's the way I worked it out," he
> said. "Or maybe if you've had a dress a long time that you wanted to wear and
> you hadn't the chance of putting it on and showing it off because all the men
> were away; I mean if you were a woman. I worked it out that maybe if you're
> one kind of woman any kind of uniform looks all right to you after a certain
> time." (*TS*, 266)

"Well, that was just one town," one of the traveling men replies, and the
bus driver agrees, "Yes, that was just one town." But when he picks up
his glass to drink, "something as crazy as tears was standing in his eyes"
(*TS*, 266).

A number of her short pieces of the forties attack the complacent
among her compatriots as well, those who apparently did not feel that a
war in Europe was their worry. From the beginning of her career, Kay
Boyle had despised the self-satisfaction of those who do not care deeply
about what is taking place beyond the perimeters of their own uninspired
lives, whether it be social or aesthetic ferment. In that sense her American bourgeois villains of the war years are kin to the French in-laws she
had portrayed in her novel *Plagued by the Nightingale*. Respectable members of the "decenter class," they are too nearsighted to see the implications of the conflict about to engulf the world. The title of "Major Engagement in Paris" is a bit of overt sarcasm, for the story concerns the
bitter quarrel between two American dowagers living in Paris over the
proper use of the special toothpicks that Mrs. Hodges had obtained from
her dentist. "Last war," Mrs. Hodges complains, in the midst of their

squabble in an air raid shelter, the sirens had had more "life" to them, and in the shelters they had had "card tables and the gramophone going and some *esprit de corps*" (*TS,* 206). The two women had also figured in an earlier story of the same sort entitled "War in Paris," published in *The New Yorker* in 1938 and never collected. In it, Mrs. Hodges' ultimate concern in the midst of Hitler's and Mussolini's "mischief" is how she will safely evacuate her beloved cat, Major Ainslee, from Paris.[25]

In "Battle of the Sequins," a short piece she wrote for *The Nation,* she juxtaposes a description of American matrons at home struggling bitterly over sequined blouses on a department store counter with the vision of "other women—women who skipped quickly back into a trench before the shellfire got them, dragging with them the body of a companion who had fought three winters with her feet bound in rags, as were the feet of the other women, and who now had been killed."[26] In "The Little Distance," a slick *Saturday Evening Post* story, she not-too-subtly compares the petty feuding of two suburban neighbors with the conflict rocking the world. It requires the death of one family's son in the war overseas to stop the nonsense and bring the neighbors to the realization that they have been "fighting the wrong fight." They finally learn that they must bridge "the little distance that lay between them" (*NEB,* 178).[27]

"Parables" might be a more accurate term for many of Kay Boyle's short works of the forties. While her nonfiction pieces like "Battle of the Sequins" achieve poignancy through the author's simple juxtaposition of dramatically constrasting scenes, stories like "The Little Distance" must have sent Edmund Wilson into paroxysms if he ever read them, for the characters are one-dimensional, the dialogue suited for B-grade movies, and the "moral" baldly stated. Yet Kay Boyle felt an urgent need to raise money for her causes (and her family) and, more important, to communicate her concerns to a wide audience. In such desperate times, she must have felt that the medium was less important than the message.

Despite her discouragement with the defeatism and complacency she had witnessed in France and America, Kay Boyle wrote other stories about the sparks of courage, humanity, and idealism that the war had not extinguished. "This They Took with Them" focuses on two individuals caught up in the mass exodus from Paris in June, 1940: a Mexican diplomat who had once fought with Pancho Villa, and a prim Parisian schoolteacher, whose attaché case contains the neatly folded examination papers, still uncorrected, of the fourth class of the *lycée* of the sixteenth *arrondissement*. After an ambulance catches fire, the stream of walkers parts silently around the glowing hulk and no drivers stop to take on the wounded lying on stretchers on the road bank. But the Mexican, who, as they walked, had never ceased talking to the schoolteacher in the face of her silence, stops to remain with the wounded, and she sits down beside him on the bank, thinking, *"There are men with the breath of life in them who can teach the rest of us to breathe; there are men with the breath of life in them, we can learn strength from them"* (*TS*, 298). At nightfall the Mexican persuades her to lie down, and she falls asleep with her head on this stranger's shoulder, she to murmur in her sleep the words of George Sand and he to dream of Pancho Villa riding through the lemon groves. In the midst of "the army of walkers who moved sightless and will-less as if in sleep through the incurable dream," each person had carried with him one thing, "and that was the accumulation of unalterable experience which made each of them what he was" (*TS*, 290). Despite the cataclysm, Kay Boyle had retained her basic faith in the dignity and integrity of the individual and in his or her ability to endure.

She never strays, either, from her belief that the most fundamental human need is connection with others. In story after story, she describes scenes of wartime France in which strangers band together in cafés or railroad stations simply to make human contact as the world around them collapses. "The Canals of Mars," set in New York City, follows a couple through their last hours together before the husband is shipped overseas to war. (The author has described it as "a purely factual story" written very quickly "under great emotional pressure.")[28] The soldier is a native Austrian who had spent time in a French concentration camp and later had fought the enemy surreptitiously. Despite their anguish at yet another separation, however, this time they find comfort in the fact that their grief can be shared with others. This time, the woman tells her husband, "I'm not just one woman keeping her mouth shut about what her husband's doing. I'm Russian women and Englishwomen and French-women" (*TS*, 339). The realization that the individual struggle is part of a collective one eases the agony.

In "Winter Night," published in 1946, Kay Boyle draws a delicate portrait of a little girl named Felicia and a woman sent by a "sitting parent" agency to spend the evening with her in a Manhattan apartment. The woman, in her strange accent, tells Felicia that today is an anniversary, that three years ago that night she had begun to take care of another girl who also had studied ballet and whose mother, like Felicia's, had had to go away. The difference was that the other girl's mother had been sent away on a train car in which there were no seats, and she never came back. The woman can only comfort herself with the thought that "They must be quietly asleep somewhere, and not crying all night because they are hungry and because they are cold" (*TS*, 362).

"There is a time of apprehension which begins with the beginning of darkness, and to which only the speech of love can lend security," the story begins, as the author describes the light of a January afternoon dying over Central Park (*TS*, 352). Felicia and the "sitting parent," both left alone by those they love, have found temporary security in each other. When Felicia's mother tiptoes in the front door after midnight, slipping the three blue foxskins from her shoulders and dropping the velvet bag on a chair, she hears only the sound of breathing in the dark living room, and no one speaks to her in greeting as she crosses to the bedroom: "And then, as startling as a slap across her delicately tinted face, she saw the woman lying sleeping on the divan, and Felicia, in her school dress still, asleep within the woman's arms" (*TS,* 362).

The story is not baldly didactic, but Kay Boyle *is* moralizing. By juxtaposing the cases of the two little girls left alone by their mothers and cared for by a stranger, she shows that the failure of love is a tragic loss on an individual as well as on a social and political scale.

Kay Boyle's novels of the forties have been described as variations on a formula first established in *Death of a Man*: "one part love story to one part parajournalistic reportage of momentous happenings in contemporary history," in one critic's words.[29] He comments that the chief difference between the short stories and the novels of this period lies in the author's use of a romantic plot in the latter as a framework to support the political commentary, and he rather condescendingly describes the romantic ending of one novel, *Avalanche,* as "fulfilling vicariously the adolescent fantasies of woman readers likely to be attracted to such a piece."[30] The fact is that the "romance" pervading these novels was as "realistic" an element in the author's life in the forties as were the grimmer realities of war. True to her established pattern, she was simply drawing the material of her fiction from her own experiences once more. Five years after her relationship with Joseph Franckenstein had begun and after the birth of their second child, she sounds like a honeymooning bride when she writes to Ann Watkins: "Joseph is so wonderful. I am terribly, hopelessly in love. What would have become of me had I never found him? He is absolutely a miracle." And three years after that, in 1947, she delights in repeating what *New Yorker* Paris correspondent Janet Flanner had said of him at dinner the night before, that "Joseph is what God intended, and every other man you see or meet is some horrible mistake."[31] "So I purr with delight, and beam upon my darling," Kay Boyle writes. "It does seem almost impossible that anyone could get more and more wonderful every time one sees him. But so it is." All four of the novels set in wartime France are simultaneously stories of love and war, and in two of them the lovers bear remarkable resemblance to Kay Boyle and Joseph Franckenstein.

Primer for Combat (1942) is an "armistice diary," a novel written in the form of daily entries dated from June 20 to October 2, 1940. The diarist is Phyl, an American living in France with her historian husband, Benchley, their young children who have never seen their homeland, and Phyl's sixteen-year-old brother, who, like Kay Boyle's stepson, Sindbad Vail, must return to America if he is to continue his schooling. Phyl corresponds with Nancy Cunard; she has known Marcel Duchamp, Ezra Pound, and James Joyce; and she had once visited the poet Carnevali in Bazzano, where he lay on his bed trembling violently with encephalitis. Her first husband had been a Frenchman, she was in Innsbruck one day when a bomb had been tossed into the beer garden of the inn in which she and Benchley were staying, and her husband knows she is in love with another man. It can hardly be stretching matters to say that she speaks for Kay Boyle.

The contrast between Phyl, with her "blind, hot need for action" (*PC,* 44),[32] and Benchley, who possesses the "coolest, soundest, and most objective familiarity with the past and present imaginable" (*PC,* 19) most likely is the same kind of conflict in interests that divided Kay Boyle and Laurence Vail. Too, the feelings that had overwhelmed Phyl when war began were most likely the author's as well and may explain the dramatic shift in her concerns as a writer in the forties. Phyl writes in her diary:

> It was in the first weeks of the war—only then—that the cold, determined need to be a part of what is to become of us all possessed me. But it was never so much the matter of a war as of a spectacle of monstrous human endeavor from which one could not turn away. Here the implacable break occurred, and there it will stand forever: the personal consequences were nothing; the names and places were nothing as long as I had a part. (*PC,* 150)

Phyl is in love with Wolfgang, an Austrian ski instructor, who as an enemy alien has been inducted into the Foreign Legion. The basic plot of the love story turns on her efforts to arrange his escape from the Legion via Portugal to America, where they will begin a new life together. However, the novel is not a neat roman à clef. Kay Boyle has made it clear that Wolfgang is not Joseph Franckenstein, saying, "He, that other Austrian skier, went voluntarily (not against his will) into the Foreign Legion, while Joseph, refusing to apply for a Nazi passport, chose to remain in internment camp."[33] Unlike Joseph Franckenstein, Wolfgang is also married—to a Frenchwoman with high-placed relatives. In the end Wolfgang bitterly disappoints his more principled lover by accepting the expedient route offered out of the Sahara, returning to France as a collaborationist via his wife's political connections in Vichy.

While the love story plot is the skeleton of the book, the flesh and blood are the diarist's astute observations on France's tragic defeat. She records the legends of French cowardice and German invincibility that mysteriously circulate through the despairing population, including the anecdotes of war that Kay Boyle would develop into the short stories "Defeat," "Men," and "They Weren't Going to Die." Through the diary device the author is also able to discourse on philosophical issues pertaining to the war as Phyl copies into her diary passages from her reading, ranging from Hegel and Nietzsche to Lawrence of Arabia. If it is not a great novel, *Primer for Combat* is at least a fascinating historical record set down by a sensitive and articulate eyewitness.

On the back of the novel's red, white, and blue dust cover, the author exhorts her readers to buy war bonds because "It is no longer a matter of personal choice as to how little or how much we can give; it is now a matter of the survival of ourselves as individuals, and of the survival of that freedom, honor, and human dignity which can be lost if we refuse to recognize our country's needs." The woman who wrote that appeal speaks with a far different voice from the one who fourteen years before had renounced her native land as a place where "each citizen functions with pride in the American conspiracy against the individual."[34] But even if her cause had changed, the fighting spirit behind the words is the same. And while she had taken a broader perspective on the issue in the forties, the root of all evil also remains the same in her estimation. Phyl's explanation for the inhumanity of the cold-eyed Gestapo officers is that they are "those to whom imagination, and thus daring, and thus a spirited temper, and thus a vision, and thus love, have not been given; and having been thus punished, they must punish in return" (*PC*, 207–8).

Avalanche (1944) was one book by Kay Boyle that received widespread attention. It was her only "great financial success."[35] Originally serialized in the *Saturday Evening Post*, it was also a Book of the Month Club selection, and two hundred and fifty thousand copies were sold to the Armed Forces. Today if a second-hand bookstore has in stock any out-of-print work by Kay Boyle, it most likely is *Avalanche*. The author believes it was the first book to be written about the French resistance, and she says she has met many former Air Force pilots and crewmen who had been required to read the book before taking off on their bombing missions over Germany so that they would understand the divided political situation in France in case they had to parachute from a disabled plane. "It's a novel, but very factual," she explains.[36]

Ironically, the success and visibility of this particular book have been responsible for considerable damage to Kay Boyle's reputation as a serious writer. The enthusiasm of the reviewer who called it a "honey" of an espionage tale was not shared by other critics.[37] In the view of some, the novel combined the worst of both worlds. The reviewer in *The Nation* found it "offensive in the extreme against the serious truth because by the introduction of italicized passages of literary exaltation and by the parade of literary mannerisms she pretends to more and better than potboiling."[38] Harry T. Moore, a long-time admirer of Kay Boyle, is more sympathetic in his appraisal: "Unfortunately, after her return from Europe during the Second World War, Kay Boyle began bending her high talent to the production of the fictional fudge of *Saturday Evening Post* serials, with results that were unsatisfactory from the point of view of her early admirers—and probably the readers of popular magazines were not very much pleased either, since a certain amount of subtlety remained amid the melodramatic scenes."[39]

Avalanche is a spy thriller leavened by liberal dashes of romance and rally-to-the-cause patriotism. Edmund Wilson's summary is nasty but to the point:

A blond heroine, half French, half American, who fled France when the Germans came, returns to work with a relief committee and becomes involved in the underground movement in the mountains of the Haute-Savoie. The villain is a Gestapo agent masquerading as a Swiss clock manufacturer, who sneers at the French so openly and makes himself in general so provocatively unpleasant that the reader is at first led to think that this character must himself be a French patriot masquerading as a German spy, and is later impelled to wonder how he has ever held down his job. The hero, Bastineau, leader of the mountain resistance, combines the glamor of Charles Boyer with the locomotive proficiency of Superman. Adored by his followers almost as a god, he constantly outwits the Germans, performs prodigies of fidelity to the Girl and, like the Frankenstein monster of the movies, is always pretending to be killed and then sensationally coming to life. The Girl herself keeps the story going only by exercising so stubborn a stupidity that it becomes difficult to understand how any underground movement could have trusted her: she is thoroughly mystified by the snarling Gestapo agent and is puzzled at finding that her old friends of the village avoid her when they see her in his company; and it takes her the greater part of the book to grasp the facts of the secret opposition, which one would think must have been perfectly plain to her from the things she has seen and heard even if she had not just come from America and so shared with the reader the advantage of having read the American papers.[40]

In the stunning climax, the jig is up and the heroine, Fenton Ravel, is captured by the Gestapo agent in an isolated cabin. On the way down the mountainside, the quick-witted captive leads him along the wrong path, he gets his foot caught in a steel trap outside the cottage of a peasant resistance member, and he has to be taken inside, where he whines his fear of getting lockjaw. Prepared to meet her fate, she blurts out his true identity to the peasant. But just as she finds herself looking down the barrel of a gun, the stillness is shattered by a wild, exultant cry: "*L'Infant'rie Alpin-e, voilà mes amours!*" (*A*, 201).[41] Bastineau, her "missing" lover, "easily, gracefully as a jumper on skis" leaps down into the room from the chimney, and after a brief scuffle, the villain is dispatched. The coming of the dashing deus ex machina is followed by that of *monsieur le curé,* who cries: "Tonight—just tonight—the news came through from Radio-Boston. The Americans have landed in North Africa!" (*A*, 206). Not only does the fate of the Allies now look bright, but the subsequent German takeover of the Unoccupied Zone of France conveniently has made it impossible for Fenton to return to her job in Lyons. The priest marries the lovers on the spot.

In *A Frenchman Must Die* (1946) the protagonist is male but also of French-American parentage. He, too, has returned from the United States to the Haute-Savoie village where he grew up in order to fight for his spiritual homeland as a member of the Maquis. But the year is 1944, France has been liberated, and the warfare is now of the urban guerilla variety between the newly-legitimate resistance group and former members of the Milice, the Vichy version of Hitler's SS. Guy Mitchie's assignment is to capture the notorious collaborationist Pliny so that he may be brought to trial for crimes against his countrymen. The suspense of the chase—over Alpine roads, into Lyons, through Paris bistros, the Ritz hotel, and the Metro, and back into the countryside—is spiced by the recurrent appearances of a lovely young woman. We had first met her when she blew up a mountain road in front of Guy Mitchie's truck, kissed him, and roared off on her German motorcycle, leaving him to walk all night to get to Lyons. Yet there was something in that kiss. . . . The hero finally learns that although she has been Pliny's personal secretary for years, she has been using her position to collect the evidence of his collaboration that could put him away for life. Pliny never comes to trial, however. He catches on to the lady's duplicity, kidnaps her, and is speeding toward the Swiss border when Mitchie finally overtakes his limousine and the villain is killed.

Avalanche and *A Frenchman Must Die* have been called "elegant potboilers." Kay Boyle's fascination with language is still evident in her descriptions of people and landscapes, although at times the style is precious, as when a resistance fighter watches a saccharine pill "drop like a parachutist into his cup of *café national* and, spinning, open its floating, white umbrella of infinitesimal foam" (*A*, 41). She freely admits, too, that the stories were shaped by commercial considerations. The *Saturday Evening Post* editor had told her that the heroine of *Avalanche* could not have two French parents; one would have to be American in order to appeal to an American audience. Practical considerations also explain the repeated appearances and disappearances of Bastineau and Danielle Monnet, the fighter with feminine mystique. Speaking specifically of *Avalanche,* the author explains that her hero had to make periodical appearances because of the serial requirements: "So I dragged him in every twenty pages, and I left it that way when it was published as a book."[42]

She probably would not take offense with the reviewer of *Avalanche* who said, "A number of Miss Boyle's admirers, unless I am mistaken, are going to rebuke her for this story, and although they are going to be right technically, they are going to be enormously wrong theoretically and practically."[43] Two years later he might have said the same thing for *A Frenchman Must Die*. The two novels are slick potboilers, but, like Kay Boyle's works of the twenties and thirties, they were written in response to the times. They are right "practically" as readable and well-informed accounts of the French resistance, a topic of vital interest in their day. And they are right "theoretically" as well. They were written in a grim period of history when readers *needed* happy endings in their fiction, at least, to keep them going in their far less happy real lives. The fine art of alienation and despair with which Kay Boyle and other serious writers had battled the unhealthy prosperity and satisfaction of the twenties would have been self-indulgent in the forties, when individuals were being crushed under the weight of a cruel external world whose problems would not go away with any amount of sensitive introspection or exercise of personal will.

While in these two novels she may not have been contributing much to the cause of serious literature, Kay Boyle was contributing to a cause she considered more important at the time. In that sense she remained a very serious writer. She explains that when she returned to the United States in 1941 and found how bitterly and cynically Americans ("both literary critics and Main Street America") believed that France had "lain down on the job," she felt she had to make them understand "how all that was simple, and good, and admirable in France had been betrayed." Of *Avalanche* and *A Frenchman Must Die*, she says, "I wanted those two books—far more than any of my others—to reach as great a number of Americans as possible, and so I wrote them, and without apology, for the *Saturday Evening Post*."[44] As for Edmund Wilson, she thought him "exceedingly stupid" for not understanding what she was trying to do in *Avalanche*: "The book was simply not literature, and it didn't need a critic to point that out." Nor does she regret having written the novel, despite whatever damage it did to her reputation. "The rewards it brought me—and I don't mean just monetary, but the many friendships—were enormous, even though literary pundits deplored my fall from grace."[45]

1939, the last of her four novels of wartime France to be published, was probably the first to be written. When interviewed upon her return to America in 1941, she mentioned that she had been working on a novel about concentration camps and had completed one version, although she planned to "do it over."[46] In a 1944 letter, she refers to her "concentration camp book" that had been "shelved," presumably out of doubt that it would sell.[47] The novel *1939,* finally published in 1948, certainly was not crafted with an eye to commercial appeal.

The narrative proper is simple, covering roughly twenty-four hours. Ferdl Eder, an Austrian ski instructor who has lived in France since before the Anschluss, reports to enlist in the French forces as soon as war is declared. But instead of being allowed to fight the Nazis, he is immediately interned as an enemy alien. The following morning—when the novel actually opens—the woman with whom he has been living for two years must resume life alone in their chalet under the smug scrutiny of the villagers. Yet this narrative accounts for only a slim proportion of the novel—itself slim at 152 pages.

The action of the book is almost entirely interior and psychological, dominated by a flashback to the moral struggle that had finally led Eder to the induction center. With the declaration of war between France and Germany, which now incorporates his native Austria, Ferdl Eder finally has been forced to commit himself to a label of national identity. His predicament is symbolically polarized into a choice between two women. On the one hand, he may continue his already ambiguous life with Corrine Audal, herself a French-American who had left her husband at the first flash of passion to live with Eder on the mountainside. Yet he wishes desperately to see his mother, still grieving for her lost son, and all he has to do to meet her in the relative safety of Italy is to walk across the border bearing a passport of "one man's Germany" (*1939,* 144).[48] Eder goes as far as a French border town before making the final decision to tear up the stiff new passport before it has been validated, thereby accepting the more difficult and dangerous though more principled role of man without a country. An individual with an inborn Teutonic love of order, he chooses to cast his lot with the French, a people who still retain "a rather sardonic respect for life," not having acquired "the habit of seeing it collectively" (*1939,* 68).

The style of the novel is complex, reminiscent of *Monday Night* and *The Crazy Hunter.* The author experiments with shifts in time and narrative voice, lavishly employing flashback, long mid-sentence parenthetical asides, italicized internal monologues and imaginary conversations, and multiple points of view that the reader must sift through to reconstruct the "truth." While the sentiments expressed in the novel are vintage Boyle, the flavor of the syntax once again is decidedly Faulkner. Of Eder's high standing in the village, Corrine thinks, "Physical beauty or physical courage or even physical love were not the words of explanation for the legend, for in the end there is no name for the fabulous power (like the sign of the cross made on the air confounding evil) which is the heart's passionate, unblemished sign giving permanence to what other men have only dreamed about or written books to, or at best known in their flesh just once and for a little while a long time back" (*1939, 25*).

When one reads Kay Boyle's wartime novels in the order of their publication, *1939*, coming after *Avalanche* and *A Frenchman Must Die*, seems an anachronism, its very title dating it, its style a throwback to her Faulknerian phase of the late thirties. Yet in another sense, its publication following those two works is most appropriate, for however accidentally, it signals another shift in her direction as a writer—a conscious return to more "serious" art created with little concern for its marketability.

Although she did it often enough and somewhat successfully, Kay Boyle never found it easy to write commercial fiction. Despite her retrospective defense of *Avalanche,* the actual writing of it had been torture. Her frustration is apparent in a letter she wrote to Bob Brown in January, 1943:

> I am working hard on this blasted serial, which I wish I could collaborate on, but which I feel I must bang out alone. I've got fifty thousand words to go, and God, it goes slowly. I MUST stop being a precious, careful writer, and get the rough copy hacked out somehow. But I bog down over the turn of a phrase, and there I am. Today, both of the children have been ill, and so I've got only four pages done of the eight I've stipulated to myself that must be done per day.[49]

Even while producing potboilers, she had not lost her discrimination and taste. Referring to a "slick" story she was working on, she wrote to her agent, "If it isn't the worst story ever written, I'll eat the entire manuscript, carbons and all. And being the worst, it must sell to 'Woman's Home Companion' immediately. The trouble is that writing a bad slick takes just as much sweat and tears on my part as writing a good story. If only the slick ones came easy, everything would be fine. . . . Don't, for heaven's sake, have anyone send it to 'The New Yorker' during your absence. I would die of outrage and shame."[50]

During the war years Kay Boyle had been profoundly moved by the sacrifice and sense of honor she had witnessed in many people. The patriotism that was so marketable then was truly sincere. Joseph Franckenstein was, to her, a model of the dignity and integrity with which an individual might face the challenge of war, and her tributes to him in print went far beyond endowing her heroes with his Austrian nationality, skiing prowess, and rugged good looks.

Two of her most serious works of the forties were inspired by her husband's experiences while training for the United States ski troops in the Colorado Rockies. In 1944, the same year in which *Avalanche* appeared, she published *American Citizen Naturalized in Leadville, Colo-*

rado, a long poem printed as a fifteen-page monograph—hardly a lucrative genre. She dedicates the work to her friend Carson McCullers, whose husband was also serving overseas, and in the first few lines she describes her poem as "the waltz/ Of the wives whose men are in khaki" (*AC,* 7).[51] *American Citizen* is a fervent expression of faith in their fight. Two decades earlier the champion of the defiant exile, Kay Boyle now sings of the common cause, of sisterhood and solidarity.

Like the priest in *A Farewell to Arms* who says that in his home region a man may love God and it is not a dirty joke, Kay Boyle now sees individual submission to the collective need as a matter of pride and honor, not of irony. The poem ends:

> When generations play the individual's tragedy
> And triumph out, then we are marvelously and faithfully
>   portrayed. Shall we
> Despair that men we love move from the wings and
>   take their
>   part in history?
> Let us say only
> That their names are there.
>
>   (*AC,* 15)

If the poem is sentimental, perhaps it is because Kay Boyle, like F. Scott Fitzgerald, has always possessed an acute sense of living in history without sharing his simultaneous ability to view his surroundings with detachment. Rather than showing her to be quite a different kind of writer than she had been in her own and the century's twenties, *American Citizen* simply provides more evidence of her consistent tendency to fling herself passionately and uncompromisingly into the stream of her times, with a romantic trust in the validity of her own emotions.

In the same spirit as this poem, *His Human Majesty* (1949) marks a decisive shift in Kay Boyle's work back to more serious art. As in her other novels of the forties, she draws her material for this one from topical events and personal experiences. But in it she goes far beyond the basic formula of one part love story to one part parajournalistic reporting on contemporary history to attempt to create from these familiar materials an allegory of mythic proportions concerning nothing less than the human condition.

She began the work that would become *His Human Majesty* in the autumn of 1943. Originally she intended a group of short stories about the men in the ski troops training in Leadville, Colorado, but soon, she says, "I realized I was writing a novel."[52] In 1946 she announced plans for the book's partial serialization in the *Atlantic Monthly* under its working title, *Enemy Detail,* but the serialization never occurred, and Simon and

Schuster, which had planned to publish the novel later that year, did not. Instead, Whittlesey House, a division of McGraw-Hill, published the book in 1949, and the final version consists of two parts, each a short novel in itself: the original "Enemy Detail" and "Main Drag."

The change in publishers may account for the changes in the work itself. Edward Aswell, who had left his position at Harper & Brothers to become editor-in-chief at Whittlesey House as well as vice-president of McGraw-Hill in 1947, was enthusiastic about the book. After receiving from Ann Watkins a copy of a memo describing his reaction to "Enemy Detail," Kay Boyle said, "my whole life and outlook have changed."[53] In Aswell's first letter to the author as her new publisher he tells her that he had read "Enemy Detail" in one night then rushed to Ann Watkins' office the next morning, where he talked about it like a drunken man. He felt that it was a great book and that in it she was writing at the top of her bent. He pledged his every effort in helping the novel achieve for its author the new recognition and level of success that he felt must inevitably follow.[54] Kay Boyle dedicated the book to Edward Aswell, "whose devotion and understanding gave the men who live in it their life."

In 1944, when she was also busy writing *Avalanche* and other "slick" stories, she had written to Ann Watkins, "it is such a satisfaction to write about these men that I feel it probably will not sell at all." She continues:

> It's only when I put myself through really agonies of self-contempt and shoddiness that I can write anything that sells. That's the way I feel, anyway. This book (or whatever it is) I love writing; perhaps because Joseph is one of the principal men in it. So it will probably have to be shelved as my concentration camp book was. But when I've done two or three pieces—stories or chapters or whatever you wish to call them—you shall decide.[55]

By 1947 she had returned to France, but she was still working on the novel set in Leadville. She told her agent, "I feel really ridiculous sitting here writing this novel about the issues of 1944 with a revolution taking place around us, but the book MUST be finished, and I must try to make the human issues involved important enough to have a significance beyond the story itself—perhaps some kind of answer to the questions people, in wartime or in peacetime, ask themselves and ask others concerning truth and loyalty—and fidelity."[56]

Her high intentions are apparent in the novel's epigraph, a passage from Plate 55 of William Blake's *Jerusalem*.

> Silence remain'd & every one resum'd his
> Human Majesty.
> And many conversed on these things as they
> labour'd at the furrow,
> Saying: "It is better to prevent misery than

to release from misery:
It is better to prevent error than to forgive
the criminal.
Labour well the Minute Particulars, attend to
the Little-ones,
And those who are in misery cannot remain so
long
If we but do our duty. . . .

In Blake's mythology, the "fall" is not of man away from a transcendent God, but the fragmentation of "Universal Man," who is himself God and all the cosmos as well. Original sin in this scheme is what Blake calls "selfhood," the attempt of the isolated, exiled parts of Universal Man to exist self-sufficiently. The conflict between the fragments in the fallen world ultimately will lead to an apocalypse and result in a "Resurrection to Unity," a return to the original "Universal Brotherhood of Eden/The Universal Man."[57] In Blake's universe, redemption will come through human imagination and vision, embodied most potently in the poet. In Kay Boyle's universe, the power that will redeem humanity from its destructive fragmentation is love. It would be foolhardy to seek in this novel an elaborate personal mythology such as Blake or Yeats had created, but certainly Boyle had striven to endow her ski-troop novel with universal significance, and she colors her narrative with strong mythic overtones. Thus qualified, Part One, "Enemy Detail," might be called "The Fall" and Part Two, "Main Drag," "Redemption."

The two parts of the novel are unified by the protagonist—English-American, an expert skier and natural leader of men, who holds a Ph.D. in classical languages from Cambridge. In "Enemy Detail" we soon sense that this quiet, dignified soldier is special, set apart by his idealism. While the other men talk of wives and girlfriends, Fennington's only "love" is Augusta Tabor, a paragon of womanly strength and virtue, whose century-old diaries he had read in the camp library. He alone feels a special affection for Pater, an unassuming former newspaper writer, older than the other men, incongruously married to a Hollywood star, and singularly inadept at the game of war.

But the night his wife visits the camp, Pater is in jail for bungling a training exercise, and she and Fennington fall instantly in love. The next day Fennington is racked by equal and opposite reactions: his passion for Pater's wife and his wrenching guilt for betraying a friend. When a messenger rushes into camp to get help for a woman and an injured companion lost in the subzero night, Fennington eagerly accepts the task, "believing now that this trial was offered as atonement, perhaps believing that, through atonement, he would be reprieved again from love" (*HHM*, 89–90).[58]

But Fennington's is not the only betrayal: the stranded woman is Pater's wife and her companion a young German prisoner of war, an old friend whom she had come to the camp to rescue. Ironically, it is she and not the injured escapee who dies from exposure, and "Enemy Detail" ends with a double blow for Fennington: along with his integrity and self-respect, he has lost a woman he could have loved for the rest of his life.

The theme of Fennington's corruption and guilt runs quietly through "Main Drag," Part Two of the novel, nearly submerged for a time beneath the varied conflicts involving other characters in the camp and nearby town. Tension and bigotry build among the men as rumors circulate that their outfit will not be shipped overseas because of the questionable loyalties of its many foreigners. A waitress whose husband is overseas talks a traveling salesman into driving her to Denver in a blizzard so that she might visit her ailing father-in-law; in the packed car a soldier who had planned to go AWOL that night rescues her from a backseat rape.

The waitress, significantly, is named Augusta. An old miner, her grandfather, tells Fennington that she is a descendent of Augusta Tabor, the pioneer whom Fennington had regarded as the incarnation of female strength, honor, and fidelity. As the miner relates the simple history of his granddaughter's love for her husband, Curley, "it took on the quality of a parable, and in listening to it one heard the echo of man's still unrelinquished faith ringing against its actual and enduring stone."

The spotlight returns in the end to Fennington's inner struggle. The inevitable telegram reaches Augusta while he is in the bar. He takes her home, and in the stillness of the empty house he realizes that love is the only validation of human significance:

> Perhaps the death of man, he thought as he and the girl sat near to each other in the growing dark, had its part in grief only if by his dying the vessel of love was broken; perhaps if the fluid which flowed in his body did not flow as well in the veins of a woman who lay sleepless for him in her bed at night, then his death was nothing but bones returning to the eager soil. (*HHM*, 285–86)

Watching Augusta, he knows that "he had come to the end of one season, and the beginning of another, and that he was ready for the changes that would come" (*HHM*, 288). With a "savage sense of his reprieve," he kisses her, and the promise of a new life together is sealed.

Like his romance with Pater's wife and like most other love affairs in Kay Boyle's fiction, this one begins instantaneously and impulsively. The cynical will charge that the relationship is absurdly sentimental, that the author is catering to the "lady reader's" appetite for romantic fluff. But again it must be remembered that the love affairs in her own life had equally "romantic," equally "impossible" beginnings. It seems clear that the reader is to take such love seriously as Kay Boyle demonstrates once again her romantic preference for intuition over reason. The love Fennington will share with the modern-day Augusta will be the expiation of his guilt and the full realization of his humanity.

When his company finally is called into service and the troop train pulls away from the mountains and toward the war, Fennington says to a friend, "Men don't go to war alone . . . their women go with them" (*HHM*, 295). Yet the author is careful not to leave the reader with a sweet aftertaste. In the final paragraph, the friend, the camp cynic, replies, "That's bleedin' fancy thinking for a Pfc" and adds with typical black humor, "Speaking of stripes . . . there's a guy over there that's got thirteen of them." He jerks his head toward a coffin draped with the American flag.

As she was writing this novel, Kay Boyle had told her agent that she wanted "to make the human issues involved important enough to have a significance beyond the story itself." Her depiction of the mountain infantry training camp is based on what she saw at Leadville, and in its evocation of scene is almost photographically realistic. Yet the camp is also a microcosm. While its men and women retain their idiosyncratic personalities, they represent the entire spectrum of humanity in its various fragmentations by nationality, values, and temperament. Throughout the novel the author employs words like "atonement," "reprieve," and "parable" to describe events. The Colorado army camp becomes "this universe created by man's incapacity" (*HHM*, 120); the man who must be rescued from a crevasse is "the nameless and faceless figure in this allegory of heaven and hell they played" (*HHM*, 100).

The root of misery and evil in Kay Boyle's universe is the absence or failure of human bonds. The most fundamental division of humanity is by gender, and the author deplores the rigid roles that keep men and women from fully understanding one another. A French boy complains, "They offer you one of two parts, women do: you can be either master or servant, if you can take the stink that rises from either" (*HHM*, 119). Yet in his own view, women are either mothers or *putains*; there is nothing in between, he says. As a solution to this form of fragmentation, the author offers the example of man and woman fused into a single "vessel of love" (*HHM*, 285).

Humankind in this book is also divided by character into idealists and cynics. One villain is "Don Juan" Cooper, a soldier who knows nothing at all of love and a great deal about lechery. The others in the company despise him for his lewd speculations as to the fidelity of Pater's wife, speculations that defile the honor of every woman back home and shake the faith of each lonely man. The young soldier who rescues Augusta from Cooper's backseat advances on the ride to Denver is fighting "not only for one woman, but for peace, or at least for the symbols of peace she had offered them, for the high schools, the gas stations, the small imperishable hopes which war had betrayed" (*HHM,* 198).

Finally, the bigotry that has brought the entire world to war is manifested in the prejudice the native-born American soldiers feel for their foreign colleagues in the camp. Anyone who speaks with an accent or does not care about baseball scores is derisively labelled a "Latvian," and in their ignorance, these "real" Americans include American Indians in that category. In a powerful scene, a stereotypical Texan redneck plays a sadistic game with Rudi Mendl, a Jewish soldier born in Berlin, and nearly murders him. Through flashbacks we learn that the Texan's hatred for the foreigner is based on his lack of self-respect and his shame for his own background. It is the same psychology that Kay Boyle had seen operating in nazism, which made the Jew a scapegoat for German frustrations and failures.[59]

Yet she retains her faith in the capacity of humanity to recognize the spark of divinity within each individual. At Rudi Mendl's naturalization ceremony, Fennington quotes a line from Blake: "Silence remain'd and everyone resum'd his Human Majesty" (*HHM,* 268). He had learned it from Pater, and it summarizes Kay Boyle's belief that the schisms between people might be bridged by the power of a love that is Christian in spirit if not in name. It is also through Mendl that she states the central theme of the novel and, indeed, of nearly all her fiction when he says: "I believe that we are all lost, all of us, unless we can make a brotherhood of men, of all men. . . . Out of the great common suffering that has been our experience, we can make a brotherhood of man, we can make a great common love" (*HHM,* 233). As romantic love is Fennington's reprieve on an individual level, so brotherly and sisterly love must in the end be the salvation of all humanity.

Kay Boyle believes that the quality of each individual's values has everything to do with the future of humankind. Through Fennington's personal struggles, she demonstrates that a human being's sanity and peace of mind depend upon his honor, integrity, faith, and respect for himself and others—in short, upon his capacity to exercise his inborn divinity, his "human majesty." War is simply a magnification of the struggles that have raged on a personal level in the microcosm of the camp. At the end of the novel, when the men set off by train toward Europe and the war, it is in a mood of confidence and satisfaction. It is as though after struggling to define their own identities—their capacities for courage or cowardice, honor or betrayal—they realize that facing evil in such a clear-cut form as the Nazis will be simply a continuation of the same struggle.

From *This Quarter* to the *Saturday Evening Post*, from *The Crazy Hunter* to *Avalanche*, Kay Boyle's fiction underwent a dramatic alteration. Some would call it a nosedive. In many of her works of the forties, her writing style had gone from subtle to slick, her intricate method of gradual revelation often giving way to action-packed plot and baldly stated moral. Yet, paradoxically, the change in her writing was born of a steadfast consistency in her view of the artist's role. The serious writer, she has always believed, shoulders a moral responsibility to speak aloud "the inarticulate whispers of the concerned people of his time." [60] The same sense of mission that had fired her rebellion in the twenties against the forces that would extinguish artistic individualism fueled in the forties her commitment to exposing the evil of social forces that undermine the value of individual life.

The mission itself *had* changed. In 1945 Caresse Crosby wished to begin a new literary quarterly and asked her friend if she would contribute a portion of the aviation epic for which she had received a Guggenheim fellowship in the early thirties. Kay Boyle replied: "I got out my aviation poem last night and re-read parts of it. It all sounds so childish now that I can't think it would add much to your quarterly."[61] After she had witnessed in war both the cruelty and the grandeur of which men and women are capable, for the writer simply to "express" a personal vision without regard to his or her fellow human beings must have come to seem to her more self-indulgence than revolution. Kay Boyle in the 1940s came to feel it imperative to communicate plainly her fervent belief in the desperate need for human connection. For the rest of her life, she would continue to speak in the plural of the need for love.

7

In the Wake of War

When Kay Boyle spoke of herself as a writer in 1951, it was with a mature voice. There would be no more radical changes in the purpose or manner of her art. For the rest of her career, the message would take precedence over the medium in her writing. Approaching fifty (and having become a grandmother), she maintained that she was a private person, yet she also acknowledged that as a writer she must never shut herself away from the social world:

> I work in a small room where no current of air can disturb either my papers or the heart's precarious flame. If I must go away from my little room, I am impatient. I want to be closed in there, feeding the fire at peace.
>
> Except I do not want to be closed away from the sound of some voices. For who can live in a country without knowing what the people living in it think? The part of the writer is to fuse himself with man, and to speak for all men, or else to speak to all men of a common experience. It is not his role to establish himself as an exceptional figure, and he is uneasy when asked to appear as a writer, an artist, and not as a common man.[1]

Kay Boyle had come a long way from her damnation of the "plain reader."

In late 1946, she returned to Europe for a second long stay, and nearly all her fiction of the late forties, the fifties, and the early sixties is drawn directly from her experiences and observations in a world racked by war. With a few notable exceptions, her works of this period stand not so much on their aesthetic merits as on their vivid depiction of a turbulent time in contemporary history and on their impassioned social messages.

In November, 1946, "Miss Kay Boyle, about to leave for Europe, and wearing the narrow black frontier pants and black Western shirt that she calls her 'cowboy' outfit, received the press in the kitchen, apparently the least cluttered room in her flat," according to a *New York Times* reporter.[2] (The "flat" was a handsome brownstone house on East 87th Street.) The author had "several projects on hand": she was writing a children's book that would "revolutionize the world" and a novel, "Enemy Detail," to appear in the *Atlantic Monthly,* and she had just signed on as a European correspondent with *The New Yorker*. She was preparing to make the transatlantic move with her three small children, Clover, "Mousie," and "Boostie"; her husband and three older daughters were already in Europe. The reporter notes: "Her passport reads 'Kay Boyle, journalist.' It is Clover, 7 and a small fraction, who is taking over the others on this trip: Her passport lists two dependents."

Kay Boyle was returning to Europe to be near Joseph Franckenstein, then stationed with the U.S. Civilian Occupation Forces. Her foreign correspondent's passport would enable her to visit her husband in Germany and to follow up on stories there. "I did not wish to live in Germany," she explains "for my feelings about the German people were still too strong."[3] Her oldest daughter, Sharon, had been in Paris for a year working as a secretary for the French radio station, while Laurence Vail was sending Apple and Kathe to school in Mégève. Kay Boyle established a home in Paris for her three youngest children and in uniform, as was required, made trips to Germany alone.

The letters she sent back from Europe are a fascinating chronicle of everyday life in the wake of war, and they demonstrate how closely her fiction was tied to her own experiences. In fact, Kay Boyle's relationship with the "functioning world" seems to have become after 1940 the very wellspring of her creativity. She wrote to Ann Watkins from Paris in 1947: "Life is so exciting here that I could write you pages about it—but it would be more to the point to make pages of fiction about it, which I shall. . . . These trips may seem senseless, but they are not just at this time when tremendous things are taking place."[4]

Her letters from France do, nonetheless, contain pages regarding what she had seen. She describes the Parisian mothers scraping together enough money to buy little wooden paint boxes to put away for Christmas presents "and two pieces of candy to save for the great day."[5] And, while attempting to make a living by her writing, she faced her own daily dilemmas as well. She had to contend with salvaging mildewed belongings from a trunk soaked on the rough ocean crossing; entering Clover in a public elementary school off the Avenue de l'Opéra and finding a nurse for the younger children; arranging short visits with her husband in Germany; coping with electricity cuts that three nights a week curtailed her typing hours; and dealing with neighbors in thin-walled hotels who cleared their throats to protest the "undue tapping" late at night. Food was in short supply. On one day she had spent six hours in various offices trying to obtain milk ration cards for her "babies," and several of the letters to Ann Watkins contain lists of supplies she needed from America, including such things as condensed milk, canned orange juice, toothpaste, toilet paper, and extension cords. On top of all this, she had to face a three-year-old son who "about twenty times a day" would look at her "very tragically" and say, "I want to go home. Not hotel home, my home with kitchen and Edie Mae."

But as usual, Kay Boyle seemed to take all in stride and wrote to reassure her agent:

Please continue to have faith in me, I am fighting against 12 million interruptions and demands and frustrations a day. But SOMEHOW I'll do what there is to be done. I've got to. Don't lose confidence. I've finished books and made dead-lines and made money just in the nick of time and I'll do it this time if you and Ross and Aswell stand by me to the end.[6]

She even had the energy to encourage a fellow writer having difficulties to stick with it: "The actual work of writing is about as depressing as anything in the world, I think, but the accumulated pages give life a meaning. I know all this is banal, but there is truth in it—and I know that remembering this often gives me comfort when I think I just can't sit another hour or another night and bang out the necessary explanations for those who will not read, anyway, and will not want to understand."[7]

In May, 1948, she left France with her three small children to join Joseph Franckenstein in Marburg, Germany, where he had a job with the military government in the Liaison and Security Office. "The children were speechless at the sight of the destroyed cities, and everything still seemingly so recently bombed, with the radiators and bits of bed-steads still hanging from the twisted rafters," she wrote to Ann Watkins. After settling into one of the homes confiscated from Nazis by the occupation government, she did not like the position in which she found herself—"a conqueror, well-fed, well-housed, in a defeated but still bitterly defiant country."[8] Of life in the military establishment, she said, "I can't tell you how truly strange I feel. It is utterly American here—utterly middle-west—handsome American cars, etc., etc., etc., endlessly—but combined with the hard bitter population it is strange indeed. I want to write stories madly—the feeling of the people—and have made copious notes."

In addition to writing short stories for *The New Yorker* and a number of pieces, both fiction and nonfiction, that appeared in *The Nation* in the late forties, Kay Boyle took an active interest in community affairs. She was encouraged by the success of her husband's campaign among the German residents of Marburg to raise money for an iron lung and wrote to Ann Watkins (along with a request for a donation): "It's wonderful to see how a little clear-thinking and clear-speaking can make people act like human beings. The Germans in this bigoted little town are acting really democratic—all working for a common purpose in which the common-weal is concerned, writing things in the paper about it instead of writing fuzzy articles about Goethe and Schiller, and all kinds of people meeting and talking and forgetting their cultural status and acting like responsible citizens. It's exciting."[9]

Yet, if she would later admit that she had come to Germany with an "almost completely loveless" attitude (*SM,* 2),[10] she did not care, either, for many of her countrymen involved in the military occupation. Late in 1948, the family moved to the American base at Frankfurt, which was, she told Ann Watkins, "as near to living in suburbia as possible—if you turn your head from the ruins."[11] She describes the American children screaming at Clover, "Mousie," and "Boostie" in the street that they were not *real* Americans because they had a French car, and the four American boys who chased Clover with a lead pipe and tore her ski-pants. ("How is it that so many Americans grow up into decent human beings when as children they are invariably monstrous?" the author wondered.) Kay Boyle did not find the adults much more agreeable and said "one must be on the watch every instant to keep them from knowing what one really feels, thinks and cares about. 'No, I don't play bridge; I don't have time for it.' 'No, I don't think the war should be started as quickly as possible so as to get it over with.' " She often felt compelled to explain to "worthy Germans" that the Americans in the military government were not necessarily representative of the best of her country, "each with his mean ambition, his small grudge, his personal vanity," and said, "I cannot bear people in uniform, anyway." She detested what she saw as "the military madness" that was "making us fools in the eyes of every thinking person on this soil."[12] With characteristic fervor she wrote:

What would I suggest? An occupation by intellectuals, artists, an occupation by people who would be aware of what is going on in the German minds, and in their cellars, not this show of uniforms we have. An occupation by intellectuals would give the Germans an awareness of their past monstrosities, a hatred of brutality, a realization of what a new future might be—give them a hope of resurrection, an understanding of atonement . . . I wish to God I could help do something about it here.[13]

Thus it was the supreme bitter irony, given Kay Boyle's passionate commitment to freedom of thought and to personal liberty, when in 1952 her husband, a war hero decorated for his OSS work, was brought before a consular panel for a McCarthy-style loyalty hearing. The charges against Joseph Franckenstein were vague, but whatever case the accusers felt they had against him certainly involved his wife as well. Kay Boyle was accused of having sponsored or endorsed six subversive organizations and of being a Communist party member. As she puts it, "The charges against me consisted of such absurd items as a ten-dollar cheque sent by me to a Bill of Rights rally in New York which was sponsored by

Eleanor Roosevelt and Paul Robeson; and of such fabrications as my attendance at weekly Communist Party meetings with Louis Budenz (a government informer) in New York, during the war, while my husband was serving in the U. S. Armed Forces."[14]

Franckenstein's defense included bringing forth witnesses to testify not only to his loyalty to the United States, but to Kay Boyle's as well. At the hearing held on October 20 and 21 in Mehlen, Germany, one of the most colorful and eloquent testimonies was given by Janet Flanner, *The New Yorker*'s "Genêt." She was known for her anti-communist sentiments and had been a friend of Boyle's since 1929. She was fond of Joseph, too, and always called him "the gent God meant."[15] In answer to the posed possibility of Boyle's secretly being a communist, Flanner replied that her friend had always had "a curious quality of American illumination": "It was a kind of American democratic radiance that came out of her. Everything she said, everything she did; for one thing the spontaneity of her speech. It was no good asking Mrs. Franckenstein what she thought, because she would tell you. If you didn't expect to know, you'd better not ask her."[16] In Flanner's opinion, Kay Boyle had "an illuminating, obstinate, strong core of downright Middle-western democratic Americanism." There was never any "mollycoddle lollipopping about her," Flanner stated. To be with Kay Boyle "was like going back home without having to take the boat." As for a contribution Boyle had allegedly made to a suspect antifascist organization, Janet Flanner explained that nearly everyone on *The New Yorker* staff, including herself and Dorothy Parker, had contributed five or ten dollars along with "a roster of practically everybody who could read and write in the United States of America, including people who had no more political sense than turtles." She added that if Kay Boyle had contributed perhaps it was also because she was the mother of six children: "She is extremely maternal. Tell her a hard luck story and she digs into her pocket."

But not everyone at *The New Yorker* was so supportive. In the late spring of 1952, Katherine White had responded to the author's request for her written support by saying that she was deeply distressed by news of the hearing—but neither she nor E. B. White offered to write a letter on her behalf. William Shawn wrote to the officials that Kay Boyle had been a close friend of the magazine's late editor, not mentioning Harold Ross by name, implying that he himself knew too little about her to vouch for her loyalty. Gus Lobrano, *The New Yorker*'s fiction editor at that time, whom Kay Boyle says she knew better than Shawn, "wrote (in his 'To Whom It May Concern') that my warm heart and my great feeling for humanity might have made me an unwitting tool of a foreign power." "Had Harold Ross been alive, the story would have been quite a different one," she adds.[17] When the Franckensteins' American lawyer in Germany, Benjamin Ferencz, director of the Jewish Restitution Committee, read these letters, he threw up his hands in despair. The day before the hearing, he said they would just have to lay before the panel the many recommendations they did have (including those of the *Wall Street Journal*, the *Ladies' Home Journal*, the *Saturday Evening Post*, and Edward Aswell's from McGraw-Hill) and hope that the panel would not ask for a letter of support from *The New Yorker*. It was the first thing the prosecutor asked to see.[18]

Even before the outcome of the hearing was announced, Kay Boyle had been devastated by the proceedings. She recalls that after the hearing she had gone home, opened all the windows of their flat in the American enclave and played at full-volume Paul Robeson's recording of "That's America to Me."[19] A few days after the trial, she wrote to Ann Watkins that she was confident the panel would make the right decision but felt "so depressed, so crushed even, by the humiliation, the degradation, the shocking injustice of all this, that I can only feel numbly for some sort of action to take to help keep this kind of thing from happening to other honest people."[20] She added that Joseph had aged ten years and was haggard, "his heart, let us hope, only temporarily broken—but broken without any doubt." She was deeply disturbed not only by the personal consequences of the hearing but by the deeper implications of such witch-hunting in an ostensibly enlightened, democratic society. She felt that the members of the panel were "frightened" men, who instead of "seeking through fact to reach the essence of truth," were "out of caution, seeking a pattern that they could recognize and condemn."[21] She wrote, "The pattern they tried to fit me into was: Sacco and Vanzetti in 1927, the Spanish Loyalists in 1936, the 'Communist dominated' French Resistance in 1941, and in the 1950's no more was necessary than the single vile word, 'peace.' " For the first time in her life, she felt like "joining something" to prevent such a thing from happening again—"that being an American is not enough."

Yet even her faith in a fair outcome of the hearing was betrayed. Joseph Franckenstein was unanimously cleared by the Consular Board. Several of its members even wept as Benjamin Ferencz delivered his closing address. But shortly afterward, two of McCarthy's subcommittee staff members, Roy Cohn and G. David Schine ("two later discredited young scoundrels," Kay Boyle calls them), arrived to look through the files of those employees who had had loyalty-security hearings.[22] Within twenty-four hours, Joseph Franckenstein (along with every other Foreign Service officer who had been tried) was fired as "surplus." Then *The New Yorker* withdrew Kay Boyle's accreditation.

As she tells it, William Shawn informed her agent "that *The New Yorker* had been considering with-drawing my accreditation even before the hearing, as I had not been sending enough stories in. This was his ignoble way out of a situation he must now view with shame."[23] She asked Ann Watkins to inform Shawn that no work of hers would ever again see publication in that magazine. Following what Boyle calls her "firing" by *The New Yorker,* the American Civilian Occupation Forces in Germany proposed a regulation that no wife of a Foreign Service officer could be accredited as a journalist. *The Stars and Stripes* reported this on its front page, pointing out that such a regulation would affect only two people: Sonia Tomara (Mrs. William Clark), a foreign correspondent for the *Herald Tribune* who had testified for the defense at the Franckenstein hearing, and Kay Boyle. (The regulation was never enacted.)

The family returned to the United States and settled in Rowayton, Connecticut, where Franckenstein was, in his wife's words, "reduced" to teaching in a young ladies' school. Kay Boyle was bitter. She wrote in October, 1953, "I lost a year's work on this blasted unAmerican activities thing and feel like suing the government in my fury at what it has done to Joseph's faith in America as well as to our finances."[24] But she had lost not only a year's work. She found herself blacklisted. In the years that followed, her agent was unable to place any of her stories. For several years Kay Boyle's writing was interrupted as she took on teaching, book reviewing, and other "odd jobs to meet the weekly bills." Her son, Ian, contributed the earnings from his newspaper route, and her daughters, Clover and Faith, started a little neighborhood summer school where they taught art, dance, and dramatics to six-, eight-, and ten-year-olds to help the family fortunes.

In 1957, when Katherine Anne Porter was unable at the last minute to teach a six-week lecture course on the short story at the University of Delaware, Kay Boyle was invited to take her place. She was terrified at the prospect, confiding to Bob Brown, "I don't know anything about the short story," but the pay was too good to refuse. Miraculously, it seems that her idealism was intact: "I have to do one big public lecture (and if I live through all this, I'll never be the same) and I want to do this lecture on the power of the individual to change the course of history."[25]

The couple fought Franckenstein's dismissal from the diplomatic service for nine years.[26] In 1962 he was reinstated, with apologies from the State Department, but the false accusations, the blacklisting, and the time and resources required to fight the charges had "exacted immeasurable harm on their personal and professional lives," in the words of a friend.[27] The injustices Kay Boyle and her husband had suffered at the hands of their compatriots fueled her determination to speak out on social issues in her fiction.

Beginning in the war years, her writing had been motivated by a powerful sense of moral responsibility. She had seen the devastating effects of fascism and felt it her duty to report what she had witnessed. Soon after the loyalty hearing in 1952, she had written to Edward Aswell, her editor, saying that she felt she must put aside work on a book for which they had contracted. "If life were calmer and the demands of conscience and responsibility less pressing," she would be writing the promised book right then, she said, "But I do not feel I can write it now." She explained: "Your book—the other book—is to be poetry, a luxury almost in these days."[28] In such turbulent times, Kay Boyle felt, things had to be said quickly in the hope that through fiction the eyes of American readers might be opened to critical issues concerning the very future of humankind.

In her postwar fiction, Kay Boyle continued to draw from her immediate experiences—a practice established in her earliest days in France when she wrote about the struggles of a young American bride living with her French in-laws. In the late forties and the early fifties while she was living in Europe, she wrote extensively about the postwar problems she had observed in Spain, France, and Germany. After her return to the United States in the mid-fifties, contemporary America would become the setting of much of her fiction, and she would focus her concern on the social problems of her native land.

As a writer with a social conscience, she felt a special commitment to speak of Spain, the nation that had been the first victim of fascism in the dress rehearsal for World War II, but whose liberation had not come with the rest of Europe's at the end of the war. "Who, in our time, remained an outsider, and aloof from the drama of Spain's civil war?" she asked. "The honor of all men was implicated in that struggle, for the issue of man standing weaponless and alone before organized power had never been more heroically defined."[29] She expressed contempt for her literary contemporaries who had failed to lend their artistic gifts and their influence to the protest against tyranny, and it is interesting that of the three writers she specifically indicts, two already had lost her admiration years earlier when they had failed to take their part in that day's battle of honor—the Revolution of the Word. Without comment, she convicts them with their own words:

"You are all mad," wrote Ezra Pound in 1937. "Spain is an emotional luxury for sap-headed dilettantes." "If I were a Spaniard I should be fighting for Franco," wrote Evelyn Waugh in the same year. "As an Englishman I am not in the predicament of choosing between two evils. I am not a fascist nor shall I become one unless it were the only alternative to Marxism." And T. S. Eliot opened the door a little way and whispered: "While I am naturally sympathetic, I still feel convinced that it is best that at least a few men of letters should remain isolated, and take no part in these collective activities."[30]

Less than a month after those words appeared in *The Nation,* Kay Boyle arrived in Spain on April 16, 1947. What she saw there inspired a short novel entitled "Decision," which first appeared in the *Saturday Evening Post* in 1948 as "Passport to Doom" (not her title, she has made clear).[31] It was published with "The Crazy Hunter" and "The Bridegroom's Body" when those works were reissued in 1958 in a volume entitled *Three Short Novels,* itself republished in 1982. "Decision" was a work that meant a great deal to Kay Boyle. Coming after a series of frankly commercial works, including *Avalanche* and *A Frenchman Must Die,* "Decision" was written without regard to its marketability: "It will sell nowhere, but it is one of the most interesting things I have ever written, and I am going to stick to it whatever bankruptcy or disaster occur."[32] In the midst of her work on the piece, she had told her agent that she honestly believed it was "one of the best things I've ever done (in a class with 'Monday Night' and 'The Crazy Hunter'") and that the whole year 1947 would be justified for her if she could "bring it off" as she hoped to.[33] "I feel as if my whole future and honor depended on the writing of this piece," she said in still another letter, "because it will show to both of us and to others who may read it, that I can still write—and not in an emotional, overwrought way, but in a matured, disciplined way."[34]

The narrator of "Decision" is a foreign woman (wearing white earrings) who has come to Madrid to find one Manuel Jeronimo. She has papers to give him that his sister in Paris had worked months to obtain—papers that would allow him to leave Spain, where he has been in and out of prison for years on political charges. In meetings with Manuel's wife, his relatives, and his friends, the narrator learns of the resisters' courage and what it means to be a Spaniard out of favor with the fascist regime. The "proprietor" of the "Republican Hotel," a hideout in one of the cave dwellings surrounding Madrid, tells the woman: "I swear if you try to give Manuel papers to get him out of the country, he'll laugh in your face. He's Spanish, I tell you, he's crazy. He'd cut out his heart, if you asked him, but if you gave him a passport to get him away, he'd tear it in half—" (*TSN,* 231). Still, all agree that he must make his own decision. When the narrator learns that Manuel and a friend, Eleuterio Garcia, have been arrested again, she visits the prison with Garcia's wife, only to learn that the inmates have rioted to protest conditions and visitors will not be admitted. To quell the disturbance, the guards had gone through the galleries and removed every third man, no matter what he was in for. The next morning she reads in the newspaper that several executions had taken place at the prison. In the list of names that follows are Jeronimo's and Garcia's.

"Decision" is a tribute to the courage of the Spanish people as much as it is a condemnation of the fascist government. Repeatedly the author emphasizes the gaiety of the oppressed—Señora Garcia's giddy laughter as she costumes and coifs the foreign woman to get her past the prison guards as a Spaniard, the Garcia children's giggling and cavorting after a butterfly on the prison grounds—and the narrator thinks, "This is in itself the answer, the final outwitting of them, the thing which they have sought to touch and have not touched. It is levity that gives drama a noble face, and yet saves it from its own depravity" (*TSN*, 261).

According to the author, the title "Decision" was intended to carry several meanings: "my own to write it, and that of the Spaniard in the story, and the decision which the situation itself must present to each of us."[35] Yet within the context of the story, there is a bit of irony in the word, too, for, as a compatriot of Manuel points out to the narrator, there *are* no complicated decisions to be made when one lives under a totalitarian system: " 'You are either every third man who is taken out and shot, or else you are not,' he said, 'but one is not permitted a decision. There is no choice that he can make, except the profounder choice which lies between good and evil' " (*TSN*, 260). It is that "profounder choice" with which the author intended to confront her readers.

The desire to make the American reading public aware of another critical situation in postwar Europe motivates her fiction set in France. Kay Boyle was distressed by the distorted picture Europeans were getting of America on the basis of "the ostentation, the big dinners, big mansions, general laxness, which typifies our headquarters establishments throughout Europe."[36] She was appalled at the insensitivity and arrogance of military personnel that could bring the French to call the American "l'occupant," as they had called the German just a few years before.

In "French Harvest," one of her many short stories of postwar France, Kay Boyle writes that there were many in Paris who remembered nothing of the armies that had lingered on their territory "except the GIs who had climbed one night onto the Jeanne d'Arc statue which stands at the Place des Pyramides and straddled in drunken triumph her gilded horse, riding like liberators behind her armored figure, aping even the gesture of the lifted sword; or remembered those other GIs who had removed the swinging doors of the ladies' rooms in restaurants, because of the word '*dames*' stenciled on them, and had borne them through the streets of Paris on summer evenings, roaring their shameless songs aloud" (*NEB*, 303). Yet she had little sympathy, either, for the petty Parisian hotelkeeper who could forget the gas chambers and deportation trains and say, "there was one thing about the Germans: Whatever they did in other countries there was nothing to complain about what they did to our hotel rooms—never a broken window, never a scratch on the furniture" (*NEB*, 304).

It was Kay Boyle's concern over the dangerous rift between France and America—the cradles of democracy—that compelled her to write *Seagull on the Step* (1955), and once more she was willing to sacrifice artistic quality in order to gain the wide hearing she felt this issue must have. In outlining her novel to her agent, she said that she wanted to write something "which might explain France now as 'Avalanche' explained France in the year I wrote it," and she wanted to write it "in 'Saturday Evening Post' terms."[37] The theme of the book, she explained, would be that "the French don't want Communism and they don't want war, but they may get both if we don't do something very, very fast about getting the democratic French and the democratic Americans together."[38]

The idea for such a book grew out of conversations early in 1952 with her French son-in-law, Michel Sciama, her oldest daughter's husband, who had fought for two years in the Resistance before being captured by the Nazis and imprisoned in the Buchenwald concentration camp until the end of the war. She patterned the hero of her novel after him. The hero's name is also Michel, although his last name, Vaillant, obviously was chosen for its symbolic value. She dedicated the novel "in love" to "those young people who are the flesh and spirit of the new France (and who have, in consequence, no time or need to read these pages), among them my children who are there."

As the vehicle of her message, the author chose the murder mystery and laced it with romance. Mary Farrant, a young woman from Ohio, leaves Paris and her fiancé, an American diplomat, in order to respond personally to a letter to the editor from one Michel Vaillant—an open invitation "to an American" to come see what he was trying to do in the coastal village of Abelin.

As Mary recuperates from a bus accident on the road to Abelin in which twenty-five of her fellow passengers were killed, she finds herself in the middle of a dispute that has split the town into two semi-armed camps: the mayor, the doctor, and the real estate people, who want to preserve the status quo and line their pockets by promoting tourism, versus the workers, led by Vaillant, who are hurt by the artificially inflated cost of housing and who want more popular control of local affairs. Symbol of the conflict is a half-finished casino, and when the town officials (the bad guys) learn that Mary has high connections with the American foreign service, they curry her favor in the hope that she will talk her fiancé into helping finance their project.

Mary, however, has already pledged allegiance to Vaillant. When the officials in power learn that Peter Cornish has finally located his missing bride-to-be and is driving down from Paris to retrieve her, Michel Vaillant is slapped in jail on false charges of having cut the bus's brake lines. Mary is spirited away to the secluded home of the lecherous Dr. Angelo, who plans either to sway her to the "establishment's" side or kill her. Mary is saved by the arrival of the priest, a friend of Vaillant, who as a ruse to liberate her, insists the doctor accompany him immediately to attend someone gravely ill. They bring Mary's untouched lobster dinner along, and when the abbey cats eat it, several of them die. Dr. Angelo's villainy is clear, not only in this attempted murder but in the successful food-poisoning murders of his own wife and a wealthy townsman—crimes committed with the intention of acquiring the man's estate by marrying his wife.

But in the corrupt village, truth is often inconsequential when legal justice is dispensed, and it appears that Vaillant may be convicted of murdering the bus passengers unless another honest witness can be found to counter the perjured prosecution. The only person who can save Vaillant now is Marrakech, a mute, deformed Algerian and the town outcast. In the final chapters the reader is led on a mad search for him through the village streets and the quays which culminates in a melodramatic cliffside scuffle in which Dr. Angelo is prevented at the last moment from feeding the beggar some suspicious mussels but succeeds in causing him to fall to his death. Mary, however, falls into the arms of Michel Vaillant, who miraculously appears on the scene, and the search party returns to Abelin to find the casino entirely dismantled by the populace loyal to Vaillant.

Still, it appears that Angelo will get away with murder until Mary, toying with a hollow wooden seagull Marrakech had carved for Dr. Angelo (with the word *Amour* written across its breast) discovers a picture story hidden inside. The mute Algerian had drawn it with pride, indicating he had paid his debt to the doctor who fed and housed him: he had followed the doctor's instructions and carefully cut the bus's brake lines. The story ends with a jousting match in the water between Michel Vaillant and Peter Cornish. They are "doing it for a woman," a bystander tells the bewildered Mary as she joins the crowd of spectators on the quay. We have no doubt as to which man will win her.

The mystery and love story, however, are only packaging for a social allegory of contemporary France. The author is not subtle about the book's symbolic intent: "Maybe this bus is France, and maybe I'm premier!" the driver shouts to his passengers, who include obvious representatives of the military, the merchant class, the clergy, the foreigner and the *haute bourgeoisie* (*SS,* 113).[39] When the driver learns that the Algerian outcast Marrakech is riding under the bus, he shouts, "put him into the bus and he'll act as representative from the colonies! This is France on four wheels, and it can't be France without him here!" (*SS,* 32). In this allegorical warning of what might happen to France, the bus is destroyed when the hand of greed and corruption causes it to career out of control. Nor has Kay Boyle abandoned her concern for the failures of love on a personal scale. It is sad and ironic that Marrakech's innocent devotion was twisted by the doctor to the destruction of life.

The characters play symbolic roles as well. Mary Farrant represents the guileless New World idealism on which the democratic system was founded; she is "the wheatfields of Ohio, and the apple trees" (*SS*, 239). Peter Cornish, however, is the impeccably groomed but "ugly" American who drives a car so big it cannot pass through the village streets—a provincial unable to understand either the language or the needs of Europeans. "It's because of the things he's owned all his life!" Mary claims. "He's always had something to put between himself and what other men are" (*SS*, 198–99). It is Michel Vaillant who embodies "the flesh and spirit of the new France," and although Peter Cornish is incapable of responding to his call, Vaillant passionately explains to him his—and Kay Boyle's—dream: "With one quarter of my country voting Communist and the other three quarters split in a dozen ways, I have to speak, I have to act. I have to believe that it's me—the good European—and you—the good American—who together will find the energy and honesty to build our own defense" (*SS*, 205).

Judged as a work of literature, *The Seagull on the Step* is not one of Kay Boyle's more admirable efforts. The plot rides on remarkably fortunate coincidences; the characters are largely of the soap commercial variety that Edmund Wilson had deplored a decade earlier; the dialogue is improbable (in the opening pages, Mary Farrant earnestly explains her life history to the strangers on the bus); and the symbolic and allegorical elements are baldly stated. As one critic wrote, "The sincerity of her anguish is more moving than the story in which she has sought to embody it."[40] The book was not a critical success, but it is significant as a clearcut example of the polemical turn Kay Boyle's writing had taken in the postwar years. It was a book in which she had invested much emotion. She wrote to her editor, Edward Aswell, of the American officials in Europe, saying: "They have so misrepresented you and me, so garbled the truth of America, so abbreviated her eloquence, so wounded the pride of men whose language they do not know, that I feel they have all but lost the cause for us. Perhaps the harm they have done can never be undone—certainly not in our lifetime, and not by this book, but I have written it just the same."[41] Aswell, however, had not been able to share her belief in the book, and their relationship as author and editor came to an end in 1954. To the deep personal regret of Aswell, who had told Kay Boyle that his faith was in her but not necessarily in everything she wrote, *The Seagull on the Step* was published by Alfred A. Knopf.

It is ironic that Kay Boyle's finest works of the postwar period were written about the country she cared for least. *The Smoking Mountain:*

Stories of Postwar Germany (1951) demonstrates that her fiction is at its best when fervor and sentiment are tempered by a shot of acid. The book is a vintage blend of vivid reporting, sensitive commentary, and skillfully crafted fiction. It is dedicated to Harold Ross, founder and senior editor of *The New Yorker,* "who wanted fiction out of Germany," and five of the eleven stories in the collection were originally published in that magazine while she was a correspondent.

In the introduction she explains that she had come to Germany after the war "without eagerness, abhorring this country's immediate past, knowing that those Germans who had been free and fearless men had, in our time, been exterminated by their countrymen, or else that one had known them as refugees on foreign soil" (*SM,* 1). While visiting displaced persons camps in the American zone in 1947, she had heard "stories of individual, if unwilling acceptance of that state" and compared that with "the quality of French and Spanish acceptance of the individual obligations to liberty." When she then came to live in Germany in 1948, she says, she committed herself to "a painstaking and almost completely loveless search for another face of Germany" (*SM,* 2).

But she was to be disappointed. In the seventy-seven page nonfiction introduction to the book, she presents a brilliant journalistic account of a denazification trial she had witnessed in Frankfurt in 1948. The former Gestapo official accused of participating in fifty-six cases of murder appears oblivious to the proceedings. While 157 witnesses give their accounts of his reign of terror, he makes no movement except to surreptitiously eat peanuts, which his fingers are busily shelling out of sight below the panels of the dock. Among the passages describing the courtroom scene, the author intersperses other accounts of Germans she has known and the effects the war has had on them. She muses on the duality of a culture that could produce Goethe, Heine, Nietzsche, and Mann on the one hand and Hitler on the other. And she expands on Nietzsche's observation that " 'The German soul has passages and galleries in it, there are caves and hiding places, and dungeons therein' " (*SM,* 40).

The book's title is taken from a passage by the German novelist Theodor Plievier, which she quotes as its epigraph. Plievier speaks to the "wretched German people," who had reached "lofty heights" in art, science, law, and languages and who had established guilds and free crafts but who had allowed one aspect of their "complex social constitution" to expand, grow all-powerful, and swallow up everything else until "the people ceased to exist as a people and became nothing but fuel for the monstrous, smoking mountain, the individual became nothing but wood, peat, fuel oil, and finally a black flake spewed up out of the flames." The tragic point of the book is that war and defeat have taught the Germans who live in its pages nothing—that they have come to no recognition of guilt and feel no responsibility for the catastrophe launched by their nation.

Any hope the reader may have that defeat would mark a new beginning for Germany is neatly dashed in the first story of the collection, ironically titled "Begin Again." The story is actually a series of four portraits of Germans unified by the fact that each has accepted a ride from an American woman driving on the Autobahn, a road originally "built for conquest" that has become in defeat "a conduit for the voices of many people" (*SM,* 79–80). The woman's passengers are a cross-section of Germany. There is the medical student bearing a briefcase, "that emblem of the cultured, the professionally elite, that only *Herr Doktors* and *Herr Professors* are authorized to bear" (*SM,* 80). He refuses to believe that German and not Allied bombings could have been responsible for destroying Italy's artistic monuments. There is the bleached blonde "with her face painted high and Post Exchange nylons on her heavy German legs" who speaks GI slang and despises Germans, but who has acquired from her American friends a new prejudice—a loathing of "niggers." There is a young amputee who looks back with nostalgia on 1943 and 1944 ("the years when the gas chambers burned the brightest," the American woman thinks) as "the good years" when milk, butter, and eggs were plentiful (*SM,* 85). And there is the man whose Mercedes had broken down—"small-skulled and vindictive as an eagle, with the eagle's cold, belligerent eye"—whose primary objection to Hitler was that he had been a common house painter and not a university graduate. He is shocked that Franklin D. Roosevelt's sons were salesmen, "although," he says, "I have been given to understand that the father had a university education, in spite of the fact that he had Jewish blood" (*SM,* 88).

A number of the stories are devoted to exposing unsavory aspects of the German character as the author sees it. In "Fife's House," a German boy attempts to bully a guileless American child living on an army base into giving him a treasured gold watch his father had brought from Switzerland. When Fife's mother (a writer with the odd habit of typing in bed) tells Horst that the watch is not Fife's to give, Horst flings it across the room and later sets fire to the garbage cans behind the American housing unit.

German acquisitiveness and the desire to erase the past without facing its implications are also the targets of "The Lovers of Gain," another series of portraits of Germans. These are employees in a PX store who seem to have no difficulties of conscience as they obsequiously serve their former enemies and regularly accept cigarettes from the American woman who knows them only by the names of their brand preferences. The tenacity of prejudice is seen in "Adam's Death" when an American woman and her young son discover that the Jewish dentist serving a corpulent peasant population is himself starving. In "The Criminal," an American family awakens to find that their house, requisitioned from a former Nazi Blockwart, has been ransacked, although the thief had by-passed the silver and crystal to take only food. The obvious suspect is the skeletal wanderer hired by the Blockwart to tend the garden in his absence. While the American father pities the starving man, the German is eager to turn him over to the police and apologizes for his negligence in hiring him: "It is a mistake to deal with anyone who hasn't a roof over his head, and I should not have done so" (*SM*, 224). In the author's view, the "criminal" of the title is not the starving thief but the well-fed burgher who feels no compassion or responsibility for his suffering compatriot and who would deal with his infraction more harshly than would the American "enemy." His crime is nothing less than the myopic insensitivity that permitted Hitler to round up six million Jews in full view of their country-men and send them to their deaths. (As a German acquaintance had explained to Kay Boyle, "There were certain things it was better not to know" [*SM*, 35].)

The Germans who flock to see the nightclub revue in "Cabaret" are delighted by the satirical political skits. They roar with pleasure to see America depicted as a gum-chewing youth in a T-shirt with a string of canned goods clattering around his neck, France as a languorous young woman in pink lingerie, and Russia as a brute in a scarlet tunic and fur cap who chases the lady around her boudoir shouting, "Veto! Veto!" They are even amused when a German girl resembling Deitrich but wearing an American mail-order plaid skirt and saddleback shoes sings in a husky voice that she would trade her love for a Camel. But they laugh most uproariously at the final skit in which a line of booted, uniformed men with sleeve bands featuring a sheep's head with one ear hooked up and the other hooked down stomp their feet in time, cry "Baaaaa" and give a ridiculous nose-thumbing salute to their leader—a housepainter who climbs a stepladder and flings paint upon them as they continue their homage undaunted. Apparently the audience has experienced no shock of recognition at the sight of this absurd leader and his mindless followers: "for what was he but the point of a colossal joke that history had played upon the world, the burlesque of a man some other people had chosen as their leader once at some other time and in some other place? This was someone they had no use for any longer, for he had deceived them into believing he would succeed in what he had set out to do" (*SM*, 151).

If Kay Boyle seems merciless in her attack on the German mind and character, she is no gentler in her presentation of American failings. The American protagonist in "Frankfurt in Our Blood" sees Germany "like some isolated territory, like a lepers' colony, an infected island which free men conquered and who have, because of this, become ailing and evil and no longer free" (*SM*, 123). In "Summer Evening," the author presents a parade of American grotesques at a cocktail party, exposing the ugliness of the military mind—specifically, the special kind of ugliness that accompanies victory. The guests brag about the sets of Dresden dinner china, the monogrammed silver, and the handmade heirloom lace tablecloths that they have bought "for a song" from Germans too hungry to argue over the terms. One American ignores the ashtrays and purposely drops his cigarette butts over the terrace rail for the fun of watching the elderly *Hausmeister* crawl on his hands and knees through the bushes to salvage the precious tobacco.

Kay Boyle's criticism of the American system does not end with the military, however. Two of the most powerful stories in *The Smoking Mountain* treat America's own favorite prejudice—not against Jews, but against blacks. In "Home" a black GI befriends a tattered-looking German waif outside the American PX and, defying the regulations that prohibit Germans from entering, brings the child inside. He spends the bulk of a month's pay outfitting him in warm socks, shoes, and a cowboy suit. When he later discovers that the boy is a shill sent regularly by his mother to play upon and profit by American sympathies, the soldier nevertheless feels he has gained more than he has lost: "For the duration of the dream, the boy was his . . . and the soldier, who had known only leaning Negro shacks, became the provider, the protector at last, the dispenser of white-skinned charity" (*SM*, 163). The author emphasizes the fact that the black man from Mississippi feels as out of place as the German boy in the gleaming representation of "home" that is the U.S. Post Exchange. The GI cheerfully pays the outraged clerk for the merchandise, explaining, "at home, ma'am, I never had much occasion to do for other people, so I was glad to have had this opportunity offered me" (*SM*, 167).

One of the most moving pieces in the collection is "The Lost," a story about the European orphans adopted as GI mascots and left behind when their outfits went home. The tough-talking children—Czech, Italian, Polish, Hungarian—know only GI slang and speak with the accents of Brooklyn or the South. The ones they consider lucky are those whose families can be proven dead so that they might avoid repatriation and be sent to the United States to live with the GIs who had promised them homes. "I ain't no Eyetie no more," says a twelve-year-old, and he informs the director of the refugee orphan camp that his parents "was bumped off" when "we" bombed the town (*SM*, 184).

There is no doubt that Johnny Madden (born Janos) is "going to be all right"—he had seen his parents hanged in Noverzcimski in 1942. His American "buddy," Charlie Madden, is eager to give him a home in Chattanooga, but there is a problem Johnny and Charlie had not figured on. Charlie Madden is black, and the American camp director explains to Johnny that in the United States there is the "color question." She would have to place him with a white family. When Johnny comes back to her office a week later to ask "if there wasn't no change yet in that question you was talking about—the colored question over there" the answer is negative (*SM*, 204). The next day Johnny is gone, but he has left a letter for her to send to his American friend: "Yessitdy I talk to the US consil Charlie and what do ya think now? Seems my fammillys jus as good as they ever waz so Charlie I make up my mynd sudden to go back whar they waz waiting for me Im sure ya thinks its for the best Charlie so I says so long" (*SM*, 205). The story was refused by *The New Yorker* on the grounds that "there was a good deal of doubt around here about whether such things could really happen." Kay Boyle was furious. She wrote to her agent that Janet Flanner "wept tears over the story and knew—as I did—that every word of it is true."[42] She felt it imperative that Americans be told the truth not only about the ways of their recent enemy, but about themselves.

The Smoking Mountain is a collection of sad and bitter tales about the desperate need for understanding and the tragedies that result when human connections are blocked by racism, nationalism, militarism, egotism, greed, and self-deception. While in this book she most often focuses her attention on the moral failings of a particular people, the message is universal: the individual must recognize a personal responsibility to his or her fellow human beings; and when, as in the case of Germany, love fails and even the most rudimentary codes of civilization and human decency are broken, the individual must accept a share of the collective guilt. In the words of a German friend of the author, "Until there has been a national upheaval, a cleaning of our house by our own hands, the twilight will remain" (*SM*, 77).

In the early fifties, Kay Boyle had contracted to write a novel about Germany, but because of the critical political situation in France, she had felt compelled to put it aside to write *The Seagull on the Step*. The German book was to be "poetry," she had written in 1952 to Edward Aswell, "a luxury, almost, in these days." When the book about France was finished, however, she again turned her attention to writing about Germany. She produced a number of accounts for *The Nation* combining journalistic reporting with narrative techniques; contributed in 1962 to a pamphlet series of the American Jewish Committee, a monograph entitled *Breaking the Silence: Why A Mother Tells Her Son About the Nazi Era*; and contracted to write a modern history of Germany for which she received a second Guggenheim fellowship in 1961.[43]

Her German novel was published in 1960 as *Generation Without Farewell*. The book stands apart from most of her works about postwar Europe in the subtlety with which she weaves her "message" into a novel that is fully realized in artistic terms as well. Harry T. Moore has traced its kinship to the author's earliest novels of the European scene: "This book is not one of narrow-visioned propaganda; rather it is a later and richer chapter in Kay Boyle's continuing involvement with the international theme, which in our time has new phases."[44]

The novel, set in Germany in 1948, is concerned with the same problems of German culpability and remorselessness that she had explored in *The Smoking Mountain*. But in addition to vividly depicting the social problems of defeat and occupation, it is also a richly symbolic story of one man's coming to terms with his own identity. The novel integrates the concerns of Kay Boyle's early expatriate novels with her later, more overtly social works by focusing on the need for love on both the individual and collective scales.

The story centers around Jaeger, an Afrika Korps soldier who had spent three years in a Colorado POW camp and has returned to the Fatherland an alien among his own people. He is "done forever with the vainglory and the black possession of the Nibelungs of his youth" and possessed instead by the desire "to say 'hi' to whatever grim, defeated faces leaned over spade or hoe in the German gardens that he passed" in order to "free himself of the old, accursed heritage of class" (*GWF*, 4).[45] Anything German "belonged to a past that he repudiated, and to a future he did not want to share" (*GWF*, 34). Yet in the course of the novel, Jaeger will come to terms with his inescapable identity as a German and will accept his share of the responsibility of rebuilding from the ruins a new nation of free men and women.

The epigraph, a passage by Wolfgang Borchert, says of Jaeger's generation:

We are the generation without farewell. We may live no farewell, we must not, for on the stray paths trodden by our feet our wandering hearts find endless farewells. . . . We have many encounters, encounters without duration and without farewell, like the stars. They approach, stand for light-seconds beside one another, move away again: without trace, without ties, without farewell.

In his devastated land, peopled with rootless wanderers, Jaeger realizes that he must connect with others if his life is to have meaning. "A man's life must have continuity, if nothing else," he thinks, "some kind of unbroken lineage of act, of association, some kind of unbroken line of friendship, love. That's where mine ravelled out" (*GWF*, 39).

At first it appears that his need for love will be fulfilled by a woman. The sensitive and intelligent wife of a boorish American colonel, Catherine Roberts possesses an interest in understanding "the secrets of the dark forests of Germany" (*GWF*, 11) that infuriates her husband, whose one-dimensional mind sees Germany only as territory to be occupied efficiently. She feels a bond with Jaeger, whom her husband has hired to teach her German, for while Jaeger had been a prisoner of war, she considers herself a prisoner of the occupation. She tells him, "I'm reading the *Portable Plato* and the *Portable Faulkner* from the PX. I start reading the moment I get up in the morning, and I read straight through every meal, not looking up because I can't bear to see what happens to people when they win" (*GWF*, 11–12).

The author makes it clear that she intends her novel as an allegory of a quest for love and identity—for connections—in a description of the two walking together in the forest:

> It was like the prologue to some kind of symbolic play; the fern-like woods in which they wandered perhaps known as the Forest of Consciousness, and they setting out on a mystical journey that had as destination something more significant than mere earthly love. It was all heavy and German, weighted with indefinable meaning, murky, Wagnerian almost, so far from the smell of honeysuckle and little lambs eating ivy that Jaeger laughed suddenly at the awful burden it laid upon their hearts. (*GWF*, 52)

But, in an interlude between rendezvous with Catherine, Jaeger has another kind of encounter that changes and clarifies the purpose of his "journey." A newspaper reporter, he makes a day trip by train to the city of Niederstadt to cover a trial, and as he is walking through the ruined streets, he witnesses the enactment of a popular myth. As a crane scoops the rubble from foundations and cellars, "out of the cellar's, or the earth's dark, fetid depths came a figure" (*GWF*, 165), one of the survivors of the war who had been interred for years under the debris in a well-stocked air-raid shelter:

> Exactly as in every account, whether from Danzig, or Munich or Warsaw, the rags of a *Wehrmacht* uniform clung to the figure's bones, the sleeves, the trousers, hanging in shreds, slashed back and forth and up and down by outraged time. A soiled, discolored beard hung to its waist, and the long green locks of hair on its head mingled upon its shoulders with epaulettes of dust. Filth rendered indecipherable the insignia that had once designated rank, and blackened the medals that had testified to the valor of an individual or a regiment. There it stood, an emissary from the earth's exuding heart, a revenant from a war lost three years before, swaying, babbling, shaking, gesticulating, saluting, seeing nothing in the bright blaze of the lowering sun. (*GWF*, 166)

Jaeger suddenly realizes that the destination of his "mystical journey" *is* "something more significant than mere earthly love." He misses a meeting with Catherine in order to write a different story from the one he had come to report: "He wrote methodically, in a kind of benumbed, halted grief, saying that each of them, every German, must claw his way out of the depths of what he was, letting the faded, filth-encrusted insignia fall from him, and the medals for military valor drop away." On the train ride home, he takes his place with the other Germans in the "destitution of third-class carriages" and falls asleep. When he awakens, his heart is heavy with "the terrible burden of Germany" (*GWF*, 168). Jaeger cannot escape by hiding behind an adopted national identity or by retreating into the personal happiness of a love affair. He realizes that as a man of conscience he must bear responsiblity for his country's past and future; he must seek to establish human connection on a much broader scale.

In addition to presenting one man's search for identity, Kay Boyle uses this novel as a forum for some of her most fundamental beliefs. Through the figure of Seth Honerkamp, an American civilian in charge of the America House in Fahrbach, where Germans and Americans may come to read books and listen to music, she displays her regard for the well-rounded humanist and the individual of principle. Honerkamp makes himself unpopular with the narrowminded of both nationalities. When a local man dies of polio, he and Jaeger head an unprecedented community effort to buy an iron lung. When it arrives, he intends to insist that it be displayed in the lobby of the hospital, an idea opposed by the medical elite, who complain, "What private honor . . . is conferred by a degree if the common man is permitted public access to the secrets of the trade?" (*GWF*, 298). The American authorities are upset because Honerkamp refuses to censor the contents of the library. He feels it is important that Germans see the photographs of lynchings in the South so they will know that Americans are aware of injustice in their own country, "that we write of it, talk out loud about it, fight to alter it, and do not hold our heads quite so high because we know it has happened and is happening still" (*GWF*, 61). He plays recordings by black singers so that the Germans will know "that the suspect can be as great artists as any other men" (*GWF*, 64). In the end, he is dismissed and faces unspecified charges from the military government, a procedure with which Kay Boyle was bitterly familiar.

She also uses her novel to attack militarism of any nationality. While she despises the Germans who have laid away their Luftwaffe uniforms and swastika armbands "in lavender with their wedding veils and their wedding tails and their tear-soaked memories" (*GWF*, 254), she finds equally despicable the "snickering" GIs in the botanical gardens in Niederstadt who drop crackerjacks into the "open throat" of an orchid and take potshots at the backside of a terra-cotta mermaid in the garden of a requisitioned home. In her view, the best men are those who have laid aside the uniform "because it stands between them and what they cherish as the beating hearts of all humanity" (*GWF*, 90). Honerkamp (and certainly Kay Boyle) believes that "the figures who stood massive and immobile in German history" must no longer be Frederick the Great or Bismarck or Hindenburg, "or whatever others there were who stamped out the measure of the booted, belted, homicidal dance." "But, crowding the national stage until they became the corporeity of man's belief, should be Bach, Handel, Haydn, Beethoven, Schubert, right up to Orff, and not stop there" (*GWF,* 190).

Moreover, Boyle seems to view militarism as the large-scale projection of a particularly masculine brand of egotism that she finds contemptible. As in other works like "Episode in the Life of an Ancestor" and "The Bridegroom's Body," she contrasts a woman's quiet strength and generosity of spirit with the brittle egotism of a man who defines himself by his acquisitions and his authority over others. Colonel Roberts treats women brutally—in an impeccably correct manner. When his daughter, Milly, first arrives at his magnificent hillside house, he proudly awaits her praise. "Quite a place, isn't it?" he asks, but she turns away from the sight of his possessions to gaze into the valley. *"Look at the house ahead of you!* he might have been roaring at her. *Don't give a second thought to Germany!* And he thinks: *Will I have to put signs up so that you'll know window from door, officer from enlisted man, Kraut from American?"* (*GWF,* 7). Fortunately, despite her gentleness, Catherine Roberts is a tough woman and will not yield readily to her husband's bullying: "Their voices, their wills, were two rapiers crossed there in the sunlight, and, for all the lightness and delicacy of the woman's, hers was as strong as the man's and would not give" (*GWF,* 11). In the course of the novel, Colonel Roberts completely loses control over his wife and daughter as Catherine spends more and more time with Jaeger and Milly falls in love with a German stable boy. Even worse, Milly walks away disgusted and unimpressed from a fox hunt her father is directing. In the end, the colonel resorts to a bald display of power that is a true measure of his weakness. When he can no longer master "his" women, he ships them back to America.

After the war, Jaeger begins to trace the entire disaster of nazism back to the patriarchal authoritarianism traditional in the German family. He says of his father: "He beat us, and all our teachers beat us. Every German of his generation beat whoever was weaker than himself, I suppose—every German, that is, except the Jews" (*GWF,* 77). He adds, "My mother stood between my father and us, between us and the whole of Germany, taking the blows. But she couldn't go to war for us" (*GWF,* 77). Colonel Roberts' contemptuous assessment of Jaeger is that he is "on the side of women:" "Some men have a kind of weakness in them that rots them down to the core. . . . They can't take discipline, so they look around for sympathy, female sympathy" (*GWF,* 78), he says. In the same vein, Kay Boyle found as she was writing her modern history of Germany that the "only good chapters in that book" were about the

women of Germany. "They were the first women to have a peace movement in the world. They were against every war their men foisted upon
them."[46] She decided to scrap much of the original manuscript and turn
her work into a book about German women, to be called *The Noblest
Witnesses*. Kay Boyle has said, "I believe very strongly that if more
mothers had political power, government positions, we would have a
more rational world."[47]

Generation Without Farewell is a rich and complex novel in which Kay
Boyle endows the quest of one spiritually displaced person with universal
significance. But in counterpoint to the struggles of Jaeger is another
"hunt," also symbolic. A problem Colonel Roberts must tackle is that of
a monstrous boar loose in the woods near the base. In Kay Boyle's
"Forest of Consciousness," the beast is a multifaceted, fluid symbol,
much like Old Ben in "The Bear" (which Catherine Roberts no doubt
had read in her *Portable Faulkner*). Boyle depicts the boar as the brave,
stubborn inhabitant of the "eternal dark underbrush" that the egotistical,
acquisitive hunter seeks to eradicate in order to establish his possession of
the land. She links the shy but fierce beast with "the Jews who fought
tooth and nail for their lives" (*GWF,* 204). Jaeger takes a broader and
more cynical view of "the beast they pursue in righteous vengeance conjured into being so long ago that they cannot conceive of life without it."
In his mind, the boar is whatever unknown threatens the self-righteous
"God-fearing peace-loving men" and makes them aggressive in their
fear. Jaeger sees that his part "is to tell them that there is no giant boar:"
*"I must say to them it is not France, this beast breathing fire and brimstone
at their thresholds, not Russia, not England, or America, but that it is all
men who have another vision, another faith"* (*GWF,* 294). The paranoia
that leads to aggression—the military "hunt" mentality—is not a peculiarly German trait, however. To the American colonel, "peace is the
interval allowed us in which to recognize the enemy . . . and war is the
corrective action that recognition of him must eventually take" (*GWF,*
286).

In the wake of World War II, it may appear that Kay Boyle had broken
with her previous concerns and traded aesthetics for polemics. Yet despite the differences in the style and substance of her fiction, she had
maintained her firm belief in love as the sole source of meaning in human
life. Only the scope of her vision had changed. In *The Seagull on the Step,*
Michel Vaillant speaks to Mary Farrant of love, but "not about love
between men and women, nothing like that, but love between brothers
and whatever it is between people who feel the same way about things,
about paintings, or politics" (*SS,* 160).

Her view of the artist's role also had changed. Twenty-six years after
Kay Boyle had signed the *transition* manifesto calling for the Revolution

of the Word, she published a new manifesto, entitled "A Declaration for 1955." In 1929, Kay Boyle had believed that "Pure poetry is a lyrical absolute that seeks an a priori reality within ourselves alone" and that the artist ought not to be concerned "with the propagation of sociological ideas, except to emancipate the creative elements from the present ideology."[48] The writer, she believed in 1955 and still believes, bears a heavy moral responsibility to the world in which she or he lives. She agrees with Thomas Mann that it was the intellectuals who had allowed a dictator to come to power in Germany: "Had they, through their works and by their vision, made richer promises than those he made, the man called Hitler would have been forced into exile instead of the writers of a country that he brought finally to defeat." [49] She believes, too, that American writers must act to check the more insidious evil infecting their own country. "I warn the sponsors of television programs that the salesman with glassy eye, and voice rising in hysteria, who, his back to the wall, offers foam-rubber pillows free, absolutely free, presages the end," she writes, and she states clearly her vision of the artist's duty in the modern world:

> It has long been established that the writer, the artist, must partake of the world he finds about him if his work is to come alive and stay álive. But in an epoch such as this, when the collective material manifestations have outdone those of the individual spirit, the artist, the writer, the believer, is unsure. Escape, exile, becoming the member of a group, whatever its nature, is not the answer; nor is that inner exile, that complete detachment of the spirit from the impingement of reality, which the intellectuals of totalitarian states have learned to endure. Now, in our time, it is clear that it is not the artist, the writer, the individual, who must seek to be accepted by the world he sees, but the scene itself that must be transformed by the higher standards of the individual to acceptability. . . . His concern must be with that belief which seeks, in Toynbee's phraseology "a higher level of conduct" both in act and in art.[50]

In the mature voice with which she has spoken since the end of World War II—the most devastating and far-reaching breakdown of connections in human history—Kay Boyle asks in her "Declaration" no less of her fellow writers than "the transforming of the contemporary scene."

She makes the same appeal in her fiction as well. "The hands of the musicians, the poets," Honerkamp says in *Generation Without Farewell*, "the hands of these men who attest to the only absolute truth we know, must reach out and grasp one another's, stretching from one century into the next, from death through life, stretching into the only kind of afterlife of which we can be certain. You see that don't you? You understand that don't you . . . ?" (*GWF,* 191). In the postwar decades that is the goal Kay Boyle has pursued in her own writing.

8

Back Home: "It Might Just Save the World"

About six blocks from the corner of Haight and Ashbury streets in San Francisco stands a four-story Victorian house, white with ivy-green trim. A flight of steps leads up to the front door, set in an alcove flanked by four white columns. In the summer of 1979, a stark black and white poster addressed passersby from behind the door's beveled glass pane. A pair of hands clutched strands of barbed wire atop a brick wall; the legend below read: "Human Rights? Who Cares? Amnesty International." On the top floor is a "real Montmartre apartment"[1] where Kay Boyle spent the better part of seventeen years writing in bed with a typewriter resting on her knees (a habit she traces back to her nomadic early days with Laurence Vail, when she did much of her writing in hotel rooms).[2] She left San Francisco in 1980, intending at first to go to Ireland, then settled for several years in Cottage Grove, Oregon, near her son, and finally moved back to live across the Bay in Oakland in the spring of 1985. But the house at 419 Frederick Street remains the symbolic home of Kay Boyle the political activist.

She had first come to San Francisco in unhappy circumstances. In the autumn of 1962, after nearly a decade of fighting his dismissal from the Foreign Service and teaching school in Rowayton, Connecticut, as well as night classes in French at Columbia University, Joseph Franckenstein had been reinstated by the State Department and appointed cultural attaché in Teheran. When Kay Boyle and their son joined him there six months later, he was already dying. Surgeons at the American military hospital in Landestühl, Germany, operated for a brain tumor in the summer of 1963, and when they found it malignant, transferred him by ambulance plane to Walter Reed Hospital in Washington, D.C. There the diagnosis was lung cancer. When it became clear that he would not recover, Kay Boyle had sent out word that she needed a job to support the family. The best of the many offers she received came from San Francisco State College—full professor status (although she held no degrees) and a good salary. In September the couple flew to San Francisco, where Joseph was taken from the plane by ambulance to the Army hospital in the Presidio. He died on October 7, 1963, at the age of fifty-three.

When a friend suggested that she buy a house with Joseph's GI and State Department insurance payments, Kay Boyle was not sure she wanted to settle so far from her friends in the East, "but the tenor of least resistance to circumstances was established and I functioned almost without will," she recalls.[3] Her two youngest children, Ian and Faith (carrying her first child, Geordie, in her arms), looked all over San Francisco while Kay committed herself "wholly and willessly" to the demanding job of teaching four courses at San Francisco State. Her only stipulation to her children was that the house be in a mixed neighborhood. "Frederick Street was the right place, and the house (a tenement when I bought it for almost nothing) was the right place," she says. Five families had been living in it and it was a mess. During the winter of 1963–64, her son and daughter and a number of her students "worked like demons to put everything into order, and resurrecting the garden, which had been used as a garbage dump." With its crisp green and white paint and the gleaming gold leaf that accents the carvings above the door and the scrollwork between the first and second floors, the restored house stands out from its undistinguished pastel companions on the block. In its immaculate appearance, it recalls Caresse Crosby's description of the owner: "Kay is always neat as a needle. I have never seen 'her hair down' not even when she tossed and turned with fever. She is like a breeze or a bird's wing."[4]

For the nearly two decades that she lived there, Kay Boyle's door was always open to those whose struggles she supported: blacks, American Indians, students in dissent, pacifists, and "those who work for the liberation of all groups and peoples."[5] To help pay the mortgage, she rented the second floor to students "on an integrated basis,"[6] and she would loan the use of the main floor to various groups whose causes she believed in. The sitting room, its bay windows hung with scalloped shades, and the adjoining dining room, where floor-to-ceiling bookcases covered the entire east wall, became classrooms for a number of professors as well as herself during the 1968–69 student and faculty strike at San Francisco State. The house was a sanctuary for runaway girls from Haight Street and for just-released prisoners with no place to go.[7] In 1970, when Kay was away for two semesters teaching at Hollins College in Virginia, it was commandeered briefly by members of a Boston cult who had chosen it, unbeknownst to the owner, as the site of their new West Coast commune. Beginning in 1973 it was the twice-a-month meeting place for U.S. Group 80, the chapter founded by Kay Boyle, of Amnesty International, the Nobel Prize-winning organization advocating the rights of political prisoners around the world.

Early in 1978 the *San Francisco Chronicle* asked eight contemporary authors to send quick sketches of how they saw themselves. Kay Boyle's submission was a line drawing of an angel in flight, complete with wings and halo, carrying a small round bomb in each hand. Her caption reads: "Since receiving several volumes of censored data through the Freedom of Information Act, I see myself as a dangerous 'radical' (they themselves put it in quotes) cleverly disguised as a perfect lady. So I herewith blow my cover."[8]

While her concern for political and social issues is nothing new, Kay Boyle has been especially active and outspoken in the past two and one-half decades in her support of various liberal causes. In 1962 she picketed First Lady Jacqueline Kennedy as she christened a Polaris submarine in New London, Connecticut. In July, 1966, she travelled to Cambodia with a group called "Americans Want to Know," a combination of pacifist organizations including the Friends Service Committee and the Women's International League for Peace and Freedom, among others. They went to look into U.S. and South Vietnamese claims that the Viet Cong were using Cambodia for supply lines and refuge—claims the group feared would be used as a pretext for extending the war into that country—and they traveled the Ho Chi Minh and Sihanouk Trails day and night without finding any evidence of such military action. She returned of the opinion that "President Johnson is a vain, stupid, prejudiced man, and will leave the White House as the most discredited President in history."[9] That same summer, every morning between nine and eleven o'clock, she maintained a solitary vigil, dressed in black, in front of the California Funeral Service in San Francisco, where the military dead were "processed" on their return from Vietnam. "In time, many protesters against the war in Vietnam joined me in the vigil: fellow professors from State, personal friends, and members of anti-war groups, everyone dressed in black," she says.[10] In 1967 Kay Boyle was arrested and imprisoned twice, in October and in December, with groups of demonstrators who had staged sit-ins at the Oakland Induction Center to protest the war in Vietnam.

As a faculty member at San Francisco State, she was active in campus demonstrations by black and third-world students. During the strike that shut down the university for several months in 1968 and 1969, she helped to found the Faculty Action Committee, whose members vowed to stand between members of the police Tactical Squad and students, acting as a buffer to prevent "real violence."[11] At eight o'clock on the morning of December 2, 1968, the acting president, S. I. Hayakawa, scrambled aboard a student-operated sound truck and ripped out the wires. Angered because he had claimed several times in public that he was "only following orders," Kay Boyle called out from the picket line, "Hayakawa

Eichmann!" She was fired on the spot. Later that morning, when interviewed by the press, Hayakawa maintained that he had not said, "Kay Boyle, you're fired," but "Kay Boyle, I'm surprised that a distinguished writer like you should behave like a member of a lynch mob!"[12] He added that he had no authority to fire her, that such an action had to go through various university committees. Along with the young man whose truck had been damaged and another professor "whom Hayakawa had maligned," Kay Boyle brought suit against him, which involved a "long and tedious academic senate hearing." They won. Hayakawa was asked to pay the truck owner $25,000 for damages and to apologize publicly to Kay Boyle and her colleague. But, as acting president of the university, he had the final review of all academic hearings, and, according to Kay Boyle, "treated the whole matter as a huge joke." He wrote a tongue-in-cheek letter to himself (which the *San Francisco Chronicle* featured on its front page) scolding himself for his ungentlemanly conduct. He complied with none of the penalties. Five years after the confrontation, the *Chronicle* reported on December 18, 1973: "Novelist Kay Boyle and her old adversary, Doc Hayakawa, now have something in common: each teaches only one course at S. F. State, for a piddling $300 a month. 'At least he gets to address Rotary Clubs,' adds Kay, 'but, frankly, I'm starving.' "[13]

In addition to her activities with Amnesty International, in the midseventies she worked on behalf of political prisoners as a member of the Committee for Intellectual and Artistic Freedom in Iran. In 1976 Boyle fulfilled a lifelong dream and visited Ireland for the first time: "Ever since I was seventeen or eighteen I wanted to get to Ireland to fight for the IRA. I never could get away—there were children, family responsibilities." [14] Nor has she been above concerning herself with social problems on smaller scale. She picketed the house of a Haight-Ashbury landlord who had raised rents to levels she considered excessive, and her neighbors suggested a "Kay Boyle for President" movement.

When her two-thousand-page security file was released to her in 1979 under the Freedom of Information Act, it became apparent that she had not made herself popular with the establishment. The dossier contained a report that she had had a clandestine affair with Ezra Pound before World War I. "I would have been no more than ten," she was reported as saying. She never met the poet until well into the 1920s, she explained, "and I didn't like him then."[15]

In November, 1967, just after her release from what she called "my first jail sentence," she wrote to her old friend (herself involved in an Italian-based world federalist movement): "As you must realize, darling Caresse, revolution is on its way—we are very close to it. These are crucial times and I am glad to be taking my part in the protest against armed authority."[16] Ever since she returned to the United States from Germany after the 1952 loyalty hearing, much of what Kay Boyle has written has been directed to the cause of world peace.

Even before the war in Vietnam had become an issue, Kay Boyle was on record against the Cold War. In works such as *The Smoking Mountain* and *Generation Without Farewell,* she had protested war in that heyday of peace and prosperity—the fifties. She recalls that soon after the end of World War II an editor of *Collier's* planned to devote an entire issue to the subject "If the Soviet Union Invades America." On the cover would be a picture of Stalin standing on the White House steps, and Boyle was asked to write an article from the point of view of mothers with children trying to live under communism in America. "What in the name of God are you talking about?" was her reply, and she turned down the five thousand dollars offered for the piece.[17] While Kay Boyle has been known at times to bend her artistic standards in order to make a living, she has never compromised her political convictions.

The arraignment of twenty-seven men and women arrested on May 3, 1960, in New York City for refusing to take shelter during a civil defense drill is the subject of her essay, "The Triumph of Principles," first published a month later. Kay Boyle had been among the demonstrators that day and was in the courtroom as the twenty-seven were being charged. She lauds them as "representatives of all of us who believe in the totally impractical value of drills and shelters against nuclear attack; and who believe that the insistence upon such drills is the cruelest kind of deception; for it is a deception which scales down to quiet human acceptance the ghastly finality of nuclear war" (*ED,* 136).[18] When the magistrate lectured the defendants that "in America we have always expressed our opinions by means of the ballot box, and not by public demonstration, not by defiance of the law," she writes that "the laughter in the courtroom was the laughter of many generations of Americans, for surely nothing more historically inaccurate could have been said" (*ED,* 136). She then uses a technique she has employed in her fiction as a multitude of ghosts approaches the bar, and individuals such as John Brown, Thoreau, and Emerson step forward to address the oblivious judge. It is interesting that the author calls upon leading figures of the nineteenth-century romantic movement in American literature to express faith in individual idealism as a political force, for they were also the unacknowledged predecessors of the Revolution of the Word to which she had so zealously committed herself decades earlier.

The essay is included in the 1972 anthology of pacifist literature that she coedited with fellow San Francisco State professor Justine Van Gundy, *Enough of Dying! Voices for Peace.* In her introduction to the book, the author who had devoted most of the early forties to writing in defense of the Allied cause in books like *Primer for Combat, Avalanche,* and *A*

Frenchman Must Die, had come to believe that even "good" wars, such as World War II, must be invalidated as "justifiable acts" because of their "total failure" to achieve their goals:

> Gandhi once said that history as we know it is a record of the wars of the world. Lacking a history of peace and the enlightenment it would have offered, we have sought to condone the uncondonable alternatives to peace by such words as "necessity" or "defense" or "liberation of peoples." In our time nonviolent men justified in these terms World War I, the Spanish Civil War, and World War II; but the total failure of these conflicts to achieve their goals invalidates them as justifiable acts. The horror of Hiroshima and Nagasaki followed the horror of Hitler's "final solution" and prepared the way for the subsequent mass annihilation of the people of Southeast Asia. Not only as humane women and men, but also as pragmatists, testing the validity of our concepts and our acts, we know that war has failed to serve the best interests of man. (*ED,* 5)

As she had demonstrated twenty years earlier in the nonfiction introduction to *The Smoking Mountain,* Kay Boyle is a fine journalist capable of expressing her political views in vivid and powerful essays. Much of her nonfiction is urgent in tone. "A novel takes at least two years to write," she explains in her 1970 essay collection, *The Long Walk at San Francisco State,* "and the young can't wait that long to have the story of their lives and deaths dredged out of the ruins" (*LW,* 5–6). The four essays in that volume are clear, direct, and at times eloquent, and they are colored with brilliant passages of description in which the author draws on her talents as a narrative writer. While the title piece chronicles the campus strike, two others discuss problems of racial injustice, and in the final essay she cries out against the war in Vietnam.

"Seeing the Sights of San Francisco" is a bitter parody of the travelogue. Among the "spots of interest" she describes is "the fabulous Golden Gate Cemetery," where "practically every well-tended inch of that vast, flowering expanse is now symmetrically covered with gleaming white headstones" (*LW,* 141–42). The tour also includes a stop at the Port Chicago (California) Naval Station where a young man with longish hair and a blond van Dyke beard, looking more like an "old-time frontier preacher" than a "hippie," maintains a daily vigil to protest the shipment of explosives and napalm from there to Vietnam (*LW,* 148). We are also treated to an "off-beat outing" to a mortuary home in the Mission District that won the government contract in 1966 after brisk competitive bidding. There the sightseer can observe the arrival of trucks from Travis Air Force Base equipped with tiers of shelves carrying long aluminum containers stencilled "DO NOT TIP," their contents packed in ice. A chat with the mortician reveals Kay Boyle's loathing of the commonplace acceptance of this outrage and of the mercantile mentality that infects our culture. The bodies of the soldiers killed in Vietnam are accompanied to their final destination by a military escort, who often spends the night in the bereaved family's home. "It's a kind of status thing, and the family appreciates it very much," the mortician explains, and he modestly points out, "We give the same care and attention to the preparation of service-men as we would if they were on a retail basis" (*LW*, 145–46). As has nearly always been her practice, the author bases her writing on personal experience: she had regularly picketed the Port Chicago Naval Station and the Valencia Street funeral parlor, whose manager, "a very coopera-tive and understanding young man," had explained to her and "truly believed" that sending a soldier to accompany each body home was a great consolation to the family and that many families made a social event of it.[19]

Kay Boyle's postwar political writing is less successful when she tries to express her fervent convictions through fiction. *The Underground Woman,* (1975) is too didactic and obviously allegorical to be good fiction and too elaborately adorned to be good propaganda. The author herself concedes, "In a way it's not a good book," explaining that she was not sufficiently detached from its conflict to make it effective fiction.[20]

The protagonist, Athena Gregory, is a very thinly disguised Kay Boyle. She is a widow in her forties instead of her sixties, has three children instead of six, teaches mythology rather than writing at a San Francisco college, and on the merit of three books she had written instead of over thirty, "got into the academic world by the back door" and cannot afford to get out again (*UW*, 27).[21] Still, she lives in a four-story Victorian house (white with green trim and gold-leaf scrollwork) in a racially mixed neigh-borhood, and she owns a large collection of white earrings.

The novel opens as she is herded into a paddy wagon along with others arrested in an anti-war demostration at an induction center. Among her companions in crime are a well-known folk singer and her mother. (Kay Boyle was arrested in October, 1967, along with Joan Baez and *her* mother, who became her close friends.) While serving her ten-day sen-tence (she refuses bail), Athena is deeply impressed by the contrast be-tween the long-term prisoners, mainly black and Hispanic, and the ar-rested demonstrators, "these ladies who were no more than vacationing here" (*UW*, 105). The demonstrators attempt to raise the social con-sciousness of their fellow inmates by restoring the iris beds in the yard behind the women's dormitory, stitching the words "peace" and "love" inside the men's underwear in the prison laundry sewing room, and lead-ing a strike. Several weeks later, as Athena and her new friend, the folk singer's mother, climb the hills of Angel Island and gaze upon the ruined brick buildings where Chinese immigrants seeking work on the mainland had once been detained, they both are overcome with guilt for "visiting abandoned islands like tourists" and for nearly forgetting about the others left behind bars. They demonstrate again and get arrested, and the book ends as they file into the paddy wagon once more and greet their old companions who have also come back.[22]

But Athena has personal as well as public problems to bear. She misses terribly her husband, who had died five years earlier. Rory had hiked with her through the "forests and fields of Europe"; had trained at an army ski camp near Leadville, Colorado; had been a foreign service officer in Germany after the war; and had died a terrible death of lung cancer. She suffers, too, from the loss of her youngest daughter to a diabolical East Coast commune led by a dictator who calls himself "Pete the Redeemer." Her letters to Melanie and the grandchildren are returned unopened; her daughter has rejected her because she will not see "reality"—that Pete is the savior of the world. After Athena has been released from jail, she is awakened at four o'clock one morning to find her hallway jammed with rucksacks and electronic musical equipment and her sitting room and dining room filled with cult members intending to establish their West-coast commune in her house. Others are fixing dinner in her kitchen. "We're on a more basic time schedule, the calendar of the tides. It's evening for us now," Lucky the Disciple explains to her, and he adds, "Like, through our time cycle with the tides we're getting closer to the movement of the planets. Let us bring you back from chaos, Athena" (*UW*, 226).

The dialogue sounds absurd, but this part of the story is tragically true to life. In the mid-sixties, Kay Boyle's youngest daughter, Faith, and her husband had become involved in a cult led by Mel Lyman, author of *Autobiography of a World Savior*, which *Rolling Stone* magazine described as "a rambling, abstract, 80-page riddle . . . based loosely on the Superman-Krypton plot." Early in 1967, Boyle took a semester's leave of absence from San Francisco State to teach at the University of Massachusetts in Amherst and went to live with her daughter, son-in-law, their two young children, and half a dozen other cult members in Boston's Roxbury ghetto. When the heat went off in the house and she had found her grandchildren lying in bed "literally blue with cold," a commune member had said to her, "*Beautiful* . . . It's just *beautiful* to see children cold like that. Children should be cold and hungry all the time—then they're close to reality." On a later visit, she was horrified to find a photograph of mass-murderer Charles Manson in the children's playroom; she was told that the flowers under the picture were changed daily.[23] The author says of her stay at the commune, "I lasted three weeks and then I threw a frying pan at someone." She moved to a two-room apartment nearby so that she could continue to help Faith with her communal duties. Still, there is an ironic element of history repeating itself in the situation. She says: "I can understand some of this. I left home at seventeen, outraged by my father and grandfather's traditional, conventional lives. I never saw them again. I'm not even against communes."[24] Indeed, in the twenties she had lived in one herself—Raymond Duncan's colony in Neuilly.

Early one morning in the fall of 1970, commune members took over Kay Boyle's San Francisco home as described in *The Underground Woman,* except that she was away at the time as a writer-in-residence at Hollins College in Virginia and her son was a member of the group. Following his graduation from San Francisco State as a music major in 1969, Ian Franckenstein also had been drawn into Mel Lyman's commune. The group took over the kitchen and the entire main floor of Kay Boyle's house and "made life unbearable" for the student-tenants whom she had left in charge of the place.[25] One of the Lyman people, David Gude, Faith's husband, told Boyle over the phone that she was a capitalist who wanted to own property to indulge her whims, and he said, "We are going to have that house if we have to burn it to the ground."[26] It is a line she quotes verbatim in the novel. In "real life" the problem was solved through the ingenuity of Kay Boyle's "tried and true and tireless attorney," Robert Treuhaft, who drew up a deed for the sale of the house for one dollar to her neighbor, Reginald Major, head of the Economic Opportunity Program at San Francisco State.[27] Major then served legal notice on the Lyman family, evicting them from his property. The episode is nearly identical in the novel except that Athena's black neighbor, Luchies McDoniel, is an upholsterer, and there is an element of romance in their friendship. While Ian Franckenstein freed himself from the commune after four years, Faith remains with the Lyman group, has five children, and for years has been estranged from her mother, her brother, and her four sisters.

The Underground Woman is interesting as a first-hand record of a turbulent time in contemporary history and moving as an account of the author's painful loss of her daughter. It is not a successful work of literature. In sharp contrast to the subtle and complex fiction she had written earlier, this novel is baldly allegorical. Much is made of Athena's mythological name. "I've known since the moment I was born and drank it in with my mother's milk . . . that you named me Athena in the expectation of shaping me into the answer to some question you were asking of life. And I couldn't be the answer. I was not the protectress of cities, for I do not like cities, and I was also the wrong one to be designated as the goddess of war," she had written her father when she left home as a teenager, never to return (*UW,* 12). Athena dubs the folk singer and her mother "Callisto" and "Calliope," and compares her loss of her own daughter to the story of Demeter and her lost daughter, Persephone. *"I have been taught that mythology transcends the individual and contains the*

life stories of all men and women," she muses (*UW,* 195). One critic has
astutely remarked:

> The novel's problem lies just here. Good fiction feeds upon the particular;
> imprecision will dent it, a muddled goodwill toward men will corrode it abso-
> lutely. Miss Boyle generalizes her characters by identifying them with Greek
> myths; her generalizations about man's estate should have been left to her
> readers to infer. We are all one body, she seems to say, and our virtue will move
> mountains. Probably, if one must emphasize this theme, he had better follow
> Tolstoy's course and abandon fiction for moral essays.[28]

Even if one were to accept the mythology device, per se, problems in its
use remain. There are times when the author seems to forget that only
Athena ought to be aware of the allegory she is creating in her own mind.
Watching two prisoners cleaning the yard, she thinks "they might have
been mistaken for Gertrude Stein and Alice B. Toklas" (*UW,* 85).
Athena mentally develops the analogy for two pages, but the material
seems to have slipped out of hand when "the travesty of Gertrude Stein"
twice addresses her companion aloud as "Alice" (*UW,* 87–88). Improbable dialogue is another problem. As the prisoners walk from the van into
the "lower regions" of the jail, Calliope formally bows to Athena and
says, "Enter, Noble Etruscan!" This exchange follows:

> "No, that can't be right," said Athena, looking in wonder at her. "They were
> enemies of the Greeks, you know, and my name's Greek, Athena. . . ."
> "But your head, it's like the ones in profile on the sides of the black, buc-
> chero pottery." (*UW,* 17–18)

Even in passages of description, long Boyle's forte, the book is disap-
pointing. Instead of the fresh, crackling figures of speech that have
marked her fiction for decades, we find policewomen looking "smart as
whips" in their uniforms, prisoners packed "cheek by jowl" in visiting
cages, and mattresses "flatter than pancakes." At times the omniscient
narrator uses slang one would expect to find only in dialogue: verbs such
as "ripped off" and "bopped" (as in "she bopped over to the window"
[*UW,* 87]).

Yet while "this novel is perhaps a lesser Boyle," in the words of one
kind critic,[29] *The Underground Woman* is nevertheless a consistent Boyle.
In her latest novel as in her first collection of short stories, written nearly
fifty years before, she is concerned with the need for love and distressed
by its failures, and she treats that recurring theme on both the private and
public scale. The two levels of human understanding are interdependent,
in fact. Athena says, "if we can't speak to one another out of our own
limited, circumscribed lives, then the wider reconciliations can't possibly
take place" (*UW,* 177). In her personal life, bonds have been broken: she
had repudiated her father, her daughter has repudiated her, and she has

lost her beloved husband to death. Yet Athena realizes that her life will have meaning only in connection with the lives of others. There is a camaraderie in the paddy wagon the second time around, and as she files into the underground hall of the prison, Athena apparently believes that the prison is the only place where she has a hope of maintaining a purposeful existence: "Oh reality, hold me close, hold me close, the underground woman asked of the barren walls" (*UW,* 264).

Kay Boyle is angered by allegations that she has been indiscriminate in choosing her causes and that her involvement in social issues has hurt her writing in recent years. "I have spent all my life—even from my childhood—concerned about these matters."[30] Certainly racial prejudice has been one of her life-long concerns. In the early thirties, at the beginning of her career, she had spoken out against racism in such stories as "White as Snow," "One of Ours," and "Black Boy," a work in which she takes particular satisfaction.[31] Even in *The Smoking Mountain,* an indictment of the aspects of the German mentality that made nazism possible, she makes it clear in two of the pieces, "Home" and "The Lost," that the Germans have no monopoly on bigotry.

In more recent years she has continued to express her abhorrence of racism, often abandoning the mode of fiction, with its requirements for subtlety, in favor of the more direct form of the essay. In 1957 three articles about racism in America appeared in *The Nation,* where she had published so many of her sketches and essays about injustice in postwar Europe.[32] In two of the four pieces in *The Long Walk at San Francisco State*—"Notes on Jury Selection in the Huey P. Newton Trial" and "No One Can Be All Things To All People"—she discusses the injustices surrounding the murder trial of Black Panther Party leader Huey Newton, accused in the shooting death of an Oakland policeman. She also expresses her support of the party's aims as well as her distaste for the white-dominated legal and police system in our country. In the title essay, devoted to civil disturbances at San Francisco State, she attacks the traditional system of higher education, which she feels often places black and third-world students at a disadvantage.

Kay Boyle had continued to write some fiction, too, on the subject of racial relations. Fourteen of the twenty stories collected in *Nothing Ever Breaks Except the Heart* (1966) deal with "old" subjects; they are listed in the table of contents under the heading "War Years" and "Military Occupation," beginning with the story "Anschluss," first published in 1939. Of the six stories in the section called "Peace" (the title no doubt intended to be ironic), two deal specifically with failures of compassion and communication between races.

One of them, "One Sunny Morning" presents an innocent white boy's initiation into the cruel realities of racial prejudice in America. A lonely child spending the summer with relatives, he is sent on an errand to visit a "colored" family living in a shack outside a Delaware town, and he responds warmly to the young mother's hospitality. She is worried about the family Ford that had flooded and stalled in the road in front of the house. She had promised her husband she would move it, but she lacks the confidence to try. When a white truck driver finds his way blocked by the car and approaches the black woman in an outrage, the boy witnesses for the first time in his life the awesome fury of blind hatred. In a passage reminiscent of Boyle's early experimental style, in which external objects are reshaped in the mind of the perceiver and reality is psychological, the angry truck driver takes on monstrous proportions in the eyes of the terrified child:

> His body had certainly grown too big to pass through the opening of the truck door, but still his bare arm struck it wide, and he squeezed past it and jumped down on the road. And now, as he came toward them, he took on the proportions of a carnival figure in a department-store parade. The face had relinquished its resemblance to that of any man the boy had known. The eyebrows sprang in whitish bristles above the baby-blue, ballooning eyes, and the pink lids had grown as big as tents as he advanced. He had reached the path now, and he surged forward, inexorable as a tide, toward the steps, toward the porch on which they stood. "There's four trucks coming fast, so get that tin can out of the way before I haul you in for murder!" he was shouting, the actual substance of his voice filling all space so now there was no air left to breathe. *So we'll have to suffocate,* the boy thought in reeling panic. . . . The truck of gravel, the broken Ford, the rusted bicycle that leaned, no larger than a cricket, against the tree, were blotted out by the tower of flesh in the faded overalls. It had pushed aside the landscape until nothing but the fury of one man was there. The floating head seemed to be tangled in the top branches of the shade trees as he came, shouting aloud his abuse. So we're going to die, the boy thought doggedly; *Alice and Ezra and the lady and me, we're going to die.* (*NEB,* 57–58)

Finally the child summons his courage and runs out into the road to back the shuddering jalopy into the driveway himself, and at once the truck driver resumes normal dimensions. The boy "sat on the cracked leather and the mildewed stuffing of the split-open seat, not hearing, and having forgotten it was not for this moment of pride that he had come, but for something else entirely" (*NEB,* 59). The point is as simple as a Sunday School lesson: "It is blessed to help one another." But the author's handling of the situation is delicate, and in this story of a lonely child achieving new awareness and self-respect through his dealings with others who are outcast in a different way, she conveys without preaching her continuing belief in the need for compassion and understanding.

The tone of "The Ballet of Central Park"—the story of a privileged white girl's ill-fated attempt to turn armed black and Hispanic street boys into performers in her original ballet—is not so subtle. The author's voice is obtrusive, and it is obvious from the first lines that this is fiction with a message:

> This is a story about children, and about what happened to two or three of them in New York one summer. It is a story that has to be written quickly before it is too late. "Too late for what?" may be asked at once, and to that there is no answer. It would be dramatic, but scarcely true to say: "Before something happens to all the children in the world." (*NEB*, 32)

While these two are the only pieces in the collection specifically concerned with racial problems, the other stories in the "Peace" section also deal with the failures of love. In "Should Be Considered Extremely Dangerous," "Evening at Home," and "Seven Say You Can Hear Corn Grow," the author expresses distaste for members of the "establishment"—whether they be parent, policeman, or hospital nurse—made callous and spineless by their power and their adherence to convention. At the same time she displays sympathy for the weak, the misunderstood, the downtrodden, and the outcast through characters ranging from a fugitive criminal, to a well-dressed woman passed out drunk on the steps of a church, to an imaginative teenage boy. Kay Boyle was reportedly "chilled" by a reviewer's comment that the stories in *Nothing Ever Breaks Except the Heart* are sympathetic to "people of the lower scale," yet she laughingly admitted, "Without realizing it I brought up all the children to be afraid of the rich—I've made them my villains."[33]

While social concerns have dominated Kay Boyle's work of recent decades, she never has lost the almost religious devotion to the Word with which she began her career in the twenties. She had started out as a poet, and William Carlos Williams had always said it was just by mistake that she had written prose. (He got very angry if anyone called her a prose writer, she told an interviewer in 1964.) "I definitely changed—tried to write less poetically in my stories—and I regret it in a way, and I feel now, in my dotage, that I am going back more to the poetic method."[34]

Some of her fiction of the sixties and seventies does show a return to a more poetic method. In some works, such as *The Underground Woman*, with its layer of myth and allegory, the "poetry" is self-conscious and obtrusive ornament. Yet in others, such as "One Sunny Morning," the poetic elements are woven subtly into the fabric of the story, enhancing the significance of a scene. But besides resurrecting the poetic method in some of her fiction, Kay Boyle has returned to the genre of poetry itself. *Collected Poems* (1962) was her first volume of poetry to appear since *American Citizen Naturalized in Leadville, Colorado* was published in 1944, and it was followed in 1970 by *Testament for my Students and Other Poems*. Both collections contain a number of pieces originally part of the

Glad Day volume (1938), and *Collected Poems* features excerpts from *American Citizen*. Still, over half the poems in the 1962 volume and two-thirds of them in the 1970 book are new. Her most recent book is a volume of previously uncollected poetry: *This Is Not a Letter and Other Poems* (1985).

Like her fiction, many of her poems of the most recent decades reflect the author's social concerns. Her topical titles include "A Poem about Black Power," "The Jews among the Nations," and "The Lost Dogs of Phnom Penh," written in Cambodia in 1966. The title work of the second volume, "Testament for my Students, 1968–1969," expresses her solidarity with the young protesters at San Francisco State and contains a six-paragraph prose story in which the author caustically ridicules the pedants of the white educational establishment.

But her commitment to social justice has not replaced her reverence for art and for its creators. Two major projects of the sixties were labors of love in memory of friends of the expatriate years. In fulfillment of a decades-old promise to the ailing poet, she compiled and prefaced and finally succeeded in finding a publisher for *The Autobiography of Emanuel Carnevali* (1967), twenty-five years after his death. In 1968 Robert McAlmon's 1938 memoirs, *Being Geniuses Together,* were resurrected, edited by Kay Boyle with chapters of her own recollections alternating with his to create what the dust cover calls "A binocular view of Paris in the '20s." Her sole reason for compiling the book, she says, "was to make known all that McAlmon, the wrongfully discarded personality of Paris in the '20's and '30's, had done for expatriate literature."[35] She felt "very bitterly" that McAlmon's work had not been appreciated, and upon the republication of the joint memoirs in paperback in 1984, said, "I think the real meaning of autobiography, the real reason for it, should be to defend those who were unjustly treated and dealt with it in one's own time. And I felt that McAlmon was very unjustly dealt with."[36]

Her own *Collected Poems* is dedicated to William Carlos Williams, "who, as man and poet, illuminates the way." Besides reprinting her previously published tributes to poets—"A Valentine for Harry Crosby," "A Communication to Nancy Cunard," "A Christmas Carol for Emanuel Carnevali," and "A Comeallye for Robert Carlton Brown" among them—her 1962 and 1970 collections contain new tributes to men and women of letters. They include "Two Twilights for William Carlos Williams," "A Dialogue of Birds for Howard Nemerov," "For James Baldwin," and "For Marianne Moore's Birthday, November 15, 1967." Many of the poems in her 1985 collection also are dedicated to writers, including James Joyce, Babette Deutsch, and Jessica Mitford. Currently she is working on what she describes as "a very long poem to Samuel Beckett," four sections of which are included in *This Is Not a Letter.*[37]

In "Testament for my Students" she quotes from the works of several of her students at San Fransisco State, Woodie Haut, Shawn Wong, Rebhun, Alvarado, Victor Turks, and Chris Miller—those young poets who each year "came jogging down that hall/Bearded or not" (*TFS*, 13).[38] In the America of the sixties, Kay Boyle recognized the same youthful spirit of rebellion against conformity that had fired the literary revolution in Paris in the twenties. Aesthetics was a moral and political issue then, and in the sixties and early seventies, her work continued to testify to the bond between poetry and politics. "Testament for my Students" ends:

> You were not afraid of death, sweet emissaries from Arizona
> Montana, Mass., and Illinois; or of mace, or of handcuffs and clubs
> And there's one thing more: you bore the terrible knowledge
> That colonized men and poets wear their sharpest pain on the surface
> Of their flesh, like an open sore
> But this year the writers you honored were, with the crack of a baton
> Turned suddenly to stone. Their tongues were hacked from their throats
> By bayonets, and the blows came steadily, savagely, on the exquisite
> Brittleness of bone. What good were the poets to you then, Baudelaire,
>   Whitman
> Rimbaud, Poe? "All the good in the world!" you shouted out
> Through the blood in your mouths. They were there beside you on
> The campus grass, Shakespeare, Rilke, Bronte, Radiguet
> Yeats, Apollinaire, their fingers on the pulse in your wrists
> Their young arms cradling your bones. (*TFS*, 18)

From her days as an avant-garde writer in Paris in the twenties, Kay Boyle has maintained a reverential regard for the Word. In more recent years she has denounced the corruption of language and warned of its dire effects on human conscience and behavior in a manner reminiscent of George Orwell. An obvious example of the way in which language may corrupt thought is the case of Nazi Germany, and she has written of the ways in which the linguists of the Nazi states made a political weapon of the German tongue, "a weapon more effective than any history had ever known before—a total weapon—that degraded the dignity of human speech to the level of baying wolves."[39] Yet she fears that the American language is being corrupted by Madison Avenue and the military establishment: "The things that are said and written day after day in a country not only affect the character of that country but they shape its destiny. It is as serious as that." [40] She states her case most fluently in her introduction to *Enough of Dying! Voices for Peace*:

> Psychologists tell us that the lack of an adequate means of communication, either spoken or written, plays a major part in the problems and tragedies of the alienated and the delinquent. Barriers isolating the disturbed psyche can be broken down by language, but the language that breaks down the barriers bears

the responsibility of shaping the identity of those who are reached by and given, speech. If the words offered the inarticulate to woo them into the company of other men are "saturation bombing," "body count," "antipersonnel bombs"— words used by the deranged who are in power in a tragically deranged society— then the alienated have been given a vocabulary that prepares the death of other men. (*ED*, 2–3)

She has said that for the writer, there seem to her to be two requirements of equal importance (aside from the ability simply to communicate): "The first thing, an acute awareness of words, of language, is almost a disease in itself, but it is seldom, unfortunately, a contagious disease. The other requirement as I see it, is an awareness of life, so pressing, so keen that it threatens with every instant to absorb all the time and energy which rightly should be given by the writer to writing itself."[41] Her publisher, Alfred Knopf, had said to her one evening at dinner in the early sixties that it was the business of the writer to redeem the word from the corruption it had undergone in recent times. Kay Boyle no doubt would agree but might add that it is the writer's business to redeem the *world* as well.

In 1975, she complained of her students, "They're absolutely apathetic. . . . They just write about I love you and the stars are out, and he deserted me and why do I have to suffer like this." She continues: "I don't want them to write personal things. Some of them get very upset when I say 'Well, look, try leaving out 'I' for the next few weeks. They don't like that. The 'I' to them is terribly important."[42] Today she says that she prefers public writers to private writers.

Boyle's own best work of recent decades is a melding of the private and public, in which she evokes the particular experience as a vehicle for the communication of broader concerns. Her poem "For James Baldwin" (1969) is the quintessential example of the art of Kay Boyle in contemporary America—the expression of love for a friend and fellow writer, but more than that, an open call for justice and understanding:

Black cat, sweet brother,
Walk into the room
On cat's feet where I lie dying
And I'll start breathing regularly again.
Witch doctor for the dispossessed,
Saint tipping your halo to the evicted,
The world starts remembering its postponed loyalties
When I call out your name. I knew you hot nights
When you kept stepping
The light fantastic to music only the wretched
Of the earth could hear; blizzards
In New Hampshire when you wore

A foxskin cap, its tail red as autumn
On your shoulder. In the waters of the Sound
You jumped the ripples, knees knocking,
Flesh blue with brine, your fingers
Cold as a dead child's holding mine.

You said it all, everything
A long time ago before anyone else knew
How to say it. This country was about to be
Transformed, you said; not by an act of God,
Nothing like that, but by us,
You and me. Young blacks saw Africa emerging
And knew for the first time, you said,
That they were related to kings and
To princes. It could be seen
In the way they walked, tall as cypresses,
Strong as bridges across the thundering falls.

                    In the question period once
A lady asked isn't integration a two-way
Street, Mr. Baldwin, and you said
You mean you'll go back to Scarsdale tonight
And I'll go back to Harlem, is that the two ways
You mean?

We are a race in ourselves, you and I,
Sweet preacher. I talked with our ancestors
One night in dreams about it
And they bade me wear trappings of gold
And speak of it everywhere; speak of it on
The exultant mountain by day, and at night
On the river banks where the stars touch fingers.
They said it might just save the world. (*TFS,* 19–20)

Epilogue: Tunes of an Aeolian Harp

Kay Boyle's contemporaries in the twenties and thirties assumed she would be one of the literary stars of their generation. In a review in *The Nation*, Gerald Sykes said of her in 1930, "It is time . . . to cease to regard her as a mere lower case révoltée and to begin to accept her for what she is: more enterprising, more scrupulous, potentially more valuable than nine-tenths of our best-known authors."[1] Katherine Anne Porter entitled her 1931 review of Boyle's first two books "Example to the Young," and in it she said, "Gertrude Stein and James Joyce were and are the glories of their time and some very portentous talents have emerged from their shadows. Miss Boyle, one of the newest, I believe to be among the strongest."[2] In 1933, Robert Cantwell called her "one of the most eloquent and one of the most prolific writers among the expatriates," saying, "It is noteworthy how much Kay Boyle gets out of the casual coming together of her people, what untold dangers and mysterious excitement she finds in their first impressions of each other—out of the tormented relationships and the eventual flight."[3] And in 1938, Mary M. Colum of *Forum* equated her talent with that of a recognized "great," saying, "Kay Boyle is Hemingway's successor": "Each has the observational facility of the newspaperman, with the poet's power of meditating on life; their work stands out from any other type of fiction written in any other country, in both content and technique."[4]

But acclaim for Kay Boyle's work nearly always has been contained within small circles. Her only popular success was *Avalanche*—the book that, on literary grounds, probably least deserved it and which earned her the damaging ridicule of that most influential critic, Edmund Wilson. Despite her distinguished and prolific career, her work is not widely known today, and only a handful of her books remain in print.

What happened? There is surely a good deal of truth to Harry T. Moore's theory that she was a victim of bad timing. Her first novel, *Plagued by the Nightingale*, appeared in 1931, financially a bad year, and that book, along with her other early novels—subtle, artistic studies of individuals engaged in personal struggles—"were hardly calculated to bewitch the liberal left," whose ideology dominated literary criticism in the thirties. He explains that although "her novels were implicitly critical of bourgeois society," they did not belong to the "marching-marching, make-my-bread, in-dubious-battle, hammer-and-anvil school that was establishing itself as the mood of the decade."[5] It is ironic that starting with the onset of World War II, she *did* come to write a good deal of rather didactic fiction in support of liberal social causes—fiction that in the thirties might have earned her critical and popular acclaim. Once more, her timing was off.

Her reputation has also suffered at the hands of critics who repeatedly devalued her work on the basis of its subject matter. It appears as though her subject matter—often the trials of a woman alone groping for an identity and a context in which to live—simply did not interest critics concerned with more "substantial" issues. The complaint that echoes in reviews of Kay Boyle's work in the thirties is that she "continues to spend herself on trivial material," in the words of one *New York Times* reviewer.[6] This critic (interestingly enough, a woman) was referring specifically to *My Next Bride,* that heavily autobiographical novel in which the author plumbs the depths of despair of a woman alone, trapped by poverty into a kind of serfdom in an art colony, who is finally rescued from a disastrous pregnancy, physical and mental collapse, and thoughts of suicide through her friendship with another woman. Perhaps more offensive is the assessment of the *Forum* reviewer who found the book "slight, charming, and pleasantly mad."[7] Kay Boyle's concern with the human need for love and her explorations of its tragic failures—at least when expressed in terms of a woman's experience—apparently were considered so much female fluff, and by the end of the thirties, she had been pigeonholed by too many critics as a mere stylistic virtuoso.[8]

One might go on to speculate that the author took this criticism too much to heart and began to abandon the subtle, introspective work she did best in order to tackle more "substantial" issues of the social and political world. It would seem the classic case of a woman intimidated— no doubt unconsciously—after hearing too many times that her own experience lacks validity and significance. Identifying herself as a writer, rather than as a woman writer, Kay Boyle very likely may have absorbed the values of the prevailing literary tradition, in which masculine experience long has been presented as the human one.[9] As early as 1930 she had expressed a disdain for "lady novelists," and she wanted her own prose to be "direct, lucid, and lean," unlike that of most women writers, she said.[10] Even today she feels she has been more successful in her short fiction than in any other genre "because I've been able in my short stories to be less subjective, not to have that figure of an American girl, or an American woman, as a central figure, as she is in my longer fiction." She says of *Monday Night,* the book she considers most successful among her novels, "I got away from that feminine American figure, and that's why I like it the best."[11] Unfortunately, the quality of much of her fiction after 1940, in which her subject matter of war and social injustice is unarguably "significant," does not match the quality of those earlier works such as *Wedding Day, Plagued by the Nightingale,* and *Year Before Last* which sprang directly from her personal experiences of pain, loss, and bewilderment. When she takes on global issues, she certainly writes with deep conviction, but such fiction often comes off as morality play—bare allegory acted out by cardboard characters.

It is only fair to note that the author herself firmly rejects the suggestion that she might have been influenced by critics who discredited her work based on distinctly female experiences: "I am not very much interested in reviews of my work and I really do not feel that I would take the opinions of critics to heart." To prove the point, she adds: "As for reviewers, I was forced by Simon and Schuster to read Edmund Wilson's review of *Avalanche* because I had to appear on a panel defending myself from an attack by Bennet Cerf—or rather it was a radio interview. I came off very badly because I didn't know who Edmund Wilson was, and I thought him exceedingly stupid for not understanding what I was trying to do in that book."[12]

There are other, more prosaic, explanations as well as to why Kay Boyle's reputation may not have lived up to its early billing. In her effort to support a houseful of children by her writing she often faced tremendous pressures. In the forties she produced—and published—a fair amount of chaff along with the grain. She knew when she was writing a slick story, and she hated it, but she did not have the luxury of presenting to the public only her very finest works of literature. Even aside from financial considerations, motherhood in itself—the unrelenting daily responsibilities involved in maintaining a household and raising eight children (six of her own and two stepchildren)—certainly had its effects on Kay Boyle the artist. In her book *Silences,* in which she explores why women are so underrepresented in the ranks of "distinguished" writers, Tillie Olsen quotes Rilke's description of the circumstances demanded for the full functioning of artistic creation: " 'Without duties, almost without external communication,' Rilke specifies, 'unconfined solitude which takes every day like a life, a spaciousness which puts no limit to vision and in the midst of which infinities surround.' "[13] Like most women (and working class) writers, Kay Boyle could count on no one else to provide what Olsen identifies as the "homely underpinning for it all, the even flow of daily life made easy and noiseless."

Kay Boyle worked regularly under nearly impossible conditions. She wrote to her sister of her struggle to finish *Avalanche* in the spring of 1943, when her husband was in the Mountain Infantry, her mother was living with her and the children in a hotel in Denver, and Kay was pregnant with her sixth child:

> I'm afraid I'm being very adamant with mother and keeping her to an iron-bound schedule, but it is the only way I can get anything done. She takes on at 10:00 in the morning, sits out on porch with great groups of foul old ladies (she really *adores* talking to them) until 12:30—keeps an eye on Clover in the garden, changes baby's diapers, etc. Then I make lunch for Clover and me in room while mother goes to a restaurant, and she takes on again at four. In that time, I give baby lunch, make formula, and prepare orange juice. From four to six, mother looks after Clover and Fay, and at six I make baby's supper, cook soft boiled eggs for mother and Clover's supper, and then run out to a restaurant (these places are far more like diners than restaurants). This gives me 10 to 12:30 to work, and then 4 to 6, and then 7:30 until any old time I want at night. Unfortunately, I can't work late as day begins at 5:30 with Fay. But I don't think mother is being overworked—She (naturally) washes nothing for the children, but I manage to do that around seven before we have breakfast, and then do my shopping at the chain-store across the street as soon as it opens at eight. With everything going like clockwork, I shall get this blasted serial done.[14]

Ten years later nothing had changed. In 1953, she wrote to Nancy Cunard: "I am sendings you these clipping in as mad a rush as usual. It is practically impossible to do housework, shopping, cooking, and writing, and keep one's sanity."[15]

"More than any other human relationship, overwhelmingly more, motherhood means being instantly interruptable, responsive, responsible," Tillie Olsen writes in *Silences*. "Children need one *now*. . . . The very fact that these are real needs, that one feels them as one's own (love, not duty); that there is no one else responsible for these needs, gives them primacy. It is distraction, not meditation, that becomes habitual; interruption, not continuity; spasmodic, not constant toil. . . . Work interrupted, deferred, relinquished, makes blockage—at best lesser accomplishment."[16] Kay Boyle says today that she is saddened that her whole domestic life seems to have escaped the notice of most critics: "I like to tell my students that they should follow the example of Bill Williams, who was 'a full-time poet, a full-time doctor, and a full-time father.' In a sense I believe my life as a woman was as a full-time writer, a full-time mother, and a full-time stepmother."[17] But she does not claim that one can juggle these roles without paying a price. She has described her career as a writer as one of constant interruptions; and although she has no regrets about the choices she has made, she believes today that had she not been so committed to a full family life, she could have written "much better books."[18] For some very practical reasons, then, the quality of Kay

Boyle's writing has been uneven—a fact that probably has tarnished her reputation as a serious writer.

Finally, Kay Boyle's standing as an artist may be victim of her own definition of the serious artist's role. Despite her early dedication to the avant-garde aesthetic principles set forth in the 1929 *transition* manifesto, she has come to believe that the artist's work is not merely to express a perception of the world, but to attempt to transform the world to meet his or her own higher standards. "His concern must be with that belief which seeks, in Toynbee's phraseology, 'a higher level of conduct' both in act and in art," she wrote in a later manifesto, her "Declaration for 1955," and this conviction has directed her own life and art to the present day.[19] She is quite aware that such fiction as *Avalanche,* written in support of a social or political cause, is not "literature," and she does not apologize for the fact. She has admitted both privately and publicly that at times the tale itself is more important to her than the manner of its telling. She wrote to Edward Aswell in December, 1952, soon after the loyalty-security hearing, that, heeding "the demands of conscience and responsibility," she was putting aside work on the book for which they had contracted (published eight years later as *Generation Without Farewell*).[20] After the hearing and her subsequent blacklisting, she was able to produce only one book of new fiction in the fifties: *The Seagull on the Step,* written in haste and "in 'Saturday Evening Post' terms" to communicate to the widest possible audience her pressing concern for the future of democracy in postwar France.[21] "Your book—the other book—is to be poetry, a luxury almost in these days," she told Aswell.

Her 1970 collection of essays on social injustice and unrest in modern America, *The Long Walk at San Francisco State,* opens with this explanation: "There is not time to set this down in fictional terms. A novel takes at least two years to write, and the young can't wait that long to have the story of their lives and deaths dredged out of the ruins. The protest must be made in other terms and as quickly as one can" (*LW*, 5–6). Her 1985 book of essays is entitled *Words That Must Somehow Be Said.* This urgent tone pervades much of her more recent writing, and that sense of urgency probably accounts for the fact that a large proportion of her work published in the past three decades has been nonfiction. Ironically, Kay Boyle's reputation as a serious writer has suffered precisely because she has taken her writing so seriously. Over the years her sense of moral responsibility to her fellow men and women has come to outweigh aesthetic concerns. Judging her work by purely literary standards, this has been a been a diminution of her talent. She no doubt feels she has chosen the higher calling.

In recent years there have been signs that interest in Kay Boyle is finally reawakening. In the late sixties, Southern Illinois University Press reissued her first two novels in its Crosscurrents/Modern Fiction series, a series dedicated to publishing significant works that are out of print or difficult to obtain in this country. The 1979 convention of the Modern Language Association featured a special session on Kay Boyle with commentary by four scholars and a reading of her own work by the author. A book-length bibliography is being prepared by David V. Koch, special collections librarian at the Morris Library of Southern Illinois University. In June, 1980, Boyle was awarded a $15,000 Senior Fellowship for Literature by the National Endowment for the Arts, one of eight grants given to "individuals who have made an extraordinary contribution to contemporary American literature over a lifetime of creative work." With the publication or republication of six books since 1980, three in 1985 alone, she has received fresh public exposure and critical attention. Reviewers have pointed to her as an overlooked talent. In her introduction to the new edition of Boyle's short novels, Margaret Atwood notes that "Writing of this caliber ought to introduce itself, and it does." "Nevertheless," she says, "writing comes out of its own time and place, though it may transcend both by its excellence; and as America and the twentieth century have short memories, it may be appropriate to rediscover Kay Boyle once again."[22] It is high time that her contribution to twentieth-century American literature be given the recognition it deserves.

Despite the surface diversity of her works, set anywhere from the Left Bank to Leadville, Colorado, and any time from the days of George Washington to the present instant, hers is a unified vision. Kay Boyle herself sees her work as being of a piece. Surveying the body of her work, she explained in 1949:

> I feel guilt for every act of oppression that has been committed in my time, and the older I grow the more I want to write about those commonplace things that we all accept which lead to acts and eventually to states of official oppression. I began it tentatively, scarcely formulating my own thoughts and beliefs about it, in my first novels, and I am writing the same story today.[23]

"I find it very convenient to have the same feelings now that I had when I was about eight or nine because I don't have to deny anything I ever wrote and say I didn't mean that," she said in the late sixties.[24] She notes that her first novel, lost in the late twenties, was a "political novel, bringing in the Farmer-Labor party, Lincoln Steffens, and other political radicals whom Mother knew, as well as my own revolt against the men in our family, and my contempt for their views." ("I'm sure it's just as well that it was lost," she adds, "but I speak of it here to emphasize that my views—and my writing—were always consistent, to the point that I sometimes wonder if I do not suffer from arrested development.")[25]

Although her style, as well as her material, has varied tremendously, from the "language of hallucination" to the language of the *Saturday Evening Post,* her work has always been motivated by what she calls "the crusading spirit."[26] In the twenties and early thirties, her cause was the liberation of art from the stuffy conventions of literary tradition. Her contributions to the Revolution of the Word were intricate, subtle, exquisitely crafted works of psychological depth and authenticity in which she explored an individual's struggle to find meaning in life through love and connection with another individual. Beginning in the thirties, as she witnessed the rise of the fascist tide in Europe, the scope of her vision broadened to encompass the "functioning world." She wrote of racial oppression in America in stories like "Black Boy" and "White as Snow" and of the stirrings of nazism in "The White Horses of Vienna" and *Death of a Man.* However, she continued to be concerned with the individual's need for a bonding with others. In the late thirties she produced some of her finest works—*Monday Night* and the three short novels of *The Crazy Hunter*—employing a brilliant and complex style to explore with a bit more artistic detachment than before individual struggles not drawn directly from autobiography. In the forties the cause was obvious. There was a war to be won. Its victims in Europe had been her friends and neighbors, and her husband was in it, too. She dedicated her talents to the effort and in her fiction presented in a sort of stereoscopic vision private love affairs set against the background of a world in which love had failed on a massive scale. To the present day, her work has continued to be of the moment, her materials changing with the times and the times' most pressing problems. Yet in her strong stands against war and any brand of personal or social oppression, she continues to express her belief in the absolute necessity for human beings to connect with one another.

As a young avant-garde expatriate, she wrote, "I have no religion, except that of poetry, and in Poe, Whitman, and William Carlos Williams I recognize the apostles of America."[27] She always has had much in common with the nineteenth-century American romantics, perhaps more than she has recognized. This romantic perspective is another constant that binds together the works of diverse material and style that make up her canon. From the beginning of her career to the present day, she has insisted upon experiencing life first-hand, ignoring any "middlemen" of letters, religion, or philosophy. She has believed in overstepping the confines of institutions and traditions and in spurning the dictates of convention and "common sense." She has placed her faith in the intuition and the imagination and believed that no time has ever been more significant than the present instant. Her impassioned tone—whether proclaiming the Revolution of the Word or denouncing a Southeast Asian war that she considered an outrage—has always been romantic as well, in the tradition of the "barbaric yawp" that Walt Whitman sent sounding over the rooftops of the world.

The century before her, Emerson had charged, "Speak what you think now in hard words and to-morrow speak what to-morrow thinks in hard words again, though it contradict everything you said to-day."[28] Kay Boyle has lived by that advice. She has written that the serious writer must be "an aeolian harp whose sensitive strings respond to the whispers of the concerned people of his time."[29] In Paris in the twenties and thirties, she says, stories "were written in protest, and also in faith, and they were not unlike fervent prayers offered up for the salvation of man, for the defense of his high spirit, for the celebration of his integrity. . . . When I ask my students now to begin writing the pages of the prayer-book again, I remind them that it must be a different prayer-book, different from that of the twenties or thirties, different from any ever written before."[30] To Kay Boyle today as half a century ago, writing is still a mission to be undertaken with "the crusading spirit," a story is a "prayer book," and the artist is standard-bearer and seer.

Notes   Selected Bibliography   Index

Notes

Prologue: "The Crusading Spirit"

1. Kay Boyle and Robert McAlmon, *Being Geniuses Together 1920–1930*, revised with supplementary chapters and an afterword by Kay Boyle (San Francisco: North Point Press, 1984). Cited in text as *BGT*. In a letter of 29 May 1981 to Sandra Spanier, Boyle explains: "I feel, and have always felt, that inasmuch as I had married a French citizen, and was obliged by law to take on his nationality, I was not strictly speaking an expatriate. I could not regain my American citizenship until 1937, when a constitutional amendment altered the law." All letters from Boyle to Spanier are in the possession of Sandra Spanier.

2. Harry Crosby to his mother, Henrietta Crosby, 12 October 1928, in Geoffrey Wolff, *Black Sun: The Brief Transit and Violent Eclipse of Harry Crosby* (New York: Random House, 1976), 251.

3. Archibald MacLeish to Harry Crosby, 22 April 1929, *Letters of Archibald MacLeish 1907 to 1982*, ed. R. H. Winnick (Boston: Houghton Mifflin Company, 1983), 229.

4. Katherine Anne Porter, "Example to the Young," *The New Republic*, 22 April 1931, 279.

5. As of 1978, Boyle is a member of the American Academy of Arts and Letters rather than the National Institute of Arts and Letters, as several published accounts have stated. The name of the group has been changed to the American Academy and Institute of Arts and Letters; there are 250 members of the Institute and 50 of the Academy. She became a member of the National Institute in 1958, in company with Babette Deutsch and Arthur Miller, and in 1978 was elected to occupy the Henry James chair of the American Academy. "I don't like the 'class' division which Institute and Academy represent, but a vote last year to merge the honors was indignantly voted down" (Boyle to Spanier, 29 May 1981).

6. *transition*, no. 16–17 (June 1929), n.p.

7. Boyle to Doug Palmer, 24 October 1974, Pattee Library, The Pennsylvania State University, University Park.

8. Kay Boyle, "The Vanishing Short Story?" *Story* 36 (July-August 1963): 115.

9 Boyle, "The Vanishing Short Story?" 118.

10. Leo Litwak, "Kay Boyle—Paris Wasn't Like That," *New York Times Book Review*, 15 July 1984, 32.

11. Boyle to Spanier, 27 July 1981.

12. Boyle, "The Vanishing Short Story?" 118.

13. Charles F. Madden, ed., "Kay Boyle," in *Talks with Authors* (Carbondale and Edwardsville: Southern Illinois University Press, 1968), 231.

14. Boyle, "The Vanishing Short Story?" 118.

15. In "The Vanishing Short Story?" Boyle writes that the stories of young artists in the twenties and thirties "were written in protest, and also in faith, and they were not unlike fervent prayers offered up for the salvation of man, for the defense of his high spirit, for the

225

celebration of his integrity." She tells her students today that they must "begin writing the pages of the prayer-book again" (110–11).

1. Beginnings: St. Paul to Paris

1. Harry R. Warfel, *American Novelists of Today* (New York: American Book Company, 1951), 44.

2. There is some confusion regarding her date of birth. The Library of Congress and most reference works list it as 1903, but Boyle herself says she was born in 1902, and that is the date the Federal government has used in her Social Security and Medicare records.

3. A fiery-tempered man, Mr. Boyle eventually quarrelled with Mr. West, and when he was a very old man dying in poverty in Cincinnati, he wrote to his granddaughter that "the great heart-break of his life was that he was never given credit for the legal dictionary which was entirely his own work, and which is still in use today" (Boyle to Spanier, 29 May 1981).

4. Warfel, 44.

5. Dan Tooker and Roger Hofheins, eds., "Kay Boyle," in *Fiction! Interviews with Northern California Novelists* (New York and Los Altos: Harcourt Brace Jovanovich/ William Kaufman, 1976), 17.

6. "Until the 1950s copies of these poems were still in existence, but disappeared with other papers of mine (including twenty-eight letters from Harold Ross) from a university's rare book library," Boyle reports. Dedria Bryfonski, ed., "Kay Boyle," in *Contemporary Authors Autobiography Series,* vol. 1 (Detroit: Gale Research, 1984), 109. An excerpt from Boyle's autobiographical essay is the opening piece of her 1985 collection, *Words That Must Somehow Be Said.*

7. Boyle to Bob Brown (Robert Carlton Brown), "Friday," tentatively dated August 1931 by the Morris Library. All letters to Brown are in the Philip Kaplan Expatriate Collection, Morris Library, Southern Illinois University, Carbondale.

8. Bryfonski, 112.

9. Boyle to Joan Boyle, "Wednesday." All letters to Joan Boyle [Detweiler] are in the Kay Boyle Papers, Morris Library, Southern Illinois University, Carbondale.

10. Boyle to Joan Boyle, 3 October 1921.

11. Boyle to Joan Boyle, 16 June 1921.

12. Boyle to Joan Boyle, 9 November 1921.

13. Kay Boyle, letter to the editor, *Poetry: A Magazine of Verse* 19 (November 1921): 105–6. "I doubtless meant Rimsky-Korsakov," she says today (Boyle to Spanier, 29 May 1981).

14. Boyle to Joan Boyle, 12 December 1921.

15. Boyle to Spanier, 19 November 1984.

16. In *Being Geniuses Together,* Boyle writes that they boarded the SS *De Grasse* in June, 1923, but letters she wrote to her mother and Lola Ridge on ship stationery ("A bord le Suffren") are dated 26 May, 28 May, and 4 June 1923. A postcard from Kay Boyle to Ridge's husband, David Lawson, informed him of their landing in France on 5 June 1923.

17. Boyle to Lola Ridge, 28 May 1923. All letters to Lola Ridge are in the Sophia Smith Collection (Women's History Archive), Smith College, Northampton, Massachusetts.

18. Boyle, interview with the author, 22 July 1979, San Francisco.

19. Boyle to Katherine Evans Boyle, 8 June 1923. All letters to Katherine Evans Boyle are in the Kay Boyle Papers, Morris Library, Southern Illinois University, Carbondale.

20. Boyle to Lola Ridge, 20 June 1923.

21. Boyle, interview with the author, 22 July 1979, San Francisco.

22. Boyle to Lola Ridge, 20 August 1923.

23. David V. Koch, "Kay Boyle," in *Dictionary of Literary Biography,* vol. 4 (Detroit: Gale Research, 1980), 49.

24. Kay Boyle's revised edition of *Being Geniuses Together* was originally published in 1968 by Doubleday. It was republished, with an afterword by Boyle, by North Point Press in 1984.

25. Boyle to Joan Boyle, 21 November 1923.

26. *The Autobiography of Emanuel Carnevali,* ed. Kay Boyle (New York: Horizon Press, 1967).

27. Boyle to Lola Ridge, 31 December 1923.

28. Boyle to Lola Ridge, 31 December 1923.

29. Quoted by Boyle in a letter to Katherine Evans Boyle, "Friday" (late 1927).

30. Boyle to Lola Ridge, 31 December 1923.

31. Boyle to Lola Ridge, 1 April 1924.

32. Boyle to Lola Ridge, 12 May 1924.

33. Boyle to Evelyn Scott, 11 August 1924. All letters to Evelyn Scott are in The Harry Ransom Humanities Research Center, The University of Texas at Austin.

34. Boyle to Evelyn Scott, 2 January 1926.

35. Boyle to Spanier, 29 May 1981.

36. Boyle to her family, addressed as "Dearest people," 11 February 1926, the Kay Boyle Papers, Morris Library, Southern Illinois University, Carbondale.

37. Boyle to Lola Ridge, 4 March 1926.

38. At that time they knew him as Cedric Harris. He changed his name to Archibald Craig in 1927.

39. Boyle to Katherine Evans Boyle, 15 July 1926.

40. Boyle to Katherine Evans Boyle, "October something" (1926).

41. Boyle to Evelyn Scott, 5 November 1926.

42. Boyle to Evelyn Scott, 31 January 1927.

43. Boyle to Spanier, 29 May 1981.

44. Boyle to Evelyn Scott, 16 March 1927.

45. John Glassco, *Memoirs of Montparnasse* (Toronto and New York: Oxford University Press, 1970), 130.

46. Boyle to Katherine Evans Boyle, 10 March 1927.

47. Boyle to Katherine Evans Boyle, 16 March 1927.

48. Boyle to Katherine Evans Boyle, 4 April 1927.

49. Boyle to Edward Dahlberg, 24 January 1967. All letters to Edward Dahlberg are in The Harry Ransom Humanities Research Center, The University of Texas at Austin.

50. Boyle to Evelyn Scott, 31 January 1927.

51. Boyle to Evelyn Scott, 19 May 1927.

52. Eugene Jolas, "Ernest Walsh, Poet and Editor, Dies in Monte Carlo at Age of Thirty-One," *Tribune,* 26 October 1926, rpt. in *The Left Bank Revisited: Selections from the Paris Tribune 1917–1934,* ed. Hugh Ford (University Park: The Pennsylvania State University Press, 1972), 243–44.

53. Boyle to Lola Ridge, 29 November 1927.

54. Boyle to Evelyn Scott, 18 March 1927.

55. Boyle to Evelyn Scott, 28 March 1927.

56. Glassco, 195

57. Litwak, 32. Geoffrey Wolff, in his biography of Harry Crosby, names Kay Boyle as one of those "eminent survivors" of the period who have "wearied unto death of the numberless rag and junk dealers eager to rummage through the attics of their memories for bits of the gossip and pieces of the glamour of that place at that time." He adds: "And it is natural too, finding themselves reluctant prisoners of a legend, that they would if they could

drive a silver stake plumb through the heart of Montparnasse, through the terrace of the Dôme, and through the ghosts of Lady Brett and Jimmy the Barman." Wolff, 112.

58. Boyle to Katherine Evans Boyle, "Tuesday" (1927).

59. Kay Boyle, "The Crosbys: An Afterword," *ICarbS* 3 (1977): 119.

60. Since then Boyle has often wondered if Craig were entirely truthful about this. "He was very jealous of the friendships of the celebrities he knew, and liked to keep them for himself," she explains. "However, because of my admiration and loyalty to Joyce, I had no interest in seeing Gertrude Stein again, and I never did" (Boyle to Spanier, 29 May 1981).

61. Boyle, interview with the author, 22 July 1979, San Francisco.

62. Boyle to Caresse Crosby, 2 October 1931. All letters to Caresse Crosby are in the Black Sun Press Archive, Morris Library, Southern Illinois University, Carbondale.

63. Eugene Jolas, "*transition*: An Epilogue," *American Mercury* 23 (June 1931): 190.

64. Jolas, 186–87, 190.

65. Boyle to Spanier, 18 January 1985.

66. Boyle to Joan Boyle, 4 May 1927; Kay Boyle, "Brighter Than Most," *Prairie Schooner* 34 (Spring 1960): 3–4.

67. Boyle to Katherine Evans Boyle, fragment (1927).

68. Wolff, 309–11.

2. The Revolution of the Word

1. " 'This Quarter' Gets Reviewed," *This Quarter*, 2 (1925): 305.

2. Kay Boyle, "Why Do Americans Live in Europe?" *transition*, no. 14 (Fall 1928): 103.

3. Kay Boyle and Laurence Vail, "Americans Abroad," *Contempo* 3 (15 March 1933): 4.

4. Stanley J. Kunitz, ed., "Kay Boyle," in *Authors Today and Yesterday* (New York: H. W. Wilson Company, 1933), 86.

5. Kay Boyle, "Homage to Harry Crosby," *transition*, no. 19–20 (June 1930): 221.

6. Malcolm Cowley entitled his study of the literature of the twenties *A Second Flowering: Works and Days of the Lost Generation* (New York: The Viking Press, 1974).

7. Tooker and Hofheins, 18.

8. Kay Boyle, "Writers Worth Reading," *Contempo* 2 (5 July 1932): 4.

9. Boyle, "Americans Abroad," 6.

10. Kunitz, 86.

11. Advertisement in *transition*, no. 13 (Summer 1928), n.p.

12. Boyle to Spanier, 22 January 1979.

13. Tooker and Hofheins, 24.

14. Editors' notes in *Contact* 5 (June 1923): n.p.

15. Hugh D. Ford, *Published in Paris: American and British Writers, Painters, and Publishers in Paris, 1920–1939* (New York: Macmillan, 1975), 306.

16. Boyle, "Writers Worth Reading," 4.

17. Evelyn Harter, "Kay Boyle: Experimenter," *The Bookman* 75 (June-July 1932): 252.

18. Kay Boyle, "Hunt," in *Collected Poems* (New York: Alfred A. Knopf, 1962), 82.

19. Harter, 252.

20. L. A. G. Strong, review of *Plagued by the Nightingale, Spectator* 147 (18 July 1931): 94.

21. Kay Boyle, "The Only Bird That Sang," in *Collected Poems,* 81.

22. Kay Boyle, "A Letter to Francis Picabia," in *A Glad Day* (Norfolk, Conn.: New Directions, 1938), 61–62.

23. Quoted by William Carlos Williams in a letter to Kay Boyle tentatively dated 1932, in

The Selected Letters of William Carlos Williams, ed. John C. Thirlwall, (New York: McDowell, Obolensky, 1957), 129.

24. Thirlwall, 130.

25. "In This Issue," *Contempo* 2 (5 July 1932), 2.

26. Boyle, "Writers Worth Reading," 4.

27. Harter, 250.

28. Margaret Atwood, introduction to *Three Short Novels* (1958; rpt. New York: Penguin Books, 1982), ix.

29. Kay Boyle, *Wedding Day and Other Stories* (New York: Jonathan Cape and Harrison Smith, 1930). Cited in text as *WD.*

30. Boyle to Spanier, 4 June 1981.

31. Boyle, "Brighter Than Most," 1.

32. Boyle to Spanier, 30 May 1981. "We who loved him were impatient with this sort of abuse, for Bob gave all he had to others," she says. Indeed, he used part of the 14,000 pounds his father-in-law gave him in 1923 to start the Contact Publishing Company as a sorely needed outlet for artists who could not get their work published by commercial presses, and he brought out books by such writers as Mina Loy, Bryher, H.D., Marsden Hartley, Ernest Hemingway, William Carlos Williams, Mary Butts, Emanuel Carnevali, Robert Coates, Gertrude Stein, and Nathanael West. Besides publishing his first book, *Three Stories and Ten Poems,* McAlmon also financed Hemingway's first visit to Spain in 1923, only to be scorned for the entire trip because he did not share his companion's relish for bullfighting.

33. Boyle to Spanier, 12 June 1981.

34. Porter, 279.

35. Herman Melville to Nathaniel Hawthorne, 1(?) June 1851, in *The Letters of Herman Melville,* ed. Merrell R. Davis and William H. Gilman (New Haven and London: Yale University Press, 1960), 129.

36. In a letter of 18 July 1927, Boyle writes to Evelyn Scott from Stoke-on-Trent that she is thinking of leaving her "adorable daughter" there and "walking the continent" with an Englishman. She never did.

37. Richard Strachey, review of *Wedding Day and Other Stories, New Statesman and Nation,* 24 September 1932, 347.

38. Porter, 279.

3. More Fruits of the Twenties: The First Four Novels

1. Kunitz, 86.

2. Boyle to Katherine Evans Boyle, 18 July 1927.

3. Boyle to Kate Buss, 26 May 1931, the Kay Boyle Papers, Morris Library, Southern Illinois University, Carbondale.

4. Porter, 280.

5. Hart Crane to Caresse Crosby, 31 March 1932, *The Letters of Hart Crane 1916–32,* ed. Brom Weber (New York: Hermitage House, 1952), 406.

6. Harry T. Moore, introduction to *Plagued by the Nightingale* (1931; rpt. Carbondale and Edwardsville: Southern Illinois University Press, 1966). Cited in text as *PN.*

7. Porter, 280.

8. Porter, 280.

9. Richard C. Carpenter, "Kay Boyle," *College English* 15 (November 1953): 84.

10. Frank Gado, "Kay Boyle: From the Aesthetics of Exile to the Polemics of Return" (Ph.D. diss., Duke University, 1968), 77.

11. Boyle to Bob Brown, 14 October 1931. When asked whether she had intended Luc as the father of the child, Boyle was amused and incredulous that anyone might think so and again pointed out that Luc was an afterthought (interview with the author, 22 July 1979, San Francisco.)

12. In a letter of 19 March 1982 to Spanier, Boyle writes: "I know the quote about 'Hyperborean Apollo' is from Ezra Pound, but I cannot tell you the source. A book of Pound's poetry was one of the treasures I took to France with me when Richard Brault and I left New York . . . , and it was one of the books lost in the trunk I could never retrieve from Raymond Duncan's commune in 1928 or 1929."

13. F. Scott Fitzgerald, *Tender Is the Night* (1934; rpt. New York: Charles Scribner's Sons, 1962), 42. Although Kay Boyle's first novel was published three years before *Tender Is the Night* and most probably is the source of Abe North's remark, Boyle's is not the only work to which Fitzgerald alludes in his use of the nightingale image, of course. His title is taken from Keats' "Ode to a Nightingale," and he quotes a passage of the ode as the novel's epigraph.

14. Porter, 280.

15. Carpenter, 84.

16. Atwood, introduction to *Three Short Novels*, ix.

17. Kay Boyle, "Plagued by the Nightingale," *This Quarter*, no. 3 (1927): 181.

18. "Her dainty eye and her dainty sentences are once more in evidence," notes the reviewer in *The Nation*, 6 May 1931, 509. Viola Meynell remarks "the delicate art of this author's perceptions" in *The New Statesman and Nation*, 1 August 1931, 144.

19. Kay Boyle, *Gentlemen, I Address You Privately* (New York: Harrison Smith and Robert Haas, 1933). Cited in text as *G*.

20. H. S. Canby, review of *Gentlemen, I Address You Privately*, *Saturday Review of Literature*, 4 November 1933, 233.

21. Carpenter, 84.

22. Boyle to Bob Brown, tentatively dated August 1931 by the Morris Library.

23. Boyle finds the reading of the novel presented here "interesting and convincing in many ways," but adds: "I never for a moment intended to imply that Leonie and Munday would establish a heterosexual relationship. Perhaps they did. As Beckett once wrote me about the ending of *Happy Days*, how could I possibly know?" (Boyle to Spanier, 23 June 1981.)

24. Boyle to Bob Brown, tentatively dated October 1931 by the Morris Library.

25. A representative from Samuel Goldwyn, Inc., wrote to Kay Boyle's agent that while the novel was not obvious picture material, she felt that an unusually beautiful picture could be made from it with the proper screen treatment (Dorothy Modisett to Ann Watkins, 24 May 1937, the Kay Boyle Papers, Morris Library, Southern Illinois University, Carbondale).

26. Boyle to Bob Brown, tentatively dated June 1932 by the Morris Library.

27. Boyle to Caresse Crosby, 2 February 1932.

28. Caresse Crosby to Boyle, 13 July 1932, the Black Sun Press Archive, Morris Library, Southern Illinois University, Carbondale.

29. Gerald Bullett, review of *Year Before Last*, *The New Statesman and Nation*, 9 July 1932, 43.

30. Harry T. Moore, introduction to *Year Before Last* (1932; rpt. Carbondale and Edwardsville: Southern Illinois University Press, 1969). Cited in text as *YBL*.

31. Ernest Walsh to Kate Buss, 25 May 1926. Letters from Walsh to Buss are in the Kay Boyle Papers, Morris Library, Southern Illinois University, Carbondale.

32. Ernest Walsh to Kate Buss, 27 November 1922.

33. However, while acknowledging Kay Boyle's "rich and resourceful imagination" and

calling the novel "a notable advance" in her career, Robert Cantwell was troubled by a "note of artificiality" in her style. "Like her hero, Kay Boyle seems to identify excellence in writing almost exclusively with uniqueness of phrase, and with this basic conception poetry seems, indeed, a lost and futile art, and poets a haggard and desperate crew." "American Exile," *The Nation,* 20 July 1932, 61.

34. Boyle to Katherine Evans Boyle, fragment (1927).

35. Eliot reviewed the novel for the publisher but either missed the jab or ignored it. In a letter tentatively dated October 1931 by the Morris Library, Boyle writes to Bob Brown of Eliot's reaction: "He 'derived considerable pleasure and amusement from its perusal' but thought it rather an indelicate thing to print in England." She was surprised, then, when the publisher enthusiastically accepted it, offering her a thousand-dollar advance. In a letter of 23 March 1932, she confides to Brown: "I thought they'd decide agin it, because if you remember in the first half there's a good bit against Eliot, mentioning him by name in fact. And in the wire to Carnevali, the text says that 'you plant things in the Wasteland [sic] and other empty poetry.' Perhaps Eliot forgot that he wrote the Wasteland."

36. In fact, Boyle's novel was written before "The Snows of Kilimanjaro," published in 1936. "Maybe Hemingway was influenced by me!" she speculates (Boyle to Spanier, 23 June 1981).

37. Kay Boyle, notes, 20 July 1957, the Kay Boyle Papers, Morris Library, Southern Illinois University, Carbondale.

38. Review of *My Next Bride, Christian Century,* 5 December 1934, 1564.

39. Review of *My Next Bride, Forum,* 92 (December 1934): ix.

40. Edith H. Walton, review of *My Next Bride, New York Times Book Review,* 11 November 1934, 6.

41. Elizabeth Hart, review of *My Next Bride, Books,* 11 November 1934, 4.

42. Kay Boyle, *My Next Bride* (New York: Harcourt, Brace and Co., 1934). Cited in text as *MNB*.

43. Boyle recounts the meeting and specifically corrects Caresse Crosby's version of it in "The Crosbys: An Afterword," *ICarbS* 3 (1977): 117–25.

44. Boyle discusses the issue of lesbianism in letters of 20 June and 23 June 1981 to Spanier.

45. Boyle to Spanier, 20 June 1981.

46. Boyle to Spanier, 30 November 1984.

47. Boyle, "The Vanishing Short Story?" 111.

48. Boyle to Bob Brown, 26 February 1931.

4. The Thirties: Art and the Functioning World

1. Boyle to Walter Lowenfels, 15 August 1930, the Kay Boyle Papers, Morris Library, Southern Illinois University, Carbondale.

2. Kay Boyle, "Elizabeth Bowen," *The New Republic,* 21 September 1942, 355.

3. Boyle to Spanier, 30 December 1984.

4. Boyle to Spanier, 14 December 1984.

5. Ford, *Left Bank Revisited,* 130.

6. Boyle to Bob Brown, 9 July 1931.

7. Boyle to Bob Brown, tentatively dated August 1931 by the Morris library.

8. Boyle to Bob Brown, tentatively dated 1932 by the Morris Library. The particular story to which she refers is unidentified.

9. Boyle to Richard C. Carpenter, 2 February 1953. The letter is in the possession of Professor Carpenter.

10. Boyle to Bob Brown, 26 February 1931.

11. Boyle to Ann Watkins, 30 April 1934. All letters to Ann Watkins are in the Kay Boyle Papers, Morris Library, Southern Illinois University, Carbondale.

12. Boyle to Bob and Rose Brown, 3 March 1935.

13. Peggy Guggenheim, *Out of This Century: The Informal Memoirs of Peggy Guggenheim* (New York: The Dial Press, 1946), 268–69.

14. Guggenheim, 113.

15. Guggenheim, 169. In the new edition of her memoirs, *Out of This Century: Confessions of an Art Addict* (New York: Universe Books, 1979), the names of Kay Boyle and Laurence Vail are undisguised.

16. Boyle to Spanier, 6 December 1984.

17. Boyle to Spanier, 6 December 1984.

18. Boyle to Bob Brown, 1 March, tentatively dated 1932 by the Morris Library.

19. Boyle to Bob Brown, "Wednesday," tentatively dated 1932 by the Morris Library.

20. Boyle to Bob Brown, 15 April 1931.

21. Boyle to Bob Brown, "Sunday," tentatively dated 1932 by the Morris Library.

22. Boyle to Bob Brown, "Wednesday," tentatively dated October 1931 by the Morris Library.

23. Boyle to Bob and Rose Brown, "Sunday" tentatively dated October 1931 by the Morris Library.

24. Boyle to Bob Brown, 16 January 1932.

25. Boyle to Caresse Crosby, tentatively dated January-March 1930 by the Morris Library.

26. Boyle to Caresse Crosby, 5 November 1933.

27. Boyle to Caresse Crosby, "Thursday," tentatively dated June 1930 by the Morris Library.

28. Boyle to Caresse Crosby, 18 July 1933.

29. Boyle to Caresse Crosby, 7 May 1931.

30. Boyle to Bob Brown, "Monday," tentatively dated 1931 by the Morris Library.

31. A short poem, "Flight of Fish," appeared in the 16 August 1933 issue of *The Nation*, 190. A ten-page piece entitled "Two Fragments from an Aviation Epic" is included in Eugene Jolas's 1941 anthology, *Vertical*. One fragment, "The Albatross of Le Bris," is a mixture of prose and verse sections describing the eighteenth-century efforts of Le Bris to construct a flying machine. The other, "In a Long Arboreal Apprenticeship Birds Came to Fly," is a paean to the natural flight of birds.

32. Boyle, *The Autobiography of Emanuel Carnevali*, 18.

33. Boyle to Spanier, 29 May 1981.

34. Robert McAlmon to Boyle, 11 December 1933, the Kay Boyle Papers, Morris Library, Southern Illinois University, Carbondale. Boyle is sure McAlmon would have published the book had they not found an American publisher (Boyle to Spanier, 23 July 1981).

35. Boyle to Ann Watkins, 15 April 1934.

36. Boyle to Spanier, 6 December 1984. The introduction by MacLeish that Ethel Moorhead refused to allow to appear apparently has been lost. "Archie wrote me recently that he had searched for a copy but cannot find it," Kay Boyle reported soon before his death (Boyle to Spanier, 19 March 1982).

37. Boyle's new translation of the entire novel, *Babylon*, with the same illustrations by Max Ernst, was published in 1985 by North Point Press (San Francisco). The 1931 book is now a collectors' item, selling for over $4000, she reports (Boyle to Spanier, 6 December 1984).

38. Boyle to Bob Brown, 13 October 1931.

39. Boyle to Bob and Rose Brown, 3 March 1935.

40. Boyle to Spanier, 23 June 1981.

41. Boyle to Ann Watkins, 27 January 1934.

42. Boyle to Spanier, 24 September 1985; Boyle to Ann Watkins, 27 January 1934. In concept, the project recalls John Dos Passos' quasi-journalistic trilogy, *U.S.A.*. He too had employed reports of actual events in contemporary history in his "Newsreel" segments and had named the second book, published in 1932, after a specific year—*1919*. However, Kay Boyle believes that their plan was an original idea of Laurence Vail's: "It may have been inspired by John Dos Passos' trilogy, but I have no recollection of our having read this work" (Boyle to Spanier, 23 June 1981).

43. Laurence Vail to Caresse Crosby, 26 December 1933, the Black Sun Press Archive, Morris Library, Southern Illinois University, Carbondale.

44. Kay Boyle, Laurence Vail, and Nina Conarain, eds., *365 Days* (New York: Harcourt, Brace and Co., 1936). Cited in text as *365D*.

45. Boyle to Spanier, 30 December 1984.

46. Gado, 111–12.

47. Boyle to Spanier, 24 September 1985.

48. Boyle to Spanier, 6 December 1984.

49. Boyle to Spanier, 23 June 1981; 24 September 1985.

50. The strange power of an Australian water-diviner that she describes in the piece of January 16 is at the center of "Career," published in *The White Horses of Vienna and Other Stories* (1936). The Southern black preacher of the March 20 sketch who calls himself "Bishop Delicatatem" reappears in another story in that volume, "First Offense," a monologue in which the glib charlatan "explains" his history of shady dealings to a church elder visiting him behind bars. The material of the July 25 sketch of a Tyrolean doctor's politically-charged marionette show figures in "The White Horses of Vienna," while the mountainside swastika fires and the death of Chancellor Dollfuss described in the pieces of January 29, February 20, and July 27, appear both in that short story and in the 1936 novel *Death of a Man*. The humpbacked crone of a nurse attending Lady Alfalfa in the April 15 sketch is transplanted from Portugal to the Tyrol as Sister Resi in *Death of a Man*.

51. Boyle, "Brighter Than Most," 1.

52. Kay Boyle, *The First Lover and Other Stories* (New York: Harrison Smith and Robert Haas, 1933). Cited in text as *FL*.

53. Interview in Whit and Hallie Burnett, eds., *The Modern Short Story in the Making* (New York and London: Hawthorn Books, 1964), 193; Boyle to Spanier, 30 December 1984.

54. In her own account of her childhood, Boyle recalls finding the crumpled halves of a letter in her father's handwriting not far from the wastebasket on the floor of her workroom. " 'Dear Mary,' it said. 'I cannot tell you how much less than nothing my life would be without you in it—' It broke off there. I never spoke of the torn letter to anyone, and I came to believe that it was not a letter written to a woman named Mary, or to any woman, but written to himself, and left there for me to read, a piece of paper torn in two asking for something none of us could give." (Bryfonski, 110.)

55. Boyle to Bob Brown, 16 January 1932.

56. Boyle to Bob Brown, "Tuesday," tentatively dated 1932 by the Morris Library.

57. Burnett, 194.

58. Kay Boyle, *The White Horses of Vienna and Other Stories* (New York: Harcourt, Brace and Co., 1936). Cited in text as *WHV*. Several of the stories were reissued ten years later in *Thirty Stories* (New York: Simon and Schuster, 1946), and again in *Fifty Stories* (Garden City, N.Y.: Doubleday, 1980).

59. In the later editions the passage reads: " 'You don't belong in this country any more than I or anyone else belongs here. But you belong to me,' said Major Alshuster. 'I don't happen to believe in death, Mrs. Whatchername,' he said."

60. Boyle to Bob Brown, 3 May 1931. Boyle writes: "I'm puzzled by the analogy you find

between *A Farewell to Arms* and 'Maiden, Maiden.' I've tried to understand your thinking on this and I can't work it out. I'd hate to think I was ever influenced by Hemingway, and I've never heard it mentioned before" (Boyle to Spanier, 30 December 1984).

61. In *Thirty Stories* and *Fifty Stories* the passage reads, "His face was as strong as rock, but it had seen so much of suffering that it had the look of being scarred, it seemed to be split in two, with one side of it given to resolve and the other to compassion."

62. "I believe in the independence of the individual," he says in later editions.

63. In the 1946 and 1980 versions Boyle adds, "I am a young man alone, as my race is alone, lost here amongst them all."

64. Boyle to Ann Watkins, 3 July 1934.

65. Boyle, *Death of a Man* (New York: Harcourt, Brace and Co., 1936). Cited in text as *DOM*.

66. Gado, 126.

67. Mark Van Doren, "Under the Swastika," in *The Private Reader: Selected Articles and Reviews* (1942; rpt. New York: Kraus Reprint Co., 1968), 241; Boyle to Spanier, 23 June 1981.

68. Boyle to Spanier, 30 December 1984.

69. Boyle to Spanier, 30 December 1984.

70. Tooker and Hofheins, 20.

71. Boyle to Spanier, 23 June 1981.

72. Boyle to Bob Brown, 13 January 1935.

73. Boyle to Spanier, 23 July 1981.

74. Boyle to Spanier, 23 July 1981.

75. Boyle to Spanier, 14 August 1981.

76. Otis Ferguson, "The Brown Blouses of Vienna," *The New Republic*, 21 October 1936, 322.

77. Van Doren, 241–42. Boyle finds his comment "very superficial": "Is one not to write about foreign countries and current history because someone in America is 'not conversant with the foreign news'?" (Boyle to Spanier, 30 December 1984).

5. Interlude: *Monday Night* and *The Crazy Hunter*

1. Boyle, "Elizabeth Bowen," 355.

2. Kay Boyle, *Monday Night* (New York: Harcourt, Brace, and Co., 1938). Cited in text as *MN*.

3. Ford, *Left Bank Revisited*, xx.

4. New Directions republished the novel in the 1940s as part of its New Classics series, retaining the 1938 copyright date. The dedication of the original Harcourt, Brace edition reads: " '. . . those who speak it follow no political leader and take no part in any persecution or conquest; nor have they to do either with a vocabulary of the rich or the poor or any country or race; it being simply one way of communication between the lost and the lost.' (*The Man Without a Nation*)."

5. Boyle to Spanier, 23 July 1981.

6. Kay Boyle, "*The Unvanquished*," in *The Critic as Artist: Essays on Books 1920–1970*, ed. Gilbert A. Harrison (New York: Liveright Publishing, 1972), pp. 39–40.

7. Boyle to Richard C. Carpenter, 2 February 1953.

8. Boyle to Spanier, 30 December 1984.

9. William Faulkner's Speech of Acceptance upon the award of the Nobel Prize for Literature, delivered in Stockholm on 10 December 1950, in *The Faulkner Reader* (New York: The Modern Library, Random House, 1961), 4.

10. Boyle, "The Vanishing Short Story?" 115.

11. Boyle, *"The Unvanquished,"* 41.

12. *Monday Night* was the second of her books (after *Year Before Last*) to be translated into French, and it was a choice of the Paris "Book-of-the-Month-Club," *Le Livre du Mois* (Boyle to Spanier, 27 July 1981).

13. Richard C. Carpenter, "Kay Boyle: The Figure in the Carpet," *Critique* 7 (Winter 1964–65): 65–66.

14. Kay Boyle, "The Bridegroom's Body." Originally part of her collection entitled *The Crazy Hunter: Three Short Novels* (New York: Harcourt, Brace and Co., 1940), this work along with "The Crazy Hunter" is reprinted in *Three Short Novels* (Boston: Beacon Press, 1958), that collection itself reprinted in 1982 by Penguin Books. Cited in text as *TSN* (1982 edition).

15. In a letter to Spanier dated 20 June 1981 Boyle concurs with this reading, but she wishes to make clear that "there were no lesbian under-tones or over-tones" to the scene. It was "never for a moment" her intention to suggest that the story "offered a lesbian affair as a solution to the problems of the loneliness of the women involved." Speaking also of her 1934 novel *My Next Bride,* she adds, "I wanted to make a statement about the comfort and the solace that being understood brought to both Lady Glourie and Victoria—two instances in which love did not fail." Yet she is not optimistic that the "connection" the two women experience at the end of "The Bridegroom's Body" will be more than transitory. In a letter of 27 July 1981 to Spanier, she writes:

> Like Beckett, I do not like stories of success, but only stories of failure. I don't know what happened either to Lady Glourie or Miss Cafferty, but I'm pretty sure they didn't find salvation in each other. Miss Cafferty was probably shipped back to where she came from because of delinquency in performing her duty toward the swanherd's wife, and Lady Glourie probably went back to knitting the sweater for her son.

16. Kay Boyle, "Big Fiddle," in *The Crazy Hunter: Three Short Novels* (New York: Harcourt, Brace and Co., 1940). Cited in text as *CH.*

17. Carpenter, "Figure in the Carpet," 76.

18. The resemblance is entirely coincidental. Kay Boyle explains: "Living in war-torn France, I had never heard of Carson McCullers, and did not meet her, or know of her work until 1941, when we returned to the United States. Incidentally, Carson was always very much annoyed by that title, *The Heart Is a Lonely Hunter.* She had called the book *The Deaf-Mutes* and resented the fact that the publisher had discarded her title and given it the new title over her objections." (Boyle to Spanier, 23 June 1981.)

19. Boyle to Joan Boyle Detweiler, 27 June 1939.

20. Boyle to Richard C. Carpenter, 2 February 1953.

21. Boyle to Richard C. Carpenter, 2 February 1953.

22. In the 1958 collection, "Big Fiddle" was replaced by "Decision," a story set against the Spanish Civil War and originally published in the *Saturday Evening Post* in 1948 under the title "Passport to Doom."

23. Carpenter, "Figure in the Carpet," 78, 65.

24. Carpenter, "Figure in the Carpet," 70.

6. The War Years: Politics and Potboilers

1. Bernadine Kielty, "Under-Cover Stuff," *Ladies' Home Journal* 63 (March 1946): 5.

2. Edmund Wilson, "Kay Boyle and the *Saturday Evening Post,*" in *Classics and Commercials: A Literary Chronicle of the Forties* (New York: Vintage Books, Random House, 1962), 128–32.

3. Boyle to Bob Brown, 14 October 1938.

4. Boyle to Caresse Crosby, 16 February 1940.

5. Boyle to Joan Boyle Detweiler, 18 April 1939.

6. Boyle to Joan Boyle Detweiler, 27 June 1939.

7. Boyle to Caresse Crosby, 26 August 1940.

8. Boyle to Spanier, 9 July 1980.

9. Boyle to Spanier, 16 August 1981. She adds, "Joseph was a Catholic, not a Jew, but Catholics, too, were victims of Fascism, albeit not in such great numbers as the Jews."

10. Boyle, interview with the author, 22 July 1979, San Francisco.

11. Guggenheim, *Out of This Century* (1946), 268. "I wish Peggy Guggenheim had not included me in this business of detesting. I did not detest her, but felt deeply sorry for a woman who was so perpetually unloved," Boyle says. Charitably, she adds: "I think I have been able to accomplish whatever I have because I was always sustained by the love of those I lived with. Peggy never had this kind of support and devotion and so her whole life was one of frustration and consequent destruction" (Boyle to Spanier, 23 June 1981). She denies, too, that she ever quarrelled with Max Ernst, as Guggenheim also reports (Boyle to Spanier, 22 January 1985).

12. Robert van Gelder, "An Interview with Kay Boyle, Expatriate," in *Writers and Writing* (New York: Charles Scribner's Sons, 1946), 194.

13. Guggenheim, *Out of This Century* (1946), 282.

14. Boyle to Spanier, 23 June 1981.

15. Boyle to Bob Brown, 6 December 1941.

16. Boyle to Spanier, 24 January 1985.

17. Boyle to Bob Brown, 13 January 1943.

18. Boyle to Spanier, 14 August 1981. Franckenstein's military career was the stuff of which legends are made, and his activities in the OSS are recounted in two recent books about secret Allied operations during World War II: Joseph E. Persico's *Piercing the Reich: The Penetration of Nazi Germany by American Secret Agents during World War II* (New York: The Viking Press, 1979) and Fritz Molden's *Exploding Star: A Young Austrian against Hitler* (London: Weidenfeld and Nicolson, 1978). Molden, who was a personal friend of Franckenstein, writes of him: "Warm and affectionate at heart, and a fervent patriot who read poetry and quoted Rilke, he was, besides, a ferocious fighter who began his day by caroling, 'Heimatschutz! Let's do 'em, get yer knives out quick. Stick 'em in and twist 'em round, cor lads, what a kick!' " (p. 210).

Boyle notes, however, that Molden's book contains some inaccuracies. "Joseph at no time wanted to get a job teaching in Vienna, nor did he die of a broken heart over this while teaching in the mid-West." Also, Franckenstein's OSS code name was not "Hornek," as Molden reports, but "Horneck," after his ancestor, Count von Horneck. Kay Boyle has silverware engraved with his name, given to her by Joseph's mother, to prove it (Boyle to Spanier, 23 June 1981).

19. Boyle to Spanier, 14 August 1981.

20. Van Gelder, 196.

21. Boyle to Caresse Crosby, 10 January 1942.

22. Boyle to Ann Watkins, 29 March 1944.

23. Gado, 153

24. Kay Boyle, *Thirty Stories* (1946; rpt. New York: New Directions, 1957). Cited in text as *TS*.

25. "War in Paris," *The New Yorker*, 26 November 1938, 18–20.

26. Kay Boyle, "Battle of the Sequins," *The Nation*, 23 December 1944, 770–71.

27. Kay Boyle, *Nothing Ever Breaks Except the Heart* (Garden City, N.Y.: Doubleday, 1966). Cited in text as *NEB*.

28. Madden, 229, 234.

29. Gado, 126.

30. Gado, 162.

31. Boyle to Ann Watkins, 1 April 1944; Boyle to Ann Watkins, 24 February 1947.

32. Kay Boyle, *Primer for Combat* (New York: Simon and Schuster, 1942). Cited in text as *PC*.

33. Boyle to Spanier, 23 June 1981. She adds in a letter of 16 August 1981 that Joseph is the character Sepp in the novel.

34. "Why Do Americans Live in Europe?" *transition*, no. 14 (Fall 1928): 103.

35. Tooker and Hofheins, 27.

36. Tooker and Hofheins, 27. "Monsieur et Madame Rose Sélavy," to whom the book is dedicated, were Marcel Duchamp and his longtime companion, Mary Reynolds. Reynolds had worked in the Resistance before narrowly escaping over the Pyrenées and later, when she was working with the United States War Department assisting Resistance fighters in France, was instrumental in arranging Joseph Franckenstein's transfer to the OSS. Duchamp had spent weeks with Kay Boyle's party in Marseilles, waiting for an exit visa to come through from the Vichy government. The couple provided the author with many of the details of her novel, and she shared with them the profits from the book. (Boyle to Spanier, 23 June 1981.)

37. Elizabeth Bullock, review of *Avalanche, Book Week*, 23 January 1944, 2.

38. Diana Trilling, review of *Avalanche, The Nation*, 22 January 1944, 105.

39. Harry T. Moore, "Kay Boyle's Fiction," in *Age of the Modern and Other Literary Essays* (Carbondale and Edwardsville: Southern Illinois University Press, 1971), 33–34.

40. Wilson, 128–29.

41. Kay Boyle, *Avalanche* (New York: Simon and Schuster, 1944). Cited in text as *A*.

42. Tooker and Hofheins, 32.

43. Struthers Burt, "Kay Boyle's Coincidence and Melodrama," *Saturday Review of Literature*, 15 January 1944, 6.

44. Boyle to Spanier, 23 June 1981.

45. Boyle to Spanier, 14 August 1981.

46. Van Gelder, 194.

47. Boyle to Ann Watkins, 29 March 1944.

48. Kay Boyle, *1939* (New York: Simon and Schuster, 1948). Cited in text as *1939*.

49. Boyle to Bob Brown, 18 January 1943.

50. Boyle to Ann Watkins, 2 August 1947.

51. Kay Boyle, *American Citizen Naturalized in Leadville, Colorado* (New York: Simon and Schuster, 1944). Cited in text as *AC*.

52. Boyle to Ann Watkins, 29 March 1944.

53. Boyle to Ann Watkins, 2 August 1947.

54. Edward C. Aswell to Kay Boyle, 6 September 1947, the Kay Boyle Papers, Morris Library, Southern Illinois University, Carbondale.

55. Boyle to Ann Watkins, 29 March 1944.

56. Boyle to Ann Watkins, 6 December 1947.

57. William Blake, *The Four Zoas,* in *The Poetry and Prose of William Blake*, ed. David V. Erdman (Garden City, N.Y.: Doubleday, 1965), 297.

58. Kay Boyle, *His Human Majesty* (New York: Whittlesey House, McGraw-Hill Book Company, 1949). Cited in text as *HHM*.

59. For her analysis of the scapegoat phenomenon see "Jew Is a Myth," *The Nation*, 13 October 1945, 368, 372.

60. Boyle, "The Vanishing Short Story?" 115.

61. Boyle to Caresse Crosby, 14 April 1945.

7. In the Wake of War

1. "Kay Boyle," *New York Herald Tribune Book Review*, 7 October 1951, 28.

2. "Kay Boyle, Journalist," *The New York Times Book Review*, 24 November 1946, 8.

3. Boyle to Spanier, 27 July 1981.

4. Boyle to Ann Watkins, 24 February 1947.

5. Boyle to Ann Watkins, 27 November 1946.

6. Boyle to Ann Watkins, 7 November 1947.

7. Boyle to Ann Watkins, 2 August 1947.

8. Boyle to Ann Watkins, 11 May 1948.

9. Boyle to Ann Watkins, 1 October 1948.

10. Kay Boyle, *The Smoking Mountain: Stories of Postwar Germany* (New York, London & Toronto: McGraw-Hill Book Company, Inc., 1951). Cited in text as *SM*.

11. Boyle to Ann Watkins, 16 December 1948.

12. Boyle to Ann Watkins, 2 March 1949.

13. Boyle to Ann Watkins, 16 December 1948.

14. Boyle to Spanier, 14 August 1981. Budenz was also responsible for ruining the diplomatic career of John Carter Vincent, among many others, she notes.

15. Boyle to Spanier, 14 August 1981.

16. Among Boyle's papers at Southern Illinois University is a seventeen-page copy of Janet Flanner's testimony at the loyalty hearing. Boyle apparently had included it in a letter of 29 October 1952 to General Edward Greenbaum, her lawyer in New York, in which she details the case and asks for his help.

17. Boyle to Spanier, 14 August 1981.

18. Immediately upon Janet Flanner's return to Paris after testifying at the hearing, even before the outcome was known, "the wrath of God" had descended upon her. "It came in the form of a cable from Shawn, saying that she had jeopardized *The New Yorker* in appearing as a witness at the hearing," Boyle recalls. Later she learned from Janet Flanner's close friend, Solita Solano, that Flanner "had wept for hours, so stricken was she by the lack of moral courage of the editors of the magazine she had worked for for so many years." Boyle adds: "It may be asked why Janet did not resign from *The New Yorker* in protest. I can only answer that she wanted to. In a subsequent talk we had one weekend in Paris, Janet wept again and said: 'Let us never mention to each other again this shattering experience. Whatever my feelings are about it, we must recognize between us that you have a husband, six children, a distinguished writing career, while I have nothing but *The New Yorker* as husband, children, career.' From that day until her death, we never spoke of it again." (Boyle to Spanier, 14 August 1981.)

19. Charles Fracchia, "Kay Boyle: A Profile," *San Francisco Review of Books* 1 (April 1976): 8.

20. Boyle to Ann Watkins, 23 October 1952.

21. Boyle to Edward Greenbaum, 29 October 1952.

22. Boyle to Spanier, 29 April 1982.

23. Boyle to Spanier, 14 August 1981.

24. Boyle to Bob Brown, 12 October 1953.

25. Boyle to Bob Brown, 14 February 1957.

26. Their lawyers, Edward Greenbaum in New York and Benjamin Ferencz in Germany, "worked with dedication and without pay" (Boyle to Spanier, 23 July 1981).

27. Koch, 53.

28. Boyle to Edward Aswell, 17 December 1952. All letters from Boyle to Aswell are in the Kay Boyle Papers, Morris Library, Southern Illinois University, Carbondale.

29. Kay Boyle, "Spain Divided," *The Nation,* 11 June 1955, 507.

30. Kay Boyle, "Farewell to New York," *The Nation,* 8 March 1947, 272.

31. Boyle to Richard C. Carpenter, 2 February 1953.

32. Boyle to Ann Watkins, 16 June 1947.

33. Boyle to Ann Watkins, 21 June 1947.

34. Boyle to Ann Watkins, 22 June 1947.

35. Boyle to Ann Watkins, 22 June 1947.

36. Boyle to Edward Aswell, 17 December 1952.

37. Boyle to Ann Watkins, 13 January 1952.

38. Boyle to Edward Aswell, 17 December 1952.

39. Kay Boyle, *The Seagull on the Step* (New York: Alfred A. Knopf, 1955). Cited in text as *SS.*

40. Sidney Alexander, review of *The Seagull on the Step, The New York Times Book Review,* 8 May 1955, 5.

41. Boyle to Edward Aswell, 15 November 1953.

42. Boyle to Ann Watkins, 16 June 1947.

43. The book was to have been part of a series edited by John Gunther to which only fiction writers were asked to contribute. Originally scheduled for completion in 1966, it has not been published. She had started the project with the help of her husband, Joseph Franckenstein, and after his death in 1963 had gotten as far as Bismarck, but in the mid-seventies she came to the realization that the only good chapters she had written were about German women. With the agreement of her editor at Doubleday, Ken McCormick, she decided to focus on that aspect of German history. Although she terminated her relationship with Doubleday in 1980 and has not worked actively on the book for some time, she still considers it a work in progress. "I'm saving it for my *very* old age," she told the author in a telephone conversation of 16 July 1982.

44. Moore, *Age of the Modern,* 36, 32.

45. Kay Boyle, *Generation Without Farewell* (New York: Alfred A. Knopf, 1960). Cited in text as *GWF.*

46. Tooker and Hofheins, 28.

47. Barbaralee Diamonstein, ed., "Kay Boyle," in *Open Secrets: Ninety-four Women in Touch With Our Time* (New York: The Viking Press, 1972), 26

48. The proclamation appeared in the June, 1929, issue of *transition.*

49. Kay Boyle, "A Declaration for 1955," *The Nation,* 29 January 1955, 103.

50. Boyle, "Declaration," 103–4.

8. Back Home: "It Might Just Save the World"

1. Mildred Schroeder, "Author Kay Boyle Spurs New Kind of Integration," *San Francisco Examiner,* 1 July 1966.

2. Boyle, interview with the author, 22 July 1979, San Francisco.

3. Boyle to Spanier, 27 July 1981.

4. Caresse Crosby, *The Passionate Years* (1953; rpt. Carbondale and Edwardsville: Southern Illinois University Press, 1968), 248.

5. Diamonstein, 27.

6. Schroeder, *San Francisco Examiner*, 1 July 1966.

7. David Felton, "The Lyman Family's Holy Seige of America," part 2, *Rolling Stone*, 6 January 1972, 45.

8. Merla Zellerback, "When Writers Give Themselves Away," *San Francisco Chronicle*, 15 March 1978, p. 15.

9. "Kay Boyle's Bitter View of Johnson," *San Francisco Chronicle*, 15 September 1968.

10. Boyle to Spanier, 27 July 1981. They abandoned the demonstration when a television cameraman recognized among the silent protesters Jessica Mitford, author of *The American Way of Death*, and the public construed the vigil as a protest against a particular funeral establishment.

11. Bob Haesler, "Kay Boyle Assesses S. F. State," *San Francisco Chronicle*, 16 November 1968.

12. Boyle to Spanier, 27 July 1981. She notes that his story varied. Another version was, "Kay Boyle, you should be ashamed of yourself, acting like a member of a lynch mob!" For a detailed account of the incident and of the strike in general, see Boyle, "The Long Walk at San Francisco State" in *The Long Walk at San Francisco State and Other Essays* (New York: Grove Press, 1970). Cited in text as *LW*.

13. In 1973, Boyle was teaching only one course a semester at the university, having chosen "early retirement" in order to have more time for her own writing. Hayakawa also had chosen an early retirement, in order to further his political career, she reports. (Boyle to Spanier, 6 February 1985.)

14. Mickey Freidman, "A Literary Legend Who Refuses to Rest on Her Laurels," *San Francisco Examiner*, 27 September 1968. Among her current projects is a book on Irish women. A short piece drawn from her experience in Ireland, entitled "St. Stephen's Green," appeared in *Atlantic Monthly*, June, 1980. When she sold the house on Frederick Street in July, 1980, one possible plan was to settle permanently in the country she considers her spiritual home. Kay Boyle did not, in fact, move to Ireland, but to Cottage Grove, Oregon, near her son. She had hoped to go to Ireland in the summer of 1981 but could not for financial reasons. In the winter of 1981–82, she left Cottage Grove to spend nine weeks as Distinguished Writer in Residence at Eastern Washington University and a week at the University of Colorado at Boulder. She again intended to travel to Ireland as part of a trip to Europe to see her daughters Sharon and Kathe in Paris in the summer of 1982, but health problems intervened and she had to cut her visit short. As for her long-term plans, she says she is "taking one year at a time." (Boyle, interview with the author, 20 May 1982, New York.)

15. "Matters of Security," *The Washington Star*, 1 June 1979, p. A-2. She first met Pound in 1928.

16. Boyle to Caresse Crosby, 2 November 1967.

17. Tooker and Hofheins, 32.

18. Kay Boyle, "The Triumph of Principles," originally published in *Liberation* 5 (June 1960): 10–11, is reprinted in *Enough of Dying! Voices for Peace*, ed. Kay Boyle and Justine Van Gundy (New York: Dell, 1972). Cited in text as *ED*.

19. Boyle to Spanier, 27 July 1981.

20. Kathy Drew, "Kay Boyle Dedicates Self to Human Dignity," *Lost Generation Journal* 4 (Winter 1976): 22.

21. Kay Boyle, *The Underground Woman* (Garden City, N.Y.: Doubleday, 1975). Cited in text as *UW*.

22. Boyle's second visit to prison in December, 1967, during which she was separated from the other arrested demonstrators and confined in an area for dangerous inmates, is the subject of her essay "Report From Lock-Up," in Erica Jong, Thomas Sanchez, Kay Boyle, and Henry Miller, *Four Visions of America*, (Santa Barbara: Capra Press, 1977), 10–39.

23. David Felton, "The Lyman Family's Holy Siege of America," part 1, *Rolling Stone*, 23 December 1971.

24. Blake Green, "Kay Boyle—A Study in Paradox," *San Francisco Chronicle*, 17 February 1975, p. 12.

25. Boyle to Spanier, 30 January 1985.

26. Felton, "Holy Siege," part 2, 45.

27. Boyle to Spanier, 27 July 1981. Of her lawyer, Boyle adds, "He is such a great and modest man that Jessica Mitford prefers to be addressed as Mrs. Robert Treuhaft."

28. Peter S. Prescott, "Life with Daughter," *Newsweek*, 13 January 1975, 67A.

29. Doris Grumbach, review of *The Underground Woman*, *The New Republic*, 8 February 1975, 3.

30. Charles Fracchia, "Kay Boyle: A Profile," *San Francisco Review of Books*, 1 (April, 1976): 8.

31. Boyle has said that she especially likes "Black Boy" "because it is so completely simple, and moral without moralizing" (Burnett, 194). "I have no 'favorites' among my stories or books. I am highly critical of them all," she says today. (Boyle to Spanier, 30 January 1985.)

32. See "So Slowly We Move," 4 May 1957; "No Time to Listen," 16 November 1957; and "City of Invisible Men," 21 December 1957.

33. Schroeder, *San Francisco Chronicle*, 1 July 1966.

34. Madden, 232.

35. Boyle to Spanier, 23 March 1982.

36. Litwak, 32.

37. Boyle to Spanier, 4 June 1981.

38. Kay Boyle, *Testament for My Students and Other Poems* (Garden City, N.Y.: Doubleday, 1970). Cited in text as *TFS*.

39. Madden, 217.

40. Madden, 219–20.

41. Madden, 216.

42. Drew, 14.

Epilogue: Tunes of an Aeolian Harp

1. Gerald Sykes, review of *Wedding Day and Other Stories*, *The Nation*, 24 December 1930, 711.

2. Porter, 279.

3. Robert Cantwell, review of *Gentlemen, I Address You Privately*, *The New Republic*, 13 December 1933, 136.

4. Mary M. Colum, review of *Monday Night*, *Forum*, 100 (October 1938): 166.

5. Moore, introduction to *Plagued by the Nightingale*, viii.

6. Walton, 6.

7. Review of *My Next Bride*, *Forum* 92 (December 1934): ix.

8. A 1972 study of freshman composition textbooks found that only a tiny percentage of the essays provided as models of logical argument or persuasive content was written by women. Yet female authors were more "generously" represented (at a proportion of 12 to 17 percent) in essays illustrating stylistic techniques. Jean S. Mullen, "Women Writers in Freshman Textbooks," *College English* 34 (October 1972): 79–84.

9. Elaine Showalter describes the problem in "Women and the Literary Curriculum," *College English* 32 (May 1971): 856: "Women are estranged from their own experience and unable to perceive its shape and authenticity in part because they do not see it mirrored and

given resonance by literature. Instead they are expected to identify as readers with a masculine experience and perspective, which is presented as the human one."

10. Kunitz, 86.

11. Tooker and Hofheins, 17.

12. Boyle to Spanier, 27 July 1981.

13. Tillie Olsen, *Silences* (New York: Dell, 1979), 12.

14. Boyle to Joan Boyle Detweiler, 27 May 1943.

15. Boyle to Nancy Cunard, 2 December 1953, The Harry Ransom Humanities Research Center, The University of Texas at Austin.

16. Olsen, 18–19.

17. Boyle to Spanier, 28 April 1983.

18. Boyle, interview with author, 17 May 1983, New York.

19. Boyle, "A Declaration for 1955," 103.

20. Boyle to Edward Aswell, 17 December 1952.

21. Boyle to Ann Watkins, 13 January 1952.

22. Atwood, introduction to *Three Short Novels*, vii.

23. Ralph Thompson, "In and Out of Books," *The New York Times Book Review*, 10 April 1949, 8.

24. Madden, 231.

25. Boyle to Spanier, 27 July 1981.

26. Madden, 231.

27. Kunitz, 86.

28. Ralph Waldo Emerson, "Self-Reliance," in *The Collected Works of Ralph Waldo Emerson*, vol. 2, ed. Joseph Slater (Cambridge, Mass., and London: The Belknap Press of Harvard University Press, 1979), 33.

29. Boyle, "The Vanishing Short Story?" 115.

30. Boyle, "The Vanishing Short Story?" 111.

Selected Bibliography

Primary Sources

Novels

Boyle, Kay. *Plagued by the Nightingale*. 1931; rpt. Carbondale and Edwardsville: Southern Illinois University Press, 1966, with an introduction by Harry T. Moore.

————. *Year Before Last*. 1932; rpt. Carbondale and Edwardsville: Southern Illinois University Press, 1969, with an introduction by Harry T. Moore.

————. *Gentlemen, I Address You Privately*. New York: Harrison Smith and Robert Haas, 1933.

————. *My Next Bride*. New York: Harcourt, Brace and Co., 1934.

————. *Death of a Man*. New York: Harcourt, Brace and Co., 1936.

————. *Monday Night*. New York: Harcourt, Brace and Co., 1938.

————. *Primer for Combat*. New York: Simon and Schuster, 1942.

————. *Avalanche*. New York: Simon and Schuster, 1944.

————. *A Frenchman Must Die*. New York: Simon and Schuster, 1946; rpt. New York: New Directions, 1957.

————. *1939*. New York: Simon and Schuster, 1948.

————. *His Human Majesty*. New York: Whittlesey House, McGraw-Hill Book Company, 1949.

————. *The Seagull on the Step*. New York: Alfred A. Knopf, 1955.

————. *Generation Without Farewell*. New York: Alfred A. Knopf, 1960.

————. *The Underground Woman*. Garden City, N.Y.: Doubleday, 1975.

Collected Stories and Short Novels

Boyle, Kay. *Short Stories*. Paris: Black Sun Press, 1929.

———— *Wedding Day and Other Stories*. New York: Jonathan Cape and Harrison Smith, 1930.

————. *The First Lover and Other Stories*. New York: Harrison Smith and Robert Haas, 1933.

————. *The White Horses of Vienna and Other Stories*. New York: Harcourt, Brace and Co., 1936.

————. *The Crazy Hunter: Three Short Novels*. New York: Harcourt, Brace and Co., 1940.

————. *Thirty Stories*. Introduction by David Daiches. New York: Simon and Schuster, 1946.

———— *The Smoking Mountain: Stories of Postwar Germany*. New York, London, and Toronto: McGraw-Hill Book Company, 1951.

——. *Three Short Novels*. Boston: Beacon Press, 1958; rpt. New York: Penguin Books, 1982, with an introduction by Margaret Atwood.
——. *Nothing Ever Breaks Except the Heart*. Garden City, N.Y.: Doubleday, 1966.
——. *Fifty Stories*. Introduction by David Daiches. Garden City, N.Y.: Doubleday, 1980.

Poetry

Boyle, Kay. *A Glad Day*. Norfolk, Conn.: New Directions, 1938.
——. *American Citizen Naturalized in Leadville, Colorado*. New York: Simon and Schuster, 1944.
——. *Collected Poems*. New York: Alfred A. Knopf, 1962.
——. *Testament for My Students and Other Poems*. Garden City, N.Y.: Doubleday, 1970.
——. *This Is Not a Letter and Other Poems*. Los Angeles: Sun & Moon Press, 1985.

Other Books

Brooke, Gladys Palmer. *Relations and Complications; Being the Recollections of H. H. the Dayang Muda of Sarawak*. Ghostwritten by Kay Boyle. London: Lane/ Bodley Head, 1929.
Boyle, Kay, trans. *Don Juan,* by Joseph Delteil. New York: Jonathan Cape and Harrison Smith, 1931.
——. *Mr. Knife, Miss Fork,* by René Crevel. Paris: Black Sun Press, 1931.
——. *The Devil in the Flesh,* by Raymond Radiguet. Paris: Crosby Continental Editions, 1932; New York: Harrison Smith, 1932.
Boyle, Kay, Laurence Vail, and Nina Conarain, eds. *365 Days*. New York: Harcourt, Brace and Co., 1936.
Bedwell, Bettina. *Yellow Dusk*. Ghostwritten by Kay Boyle. London: Hurst and Blackett, 1937.
Boyle, Kay. *The Youngest Camel*. Illustrated by Fritz Kredel. Boston: Little, Brown and Company, 1939, and London: Faber and Faber, 1939.
——. *Breaking the Silence: Why a Mother Tells Her Son about the Nazi Era*. New York: Institute of Human Relations Press, 1962.
——. *Pinky, the Cat Who Liked to Sleep*. Illustrated by Lillian Obligado. New York: Crowell-Collier, 1966.
——, ed. *The Autobiography of Emanuel Carnevali*. New York: Horizon Press, 1967.
Boyle, Kay, and Robert McAlmon. *Being Geniuses Together 1920–1930*. Rev. ed. Garden City, N.Y.: Doubleday, 1968.; rpt. San Francisco: North Point Press, 1984.
——. *Pinky in Persia*. Illustrated by Lillian Obligado. New York: Crowell-Collier, 1968.
——. *The Long Walk at San Francisco State and Other Essays*. New York: Grove Press, 1970.
Boyle, Kay, and Justine Van Gundy, eds. *Enough of Dying! Voices for Peace*. New York: Dell, 1972.
Jong, Erica, Thomas Sanchez, Kay Boyle, and Henry Miller. *Four Visions of America*. Santa Barbara: Capra Press, 1977.
Boyle, Kay, trans. *Babylon,* by René Crevel. San Francisco: North Point Press, 1985.
Boyle, Kay. *Words That Must Somehow Be Said: The Selected Essays of Kay Boyle, 1927–1984*. San Francisco: North Point Press, 1985.

Uncollected Short Fiction

Boyle, Kay. "Passeres' Paris." *This Quarter,* no. 1 (1925): 140–43.
——. "Flight." *This Quarter,* no. 2 (1925): 161–71.
——. "Collation." *Calendar of Modern Letters* 3 (October 1926): 171–74.
——. "Plagued by the Nightingale." *This Quarter,* no. 3 (1927): 165–203.
——. "Written for Royalty." *transition,* no. 13 (Summer 1928): 60–64.
——. "War in Paris." *The New Yorker,* 26 November 1938, 18–20.
——. "Poor Monsieur Panalitus." *The New Yorker,* 20 January 1940, 19–22.
——. "St. Stephen's Green," *The Atlantic Monthly* 245 (June 1980): 41–44.

Uncollected Poems

Boyle, Kay. "Monody to the Sound of Zithers." *Poetry: A Magazine of Verse* 21 (December 1922): 124–25.
——. "Morning." *Broom* 4 (January 1923): 121.
——. "Shore." *Contact* 5 (June 1923): n.p.
—— "Harbor Song." *Poetry: A Magazine of Verse* 25 (February 1925): 252–53.
——. "Summer." *This Quarter,* no. 1 (1925): 40–42.
——. "Three Poems." *Poetry: A Magazine of Verse* 29 (February 1927): 250–51.
——. "Carnival 1927." *This Quarter,* no. 3 (1927): 117.
——. "Comrade." *This Quarter,* no. 3 (1927): 118.
——. "For an American." *This Quarter,* no. 3 (1927): 111–15.
——. "Poems." *This Quarter,* no. 3 (1927): 116.
——. "To America." *This Quarter,* no. 3 (1927): 109–10.
——. "And Winter." *transition,* no. 5 (August 1927), 114.
——. "Letter to Archibald Craig." *transition,* no. 13 (Summer 1928): 188–90.
——. "The United States." *transition,* no. 13 (Summer 1928): 186–87.
——. "Dedicated to Guy Urquhart." *transition,* no. 18 (November 1929), 85.
——. "Flight of Fish." *The Nation,* 16 August 1933, 190.
——. "Flying Foxes and Others." *The Nation,* 18 October 1933, 444–45.
——. "Two Fragments from an Aviation Epic." *Vertical: A Yearbook for Romantic-Mystic Ascensions.* Ed. Eugene Jolas. New York: The Gotham Bookmart Press, 1941, 20–29.

Articles

Boyle, Kay. Letter to the editor. *Poetry: A Magazine of Verse* 19 (November 1921): 105–6.
——. Review of *In the American Grain,* by William Carlos Williams. *transition,* no. 1 (April 1927): 31–35.
——. "Unrecommended List." *This Quarter,* no. 3 (1927): 272–73.
——. "Mr. Crane and His Grandmother." *transition,* no. 10 (January 1928): 135–38.
——. "Why Do Americans Live in Europe?" *transition,* no. 14 (Fall 1928): 102–3.
——. "Homage to Harry Crosby." *transition,* no. 19–20 (June 1930): 221–22.
——. "Writers Worth Reading." *Contempo* 4 (5 July 1932): 4.
Boyle, Kay, and Laurence Vail. "Americans Abroad." *Contempo* 3 (15 March 1933): 4.
Boyle, Kay. "The Unvanquished." In *The Critic As Artist: Essays on Books 1920–1970,* edited by Gilbert A. Harrison, 38–41. 1938; rpt. New York: Liveright Publishing, 1972.
——. "Elizabeth Bowen." *The New Republic,* 21 September 1942, 355–56.

———. "Battle of the Sequins." *The Nation,* 23 December 1944, 770–71.

———. "The Silent Women." In *They Were There: The Story of World War II and How It Came About by America's Foremost Correspondents,* edited by Curt Riess, 228–31. New York: G. P. Putnam's Sons, 1944.

———. "Jew Is a Myth." *The Nation,* 13 October 1945, 368, 372.

———. "Farewell to New York." *The Nation,* 8 March 1947, 271–72.

———. "Monument to Hitler." *The Nation,* 12 April 1947, 417–19.

———. "Isabelita Has Lost Her Reason." *The Nation,* 24 May 1947, 628–29.

———. "Isabelita's Trial." *The Nation,* 11 October 1947, 393–94.

———. "Hans Jahn Fights Rearmament." *The Nation,* 15 December 1951, 519–21.

———. "Farewell to Europe." *The Nation,* 12 December 1953, 526–28.

———. "A Declaration for 1955." *The Nation,* 29 January 1955, 102–4.

———. "Spain Divided." *The Nation,* 11 June 1955, 506–7.

———. "They Sing of Love: A German Vignette." *The Nation,* 10 September 1955, 224–25.

———. "So Slowly We Move." *The Nation,* 4 May 1957, 90–93.

———. "No Time to Listen." *The Nation,* 16 November 1957, 341–42.

———. "City of Invisible Men." *The Nation,* 21 December 1957, 475–76.

———. "The Imposed Revolutions." *The Nation,* 4 January 1958, 14–15.

———. "Brighter Than Most." *Prairie Schooner* 34 (Spring 1960): 1–4.

———. "The Vanishing Short Story?" *Story* 36 (July-August 1963): 108–19.

———. "Saluting Kings and Presidents." *The Nation,* 7 February 1972, 184–87.

———. "Sisters of the Princess." *The Nation,* 6 March 1976, 261–62.

———. "The Crosbys: An Afterword." *ICarbS* 3 (1977): 117–25.

Secondary Sources

Advertisement for Kay Boyle and Archibald Craig's poetry anthology. *transition,* no. 13 (Summer 1928): n.p.

Alexander, Sidney. Review of *The Seagull on the Step,* by Kay Boyle. *The New York Times Book Review,* 8 May 1955, p. 5.

Bourjaily, Vance. Review of *Fifty Stories,* by Kay Boyle. *The New York Times Book Review,* 28 September 1980, 9, 32.

Bryfonski, Dedria, ed. "Kay Boyle." In *Contemporary Authors Autobiography Series.* Vol. 1. Detroit: Gale Research, 1984.

Bullett, Gerald. Review of *Year Before Last,* by Kay Boyle. *The New Statesman and Nation,* 9 July 1932, 43.

Bullock, Elizabeth. Review of *Avalanche,* by Kay Boyle. *Book Week,* 23 January 1944, 2.

Burnett, Whit and Hallie, eds. *The Modern Short Story in the Making.* New York and London: Hawthorn Books, 1964.

Burt, Struthers. "Kay Boyle's Coincidence and Melodrama." *Saturday Review of Literature,* 15 January 1944, 6.

Canby, H. S. Review of *Gentlemen, I Address You Privately,* by Kay Boyle. *Saturday Review of Literature,* 4 November 1933, 233.

Cantwell, Robert. "American Exile." *The Nation,* 20 July 1932, 61.

———. Review of *Gentlemen, I Address You Privately,* by Kay Boyle. *The New Republic,* 13 December 1933, 136.

Carpenter, Richard C. "Kay Boyle." *College English* 15 (November 1953): 81–87.

———. "Kay Boyle: The Figure in the Carpet." *Critique* 7 (Winter 1964–65): 65–78.

Centing, Richard R. "Kay Boyle: The Cincinnati Years." *Ohioana Quarterly* 15 (1972): 11–13.

Churchill, Allen. *The Literary Decade*. Englewood Cliffs, N.J.: Prentice-Hall, 1971.

Colum, Mary M. Review of *Monday Night*, by Kay Boyle. *Forum* 100 (October 1938): 166.

Cowley, Malcolm. *A Second Flowering: Works and Days of the Lost Generation*. New York: The Viking Press, 1974.

———. *Exile's Return: A Literary Odyssey of the 1920s*. New York: The Viking Press, 1951.

———. "The Last of the Lost Generation." *Esquire* 60 (July 1963): 77–79.

Crosby, Caresse. *The Passionate Years*. 1953; rpt. Carbondale and Edwardsville: Southern Illinois University Press, 1968.

Diamonstein, Barbaralee, ed. "Kay Boyle." In *Open Secrets: Ninety-four Women in Touch With Our Time*. New York: The Viking Press, 1972.

Drew, Kathy. "Kay Boyle Dedicates Self to Human Dignity." *Lost Generation Journal* 4 (Winter 1976): 14–23.

Felton, David. "The Lyman Family's Holy Siege of America," part 1. *Rolling Stone*, 23 December 1971, 40ff.

———. "The Lyman Family's Holy Siege of America," part 2. *Rolling Stone*, 6 January 1972, 40ff.

Ferguson, Otis. "The Brown Blouses of Vienna." *The New Republic*, 21 October 1936, 322.

Ford, Hugh D. *Four Lives in Paris*. New York: Horizon Press, 1985.

———. *Published in Paris: American and British Writers, Painters, and Publishers in Paris, 1920–1939*. New York: Macmillan, 1975.

———, ed. *The Left Bank Revisited: Selections from the Paris Tribune 1917–1934*. University Park and London: The Pennsylvania State University Press, 1972.

Fracchia, Charles. "Kay Boyle: A Profile." *San Francisco Review of Books* 1 (April 1976): 7–9.

Friedman, Mickey. "A Literary Legend Who Refuses to Rest on Her Laurels." *San Francisco Examiner*, 27 September 1968.

Gado, Frank. "Kay Boyle: From the Aesthetics of Exile to the Polemics of Return." Ph.D. diss., Duke University, 1968.

Glassco, John. *Memoirs of Montparnasse*. Toronto and New York: Oxford University Press, 1970.

Green, Blake. "Kay Boyle—A Study in Paradox." *San Francisco Chronicle*, 17 February 1975, 12.

Grumbach, Doris. Review of *The Underground Woman*, by Kay Boyle. *The New Republic*, 8 February 1975, 3.

Guggenheim, Peggy. *Out of This Century: Confessions of an Art Addict*. New York: Universe Books, 1979.

———. *Out of This Century: The Informal Memoirs of Peggy Guggenheim*. New York: The Dial Press, 1946.

Haesler, Bob. "Kay Boyle Assesses S. F. State." *San Francisco Chronicle*, 16 November 1968.

Harrison, Gilbert A., ed. *The Critic As Artist: Essays on Books 1920–1970*. New York: Liveright Publishing, 1972.

Hart, Elizabeth. Review of *My Next Bride*, by Kay Boyle. *Books*, 11 November 1934, 4.

Harter, Evelyn. "Kay Boyle: Experimenter." *The Bookman* 75 (June-July 1932): 249–53.

Hoffman, Frederick J. *The Twenties: American Writing in the Postwar Decade*. New York: The Viking Press, 1955.

"In This Issue." *Contempo* 2 (5 July 1932): 2.

Jackson, Byron K. "The Achievement of Kay Boyle." Ph.D. diss., University of Florida, 1968.

Jolas, Eugene. "Ernest Walsh, Poet and Editor, Dies in Monte Carlo at Age of Thirty-One." In *The Left Bank Revisited: Selections from the Paris Tribune 1917–1934*, edited by Hugh Ford, pp. 243–44. University Park: The Pennsylvania State University Press, 1972.

———. "Transatlantic Letter." *transition*, no. 13 (Summer 1928): 274–77.

———. "*transition*: An Epilogue." *American Mercury* 23 (June 1931): 185–92.

"Kay Boyle." *New York Herald Tribune Book Review*, 7 October 1951, 6, 28.

"Kay Boyle, Journalist." *The New York Times Book Review*, 24 November 1946, 8.

"Kay Boyle's Bitter View of Johnson." *San Francisco Chronicle*, 15 September 1968.

Kielty, Bernadine. "Under-Cover Stuff." *Ladies' Home Journal* 63 (March 1946): 5.

Knoll, Robert E., ed. *McAlmon and the Lost Generation: A Self-Portrait*. Lincoln: University of Nebraska Press, 1962.

———. Review of *Collected Poems*, by Kay Boyle. *Prairie Schooner*, 37 (Spring 1963), 176–78.

Koch, David V. "Kay Boyle." In *Dictionary of Literary Biography*. Vol. 4. Detroit: Gale Research, 1980, 46–56.

Kunitz, Stanley J., ed. *Authors Today and Yesterday*. New York: H. W. Wilson Company, 1933.

Litwak, Leo. "Kay Boyle—Paris Wasn't Like That." *New York Times Book Review*, 15 July 1984, 1, 32–33.

Ludwig, Richard M. and Marvin B. Perry, Jr., eds. *Nine Short Novels*. Boston: D. C. Heath, 1952.

McMillan, Dougald. *transition: The History of a Literary Era 1927–1938*. New York: George Braziller, 1976.

Madden, Charles F., ed. *Talks with Authors*. Carbondale and Edwardsville: Southern Illinois University Press, 1968.

Marini, Myra. Review of *Year Before Last*, by Kay Boyle. *The New Republic*, 13 July 1932, 242.

"Matters of Security." *The Washington Star*, 1 June 1979, p. A-2.

Meynell, Viola. Review of *Plagued by the Nightingale*, by Kay Boyle. *The New Statesman and Nation*, 1 August 1931, 144.

Moore, Harry T. "Kay Boyle's Fiction." In *Age of the Modern and Other Essays*. Carbondale and Edwardsville: Southern Illinois University Press, 1971.

Moorhead, Ethel. Introductory memoir. In *Poems and Sonnets*, by Ernest Walsh. New York: Harcourt, Brace and Company, 1934.

Olsen, Tillie. *Silences*. New York: Dell, 1979.

Porter, Katherine Anne. "Example to the Young." *The New Republic*, 22 April 1931, 279–80.

Pratt, Annis. "The New Feminist Criticism." *College English* 32 (May 1971): 872–78.

Prescott, Peter S. "Life with Daughter." *Newsweek*, 13 January 1975, 67A.

Review of *My Next Bride*, by Kay Boyle. *Christian Century*, 5 December 1934, 1564.

Review of *My Next Bride*, by Kay Boyle. *Forum* 92 (December 1934): ix.

Review of *Plagued by the Nightingale* by Kay Boyle. *The Nation*, 6 May 1931, 509.

"Revolution of the Word." *transition*, no. 16–17 (June 1929): n.p.

Rothman, N. L. "Kay Boyle's Stories." *Saturday Review of Literature*, 8 February 1936, 6.

Schroeder, Mildred. "Author Kay Boyle Spurs New Kind of Integration." *San Francisco Examiner*, 1 July 1966.

Sharp, Roberta. "A Bibliography of Works by and about Kay Boyle." *Bulletin of Bibliography* 35 (October-December 1978): 180–91.

Showalter, Elaine. "Women and the Literary Curriculum." *College English* 32 (May 1971): 855–62.

Strachey, Richard. Review of *Wedding Day and Other Stories*, by Kay Boyle. *New Statesman and Nation*, 24 September 1932, 347.

Strong, L. A. G. Review of *Plagued by the Nightingale*, by Kay Boyle. *Spectator* 147 (18 July 1931): 94.

Sykes, Gerald. Review of *Wedding Day and Other Stories*, by Kay Boyle. *The Nation*, 24 December 1930, 711.

Thirlwall, John C., ed. *The Selected Letters of William Carlos Williams*. New York: McDowell, Obolensky, 1957.

" 'This Quarter' Gets Reviewed." *This Quarter*, no. 2 (1925): 305–10.

Thompson, Ralph. "In and Out of Books." *The New York Times Book Review*, 10 April 1949, 8.

Tooker, Dan, and Roger Hofheins, eds. *Fiction! Interviews with Northern California Novelists*. New York and Los Altos: Harcourt Brace Jovanovich/ William Kaufman, 1976.

Trilling, Diana. Review of *Avalanche*, by Kay Boyle. *The Nation*, 22 January 1944, 105.

Van Doren, Mark. *The Private Reader: Selected Articles and Reviews*. 1942; rpt. New York: Kraus Reprint Co., 1968.

Van Gelder, Robert. *Writers and Writing*. New York: Charles Scribner's Sons, 1946.

Walsh, Ernest. *Poems and Sonnets*. New York: Harcourt, Brace and Company, 1934.

Walton, Edith H. Review of *My Next Bride*, by Kay Boyle. *New York Times Book Review*, 11 November 1934, 6.

Warfel, Harry R. *American Novelists of Today*. New York: American Book Company, 1951.

Weber, Brom, ed. *The Letters of Hart Crane 1916–1932*. New York: Hermitage House, 1952.

Williams, William Carlos, and Robert McAlmon. Editors' notes. *Contact* 5 (June 1923): n.p.

Wilson, Edmund. "Kay Boyle and the *Saturday Evening Post*." In *Classics and Commercials: A Literary Chronicle ot the Forties*. New York: Vintage Books, Random House, 1962.

Wilson, Ted. Review of *Year Before Last*, by Kay Boyle. *Contempo* 3 (25 October 1932): 5.

Winnick, R.H.,ed. *Letters of Archibald MacLeish 1907 to 1982*. Boston: Houghton Mifflin Company, 1983.

Wolff, Geoffrey. *Black Sun: The Brief Transit and Violent Eclipse of Harry Crosby*. New York: Random House, 1976.

Zellerbach, Merla. "When Writers Give Themselves Away." *San Francisco Chronicle*, 15 March 1978, 15.

Index

SANDRA WHIPPLE SPANIER received her Ph.D. in English in 1981 from The Pennsylvania State University. In addition to her work on Kay Boyle, she has published articles on Hemingway, Salinger, Lawrence, Hawthorne, and Poe. She is assistant professor of English at Oregon State University.